Brennan vs. Rehnquist

BRENNAN
vs.
REHNQUIST

THE BATTLE FOR
THE CONSTITUTION

PETER IRONS

ALFRED A. KNOPF   NEW YORK   1994

THIS IS A BORZOI BOOK
PUBLISHED BY ALFRED A. KNOPF, INC.

Library of Congress Cataloging-in-Publication Data
Irons, Peter H.
Brennan vs. Rehnquist : the battle for the
Constitution / by Peter Irons.—1st ed.
p.   cm.
Includes bibliographical references and index.
ISBN 0-679-42436-9
1. United States—Supreme Court. 2. United States—
Constitutional law—Interpretation and construction.
3. Political questions and judicial power—United States.
4. Rehnquist, William H. [date].   5. Brennan,
William J. (William Joseph) [date].   I. Title.
KF8748.I76   1994
342.73—dc20
[347.302]   94-7708   CIP

Manufactured in the United States of America
First Edition

For my mother, Alda Hanlon Irons,

who raised all seven of her children to respect

the dignity of every person

Contents

Preface   ix

ONE   "All That's Left from Welfare Check"   3

TWO   "The Constitutional Principle of Human Dignity"   23

THREE   "One Personal Conviction Is No Better Than Another"   43

FOUR   "Beyond the Reach of Majorities"   65

FIVE   "The Greatest Dangers to Liberty"   91

SIX   "This Is a Christian Nation"   113

SEVEN   " 'No Law' Does *Not* Mean No Law"   143

EIGHT   "*Utterly* Without Redeeming Social Importance"   166

NINE   "You Are Under Arrest"   189

TEN   "Cruel and Unusual Punishment"   212

ELEVEN   "The Equal Protection of the Laws"   241

TWELVE   "Well Qualified by Character and Education"   267

THIRTEEN   "Not on a Pedestal, but in a Cage"   292

FOURTEEN   "Which Side Are You On?"   321

           Bibliographic Note   339

           Notes   343

           Table of Cases   361

           Index   367

Preface

WILLIAM J. BRENNAN, JR., AND WILLIAM H. REHNQUIST served together on the United States Supreme Court between 1972 and 1990. During these eighteen years, they headed the Court's liberal and conservative wings, and lobbied for the votes of moderate justices. They provided intellectual and political leadership to contending sides in a battle over the Constitution that affected the lives of every American. The two justices brought divergent judicial philosophies to the Court, rooted in different values and views about the relations of individuals and the state. Each won major victories, but neither won a final triumph.

Brennan joined the Court headed by Chief Justice Earl Warren in 1956, appointed by President Dwight Eisenhower, and soon became the intellectual leader of the liberals who dominated the Warren Court. After Warren's retirement in 1969, President Richard Nixon appointed Chief Justice Warren Burger and chose Rehnquist in 1971 for his commitment to reversing the Warren Court's liberal decisions. Rehnquist eagerly assumed this task, but encountered a determined adversary, as Brennan rallied the Court's moderates to resist the conservatives. After Rehnquist replaced Burger as Chief Justice in 1986, elevated by President Ronald Reagan, he and Brennan continued their struggle. Age and illness finally took their toll on the senior associate justice, and Brennan retired in 1990 after thirty-four years on the Court, his judicial legacy still largely intact.

This book recounts the constitutional battles of Justices Brennan and Rehnquist, and explores their divergent approaches to the Constitution by examining their opinions in one hundred cases that raised claims under the Bill of Rights. To use a somewhat daunting phrase, this is an exercise in "applied jurisprudence." It focuses, however, not on abstract ideas but on real people and the Court's impact on their lives. This is not the kind of "objective" study that most professors claim to produce. Readers will soon discover my preference for Justice Brennan's approach to the Constitution. But I have tried to be fair in letting each justice speak in this constitutional debate, primarily through words they wrote in their published opinions.

THIS BOOK BEGAN in 1957, when I was a high school senior in Wyoming, Ohio, an affluent suburb of Cincinnati. My father worked as an engineer for General Electric, heading a project to design a nuclear-powered airplane that never got off the ground. My school was considered one of the best in Ohio, in both academics and athletics. Every member of my senior class went to college, and the Wyoming Cowboys won every football game that year. I followed politics closely, mainly through the conservative Cincinnati *Enquirer*.

During my senior year, I wrote a letter to the *Enquirer*, which ran a column by a local reactionary named Otto Garr Teague, who screamed "Wake Up, Americans!" every morning. He repeatedly condemned the Supreme Court as soft on communism and hard on states' rights. Teague's attacks on the Court's rulings against racial segregation finally provoked me to respond. My letter—written with the aid of a thesaurus—denounced his "Paleolithic" views and argued that "the duty of the Supreme Court is to redefine the purport of the law in light of changing social trends." I was excited to see this first expression of my political views in print.

This personal story may help readers understand the perspective of this book. Since my 1957 letter, I have retained my belief that the Constitution must adapt to "changing social trends." In this regard, I share the views of Justice Brennan. But in several ways, I have more in common with Justice Rehnquist. We both grew up in midwestern suburbs, mostly white and Protestant. His hometown of Shorewood Village, Wisconsin, looks much like mine. During our high school and college years, we shared a fascination with politics, and we both liked to write about public affairs. We both have graduate degrees in political science, and have both written books about the Supreme Court and American legal history. On the surface, I have much less in common with Brennan. He is Irish and Catholic, and grew up in a polyglot eastern city, Newark, New Jersey. He studied business and finance in college, while I majored in sociology.

His father was a union officer and a Democrat, while mine opposed unions and voted Republican.

There are other reasons, however, why my first published words about the Supreme Court sound more like Brennan than Rehnquist. First, my mother's father was an Irish Catholic who started work at the age of nine in a New Hampshire shoe factory. I am conscious of his struggles with poverty and prejudice. Second, my family attended the local Unitarian church, a haven for doubters and dissenters. I have returned to this church with my doubts and dissent. Third, my father shared the Republicanism of Senator Robert Taft, a Cincinnati native who supported civil rights and liberties. I was raised to abhor racism and political repression. Before the *Brown* decision in 1954, I attended segregated schools in Delaware and wondered why there were no black kids in my classes. And my father, whose "Q-clearance" for nuclear secrets was higher than the president's, left the Atomic Energy Commission after it stripped Robert Oppenheimer of his security clearance.

In short, I am the mirror image of William Rehnquist. We are both lawyers, and we share a passion for constitutional law and history. But I disagree with virtually every opinion Rehnquist has written, and I agree with almost all of Brennan's. In reading dozens of their opinions, during and since law school, I was struck by how profoundly these two intelligent men differed over the Constitution. I also noticed that each consistently used words and phrases that the other rarely employed. The patterns were so consistent that I asked the Lexis database, which scans opinions in a flash, to check for me. According to Lexis, Brennan used the word "dignity" in more than thirty opinions; Rehnquist never did. Conversely, Rehnquist employed the word "deference" in about forty opinions, expressing his attitude toward legislative decisions. Brennan occasionally spoke of "deference," but most often to explain why he declined to defer to lawmakers.

The judicial philosophies of the two justices are distilled, I believe, in the terms "dignity" and "deference." They reflect different ideas about the core values of the Constitution. But are they antithetical, in the sense that applying one or the other to actual cases will affect the outcome? The statistical record supports this commonsense assumption. During the years that Brennan and Rehnquist served together, they both voted in 2,703 cases that the Court decided with full opinions, an average of 150 cases in each term. They voted on the same side in 1,161 of these cases, almost 43 percent. However, 888 of their agreements came in unanimous decisions, the Court's "easy" cases that are usually accepted to send a message to lower courts. Setting aside unanimous decisions, Brennan and Rehnquist agreed in only 273 of 1,815 cases in which one or more justices dissented, just 15 percent of the Court's divided decisions over a span of almost two decades. This was the lowest rate of agreement of any pair of justices over those years. And they disagreed in virtually every case that raised important constitutional issues.

Brennan and Rehnquist are almost totally opposite in background, philosophy, and judicial voting. During their years together, they battled over the Constitution, each trying to rally the Court's moderates to his side. The stakes were high—questions of abortion, affirmative action, capital punishment, and other controversial issues hung in the balance. To explore these judicial battles, I have selected one hundred cases in which Brennan and Rehnquist wrote opinions. They agreed in just two of these cases. All but seven cases matched an individual against a government agency or official. Justice Brennan voted against the government in every case; Justice Rehnquist supported the state in all but one, an obscenity prosecution of an Academy Award–winning movie. Each of the seven private-law cases pitted an individual plaintiff against a corporate defendant. Brennan sided with the plaintiff in five decisions; he supported the defendants in two libel cases. Rehnquist voted for corporations in all but one case, the "reverse discrimination" claim of a white male.

This book is structured around the major provisions of the Bill of Rights and the Fourteenth Amendment. The initial four chapters provide background and context for the case studies that follow. The first chapter examines one case, *U.S. Department of Agriculture v. Moreno*, in considerable detail, from its filing to its decision by the Supreme Court. This case illustrates the politics of constitutional litigation, the use of "social facts" by lawyers and judges, and the differing principles that Brennan and Rehnquist apply to the Constitution. The next two chapters explore the sources of these principles in the family, schooling, and early careers of each justice. The following chapter places their constitutional battles in historical context, in particular the genesis of the "strict scrutiny" test that underlies Brennan's jurisprudence. The remaining chapters look at their opinions in Bill of Rights cases, beginning with the "liberty" clauses of the Fifth and Fourteenth amendments. Separate chapters then deal with religion; freedom of speech; obscenity and censorship; the rights of criminal defendants; capital punishment; racial discrimination; the rights of aliens and other minorities; and gender discrimination and abortion. The final chapter allows champions and critics of the justices to comment on their judicial work.

This book perceives the Supreme Court as a political institution, and constitutional litigation as a form of politics. These are hardly radical— or recent—notions. "Scarcely any political question arises in the United States," Alexis de Tocqueville observed in 1835, "that is not resolved, sooner or later, into a judicial question." The Court's first major decision, *Marbury v. Madison* in 1803, drew the justices into an intensely political conflict among all three branches of the federal government. Chief Justice John Marshall did not shrink from this dispute. "It is emphatically the province and duty of the judicial department," he wrote, "to say what the law is." His opinion established the Court as the ultimate arbiter of political disputes the other branches could not resolve.

The Supreme Court remains embroiled in political disputes. Robert Jackson, who served as attorney general before joining the Court in 1941, wrote that "constitutional lawsuits are the stuff of power politics in America." Francis Biddle, who succeeded Jackson as attorney general, was asked how the Supreme Court could ignore the Constitution and uphold the wartime internment of Japanese Americans. "At the highest level," he replied, "the Constitution *is* politics." Although the justices sit across the street from Congress, and up the hill from the White House, they disavow any political role. But every Bill of Rights case that reaches the Court reflects a political dispute, and the Court's decision most often stirs a political reaction.

The cases examined in this book arose during two decades of intense political conflict in American society. William Rehnquist joined the Court in January 1972, and William Brennan retired in June 1990. These years spanned the time from Watergate to the Iran-Contra affair. The fifties and sixties had been dominated by protest movements that supported civil rights for black Americans and opposed the Vietnam War, conflicts that spilled over into the next decade. The seventies and eighties saw the rise of the feminist movement, a shift from moderation to militance by gays and lesbians, and growing despair in the black community over the persistence of racism. These social and political conflicts moved from noisy streets to the quiet chambers of the United States Supreme Court. Justices Brennan and Rehnquist—personal friends and philosophical foes—battled over these issues for two decades. This book explores the impact of their competing values on the outcomes of those battles.

A WORD ABOUT SOURCES IS NECESSARY. This is not an insider's account. I did not interview either justice for this book. Neither have I talked with former law clerks, or looked at private papers. The vast majority of quoted material is from published opinions in *United States Reports*, the Court's official record. I have supplemented this source with material from case briefs and records, published opinions from lower courts, and data from newspapers, magazines, and books.

A final word of thanks to those who helped along the way. My friend and colleague Harry Hirsch stimulated my thinking about "social facts" with his excellent book *A Theory of Liberty*, and he generously commented on early drafts of this book. Stephanie Guitton, who helped me edit the Supreme Court oral argument tapes for my book *May It Please the Court*, has provided critical views of law and social reality from a feminist and continental perspective. Jayne Cooke tracked down citations that I skipped or missed. Reference librarians at the University of California, San Diego, and at California Western Law School and the University of Washington were unfailingly helpful; I want to pay special tribute to Larry Cruse and Renata Coates of UCSD. Bonnie Fox came into my life as I was finishing this book and brought happiness with her. She is raising her daughter Haley—who is three—to live by the values she shares with me and Justice Brennan. Finally, Priscilla Long is my dearest friend and most friendly critic. For close to thirty years, we have supported each other's work in all the ways that make the hard job of writing a rewarding experience.

San Diego, California
March 1994

BRENNAN VS. REHNQUIST

ONE

"ALL THAT'S LEFT FROM
WELFARE CHECK"

THE SUPREME COURT conference began on a Wednesday afternoon, April 25, 1973, with a ritual that began in the 1880s. Each of the nine justices shook hands with each colleague, a practice designed to cement the collegiality of this very small community. There were special words of salutation for Justice William J. Brennan, Jr. This was his sixty-seventh birthday, and every member of the Court had warm feelings for the gracious, diminutive Irishman. Brennan knew that birthday greetings and handshakes would not blunt the sharp differences over today's cases. Justice James Byrnes, who served for one unhappy year in the 1940s, likened the handshake formality to "the usual instruction of the referee in the prize ring, 'Shake hands, go to your corner and come out fighting.' " Brennan, who never raised his voice or used harsh words in conference, was nonetheless a real fighter for his vision of the "living Constitution."

During this Court term, which began the previous October, Brennan had the most fights with the newest and youngest justice, William H. Rehnquist. This year was already momentous in the Court's history, dominated by the abortion decision in *Roe v. Wade*, handed down in January 1973. But *Roe* was just one of a dozen important decisions, including the issues of northern school segregation, tax support for parochial schools, obscenity, welfare rights, and sex discrimination. Brennan and Rehnquist voted on opposite sides in each of these landmark cases, and most of the less-noted ones as well.

They would resume their battle over the Constitution at this end-of-term conference. Five minutes earlier, buzzers had sounded in the justices' chambers, summoning them to discussion and decision in four cases argued the previous Monday. Actually, there were two pairs of related cases, argued separately but with overlapping lawyers. The first two involved disputes between the city and county school boards in Richmond, Virginia. A federal judge had ordered a merger of districts to break down racial segregation between the largely black city schools and the lily-white suburbs: the state board of education appealed for the suburban schools, and a federal appeals court reversed the judicial order. This time, the city appealed to the Supreme Court. The arguments featured a stellar cast of lawyers, including William Coleman, who served as the first black clerk at the Supreme Court and now spoke for the city schools, and Philip Kurland, a University of Chicago law professor who represented the state. The justices also heard from Solicitor General Erwin Griswold, a former Harvard Law School dean who appeared as a "friend of the court" for the Nixon administration, which supported "neighborhood schools" and opposed "forced busing" to foster integration.

The lawyers who argued the second pair of cases were younger and less renowned. Griswold was actually involved in both, since his office represented the U.S. Department of Agriculture, the losing party in the lower federal courts. His name appeared on the Supreme Court briefs, but he delegated the oral arguments to a pair of young assistants. Both cases challenged regulations that restricted access to the federal food-stamp program. Congress had enacted the program in 1964 as a major weapon in President Lyndon Johnson's War on Poverty. The idea behind food stamps was simple: poor people could buy stamps at a fraction of their face value and use them to purchase groceries. The federal government reimbursed the merchants for the difference in price. Almost everyone liked the program. Poor people and their professional advocates were natural supporters, but farmers and grocers also benefited and lobbied for the law.

The poverty war became a casualty of the Vietnam War after Lyndon Johnson surrendered the White House to Richard Nixon in 1969. Nixon had denounced government "waste" and pledged to slash welfare funds. But the popular food-stamp program largely escaped the budget-cutting cleaver. Congress did act, however, to purge two groups that Nixon detested from the ranks of food-stamp recipients. One was college students, who sent battalions of war protesters into the streets and hid from military service behind draft deferments. Nixon, who worked his way through college, resented students who got a "free ride" on food stamps. Another group Nixon despised was "hippies" who lived in communes, practiced free love, and smoked marijuana.

Nixon signed into law in 1971 a statute designed to remove students and hippies from the food-stamp rolls. One provision barred from the program any person over eighteen who had been claimed the previous year as a dependent by a taxpayer who was not eligible for food stamps. This amendment's congressional sponsor explained that it was aimed at "college students, children of wealthy parents." The only comment on the second amendment came from Senator Spessard Holland, a Florida Democrat, who said it would "exclude households consisting of unrelated individuals under the age of sixty, such as 'hippy' communes."

The problem with the food-stamp amendments was that they blasted a legislative shotgun at a very small target, and injured a large group of poor people who were neither rich students nor lazy hippies. The ink was hardly dry on the statute before poverty lawyers filed lawsuits to challenge both provisions. Two separate cases, one against the ban on "tax dependents" and the other against the "hippy" amendment, were quickly filed in the District of Columbia federal court. These suits were carefully calculated to take advantage of three facts. First, this court had jurisdiction over federal agencies whose actions were challenged; second, most of the District judges had been appointed by Presidents Johnson and Kennedy; and third, judicial precedent from the Supreme Court of Earl Warren supported an expansive reading of the Constitution's Due Process and Equal Protection clauses.

THE LAWYER who filed these suits was Ronald F. Pollack, director of the Center on Social Welfare Policy and Law at Columbia University in New York City. The Columbia center gave Pollack an academic image, but his actual legal home was the Food Research and Action Center, founded in 1970 and funded with grants from religious social-action groups and liberal foundations. Pollack put FRAC's mission in one sentence: "Our function is to use the law to feed people." By 1976, when *Time* magazine pictured him in an admiring full-page article on "The Hunger Lawyers," Pollack and his team of four young lawyers had filed 150 suits and won all but 4.

Ron Pollack brought a missionary's zeal to his legal assault on hunger in America. Born in New York City in 1944, he joined the Mississippi Freedom Summer crusade to register black voters in the mid-1960s. He told the *Time* reporter that in Mississippi he "saw in the starkest terms people who were extraordinarily hungry and needed government assistance." He went back to New York University's law school and graduated in 1968. That same year, he filed twenty-six suits against state agencies and the federal Department of Agriculture for "foot dragging" in food programs that Congress had funded. He won all but one case, impressing judges with thorough research and trial preparation. A government lawyer who had faced Pollack in court said, "With Ron, we have to work a little harder."

Pollack mixed litigation with lobbying for increased funding for food programs, and escorted politicians like Senator Edward Kennedy on "hunger tours" of urban and rural areas that exposed the Third World face of American poverty. He told a group of lawyers in 1970 of visiting children in the Detroit General Hospital who suffered from rickets, a disfiguring bone disease caused by malnutrition, and a Navaho reservation "where we have seen countless numbers of children who have marasmus and kwashiorkor, diseases that we thought could not exist in the United States, diseases that almost inevitably result in death." Pollack had scorn for recalcitrant government officials, and a special scorn for Earl Butz, Nixon's agriculture secretary. He complained that "it required a motion to ask the Secretary to be held in contempt of court" to gain compliance in two cases he won.

Pollack worked with a national network of poverty lawyers in preparing the suits against the regulations Butz had signed to exclude tax dependents and unrelated persons from food-stamp eligibility. The cases were filed as "class actions" on behalf of all persons denied food stamps under the regulations. But Pollack took special care in selecting the "named plaintiffs" who represented the entire class. For the "hippy" case, he chose five households around the country, from California to Florida. One actually was a "hippy commune." The suit included an affidavit from five young people in Columbia, South Carolina, who said their relationship "is far deeper and stronger than the bonds between friends or between mere roommates" and that they "consider themselves a family, not merely for the purposes of this lawsuit, but for *all* purposes." Pollack felt that even hippies—however one defined that sixties term in the seventies—had a right to food stamps if they otherwise qualified.

Pollack picked Jacinta Moreno as the lead plaintiff, a choice that was calculated to arouse sympathy. He also knew that judges would read her affidavit first. Moreno was definitely not a hippy. She was fifty-six years old and diabetic, and lived in Homestead, Florida, with Ermina Sanchez, a younger woman with three small children. Homestead is a

small city that lies between Miami and the Florida Keys and was devastated by Hurricane Andrew in 1992. Back in 1970, more than 35 percent
of its residents lived below the official poverty line; the average yearly
income of those on welfare was $838. The combined monthly income
of Jacinta and Ermina was $208; monthly food expenses for the two
women and three children were budgeted at $28. In her affidavit, Jacinta
explained, "This is all that's left from Welfare check."

Jacinta Moreno visited the food-stamp office on February 1, 1972. "I
was told I was not eligible because of our unrelated household status and
denied stamps," she said in her affidavit. "The loss of food stamps seriously
affects my household." Because of her diabetes, "I am advised to follow
a strict diet, which I am not able to adhere to due to financial inability."
She ended with poignant words: "As long as I am denied eligibility, I
will have to continue to deprive myself of necessary food, clothing and
household items, and the promise of food relief to those of us in low-
income families shall be meaningless." She signed her affidavit with
an X.

Ron Pollack gained a quick hearing from a federal judge in Washington, D.C. The complaint he filed in *Moreno v. U.S. Department of
Agriculture* alleged that "the 'anti-hippy commune' provisions of the Food
Stamp Act and regulations violate plaintiffs' rights to equal protection as
guaranteed by the Fifth Amendment to the United States Constitution."
The case was assigned to District Judge John Lewis Smith, Jr., who was
a Republican but had been appointed by President Lyndon Johnson.

Peter Brickfield, a young trial attorney in the Justice Department's
Civil Division, represented Secretary Butz during the brief hearing before
Judge Smith. Brickfield argued that equal protection was not the issue,
and that he only needed to show a "rational basis" for the law. "I don't
think Congress has to give food stamps to everyone," he said. "I think
they can be allowed to give them to whom they want." Judge Smith
asked a personal question: "I have living with me in my home a young
man, unemployed, working on an intern project. Do you mean I would
not be entitled to benefits if I required them?" Brickfield said the judge
would be denied food stamps because "Congress has determined that
people without a certain degree of relationships are not those that they
chose to give these benefits to." Judge Smith promptly ruled for Ron
Pollack and his clients. He issued a temporary restraining order on April
6, 1972, that enjoined Butz from denying food stamps to Jacinta Moreno
and all other class members. Because the suit challenged the constitu-

tionality of a federal law, Smith invoked a special statute and sent the case to a three-judge panel—on which he would sit—for a hearing on the constitutional issues.

Pollack could not have picked a better panel himself. The judges who joined Smith had both been appointed by President John Kennedy. Spottswood Robinson, who came to the bench as dean of Howard Law School—the "black Harvard" in Washington—was a civil rights veteran who joined Thurgood Marshall on the team of NAACP lawyers who argued *Brown v. Board of Education* before the Supreme Court. Robinson had argued two of the four school segregation cases decided with *Brown* in 1954. Carl McGowan had been a corporation lawyer in Chicago before his appointment to the District of Columbia Court of Appeals, but he was a firm liberal on the bench.

Peter Brickfield returned to argue for Secretary Butz at the hearing on April 14, 1972. He ran into tough questions from the outset. Judge Robinson asked him to define the term "family." "We contend that the traditional concepts of a family are related people," Brickfield replied. "We are not dealing with tradition," answered Robinson, who knew that extended families in black communities included many unrelated people. Judge McGowan asked if exclusion of "hippy communes" was based on concerns about "morality." Brickfield ducked the question, but added that "if Congress put into the legislative history that we are doing this to maintain family units, then this court must consider that as a rational basis." McGowan had a brusque reply: "But they didn't." Brickfield's response was hardly likely to win judicial votes: "That is not relevant, Your Honor."

Judge McGowan wrote the opinion for the panel in the *Moreno* case, decided on May 26, 1972. Ron Pollack could not have written a better opinion himself. McGowan had read Jacinta Moreno's affidavit and made note of her financial plight and medical needs. When he turned to the constitutional issues, McGowan wrote that "we find the case appropriate for the application of traditional equal protection analysis." This was a somewhat disingenuous statement, for several reasons. First, Pollack had based his complaint on "rights to equal protection" under the Constitution's Fifth Amendment. But that amendment has no Equal Protection clause; it guarantees "due process of law" by the federal government. The Fourteenth Amendment does require state governments to provide "the equal protection of the laws" to every person. Not until 1954, in a companion case to *Brown v. Board of Education* from the District of

Columbia, did the Supreme Court impose the "equal protection" requirement on the federal government.

A second reason that Judge McGowan was not applying "traditional equal protection analysis" was his citation, not of any Supreme Court decisions as precedent, but of a recent law review article written by anonymous Harvard Law School students. This 130-page article, published in 1969, offered an exhaustive canvass of cases that broadened the rights of racial and religious minorities and other groups—like poor people—who belonged to what Ron Pollack called "the weakest political constituencies." The *Harvard Law Review* article that McGowan cited for authority had no force as precedent, but it gave his opinion a solid basis in recent legal scholarship.

Perhaps the greatest break with legal tradition came in McGowan's citation of Supreme Court decisions that had nothing to do with the Equal Protection clause. He rested his opinion on cases that he said established "rights to privacy and freedom of association *in the home.*" These cases dealt with access to contraceptives and possession of pornography. What could possibly connect birth control and dirty movies with food stamps for Jacinta Moreno? McGowan looked beyond the Equal Protection clause to "fundamental personal freedoms" that stemmed from the First Amendment. This was hardly "traditional" legal analysis, but it avoided the problem that no Supreme Court opinion had ever sheltered poor people under the "equal protection" umbrella.

Judge McGowan then took a circular route around a 1970 Supreme Court decision that Peter Brickfield cited in his argument for Secretary Butz. This case, *Dandridge v. Williams*, had upheld a Maryland law that placed a ceiling on welfare payments, penalizing recipients with large families. The Supreme Court's opinion, from which Justice Brennan dissented, held that legislative judgments on "economic and social" issues were protected from judicial scrutiny. McGowan found a way around *Dandridge* to provide Jacinta Moreno and Ermina Sanchez with food stamps. He wrote that the Supreme Court was "careful to note that the statute there challenged did not affect 'freedoms guaranteed by the Bill of Rights' " against federal infringement. Because the "hippy commune" law was in "visible conflict with fundamental personal freedoms" of privacy and personal association, McGowan concluded that it "directly impinges on First Amendment freedoms." Adding the First Amendment to the Fourteenth, through the Fifth, was certainly not "traditional" legal analysis, but it did the job in the *Moreno* case.

McGowan took a final swipe at the argument—which Brickfield had not really made—that the "hippy commune" law was designed to promote "the fostering of morality" among the poor and hungry. The legislative effort "to combat the unconventional living arrangements" of hippies, McGowan wrote, "is not 'social and economic' in the traditional sense." Rather than fostering "the improvement of the general welfare," the law displayed a forbidden "intent to harm a politically unpopular group" who were treated differently than members of related families. From this decidedly untraditional reading of "traditional equal protection analysis," McGowan concluded that the law "denies plaintiffs equal protection of the laws." Jacinta Moreno would get her food stamps, unless the government's lawyers could persuade the Supreme Court to reverse this ruling, which continued the injunction against Secretary Butz and declared the law unconstitutional.

THERE WAS LITTLE QUESTION the Supreme Court would hear the government's appeal. The justices grant review in only a handful of the cases filed each term. Of more than 4,500 "petitions for certiorari" submitted each year, fewer than 4 percent are granted and scheduled for oral argument. Close to half the petitions are filed by prisoners, and fewer than 1 percent of these are accepted. But one frequent litigant has a phenomenal success rate, more than 70 percent since 1954. The Solicitor General of the United States decides which cases involving federal agencies should be appealed to the Supreme Court. Often described as "the tenth justice," the solicitor is the only government lawyer required by statute "to be learned in the law," and Erwin Griswold was indisputably learned and widely respected. He had none of the political taint of his nominal superior, Attorney General John Mitchell. Virtually any case he asked the Court to review would be heard.

The government filed its notice of appeal in the *Moreno* case with the Supreme Court clerk on June 23, 1972. The justices were about to begin their summer recess, and this case had no particular urgency, since Judge McGowan's order required Secretary Butz to provide Jacinta Moreno and other class members with food stamps. Justice Rehnquist, assigned to rule on motions from District of Columbia cases, extended the normal sixty days for filing petitions to October 3, the beginning of the Court's next term. Because the government had lost in the lower court, the parties switched places and the caption became *U.S. Department of Agriculture v. Moreno.* The Court should reverse McGowan's order, the petition argued, because Congress had decided that related families "represent relatively more stable living units than do groups of unrelated individuals." Congress had a "reasonable basis" for denying food stamps to "individuals who abuse the program by remaining voluntarily poor." This phrase was a code word for hippies, a term the petition avoided.

The justices voted on December 4, 1972, to review the *Moreno* case, along with *Department of Agriculture v. Murry,* an appellate ruling against the "tax dependents" provision of the food stamp law, which Ron Pollack also argued and won. The Court granted his motions to appear *in forma pauperis* in both cases, a "pauper's plea" which exempted the clients from court fees. Lawyers on both sides went to work on their briefs. The Solicitor General's office went first and filed a short brief of eighteen pages in the *Moreno* case. It relied primarily, as government lawyers had since the case began, on the Supreme Court's *Dandridge* opinion that excluded "social and economic" legislation from judicial scrutiny. The brief repeated the argument that Congress had a "reasonable basis" for denying food stamps to unrelated people and that lawmakers "could assume that traditional living units" included those persons "with the greatest need for food stamp assistance." Repeating the code word for hippies, the brief also claimed that excluding unrelated people "furthered legitimate governmental interests in efficient administration and elimination of abuses by the voluntary poor."

Pollack responded in his brief with predictable scorn. The government's "search for a rational relationship between the purposes of the Food Stamp Act and the unrelated household provision," he wrote, "has proved fruitless." The law's real purpose, he charged, was to "harmfully discriminate" against poor people like Jacinta Moreno and Ermina Sanchez, who lived together from necessity and not for "immoral" reasons. Pollack's brief— at sixty-four pages—more than three times longer than the government's, quoted from *Democracy in America,* written by Alexis de Tocqueville in 1835. Anticipating the Supreme Court by more than a century, the perceptive French visitor wrote that Americans valued the "right of association" as an "inalienable" grant of citizenship. Pollack also quoted at length an opinion of Justice William O. Douglas—who would vote on the *Moreno* case—upholding the "freedom of association" of NAACP members against state harassment. The brief was calculated to portray the household of Jacinta Moreno and Ermina Sanchez as a citadel that should be "vigilantly protected by the Supreme Court" against Secretary Butz and his minions.

The justices set the *Moreno* and *Murry* cases for argument on April 23, 1973. Solicitor General Griswold assigned the "hippy" case to A. Raymond Randolph, the youngest member of his elite staff. Only a dozen lawyers, recruited from top law schools, served in Griswold's office. Randolph graduated *summa cum laude* in 1969 from the University of Pennsylvania law school, where he had the highest grades and was elected managing editor of the law review. He served a year as law clerk to Henry Friendly, a renowned federal circuit judge in New York, before joining the solicitor's office. The *Moreno* case would be Randolph's sixth Supreme Court argument, but he lacked Pollack's trial experience. Legal brilliance would be matched against a crusader's spirit as the two young lawyers faced each other.

Chief Justice Warren Burger presided at oral argument in the *Moreno* case. President Nixon had selected Burger in 1969 to replace Earl Warren. During his 1968 campaign, Nixon blasted the Warren Court as "soft on crime," and he chose Burger largely because of his hard-line opinions in criminal cases as a federal appellate judge in Washington, D.C. Burger had often differed with Judge McGowan, his former colleague on that court. By the time of the *Moreno* argument, Nixon had named three more Supreme Court justices, one short of a majority. But five members of the Warren Court remained on the bench. If a "Burger Court" was to emerge, it still lacked at least one new justice.

Each lawyer in the *Moreno* case was allotted thirty minutes, which could be interrupted by questions from the bench. Ray Randolph went first and spent most of his time detailing the procedures for deciding who was and wasn't eligible for food stamps. In his brief discussion of constitutional issues, Randolph predictably relied on the *Dandridge* case for the proposition, as he put it, that "the Constitution does not empower this Court to second-guess officials charged with the difficult responsibility of allocating limited public welfare funds among the myriad of potential recipients." Lawmakers could "rationally conclude" that households of unrelated persons were likely to be unstable and were "not deserving of food stamps on any scale of priorities that Congress could follow." Not once did Randolph mention Jacinta Moreno or her fellow plaintiffs. He encountered few questions and sat down before his time expired.

Ron Pollack began his argument by denying that the "hippy commune" law could meet the "rational basis" test of challenged legislation. The statute was not rational, he said, because real hippies could easily change their living arrangements to qualify for food stamps. "What the provision actually does harm are the poorest of the poor, those people who cannot separate themselves as independent economic units," he claimed. He then recited the dire poverty of Jacinta Moreno, forced by "brutal necessity" to live with Ermina Sanchez.

Unlike Randolph, Pollack faced a barrage of questions, mostly about the legislative motive behind the law. Justice Rehnquist made clear his position that this issue was irrelevant to the "rational basis" test. He suggested that the proper question was "whether any reasonable person could have enacted the statute that Congress did, not whether Congress's purpose is actually carried out by the statute." Pollack responded that Congress "never produced a purpose whatsoever." He turned to sarcasm. "If we want to fictionalize," he said, the justices could try "to figure out some other purposes that Congress really intended." It seems clear that Pollack knew he would not get Rehnquist's vote and aimed his argument at more receptive justices.

There is little doubt that oral argument in the *Moreno* case had no effect on the Court's decision. Some justices have claimed that an unusually persuasive argument could influence their vote, but none has ever identified such a case. Justice Rehnquist once said that his mind was "sometimes" changed by an argument, but his consistent voting record belies this claim. Justice Brennan was even less likely to be swayed. He rarely asked questions, and his votes—like those of Rehnquist—could be predicted with great precision. For both men, oral argument was basically a judicial ritual like the traditional handshake before the Court's conference.

Chief Justice Burger presided at the April 25 conference and opened discussion of the school integration and food-stamp cases. Burger had a firm, authoritative style in conference—he looked and sounded like a Chief Justice—but his review of precedent in many cases struck some justices as thin and tendentious. Justice Lewis Powell took no part in the discussion of the Richmond cases; he was a former president of the Richmond school board and had recused himself to avoid any hint of bias. Without his vote, the justices were split, four to four. The Court's clerk later issued a terse, unsigned order that said the lower-court decision was "affirmed by an equally divided Court."

When discussion turned to the food-stamp cases, Burger announced he was voting to uphold both the "tax dependents" and "hippy commune" laws. Once the Chief is finished, discussion proceeds in descending order of seniority. William O. Douglas, placed on the Court by President Franklin D. Roosevelt in 1939, spoke next as the senior associate justice. His physical stamina had declined after thirty-four years on the bench, but his liberal principles remained strong. He evened the score by voting to strike down both laws. Justice Brennan spoke next and agreed with Douglas in both cases. Potter Stewart, Byron White, and Thurgood Marshall joined to make a five-vote majority against both laws. Significantly, all five had served under Chief Justice Warren. The three junior justices—Harry Blackmun, Lewis Powell, and Rehnquist—were divided in the two cases. Blackmun and Powell voted to strike down the "hippy commune" law in the *Moreno* case, while Rehnquist joined Burger in dissent, producing a 7–2 vote against the law. However, Blackmun and Powell voted to uphold the "tax dependent" law in *Murry*, making the final tally 5–4 in that case.

BY TRADITION, when the Chief Justice is in the majority, he decides who will write the Court's opinion. When he is among the dissenters, as Burger was in both food-stamp cases, assignment passes to the senior justice in the majority. This allowed Douglas to decide, and he split the task with Brennan, taking the "tax dependents" case for himself and giving Brennan the *Moreno* opinion. Douglas was the Court's acknowledged tax law expert, which probably accounted for the division of opinions. Rehnquist agreed with Burger to take on both dissenting opinions.

"The writing of an opinion is not easy work," Brennan has said. "It always takes weeks and sometimes months. The most painstaking research and care go into the task." In addition to legal research, Brennan noted that "Supreme Court cases often require also some familiarity with other disciplines—history, economics, the social and other sciences" outside the law. Rehnquist has written that he "eagerly awaited" his opinion assignments, and that his work "offers no greater reward than the opportunity to author an opinion on an important point of constitutional law." Of course, writing majority opinions is more rewarding, but a well-crafted dissent can sometimes—even decades later—become the heart of a new majority opinion.

Law clerks do much of the research and drafting of opinions for most justices. Each justice is now entitled to four clerks, picked from the cream of the law school crop. Clerks often write opinions, and some justices only lightly edit their work. Brennan and Rehnquist, however, are both craftsmen, and each put a distinctive stamp on his opinions, although their styles differed considerably. These differences reflect more than personality; they stem from the diametrically opposed judicial philosophies the two men brought to the Supreme Court.

The opinions that Brennan and Rehnquist issued on June 25, 1973, had no rhetorical flourish or grand sweep of doctrine. They were definitely not written by Oliver Wendell Holmes or Felix Frankfurter, masters of the language. Both opinions were relatively short. Brennan's took up ten pages in the Court's official record. The dissent that Rehnquist wrote for himself and Chief Justice Burger covered only three pages, although it referred as well to Rehnquist's five-page dissent in the *Murry* case.

Brennan first recited the procedural history and legal issues in the *Moreno* case. He then described, in detail, the financial plight of Jacinta Moreno and Ermina Sanchez, down to the last dollar of their meager household budget. He noted that Moreno's monthly welfare check was only seventy-five dollars and that she paid fifty dollars for rent, ten dollars for transportation to the hospital, and five dollars for laundry. "That leaves her ten dollars per month for food and other necessities." Brennan took these facts almost verbatim from Ron Pollack's brief, which had put them at the front. Pollack's calculated appeal for sympathy clearly worked with Brennan, whose opinions often focused on "social facts" and personal data about litigants. For Brennan, the Constitution came alive in the stories of real people who challenged an often hostile government bureaucracy.

The opinion then moved to constitutional issues. "Under traditional equal protection analysis," Brennan wrote, "a legislative classification must be sustained if the classification itself is rationally related to a legitimate governmental interest." In the case citations that followed this sentence, Brennan took a slight bow toward the *Dandridge* case the government relied on for precedent. But he had dissented in *Dandridge* and had no trouble distinguishing it from the *Moreno* opinion. He looked for the intent of Congress in passing the "hippy commune" law and found it in Senator Holland's offhand comment on the Senate floor. This statement doomed the law. "The challenged classification clearly cannot be sustained by reference to this congressional purpose. For if the constitutional conception of 'equal protection of the laws' means anything, it must at the very least mean that a bare congressional desire to harm a politically unpopular group cannot constitute a *legitimate* governmental interest." Brennan italicized "legitimate" to emphasize his scorn for the hostility Congress displayed toward hippies and the harm imposed on people like Jacinta Moreno.

Brennan's opinion liberally borrowed the language of Judge McGowan, a kindred spirit on the bench. But he shied away from the "rights to privacy and freedom of association" on which McGowan's decision rested. Brennan clearly agreed with this position, but he was writing an opinion not only for himself, but for Justices Powell, Blackmun, and Stewart as well. These more conservative justices had all joined the *Roe v. Wade* opinion establishing a "right to privacy," which protected a woman's choice on abortion. But food stamps were hardly related to abortion. McGowan had invoked privacy and association rights to counter the government's "morality" excuse for denying food stamps to unrelated people. "The Government itself has now abandoned the 'morality' argument," Brennan noted with apparent relief. He could now write a narrowly crafted opinion that would satisfy the majority's more conservative members. Brennan was an acknowledged master at tailoring his opinions to fit the cloth of his colleagues, expansive if possible but narrow if necessary.

Having abandoned the "morality" argument, the government asserted that Congress designed the "hippy commune" law to prevent fraud by excluding people who were "likely to abuse the program" by living together simply to get food stamps. Brennan answered with "social facts" drawn from an affidavit Ron Pollack secured from California's director of social welfare, who claimed the law would harm mothers and children on welfare "who try to raise their standard of living by sharing housing" with unrelated people. Brennan claimed the law would not prevent fraud but would punish "*only* those persons who are so desperately in need of aid" that they must band together to cope with poverty. He concluded that the law "is wholly without any rational basis." The opinion ended by stating that the district court's decision "is therefore *Affirmed.*"

Justice Douglas, with no need to keep the majority in line, expressed the views he and Brennan shared in a concurring opinion that rested on "associational rights that lie in the penumbra of the First Amendment." Douglas borrowed his language from *Griswold v. Connecticut*, the 1965 case that overturned a ban on birth control and articulated a constitutional "right of privacy," which the Court extended in *Roe* to abortion. Because it impacted First Amendment rights, Douglas felt the "hippy commune" law should be "subject to the closest scrutiny" and could be sustained "only on a showing of a 'compelling' governmental interest." The government had not met that heavy burden of proof, and the law failed, Douglas wrote, because it denied "the rights of people to associate for lawful purposes with whom they choose." There is no doubt that Brennan agreed completely with Douglas's concurring opinion, which utilized the "strict scrutiny" test that Brennan applied in cases where he was free to write an expansive opinion. But *Moreno* was not such a case, and he did not join a concurrence that went beyond his narrow opinion.

IN HIS DISSENT, Rehnquist insinuated that Brennan had written a political tract and not a judicial opinion. "The Court's opinion," he wrote, "would make a very persuasive congressional committee report arguing against the adoption of the limitation in question." Rehnquist agreed that "Congress attacked the problem with a rather blunt instrument" that may have injured some needy people. "But questions such as this are for Congress, rather than for this Court; our role is limited to the determination of whether there is any rational basis" for denying food stamps to unrelated people. Brennan found the law to be "wholly without any rational basis," dismissing its supposed purpose in deterring fraud. Rehnquist was more charitable. "I do not believe that asserted congressional concern with the fraudulent use of food stamps," he wrote, "is quite as irrational as the Court seems to believe."

Rehnquist chided Brennan for rejecting the possibility that the law might deter those who live together simply to collect food stamps. He cited no evidence on this issue, since the government had never provided any. For Rehnquist, evidence was not necessary; all he required was a purpose for the law that was not totally beyond reason. As he put it, Congress could have "conceivably" intended to deter fraud in the program. No member of Congress had actually said this, since the sole evidence of congressional "intent" was limited to Senator Holland's one-sentence statement about hippies. This lack of evidence did not bother Rehnquist. His "rational basis" approach to the Constitution allowed him to imagine reasons that might have motivated lawmakers to pass a statute.

Rehnquist did not invent the "rational basis" test, but he applied it with a vengeance in dozens of cases. Ironically, he had been handed this constitutional tool by the Court's leading liberal, Justice Douglas. Writing in 1955, Douglas upheld in *Williamson v. Lee Optical Co.* an Oklahoma

law that barred opticians from grinding eyeglass lenses without a prescription from an optometrist or ophthalmologist. Opticians can easily
duplicate lenses without prescriptions, but Oklahoma lawmakers had
listened to the eye doctors' lobby. Douglas deferred in this case to legislative judgment. "The Oklahoma law may exact a needless, wasteful
requirement," he admitted, but "it is for the legislature, not the courts"
to make such decisions. With no evidence of legislative intent, Douglas
simply imagined reasons the lawmakers "may have concluded" that opticians should not grind lenses without a prescription.

Douglas limited his *Williamson* opinion to laws that regulated "business
and industrial conditions." In the *Dandridge* case, decided in 1970,
Justice Potter Stewart cited *Williamson* in extending the "rational basis"
test to laws that dealt more broadly with "economics and social welfare."
Douglas, who dissented in *Dandridge*, may have felt like Dr. Frankenstein
as he watched Rehnquist turn his test against Jacinta Moreno and other
poor people. In his longer dissent in the "tax dependents" case, Rehnquist
quoted Douglas—perhaps to needle him—in *Williamson*: "But the law
need not be in every respect logically consistent with its aims to be
constitutional. It is enough that there is an evil at hand for correction,
and that it might be thought that the particular legislative measure was
a rational way to correct it." The words "might be thought" gave
Rehnquist—as they had Douglas—an escape from the lack of evidence
on legislative intent.

Rehnquist did not mention Jacinta Moreno in his dissent, nor did he
refer to any "social facts" about the food-stamp program. His approach
to the Constitution is impersonal and abstract. Only rarely does Rehnquist
write about real people, most often in criminal cases, providing graphic
details of violence against the victims of gruesome crimes. This is not to
say that Rehnquist is cold and heartless; even his judicial critics consider
him warm and compassionate. But his constitutional philosophy does
not allow sympathy to interfere with the "rational basis" test of legislation
that may, as he wrote in his *Moreno* dissent, "have unfortunate and
perhaps unintended consequences" for people like Jacinta Moreno.

The Court's opinions in the food-stamp cases were issued on June 25,
1973. Reporters scrambled to digest opinions in twelve cases on the final
day of this historic term, as well as judicial orders in more than one
hundred pending cases. The headline of the *New York Times* roundup
article announced the Court's decision that "Curbs on Political Activity
Are Fair." Over dissents by Douglas, Brennan, and Marshall, six justices

upheld a law banning political activities by federal workers. At the tag end, under the heading "Communes Get Assist," the *Times* said the *Moreno* decision would benefit "as many as 600,000 people," including "migrant workers, welfare recipients and the unemployed who are often forced to live with families to whom they are not related." The article did not mention Brennan, but it quoted Rehnquist's claim that the law was "a permissible Congressional decision" to withhold aid from "households which have been formed solely for the purpose of taking advantage of the food stamp program."

With that brief account, the *Moreno* case vanished from public view. The justices scattered to their summer homes, where they would review hundreds of petitions for the next term. The two lawyers who argued before the Supreme Court took different paths in the legal profession. Ron Pollack remained as a public interest advocate, and is now executive director of the Families USA Foundation, which adds health care, education, and employment to concerns with food for poor families. Ray Randolph left the Solicitor General's office in 1973 for private practice, but returned in 1975 as deputy to Robert Bork, who praised him as a "top-flight advocate." Randolph left the office again in 1977 and moved into corporate law at $350,000 a year. With Bork's support, he was rewarded in 1991 with nomination by President George Bush to the federal appellate court for the District of Columbia.

Secretary of Agriculture Earl Butz, the defendant in the *Moreno* case, survived the Nixon administration but succumbed in 1976 to political foot-in-mouth disease, resigning in disgrace after telling a racist "joke" to a reporter. And what about the lead plaintiff, Jacinta Moreno? There is no current record of her address, if she is still alive. She was illiterate and never read the Supreme Court opinions that Justices Brennan and Rehnquist wrote in her case. She probably never knew that her affidavit, signed with an X, helped to restore food stamps to 600,000 people who shared her poverty.

THE *Moreno* CASE is hardly famous, although the doctrinal significance of the decision was reflected by an eight-page *Harvard Law Review* analysis and by thirteen citations in the leading treatise, *American Constitutional Law*, by Harvard law professor Laurence Tribe. But there are several reasons to begin this book with a detailed account of the *Moreno* case—one longer than the combined opinions of Justices

Brennan and Rehnquist. Their conflicting approaches to the Constitution are evident in many cases more noted than *Moreno*. This relatively obscure case, however, illustrates all the themes that run through the cases treated more briefly in this book, each of which could be expanded to equal or greater length.

First, the *Moreno* case stemmed from political conflict, both ideological and partisan. From the broadest perspective, it reflected a long-standing debate over the proper role of government in alleviating poverty. The "Poor Laws" of England and colonial America offered food, clothing, and shelter to the destitute, and were opposed by those who believed that poverty was the just reward for sloth. The Social Darwinists and laissez-faire "liberals" of the nineteenth century denounced "welfare" programs, as did twentieth-century "conservatives" who fought the New Deal during the Great Depression. During the 1950s and 1960s, poverty programs became embroiled in partisan politics, with most Democrats supporting them and most Republicans opposed. Racial polarization in American politics, increasing in every election since 1964, gave many people the erroneous belief that blacks constituted a majority of welfare recipients and made the word "welfare" an epithet.

Although some conservatives supported the food-stamp program, other political factors prompted the ban on stamps for "hippies" and college students. Drug use and draft evasion were already crimes, but youth itself became suspect, and politicians voted harsh penalties for burning marijuana and draft cards. Congress aimed the food-stamp restrictions at unpopular groups, unaware or uncaring that many of the "deserving poor" would get hit. Most constitutional cases, in fact, have similar political roots. Whatever the issue, liberals and conservatives—however fuzzy these terms have become—usually line up on opposite sides. And these political conflicts quickly reach the courts. To paraphrase General Clausewitz, constitutional litigation is politics by other means.

The *Moreno* case illustrates another political factor, the role of interest groups in constitutional litigation. Few cases arrive at the Supreme Court without a sponsor, as either a party or an *amicus* organization. This is hardly new, as groups like the NAACP and ACLU have sponsored hundreds of cases since the 1920s. But interest-group litigation has mushroomed in recent years, on both the left and the right. These groups flood the Supreme Court with *amicus* briefs in cases affecting their members. Abortion cases provide an index of the rapid increase: the *Roe* case in 1973 attracted eighteen *amicus* groups, while the *Webster* case in 1989 set a record of seventy-six briefs on both sides.

The politics of constitutional litigation is obvious in most cases. Reading through stacks of *amicus* briefs—or their clerks' summaries—before oral argument, justices quickly assess the political lineup on each side. The *Moreno* case attracted no supporting briefs, but the sponsoring interest group was clearly liberal, while the Nixon administration, which defended the law, was avowedly conservative. Interest groups also fund the cases of indigent clients. There is nothing unusual or unlawful about such arrangements; expenses in complex cases often exceed a million dollars. Jacinto Moreno could not have afforded a lawyer to challenge her denial of food stamps. Ron Pollack recruited her as a plaintiff to further the political aims of the Food Research and Action Center.

The *Moreno* case also reflects the other side of constitutional litigation: judicial politics. Interest groups represent contending political factions in American society, and Supreme Court justices are equally grouped into factions of left, right, and center. Political currents shift with time, outside and within the Court, and no faction remains stable over the years. The basic polarities, however, have persisted with little change. The judicial philosophies of Justices Brennan and Rehnquist express their liberal and conservative views in the words "dignity" and "deference."

Although neither of the *Moreno* opinions used these terms, their applications were obvious. Brennan expressed his belief that Congress, in depriving Jacinta Moreno of "necessary personal and hygienic needs," had robbed her of dignity as a human being. Rehnquist made equally clear his conviction that these "unfortunate and perhaps unintended consequences" should not affect the deference the Supreme Court owed to Congress.

The *Moreno* case illustrates another aspect of judicial politics, the search for votes. The goal, of course, is to secure a majority of five justices, preferably more. During the years they served together, Brennan and Rehnquist became the acknowledged leaders of their judicial factions, in both intellectual and political terms. Combining these two skills is rare in the Court's history. Felix Frankfurter, for instance, championed the cause of "judicial restraint" for two decades, but his acerbic tongue and pen lost him votes of potential allies in many cases. Justice Frank Murphy, who served with Frankfurter in the 1940s, matched Brennan in liberal views but remained an outsider on the Court.

In *Moreno*, Brennan gained the votes of two Nixon nominees, Blackmun and Powell, by writing a narrow opinion that avoided the "strict scrutiny" test favored by judicial liberals. Considering that both justices voted with Rehnquist in more than 90 percent of divided cases that term, Brennan showed political acumen in moderating his *Moreno* opinion to satisfy his centrist colleagues. Most observers agree that Rehnquist has not had equal success in marshaling votes, but not for lack of effort. His rigidly conservative views offer little room for compromise, and Rehnquist seemed to relish, until he became the "Chief" in 1986, his "Lone Ranger" role as an often solo dissenter. In fairness, no other justice has ever matched Brennan's mastery of judicial politics.

Finally, this recounting of the *Moreno* case highlights the differing emphasis Brennan and Rehnquist place on "social facts" in their opinions. Cases arrive at the Supreme Court with a record, largely based on trial testimony and exhibits such as affidavits and documents. Experienced lawyers like Ron Pollack carefully shape trial records to include material that sympathetic justices can quote in their opinions. The briefs of *amicus* groups provide additional facts and figures. In general, liberal justices rely more on "social facts," such as those Brennan cited from the *Moreno* record. Conservatives like Rehnquist usually ignore these facts in their opinions.

All these factors, in varying degrees, are present in every controversial case the Court decides. Their influence on final decisions is often complex and unpredictable, and is affected by the personalities, philosophies, and backgrounds of the nine justices who vote in each case. And few justices in the Court's history have differed more on each measure than William Brennan and William Rehnquist.

TWO

"THE CONSTITUTIONAL PRINCIPLE OF HUMAN DIGNITY"

LATE ON A FRIDAY afternoon, September 28, 1956, the telephone rang in the New Jersey Supreme Court chambers of Justice William Brennan. Other justices had left for the weekend, but courthouse janitors were used to seeing Brennan working late. During his four years on the state's highest court, Brennan had gained a reputation as a diligent judge, dedicated to his job. He was once asked about his hobbies. "I won't be so corny as to say my work is my hobby," he replied. "My work is my work, and I love every minute of it." When Brennan picked up the phone, his caller was Herbert Brownell, attorney general of the United States. He asked Brennan to meet with him the following morning in Washington, D.C., a three-hour train trip from Brennan's home. Brownell did not explain the purpose of his request, except to say it was important.

Brennan later gave his first reaction to Brownell's call. "I assumed it had something to do with the part I'd been playing in judicial reform." A few months earlier, he had stepped in at the last minute to replace New Jersey's Chief Justice, Arthur Vanderbilt, at a conference of U.S. attorneys in Washington. Brennan spoke on a favorite topic, the need to streamline the procedures of state and federal courts to ease judicial bottlenecks and reduce the backlog of cases. Brownell presided at the meeting and listened intently to Brennan's reform proposals.

The unexpected call from Brownell prompted another thought. The press had reported three weeks earlier that Justice Sherman Minton had told President Dwight Eisenhower he would retire from the U.S. Supreme Court after nine years of service. Minton suffered from pernicious anemia and could barely hobble to the bench. A former Indiana Democratic senator and poker-playing crony of President Harry Truman, who appointed him, "Shay" Minton wrote no opinions of lasting import and left no mark on the Court.

"I have to admit," Brennan recalled, "that the possibility crossed my mind about the Supreme Court vacancy but it seemed so fantastic I dismissed the idea at once." Brennan took the train the next morning to Washington's Union Station, a short walk from the Supreme Court. "Mr. Brownell came to the station to meet me," he said, "and on the way to his house for breakfast told me the President was considering me to fill the Supreme Court vacancy. I'm afraid I couldn't say anything intelligible—I just sat there, stunned to my bones. Later I was escorted into the President's office. I thought there'd be other people, but suddenly I found I was alone in the room with him, not a soul but me and the President. It was something!" After Brennan and Eisenhower had spent thirty minutes alone, White House press secretary James Hagerty joined them for Ike's formal offer of nomination. "I never heard a man say 'yes' so fast," Hagerty recalled. Brennan admitted his eagerness for the post. "I was willing to stop the inquiries right there," he said.

Hagerty escorted Brennan into the White House press office for a brief meeting with reporters. The press secretary noted that Eisenhower had reviewed the records of several federal and state judges. "After looking over the record of Justice Brennan, and reading the laudatory letter of recommendation which Chief Justice Arthur T. Vanderbilt of the New Jersey Supreme Court submitted, the President was satisfied that Justice Brennan was the man he wanted." Brennan had a few words for the press. "This has come as a complete surprise to me," he said. "I had no inkling of my impending appointment until I arrived here this morning." However genuine his surprise, Brennan could not conceal his delight. "The New Jersey jurist looked surprised and immensely pleased about his appointment," reported the New York Times. Photographers were ushered into the Oval Office, and the front-page picture in the Times showed the new justice with a grin that outdid Ike's famous ear-to-ear smile.

The Times also noted that Brennan "is a life-long Democrat and a Roman Catholic." Reporters speculated that he owed his appointment to both political and religious factors. Just a month after choosing Brennan, Eisenhower would face the voters in a rematch of his 1952 campaign against Adlai Stevenson. Polls showed a comfortable GOP lead, but several key northern, industrial states held the electoral balance. Eisenhower might win some wavering votes by naming a Catholic Democrat from an urban, northeastern state to the Supreme Court. What some called the "Catholic seat" on the Court had been vacant since the death of Justice Frank Murphy in 1949. There is no evidence that Brennan's appointment shifted the election results, let alone a single vote. Ike remained in the White House for a second term, and buried Stevenson in an electoral avalanche. In Brennan's home state, Eisenhower swamped his opponent by a margin of almost two to one. But if Brennan's nomination was a calculated political ploy, the voters "elected" him to the Supreme Court for a thirty-four-year term, and he outlasted every senator who voted to confirm him.

Brennan took his seat on the Supreme Court bench on October 16, the day after Minton's formal retirement. Because the Senate, whose "advice and consent" is required for Supreme Court nominations, was in recess for the election campaign, the appointment was temporary. The Senate would hold hearings and vote after the new Congress met in January 1957. Hardly anyone doubted Brennan's confirmation, probably without dissent. The conservative dean of American columnists, Arthur Krock of the *New York Times*, bestowed his imprimatur on Brennan as a deserving "representative of what an American can, with honor and integrity, achieve without the birthright of social and economic privilege." Bernard Shanley, President Eisenhower's appointments secretary and a boyhood schoolmate of Brennan, praised his friend in less exalted words. "They don't come like this guy. This is the American saga, the American dream."

WILLIAM JOSEPH BRENNAN, JR., came to the Court from a childhood in Newark, New Jersey, a city of tough streets and rough-and-tumble politics. His father came over from County Roscommon, Ireland, in 1893, at the age of twenty. Schooling in rural Ireland stopped after six grades, but Bill Brennan had a strong back and could lift a shovel all day long. He began in Trenton, firing a boiler in a licorice factory, but he disliked both the city and the smell, and moved to Newark, where he spent many years shoveling coal into the furnaces of the Ballantine brewery. Brennan soon became a union man, and joined Local 55 of the International Brotherhood of Stationary Engineers and Oilers. But the local was run by "grafters," and dissident members turned to Brennan for honest leadership. He wound up as business manager of Local 55 and delegate to the Essex County Trades and Labor Council.

After several years in union politics, Brennan ran for public office in 1917 as a Newark city commissioner. He was elected on his first try, and was returned to office every four years until 1929, topping the ticket in his last two elections. His fellow commissioners made Brennan the director of public safety, heading the police and fire departments. "No one ever accused Brennan of grafting," wrote an admiring reporter. "He was a strict ruler—many thought him too strict, especially with the police, from whom he demanded adherence to high standards of conduct." This principle of being "firm but fair" also characterized Brennan's approach to his children. He had married Agnes McDermott, another Roscommon emigrant, in 1903, and they raised eight children, four girls and four boys.

Bill Junior was the second child, born on April 25, 1906. Even in grade school, he followed his father's example of hard work. He labored six days a week as a "butcher boy," four hours after school and all day Saturday. During high school, Brennan held several jobs, working as a grease monkey in a garage, making change for trolley passengers, and delivering milk in a horse-drawn wagon with his brother Charlie. Brennan later made light of his teenage jobs. "I'm no Horatio Alger," he said. He joked that his purpose in working "was to keep me in custom-made clothes." Brennan was a gay blade as a young man in the Roaring Twenties, but he also absorbed from his father the virtue of hard work and his vision of a just society.

The visitors to the Brennan home included many lawyers, and Bill Junior was entranced by their discussions of law and politics. He remembers his father's advice on a career. "Lad, you argue well around the house and I've no doubt you'll make a fine lawyer. But as for politics, I think you'll be happier out than in." Brennan heeded this counsel and headed straight for Harvard Law School after graduating with honors in 1928 from the University of Pennsylvania's Wharton School of Finance and Commerce. A week before commencement, Brennan married his high school sweetheart, Marjorie Leonard. To save on expenses, she remained at home in New Jersey, working as a newspaper proofreader, while Brennan lived a spartan life in Cambridge. He excelled in law school, and devoted his spare time to the Harvard Legal Aid Society, which provided student lawyers to indigent people in the Cambridge and Boston courts. His experience in these municipal courts gave Brennan firsthand exposure to the "justice" meted out to the poor.

Brennan worked even harder after his father died, a year before his graduation from Harvard in 1931. When he returned to Newark to join the city's biggest law firm, Brennan moved into labor law, but on the opposite side of the table from that his father had occupied. He represented companies like Western Electric in negotiations and labor disputes with their workers, but retained his father's reputation for being firm but fair as a lawyer. Brennan's firm rewarded his hard work with a partnership in 1937. World War II interrupted his law practice, but he continued his legal career as an Army major, assigned by the Ordnance Department to settle labor disputes in defense factories. He did troubleshooting all over the country, including for the chaotic West Coast aircraft industry, plagued by manpower shortages and strikes. By the war's end, he wound up as a colonel, with glowing recommendations from high-ranking officials.

When he returned to practice in Newark, Brennan joined a group of Young Turks who threw themselves into an effort to reform New Jersey's archaic legal system, which tossed cases—almost randomly—into fourteen separate courts. His work attracted the attention of Governor Alfred Driscoll, a Republican who paid little heed to party labels in choosing judges. In 1949, Driscoll tapped Brennan for the state Superior Court, where he gained valuable trial experience and learned firsthand about the deficiencies of the courts in dispensing justice. Governor Driscoll kept his eye on Brennan, was impressed by what he saw, and elevated him to the state Supreme Court in 1952.

STATE COURT JUDGES, even those on Supreme Court benches, devote most of their time to mundane cases that raise issues of state law and involve fields such as wills, contracts, and municipal regulations. One of the first cases Brennan decided in New Jersey's highest court raised the question of whether a manure barn should be classified as a residence or a business under zoning laws. State judges, of course, are bound like their federal counterparts by the Supremacy clause of the U.S. Constitution, which declares invalid any state law that conflicts with federal guarantees. During his four years on the New Jersey Supreme Court, Brennan wrote about one thousand pages of opinions and dissents, in more than one hundred cases. Only a handful dealt with federal constitutional issues, and they show Brennan as a careful and cautious judge, respectful of precedent but also concerned with "social facts" that moved the court beyond legal abstractions. Of this modest number of cases, four opinions illustrate Brennan's approach to constitutional issues during his formative years as an appellate judge.

One of Brennan's first opinions took a narrow approach to the privilege against self-incrimination. The Fifth Amendment of the U.S. Constitution protects every defendant in federal court from becoming a "witness against himself." Brennan faced the question of whether the federal privilege applied to New Jersey cases. The case involved charges against James Christy and "Patsy" Pillo, identified in press reports as having "corruptly taken money and permitted gambling games" at the Maple Shade Casino in Burlington County. The two men were called before a grand jury, but claimed the privilege against self-incrimination and refused to answer questions about payoffs.

Brennan's opinion, which generally upheld the grand jury's right to compel answers from Christy and Pillo, acknowledged that "compelling a person to convict himself of crime" was "abhorrent to the instincts of an American." But he stepped back from what he called the "extreme and over-generous interpretation and application" of the Fifth Amendment by the U.S. Supreme Court. Brennan noted that the privilege "does not apply to the several states." While correct as a matter of precedent, this ruling was not compelled by New Jersey law. Because the privilege *was* protected by state law, decisions of the U.S. Supreme Court could provide Brennan with guidance in deciding its scope. He gave the state privilege a narrow reading. "The trial judge is not to accept the witness' mere statement that the answer will tend to incriminate him," he wrote. "It is for the court to say whether his silence is justified." Writing after Brennan's appointment to the U.S. Supreme Court, but before he took his seat, one commentator said that Brennan's opinion "cut the heart out of" the privilege. This friendly critic wrote that whether Brennan "will be equally harsh with the politically heterodox—for whose protection the self-incrimination concept was originally evolved—remains to be seen."

Brennan showed more respect for the federal Constitution in a 1953 opinion that involved his father's former office of public safety director in Newark. He might have asked Chief Justice Vanderbilt for the opinion for just this reason. At any rate, his father's successor, a man named Keenan, denied a license to the Adams Theater because he considered its burlesque shows to be lewd performances. A city ordinance gave the public safety director the discretion to decide which theatrical performances offended "decency and good order." Brennan's opinion, striking down the ordinance, cited a long string of U.S. Supreme Court decisions that prohibited any "previous restraints upon free expression." He noted that deciding whether a "play, show, or motion picture is lewd and indecent more often is a controverted question than a matter upon which all will agree."

Brennan reached back for precedent to a 1934 opinion of federal judge Augustus Hand striking down a ban on James Joyce's controversial novel *Ulysses*, which includes graphic scenes of sexual fantasy. Brennan agreed with Hand that "the mere fact that sexual life is the theme of the presentation" or that characters use "vulgar language" does not make a book or play "lewd and indecent." Early in his judicial career, Brennan displayed a penchant for finding guidance not in ancient cases but in current scholarship. His opinion quoted at length a book entitled *Burlesque as a Cultural Phenomenon.* "The pièce de résistance is the girl who disrobes, partially or entirely, and this act varies with the political season and the locality," the author noted. The burlesque operator knows "that he is giving a sex show, sans excuses, sans philosophy and above all, sans clothes." One gets a hint from this opinion that Justice Brennan doubted that his father, who enjoyed Irish conviviality, would have denied a license to the Adams Theater.

Like his father, Brennan may have been soft on burlesque, but he was hard on union corruption. One of his opinions rejected claims that the federal Constitution prohibited the barring from union office of a person who had been convicted of state crimes. James Calabrese, who served a sentence for extortion, was later elected treasurer of Local 1247 of the International Longshoremen's Association. New Jersey law denied union office to anyone whose conviction involved "moral turpitude," which Brennan extended to Calabrese's crime.

Calabrese based his challenge to the state law on five provisions of the federal Constitution, including prohibitions against "bills of attainder" and protections of the Due Process and Equal Protection clauses. "None of these grounds has substance," Brennan wrote. He relied on the state's "police powers" to protect its waterfronts against "criminals, racketeers and hoodlums" like Calabrese. Brennan cited "social facts" from a legislative report that "criminal elements are firmly entrenched on the waterfront" and that "gambling, the narcotics traffic, loansharking, shortganging, payroll 'phantoms,' the 'shakedown' in all its forms—and the brutal ultimate of murder—have flourished virtually unchecked" in New Jersey ports. On the constitutional scale, Brennan placed a heavier thumb on the state's "police powers" than on Calabrese's claim that he had been duly elected by the union's members. Brennan felt that control of unions by "criminal elements" threatened "free collective bargaining" and other "lawful means" to settle labor disputes. "The first and immediate need" of the law, he wrote, "was to break the grip of the racketeers and hoodlums." His father would certainly have agreed with this opinion.

Brennan did not write the opinion in the fourth New Jersey case, but its holding brought him trouble in Senate confirmation hearings. This case involved a decorated war veteran, James Kutcher, who lost his legs on a Pacific island. Brennan had lost his younger brother Charlie on another Pacific island. The case also came from Brennan's hometown of Newark, where Kutcher lived with his father, Hyman, in a low-rent housing project. Officials of the Newark Housing Authority demanded that Hyman Kutcher and other project residents sign a statement that no member of their households "is a member of any organization listed by the Attorney General of the United States as subversive." Tenants who did not sign would be evicted. Hyman Kutcher refused to sign the statement. His son was not only a disabled veteran but was a member of the Socialist Workers Party, a Trotskyite group listed by the U.S. attorney general as a Communist organization.

The New Jersey Supreme Court, without dissent, issued a narrow ruling in the case, holding that the attorney general had not formally designated the Socialist Workers Party as a "subversive" group. The justices also agreed that membership in the party did not provide "reasonable grounds for belief in the tenant's disloyalty" under state law. The court held that the Housing Authority was "subject to the requirements of due process" and that the Kutcher family was protected "against an arbitrary exercise of the powers of government." This opinion, issued in 1955, reflected judicial revulsion at the excesses of McCarthyism.

Earlier that year, Brennan had spoken out in public against the contempt for the Constitution displayed by Senator Joseph McCarthy and other congressional inquisitors. In a speech to the Monmouth Rotary Club, Brennan deplored "secret hearings released to the press, the shouted epithet at the hapless and helpless witness." It was not accidental that Brennan made this speech in the county that housed Fort Monmouth, the site of McCarthy's attack on the U.S. Army for "coddling" Communists in its ranks. By the time Brennan spoke, McCarthy's grip of fear on the nation had already been loosened by a feisty Boston lawyer named Joseph Welch. During the televised "Army-McCarthy" hearings in June

1954, Welch finally responded to weeks of the senator's bullying: "Have you no sense of decency, sir?" After several more exchanges the audience erupted in applause, and McCarthy's slide from power began. In December 1954, the Senate "condemned" its rogue member by a 67–22 vote. Two months later, Brennan expressed in his Rotary Club speech his "pure joy and relief that at long last our collective conscience has sickened of the excesses and is demanding the adoption of permanent and lasting reforms to curb investigatory abuses."

JUSTICE BRENNAN felt anything but joy when he encountered McCarthy, for the first and only time, at the Senate hearing on his nomination in February 1957. Following his recess appointment, Brennan had sat on the Court for more than four months, and his confirmation was a formality. He appeared before the Senate Judiciary Committee, whose members showered him with praise. McCarthy was not a committee member, but he took a seat and demanded to question Brennan. The two men sparred for almost an hour.

McCarthy got right to the point. "As the committee is well aware," he began, "the Supreme Court will have a number of cases before it in the months ahead concerning the Communist conspiracy, and concerning congressional efforts to expose the conspiracy." Recalling the speech that made him famous in 1950, McCarthy waved a sheaf of papers and claimed they contained evidence that "Justice Brennan has demonstrated an underlying hostility to congressional attempts to expose the Communist conspiracy." Wyoming Senator Joseph O'Mahoney, who detested his colleague, interrupted, saying that "the documents which you have in your hand are mere typewritten papers. I want you to identify them. What are they?" McCarthy continued to wave the papers and said they were "statements that come from the mouth of Justice Brennan." After much fencing between the two senators, McCarthy identified the papers as copies of two speeches Brennan had given, one to the Charitable Irish Society in Boston and the other to the Monmouth Rotary Club. Despite McCarthy's pose of having uncovered hidden evidence, there was no secret source of the papers he waved. A member of McCarthy's staff had called Brennan's secretary, who sent the speeches right over.

The two speeches, in fact, were almost identical in wording and entirely patriotic in tone. They both professed belief in America as God's country. Ever since the Constitution's ratification, Brennan told his audiences, "all branches of government in America have followed a course of official conduct which openly accepts the existence of God as the Creator and Ruler of the Universe." He pointed to the annual presidential Thanksgiving Proclamation as "a striking reflection of the acceptance by our Nation, and specifically by our Government, of the idea and existence of God." Brennan matched his praise of religion with denunciation of "the godless foe" of communism and its "deadly challenge" to democracy. "Organized atheistic society," he said, "is making a determined drive for supremacy by conquest as well as by infiltration." Hardly anything in Brennan's speeches could offend anyone who believed in God and opposed communism. Even McCarthy conceded that "Mr. Brennan is a very erudite gentleman" and "gives very good speeches on an overall basis."

But the Wisconsin senator did not attend the hearing to praise Brennan's forensic abilities. He wanted to know why Brennan had "referred to congressional investigations of communism as Salem witch hunts, and inquisitions, and has accused congressional investigating committees of barbarism." Brennan had in fact made these charges. Speaking in Boston during the Senate inquiry into McCarthy's attacks on the Army, Brennan referred to an earlier—and more deadly—inquisition of dissenters. He told his audience that he found "some practices in the contemporary scene reminiscent of the Salem witch hunts." Before the Monmouth Rotarians in 1955, Brennan defended the Fifth Amendment privilege against self-incrimination with greater passion than he displayed in his 1952 judicial opinion. He now linked the "abuses which brought the privilege into being so many years ago" with abuses by "those committees inquiring into alleged subversion in Government." Congressional inquisitors had moved from "the rack and the screw" to modern methods of intimidation that came "perilously close to destroying liberty in liberty's name." Brennan did not mention McCarthy by name in either speech, but the Red-hunting senator pursued his critic into the hearing room.

McCarthy began his interrogation with a blunt question: "Do you approve of congressional investigations and exposure of the Communist conspiracy?" Brennan had a disarming answer. "I can't think of a more important or vital objective of any committee investigation than that of rooting out subversives in Government." McCarthy had not expected this agreement with his question, and suggested that Brennan had "adopted the gobbledegook that communism is merely a political party, is not a conspiracy." He again demanded that Brennan state his opinion on this issue. Brennan demurred. "I can't say anything to you, Senator, about a pending matter." Both men knew the Court had already heard argument in several cases that challenged the powers of congressional committees—including McCarthy's own panel—to compel answers from alleged Communists. But these cases were not yet decided, and Brennan consistently declined to answer questions about them. "I do have an obligation," he reminded McCarthy, "not to discuss any issues that are touched upon in cases before the Court." McCarthy ended on a note of frustration. "I just wonder if a Supreme Court justice can hide behind his robes and conduct a guerrilla warfare against investigating committees," he asked.

Brennan survived his ordeal as McCarthy's last victim of legislative torture. The Senate Judiciary Committee unanimously approved his nomination and set it for a vote on March 19, 1957. McCarthy made one last objection on the Senate floor. "Mr. Brennan's frame of mind toward the Communist conspiracy," he said, "shows his supreme unfitness to be an Associate Justice of the Supreme Court." Minutes later, the Senate confirmed Brennan's appointment by voice vote. McCarthy's solitary "No" was not even recorded in the *Congressional Record*.

McCarthy did not survive to read the opinions in the cases Brennan had refused to discuss at his hearing. His mind and body ravaged by alcohol, McCarthy died on May 2, 1957. A month later, Brennan helped to write the political obituary of his opponent. The day after he joined the Supreme Court, Brennan heard arguments in a case that tested the government's power to force union officers to swear they were not Communist Party members. Clinton Jencks, an official of the Mine, Mill and Smelter Workers union, filed the required affidavit but was prosecuted and convicted of perjury. The main witness at his trial was Harvey Matusow, an FBI informant who later admitted he had lied in dozens of trials. Jencks appealed to the Supreme Court, arguing that the government had refused to produce records that exposed Matusow's consistent perjury. "The burden is the government's," Brennan wrote in his opinion, to disclose "relevant statements or reports in its possession of government witnesses touching the subject matter of their testimony at the trial." Matusow had been a favorite witness before McCarthy's committee.

THERE IS LITTLE QUESTION that William Brennan brought with him to the Supreme Court bench a well-formed constitutional philosophy. Shaped in childhood and sharpened by law practice and judicial experience, it can be capsulized in one word: dignity. Perhaps surprising to those who consider him a convinced secularist, Brennan's philosophy is firmly rooted in his Catholic upbringing and religious faith. Of course, Senator Joseph McCarthy was also Catholic and denounced Brennan as a political heretic. But every major religion has liberal and conservative wings, and Brennan clearly absorbed the "social gospel" of the Catholic left. As with Justice Frank Murphy, who occupied the "Catholic seat" before him, Brennan's religious faith animated his judicial philosophy but did not influence his votes in cases that raised the separation of Church and State. This seeming anomaly stems from the troubled role of Catholics in American society, as a religious minority that finally achieved political influence. Thoughtful Catholics recognize that their secular status depends on constitutional tolerance.

His exposure to the Catholic "social gospel" helps to explain Brennan's devotion to "justice and fair play and simple human dignity" as the core values of the American constitutional system. Speaking to a Catholic group before his Supreme Court nomination, Brennan said the American system was "based upon the dignity and inviolability of the individual soul," linking the Declaration of Independence with the biblical injunction "Ye shall know the truth, and the truth shall make you free." For Brennan, the "truth" of the Declaration's proclamation of "God-given inalienable rights" stems from the "truth" of Christian faith. "Freedom was the promise" of that faith, Brennan said, and freedom is the promise of the Constitution. Americans sought freedom from "the absolute state," and built a society of "millions of free men working in their own way for themselves and their children." And the freedom of each required freedom for all. "Yes, this is a religious nation," Brennan said, but "not a Catholic nation, or a Protestant nation, or a Jewish nation, but increasingly a genuinely free and tolerant society," mindful of its diversity in religion, race, and politics.

From this speech emerge several themes that foreshadow Brennan's self-proclaimed "activism" as a judge. His faith was rooted, not in deference to ecclesiastical authority, but in Catholic social movements for workers' rights. There is no evidence of personal ties to Monsignor John A. Ryan or other Catholic progressives of the 1930s and 1940s, but Brennan's speeches closely matched their writings on the social and political quest for "dignity" in the workplace and community. There is a striking parallel in these speeches with the labor encyclical of Pope Leo XIII, *Rerum Novarum,* issued in 1891. "Workers are not to be treated as slaves," he wrote, "justice demands that the dignity of the human personality be respected in them." During a devastating world war, Pope Pius XII called in 1942 for "giving back to the human person the dignity given to it by God from the very beginning." Whether or not Brennan read these papal words, their message infused his father's work as an honest labor leader and the atmosphere of the Brennan household in Newark.

A second theme of Brennan's speeches is that human dignity can only flourish in a society that protects the individual from the "absolute state" and from "arbitrary" officials. Once he left the state bench and "wrestled with the Constitution" as a Supreme Court justice, Brennan found the text for his judicial sermons in the Due Process clauses of the Fifth and Fourteenth amendments. During the Constitutional Bicentennial in 1987, he elaborated this theme in a speech entitled "Reason, Passion, and 'The Progress of the Law,' " delivered in honor of Justice Benjamin Cardozo, who served on the Supreme Court from 1932 to 1938. Cardozo was an obvious judicial model for Brennan. He had been a noted judge on New York's highest court, and had stressed in his 1921 book, *The Nature of the Judicial Process,* the human element in judging.

In his Cardozo lecture, Brennan looked back to a colonial America based on "assumptions of a natural social hierarchy" of caste and class. In such a society, officials ruled with arbitrary authority, unchecked by law. The Revolution, and the Constitution that followed, changed these assumptions. "As a result," Brennan said, "Americans regarded the relationship between the government and the people in a fundamentally new way. Government officials were considered agents of the people, to whom certain limited authority had been delegated."

The Due Process clauses of the Constitution, added by the Fifth and Fourteenth amendments, were designed to limit governmental authority by protecting the "life, liberty, or property" of Americans from arbitrary official action. As Brennan put it, "Due process required fidelity to a more basic and more subtle principle: the essential dignity and worth of each individual." The Constitution required officials "to treat citizens not as subjects but as fellow human beings." Brennan added that "due process asks whether government has treated someone fairly, whether individual dignity has been honored, whether the worth of an individual has been acknowledged." Officials cannot answer these questions "solely by pointing to rational action taken according to standard rules. They must plumb their conduct more deeply, seeking answers in the more complex equations of human nature and experience."

Brennan argued that a critical element of these "complex equations" is human passion, which he loosely defined as the imposition of "personal will" on a social situation. The Constitution's Framers, he said, "operated within a political and moral universe that had experienced arbitrary passion as the greatest affront to the dignity of the citizen." One way to eliminate "arbitrary passion" is to construct a "bureaucratic model of authority" that "aspires ultimately to banish passion from government altogether, and to establish a state where only reason will reign." Brennan did not exalt "passion" over "reason" in a Rousseauian sense, preferring the "noble savage" to the enlightened intellectual. What he proposed was replacing the "arbitrary passion" of bureaucrats with a passion for human dignity. "If due process values are to be preserved in the bureaucratic state of the late twentieth century," he said, "it may be essential that officials possess passion—the same passion that puts them in touch with the dreams and disappointments of those with whom they deal."

Another central theme of Brennan's judicial philosophy is that "due process" is a concept whose meaning is not static, frozen by the Framers in 1787, but one that changes over time, as society changes. The Framers did not intend, he argued, to impose on judges an inflexible definition of "a clause that reflects a principle as elusive as human dignity." Brennan quoted Justice John Harlan, writing in 1961: "Due process has not been reduced to any formula; its content cannot be determined by reference to any code." It represents, Harlan wrote, the shifting "balance which our Nation, built upon postulates of respect for the liberty of the individual, has struck between that liberty and the demands of organized society."

The notion that the meaning of "due process" shifts over time imposes a burden on judges who share this approach to the Constitution. Placed by history within a "given age," Brennan said, judges "must draw on our own experience as inhabitants of that age, and our own sense of the uneven fabric of social life. We cannot delude ourselves that the Constitution takes the form of a theorem whose axioms need mere logical deduction." Speaking at Georgetown University—a Catholic school— in 1981, Brennan aimed these remarks at Attorney General Edwin Meese, who claimed that judges must apply the "original intent" of the Framers to constitutional provisions. Meese had launched a political assault on the Supreme Court for the Reagan administration, which was frustrated by Brennan's skill at saving Warren Court decisions from reversal by Chief Justice Warren Burger and his conservative colleagues.

Brennan responded in his Georgetown speech to Meese's demand "that Justices discern exactly what the Framers thought about the question under consideration and simply follow that intention in resolving the case before them." In a phrase widely quoted in the press, Brennan labeled this demand as "little more than arrogance cloaked as humility." He did not conceal his contempt for those who "have no familiarity with the historical record." Brennan noted that "records of the ratification debates provide sparse or ambiguous evidence of the original intention" on the interpretation of "due process" and other broad phrases in the Constitution. "Typically, all that can be gleaned is that the Framers themselves did not agree about the application or meaning of particular constitutional provisions and hid their differences in cloaks of generality."

Brennan told his Georgetown audience that "the political underpinnings of such a choice should not escape notice." He clearly meant his listeners to notice the right-wing agenda of the Reagan administration. Brennan went on to deplore the "facile historicism" of Meese's position. Any claim that the meaning of "due process" was frozen in 1787, he said, "establishes a presumption of resolving textual ambiguities against the claim of constitutional right" by minorities and dissenters. Meese and his conservative allies, Brennan argued, "turn a blind eye to social progress" and display "antipathy to claims of the minority to rights against the majority."

This last statement illustrates another important theme of Brennan's jurisprudence. "The view that all matters of substantive policy should be resolved through the majoritarian process," he says, "has appeal under some circumstances, but I think ultimately it will not do." What the principle of majority rule cannot do, Brennan argues, is "to rectify claims of minority right that arise as a response to the outcomes of that very majoritarian process." When those outcomes—in voting booths and legislative chambers—display prejudice against the "outsiders" in American society, the Constitution requires judicial intervention. In Brennan's view, judges have the power and, in appropriate cases, the duty to displace majority rule when it violates the rights of minorities. "Faith in democracy is one thing," he says, "blind faith quite another." The Constitution was designed to place fundamental rights "beyond the reach of temporary political majorities."

This defense of minority rights does not lead Justice Brennan to advocate replacing what he calls legislative "imperialism" with an equivalent judicial imperialism. The Constitution does not empower judges to impose their own personal values on its provisions. But it does require them to speak, individually and collectively, for American society as a whole. "When Justices interpret the Constitution," Brennan says, "they speak for their community, not for themselves alone." This statement, of course, begs the question of how any justice can determine which "community" is relevant to the decision of a case. Some communities are delimited by geography as local, state, or national; others are defined as ethnic, religious, or racial. And the nation can be considered a "community" as a whole. Beyond these questions are those of public opinion and personal sentiment. No justice has ever proposed that the Court rely on public opinion polls in deciding controversial cases. And no justice has suggested that personal views are superior to the Constitution's demand for impersonal judging.

Justice Brennan does not evade these hard questions. He acknowledges that judges must make "substantive value choices" when they interpret constitutional provisions and that they "must accept the ambiguity inherent in the effort to apply them to modern circumstances." Justices, he says, "read the Constitution in the only way that we can: as twentieth-century Americans." He adds these words: "We look to the history of the time of framing and to the intervening history of interpretation. But the ultimate question must be: What do the words of the text mean in our time? For the genius of the Constitution rests not in any static meaning it might have had in a world that is dead and gone, but in the adaptability of its great principles to cope with current problems and current needs."

Brennan agrees that allowing unelected judges to reverse the decisions of elected lawmakers goes against the grain of democratic government. "These are important, recurrent worries," he admits. But he does not shrink from advocating "an active judiciary" as a counterweight to "legislative irresponsibility." He cites as examples of "panic" by majorities the prosecution of those who criticized American involvement in both world wars. Judges failed in each case to protect the victims of wartime hysteria, and the results "are among the least proud moments in the Court's history."

In summary, Justice Brennan's judicial philosophy begins with his deep religious faith in the "dignity" of every person, moves to the principle that government exists to serve the needs of individuals and to protect their dignity, and ends with the notion that the meaning of the Constitution must change as society changes. Judges speak for a community that is diverse and disputatious, and they must step in to prevent majorities, permanent or temporary, from trampling on the rights of minorities. The foundation of Brennan's jurisprudence is his view of the Constitution as "a living, evolving document that must be read anew" by each generation.

THE REAL TEST of a judicial philosophy comes in judicial opinions. Justice Brennan himself has identified the case he considers the best illustration of his approach to the Constitution: *Goldberg v. Kelly*, decided by the Supreme Court in 1970. During the final battles of the federal War on Poverty, legal aid lawyers in New York City filed a suit against Jack Goldberg, the commissioner of social services, on behalf of twenty welfare recipients; all had been terminated from the Aid to Families with Dependent Children (AFDC) or Home Relief programs. Decisions to cut off aid were made without advance notice or hearings, based on administrative findings the welfare recipients could not see or challenge. They claimed the state had violated their rights to procedural due process under the Fourteenth Amendment.

The lead plaintiff was John Kelly, a young man who had been the victim of a hit-and-run driver and could not work. The complaint in the case said that Kelly's caseworker ordered him to move into a notorious welfare hotel, but he complained it was full of "drug addicts and drunkards" and left the hotel to live with a friend. Not only was Kelly terminated from welfare without notice, but the caseworker demanded and got back a check for a winter coat she had authorized for him.

Brennan wrote for five members of the Court in striking down New York's policy of "termination first, hearing later." Characteristically, he first looked at "social facts" and the policy's impact on people it actually affected. He did not discuss John Kelly's plight, but he examined the records of other plaintiffs and wrote that "Mrs. Altagracia Guzman alleged that she was in danger of losing AFDC payments for failure to cooperate with the City Department of Social Services in suing her estranged husband." Brennan also noted that "Home Relief payments to Juan DeJesus were terminated because he refused to accept counseling and rehabilitation for drug addiction. Mr. DeJesus maintains that he does not use drugs."

After discussing federal legislation on welfare funding for the states and New York's welfare-termination procedures, Brennan moved to broader issues and to "social facts" of national scope. "We have to come to recognize," he wrote, "that forces not within the control of the poor contribute to their poverty." He cited for this statement a 1965 article by Yale law professor Charles Reich, "Individual Rights and Social Welfare." The year before, Reich had published a highly controversial article, "The New Property," which argued that government entitlements such as welfare were as much a form of "property" for the poor as real estate and stocks are for the wealthy. Brennan did not quote from the article he cited, but Reich argued in it that "when individuals have insufficient resources to live under conditions of health and decency, society has obligations to provide support, and the individual is entitled to that support as of right."

Brennan added to Reich's argument his own claim that "the background of our traditions" supported a welfare system that could "bring within the reach of the poor the same opportunities that are available to others to participate meaningfully in the life of the community." There are, of course, other—and less generous—traditions in this country of casting the poor onto private charity alone. Brennan, however, looked to a tradition of public assistance, one not much older than the New Deal of Franklin Roosevelt.

From "social facts" that he read with sympathy for the poor, Brennan moved to the question of whether the Constitution provides welfare recipients rights to a pretermination hearing. He again cited a recent law review article, "Due Process and the Right to a Prior Hearing in Welfare Cases," written precisely to argue the plaintiffs' case in *Goldberg v. Kelly*. This article, Brennan said, "is particularly telling in light of the welfare bureaucracy's difficulties in reaching correct decisions on eligibility." The authors noted that more than a third of New York's welfare-termination decisions were found on appeal to be based on erroneous facts and were reversed. Brennan did not cite the statistics, but he dismissed the state's argument that "summary adjudication" is a rational means of "conserving fiscal and administrative resources."

Four years earlier, Brennan had joined the Court's majority in *Miranda v. Arizona*, which forced the police to provide criminal defendants with detailed warnings of their rights to remain silent and to have counsel after arrest. Brennan's opinion in *Goldberg* forced welfare officials to provide equivalent protections to anyone threatened with termination.

He wrote that "due process requires an opportunity to confront and cross-examine adverse witnesses." Welfare recipients share this right with criminal defendants, because their "situation becomes immediately desperate" when benefits are terminated. In addition, "the recipient must be allowed to retain an attorney" for the hearing. Brennan argued that lawyers "can help delineate the issues, present the factual contentions in an orderly manner, conduct cross-examination, and generally safeguard the interests of the recipients."

Brennan rooted the *Goldberg* opinion in his core value. "From its founding," he wrote, "the Nation's basic commitment has been to foster the dignity and well-being of all persons within its borders." Stripping needy people like Altagracia Guzman and Juan DeJesus of welfare benefits without a hearing robbed them of both sustenance and dignity. Brennan used this opinion in his Cardozo lecture in 1987 to examine a basic question: How exactly does due process jurisprudence take account of concepts as abstract as reason and passion? To some, he said, "*Goldberg* appears as a triumph of the model of reason, holding the welfare system to a demanding standard of rationality that only an even more advanced bureaucracy could satisfy." Brennan had "no regrets" about making the welfare system more rational, but he suggested that "*Goldberg* can be seen in another way." He viewed his opinion "as an expression of the importance of passion in governmental conduct, in the sense of attention to the concrete human realities at stake."

In his Cardozo address, Brennan went beyond the "social facts" in his opinion and quoted at length from the plaintiffs' brief, which recounted "the human stories that the state's administrative regime seemed unable to hear." These were stories of hunger and homelessness. "Esther Lett fainted in a welfare center while seeking an emergency food payment of $15 to feed herself and her children for three days." And "Juan DeJesus found himself homeless, living in temporary shelter provided by a friend." Brennan's point in telling these stories was to suggest that officials in every branch of government—legislators, administrators, and judges—must add to bureaucratic rationality and formality the "passion" that he called "the wellspring from which concepts such as dignity, decency, and fairness flow."

Brennan admitted that "*Goldberg* may have spawned unforeseen consequences. It may have even contributed in some ways to the formality of the welfare system. Yet I think that it also opened a dialogue that continues to this day about the responsibilities of the bureaucratic state to its citizens." Brennan was proud of his opinion for beginning a dia-logue, within the Court and outside, over what he called "the underlying vision of human dignity enshrined in the due process clause." He con-tinued that dialogue, in reality a debate, for almost two decades with Justice William Rehnquist, whose judicial philosophy stems from an entirely different background and set of values.

THREE

"One Personal Conviction Is No Better Than Another"

EARLY ON A WEDNESDAY morning, October 21, 1971, William H. Rehnquist was summoned to the office of John Mitchell, attorney general of the United States. Rehnquist worked down the hall from Mitchell in the dull gray, square-block building that houses the Department of Justice. He served Mitchell and President Richard Nixon as assistant attorney general and director of the Office of Legal Counsel, a job that made him, in Nixon's words, "the President's lawyer's lawyer."

Two other men waited in Mitchell's office. Richard Kleindienst, the deputy attorney general, came to Washington from Phoenix, Arizona, where he and Rehnquist had long been friends and allies in Republican politics. The two lawyers were only a year apart in age, and they both idolized Arizona Senator Barry Goldwater, the party's right-wing leader. After a decade of political work in Arizona, they both plunged into Goldwater's presidential campaign against Lyndon Johnson in 1964, Kleindienst as national director of field operations and Rehnquist as a speechwriter. The crushing loss to the Democrats only renewed the lawyers' determination to press for conservative principles. Four years later, Kleindienst took the same post in Nixon's presidential campaign, and this time he backed a winner. After choosing his reward in the Justice Department, Kleindienst urged a reluctant Mitchell to place Rehnquist in the Legal Counsel's office. "It's bad enough that the deputy attorney general will be a cowboy from Arizona," Mitchell groused; "two cowboys at one time would be ridiculous." But he relented and offered the job to Rehnquist, who was at best an adopted cowboy from Wisconsin.

The other lawyer who greeted Rehnquist that morning was Richard Moore, who had recently moved from Mitchell's office to the post of special counsel in the White House. Moore came to Washington from the television industry, where he had worked as a network lawyer and executive. Mitchell and Nixon both valued him more for political than legal advice; Moore was savvy and pragmatic, conscious of "image" problems, and uniquely able to bridge the gap between Mitchell's Wall Street power brokers and Nixon's West Coast partisans.

When he entered Mitchell's office, Rehnquist knew that Nixon had been working for the past month to fill not one but two vacancies on the Supreme Court. Two great justices, Hugo Black and John Harlan, had been struck by cancer, and both retired in September 1971. Attorney General Mitchell delegated Rehnquist to sort through a list of possible replacements and to summarize their strengths and weaknesses. Both men well knew the personal and political humiliation Nixon had suffered the year before when he sought a replacement for Justice Abe Fortas, who resigned after media reports of financial impropriety. Although Fortas had clearly breached ethical standards, the charges against him had partisan overtones; Senate Republicans had cried for his scalp.

Angry Democrats retaliated by rejecting two of Nixon's nominees to replace Fortas, Clement Haynsworth and G. Harrold Carswell. Both were southerners, and both were federal appellate judges. Reporters discovered financial conflicts of interest in Haynsworth's judicial rulings, and speeches in which Carswell had publicly defended racial segregation. These defeats temporarily derailed Nixon's professed drive to fill the Court with strict constructionists of the Constitution, but he recovered with the nomination of Harry Blackmun, a moderate federal judge from Minnesota, who breezed through his Senate confirmation.

With two new Supreme Court seats at stake, Nixon announced his intention to nominate a southerner and a woman. The list of candidates given to Rehnquist included two who met the test. The southerner was Herschel Friday, a bond lawyer from Little Rock, Arkansas. Friday and Mitchell—another bond lawyer—had known each other for years. The woman candidate was Mildred Lillie, a judge on the California Court of Appeals in Los Angeles. Mitchell had heard her speak at a judicial conference, and she impressed him as a strong law-and-order judge.

Nixon had already scheduled a press conference to announce the nominations when Mitchell received a call from Lawrence Walsh, who chaired the Committee on the Federal Judiciary of the American Bar Association. Walsh, who served two decades later as special prosecutor for the Iran-Contra scandal, told Mitchell that his panel refused to support either Lillie or Friday. Reporters had disclosed that Lillie's husband had been sued twenty-two times for nonpayment of debts, and that Friday's law firm had been paid $220,000 for defending school segregation in Little Rock. The ABA committee had voted, eleven to one, that Lillie was "unqualified" for the Supreme Court, and had divided, six to six, on Friday. Eight votes were required for a positive recommendation by the ABA's screening committee. Mitchell was furious, but he knew the president could not nominate anyone the ABA labeled "unqualified." He and Nixon went back to their list, guided by Richard Moore's political advice.

Nixon moved quickly to fill one of the two vacancies, persuading a prestigious Virginia lawyer, Lewis Powell, to reconsider an earlier decision not to serve because of his age. Powell was sixty-four, and two years earlier he had declined Nixon's offer to replace Abe Fortas. With the sudden collapse of Herschel Friday and Mildred Lillie as candidates, Nixon returned to Powell, who had served as president of the American Bar Association and also played a leadership role in turning Virginia from "massive resistance" to compliance with the Supreme Court's school integration orders. Powell had served on both the Richmond and state boards of education, urging a moderate course in a time of racial polarization. There was no question of his Senate confirmation.

Word of the ABA's rejection of Friday and Lillie had reached the press, and Nixon was under the gun to make a decision. He asked Richard Moore for advice. "How about Rehnquist?" Moore suggested. "He's a brilliant scholar. He's a lawyer's lawyer. Having been a clerk to former Justice Robert Jackson, he knows the Court. He is real quality." Nixon recalled his own experience as a younger, more conservative member of the Republican ticket in 1952, running with Dwight Eisenhower for the post of vice president. Appointing an older moderate and a younger conservative to the Supreme Court made sense to Nixon, and he quickly agreed to add Rehnquist to the ticket with Powell.

This was a political decision, not one the president based upon personal knowledge of the nominee. Nixon had met Rehnquist just once, during an Oval Office meeting with other Justice Department lawyers to discuss the administration's legal response to antiwar demonstrations. He was apparently not impressed, and complained later to his chief of staff, John Ehrlichman: "Do you remember the meeting we had when I told that group of clowns we had around here, Renchberg and that group—what's his name?"

When Attorney General Mitchell conveyed the president's offer, Rehnquist was probably unaware that Nixon could not remember his name. But he did not hesitate in accepting the nomination. Kleindienst and Moore congratulated their friend and wished him well. Mitchell told him that Nixon would announce the dual appointments in a national television address that evening, but not to tell anyone the news. Rehnquist and his family watched in the living room of their home in McLean, Virginia, near the headquarters of the Central Intelligence Agency. Rehnquist had met his wife, Natalie, when she worked for the CIA, and they now had three teenage children. Rehnquist knew how to keep a secret; one reporter wrote that the children "gasped when they heard their father's name. It was the first they knew of his nomination."

Nixon had not invited Powell or Rehnquist to the Oval Office, nor had the White House staff arranged "photo opportunities" for the press. Rehnquist was pictured in the *New York Times* on the doorstep of his home, with an awkward smile on his face. Nixon's televised speech was equally awkward, describing the Supreme Court as "the fastest track in the Nation" and reminding his viewers that "during my campaign for the presidency, I pledged to nominate to the Supreme Court individuals who shared my judicial philosophy, which is essentially a conservative philosophy." Although the Supreme Court was now headed by his Chief Justice, Warren Burger, Nixon complained that "some Court decisions have gone too far in the past in weakening the peace forces as against the criminal forces in our society." The president made clear his belief that "the peace forces must not be denied the legal tools they need to protect the innocent from criminal elements." This was the test he applied, Nixon said, in selecting Powell and Rehnquist for the Supreme Court.

Nixon had words of praise for both nominees. He said that Powell "has received virtually every honor the legal profession can bestow upon him." And he recited Rehnquist's academic record: Phi Beta Kappa from Stanford University and first in his class at Stanford's law school, followed by a clerkship with Justice Robert Jackson at the U.S. Supreme Court. "I would rate William Rehnquist," Nixon said, "as having one of the finest legal minds in this whole Nation today." Nixon later added the bottom line to his assessment: "Rehnquist's most attractive quality was his age; he was only forty-seven and could probably serve on the Court for twenty-five years."

WILLIAM HUBBS REHNQUIST grew up in suburban, white, Protestant, Midwest America. He was born in Milwaukee, Wisconsin, on October 1, 1924. His father, William Benjamin, was the son of Swedish immigrants and made a comfortable living as a wholesale paper salesman. He had not gone to college, but Marjorie Peck Rehnquist had a University of Wisconsin degree and spoke five languages fluently. Bill Rehnquist— known as Renny during high school—and his younger sister, Jean, went through the public schools in Shorewood, a peaceful town just a few miles from downtown Milwaukee. As the name suggests, Shorewood is on Lake Michigan and its streets are shaded with oaks and maples.

The lakefront road in Shorewood is graced with mansions built by the bankers, brewers, lawyers, and doctors who made Milwaukee a thriving industrial and financial center. The Rehnquist family lived more modestly in a tan brick house. At the time Renny attended Shorewood High, the town had about 15,000 residents; more than 90 percent were native-born Caucasians. Only nine blacks lived in the town, and they worked as live-in maids in the lakefront mansions. Shorewood had the highest educational level of any Wisconsin city; the average adult in 1940 had more than twelve years of schooling, compared with less than nine for most others. The census reported the largest employment categories as "finance, insurance, and real estate," and "professional services." Only 2 percent worked as "laborers" in Shorewood.

A reporter once asked Rehnquist about the origins of his conservative political views. "It may have something to do with my childhood," he replied with a sarcastic edge. But he was certainly right. Conversation around the Rehnquist dinner table included lively political discussion, and the entire family held strong Republican loyalties. Milwaukee had a Socialist mayor, but Shorewood was always a GOP stronghold. Bill Rehnquist sharpened his political views in high school. He was seventeen when the Japanese bombed Pearl Harbor in 1941, and he promptly volunteered as a civil-defense officer. The teenager was put in charge of a network of block captains whose job, said the local paper, was to report to the police "subversive activities which might lead to the sabotaging of our national unity."

Rehnquist graduated from high school in 1942 and accepted a scholarship from Kenyon College in rural Ohio. But he left after one quarter and joined the Army Air Corps, which trained him as a weather observer. He was posted to North Africa in 1943 and spent the next two years in Cairo, Tunis, Tripoli, and Casablanca. The German and Italian armies had been driven out of North Africa, and duty was light. When he mustered out, Rehnquist did not return to Kenyon. He was tired of cold weather. "I wanted to find someplace like North Africa to go to school," he recalled. The closest he could find was California, and the G.I. Bill paid his tuition at the palm-shaded campus of Stanford University in Palo Alto. Rehnquist already had the political bug, and he graduated Phi Beta Kappa in political science in 1948.

Ever since high school, where he served as features editor of the paper, Rehnquist enjoyed putting his political views into print. During his last year in college, he jumped into a debate in the *Stanford Daily* over the university's invitation to bring two German and Finnish officers to the campus. One letter-writer, signing himself "A Wounded Student Veteran," said that Axis soldiers had "massacred our troops" and suggested the visitors "should be taken care of the way we used to take care of their comrades when the war was a little hotter than it is now." The *Daily* ran several letters in rebuttal, with an editorial noting the "overwhelming prevalence of humanitarian sentiment" in these letters.

The letter Rehnquist wrote in response to this debate provides an early illustration of the basic political philosophy he continues to apply in judicial opinions. Significantly, he took no stand on whether the Axis officers should visit Stanford. His *Daily* editorial was entitled "Emotion vs. Reason." What bothered Rehnquist was "the implication that humanitarianism is desirable" as a moral value. "It is recognized by most moralists," he wrote, "that moral standards are incapable of being rationally demonstrated. If we accept humanitarianism as a desirable end, we must realize that the basis of this acceptance is non-rational." The opinions of "Wounded Student Veteran" and his critics struck Rehnquist as equally emotional and "non-rational." He argued that it "is logically impossible to weigh the merits of one of these emotions against the other," and that "one personal conviction is no better than another." Rehnquist concluded with emphasis that "the idea that humanitarianism is the road to world understanding is, IN MY OPINION, fallacious."

Virtually every judicial opinion Rehnquist has written over more than two decades is rooted in the five paragraphs of this letter. What he did not address was the process by which public decisions are made. Implicit in his letter, however, is Rehnquist's belief that one public policy "is no better than another." During his years since college, he has stuck by this conviction. Concerns of "humanitarianism" find no place in his judicial philosophy.

ONE DEGREE in political science did not satisfy Rehnquist. He went on to obtain two master's degrees, from Stanford and Harvard. One year in chilly Massachusetts drove him back to California and to law school at Stanford, where he graduated first in his class in 1952 and landed a coveted Supreme Court clerkship with Justice Robert Jackson. He enjoyed his stay in Washington, and Jackson's recommendation gave him the pick of law firms in Washington or Wall Street. Weather was still a consideration, and Rehnquist chose real estate law in Arizona over big-city corporate practice. Nan Rehnquist left her CIA job and moved with her husband in 1953 to Phoenix, still growing from a frontier town into a sprawling city.

Rehnquist spent sixteen years in Phoenix, working in firms that specialized in turning desert land into housing developments. The year before he arrived, Barry Goldwater broke a forty-year Democratic grip on state politics with election to the U.S. Senate, and Rehnquist joined his friend Richard Kleindienst in working to make Phoenix a Republican stronghold. They helped to push through the state legislature a law that imposed an anti-Communist loyalty oath on Arizona teachers. And they lobbied to defeat an ordinance that would require hotels and restaurants to serve all persons, regardless of race.

The Phoenix City Council met on June 15, 1964, to consider the public accommodations ordinance modeled on the federal law that Congress had recently enacted. Members of several groups, including the NAACP, testified in favor of the proposed ordinance. Only one Phoenix resident spoke against it. "Mr. Mayor, members of the City Council," he said, "my name is William Rehnquist. I would like to speak in opposition to the proposed ordinance because I believe that the values that it sacrifices are greater than the values which it gives." Rehnquist put the issue in terms of property rights. "Here you are talking about a man's private property," he said, "and you are saying, in effect, that people shall have access to that man's property whether he wants it or not." He denied the city's power to decide "who can come on your property" and argued that "the ordinance ought to be rejected." The next day, the council unanimously passed the ordinance.

Despite this expression of majority sentiment, Rehnquist continued his battle, denouncing the new law in a letter to the Arizona *Republic*. The ordinance, he wrote, "summarily does away with the historic right of the owner of a drug store, lunch counter, or theater to choose his own customers." The "right" of discrimination that Rehnquist defended had its legal roots in the "separate but equal" doctrine of *Plessy v. Ferguson*, decided by the Supreme Court in 1896. Protecting blacks against the indignity of discrimination, Rehnquist argued, would place "a separate indignity on the proprietor" who wants to serve only whites.

Rehnquist claimed in his 1964 letter that only a "small minority" would benefit from a public accommodations law. Three years later, he wrote another letter to the *Republic*, arguing that only a "small minority" would benefit from a plan to foster school integration in Phoenix. Rehnquist purported to speak for the "great majority of our citizens," who he said were "well satisfied with the traditional neighborhood school system" and did not want to see it "tinkered with" by "social theorists" who asserted "a claim for special privileges" by the black minority. The thesis of his letter was that "we are no more dedicated to an 'integrated' society than we are to a 'segregated' society." Decisions about school integration, Rehnquist argued, should "come from policy-making bodies who are directly responsible to the electorate, rather than from an appointed administrator" like a school superintendent. If the majority opposed integration, Rehnquist would not object.

REHNQUIST SPENT close to three years, from 1969 to 1971, as director of the Justice Department's Office of Legal Counsel. His primary responsibility was to advise Attorney General John Mitchell on legal issues that stemmed from federal-law enforcement. But he assumed a broader mandate from Mitchell as the department's "point man" on controversial policies, ranging from the American bombing of Cambodia to the Equal Rights Amendment. There was no shortage of controversy during these years: the Vietnam War provoked massive demonstrations around the country and sporadic acts of violence and sabotage; the government responded with mass arrests and surveillance of antiwar groups and their leaders. Rehnquist had his hands full, and churned out memoranda, policy papers, congressional testimony, and speeches on these and other issues. He enjoyed stumping the country, traveling as far as Hawaii to defend the Nixon administration against its critics.

Unlike Justice Brennan, Rehnquist had no record of judicial opinions before his nomination to the Supreme Court. But he put his opinions, personal and official, into a large stack of memos and speeches. Rehnquist wrote and spoke, of course, as an appointed official whose words reflected administration policy. But there is little doubt that he voiced his personal opinions as well, for they matched the hard-line law-and-order approach of John Mitchell and Richard Nixon.

Running through all of Rehnquist's speeches and statements is a consistent view of government and law. This view is unabashedly majoritarian, and stresses official authority and individual obedience to the majority's commands. Several speeches read like political-science term papers, sprinkled with quotations from Edmund Burke and other conservative writers. Government exists, in Rehnquist's view, to protect property and public order. The former Goldwater speechwriter sounded just like his mentor in *The Conscience of a Conservative*. "Implicit in each of our daily lives," Rehnquist wrote, "is the reliance on our right to act as we choose in areas not proscribed by law, and reliance that the law will be enforced against those who wrongfully interfere with this exercise of freedom on our part." In short, the state is essentially a police officer for the majority.

The fullest exposition of Rehnquist's political and legal philosophy came in a 1969 speech entitled "The Law: Under Attack from the New Barbarians." He delivered this speech on May 1, "Law Day" for conservatives and "May Day" for radicals, to attack the New Left and its campaign against the Vietnam War. His tone was polemical. "The very notion of law, and of a government of law," Rehnquist said, "is presently under attack from a group of new barbarians. Just as the Barbarians who invaded the Roman Empire neither knew nor cared about Roman government and Roman law, these new barbarians care nothing for our system of government and law. They believe that the relatively civilized society in which they live is so totally rotten that no remedy short of the destruction of that society will suffice."

Rehnquist did not name any of the "new barbarians," although he loosely quoted the manifesto of the "Weatherman" group, a violent offshoot of Students for a Democratic Society who planted bombs in the Capitol and other public buildings. But the scope of his disapproval went beyond the bombers to all those who engaged in civil disobedience, even the peaceful marches of Martin Luther King and the sit-in protests against segregation. Rehnquist made clear his commitment to unrestrained majority rule. "From the point of view of the majority," he said, "the minority, no matter how disaffected or disenchanted, owes an unqualified obligation to obey a duly enacted law." He dismissed those who base their protest on "matters of conscience." "Neither idealism of purpose nor self-proclaimed moral superiority on the part of the minority qualifies in the slightest way its obligation to obey the law." Not even a willingness to go to jail as the cost of conscience placated Rehnquist. "The deliberate law breaker does not fully atone for his disobedience when he serves his sentence, for he has by example undermined respect for the legal system itself."

Two years later, Rehnquist played a role in the mass arrests of the "Mayday" demonstrators who tried to shut down Washington, blocking streets and bridges. Police rounded up more than seven thousand protesters and held them for several days in a football stadium. Rehnquist argued that the doctrine of "qualified martial law" justified the dragnet arrests, although *Newsweek* reported that "other Justice Department officials later conceded privately that up to 80 per cent had been unconstitutional." Federal judges later ordered the government to pay those who were illegally arrested up to ten thousand dollars each in damages.

Several months after the "Mayday" arrests, Rehnquist spoke about civil disobedience, criticizing both violent and peaceful protest. He condemned not only antiwar protesters but Henry Thoreau, who spent a night in Concord jail for refusing to pay a tax for the war against Mexico. Thoreau's classic essay "On Civil Disobedience" inspired Mohandas Gandhi, Martin Luther King, and others who violated "unjust" laws. Rehnquist deplored this position, claiming that "even the individual who chooses to go to jail, rather than obey the law, is setting a precedent which can have the most damaging consequences to our system of government." He decried "the notion that one's own conscientious judgment is entitled to moral force superior to the moral force behind the claim of the government that a duly enacted law be obeyed." His hard-line position included the warning "that if force or the threat of force is required in order to enforce the law, we must not shirk from its employment."

A recurrent theme in Rehnquist's public statements is the defense of strong executive powers. The ultimate test of these powers is the president's authority under the Constitution as commander-in-chief of the armed forces. Presidents of all political persuasions have claimed, and used, the power to commit American troops to combat. Ever since World War II ended they have ignored the constitutional provision that only Congress can declare war on other nations. Richard Nixon provoked a conflict with Congress in 1970 when he sent American troops and planes into Cambodia to destroy Viet Cong "sanctuaries" across the Vietnam border. The "secret war" became a test of power against an increasingly antiwar Congress.

Rehnquist stoutly defended the president. Speaking to a skeptical New York bar group, he argued that "the United States has in no sense gone to 'war' with Cambodia." He asked rhetorically if the president may "lawfully engage in armed hostilities with a foreign power in the absence of a congressional declaration of war? I believe that the only supportable answer to this question is 'yes' in the light of our history and our Constitution." Rehnquist was hardly alone in asserting broad executive powers in foreign affairs, but he clearly approved Nixon's action and opposed congressional efforts to limit presidential authority in the War Powers Act.

As spokesman for a law-and-order administration, Rehnquist defended policies that included detention of criminal suspects without bail, wiretapping without judicial warrant, and police surveillance of dissenters. Each of these positions had serious constitutional problems, and Rehnquist read the Constitution narrowly in each area. Speaking in 1970, he attacked Warren Court rulings and federal laws that protected criminal defendants against excessive bail for their release pending trial. Rehnquist admitted the Constitution provides that "excessive bail shall not be required" of defendants. The answer he proposed was to make certain crimes "nonbailable" and to deny defendants any right to release before trial. Rehnquist took on the Warren Court. "With the plethora of rights recently granted him by the U.S. Supreme Court, the criminal defendant can and does do a good deal more than merely present evidence at trial." He conjured up "a heroin addict, with a $100-a-day habit," continuing to rob and steal while he waited for trial on bail. Opponents of pretrial detention without bail claim that it violates the Constitution's Due Process clause. Rehnquist replied that "due process arguments are susceptible to the balancing process and the test of reasonableness under the circumstances."

Wiretapping is another sensitive constitutional issue. The Fourth Amendment requires judicial warrants for all "searches and seizures," and the Supreme Court has ruled that wiretaps fall within this protection. The Nixon administration engaged in widespread wiretapping against antiwar activists, suspected spies, and members of Nixon's "enemies list," which included journalists and even White House officials. Rehnquist defended wiretaps as a "potent weapon" for law enforcement. And he dismissed constitutional objections to warrantless taps. In conducting "national security" investigations, he said in 1971, "the executive branch in the United States for more than thirty years has asserted the right to wiretap without securing any type of Fourth Amendment warrant."

Rehnquist also defended the government's power to conduct surveillance of citizens for political reasons. During his time in the Justice Department, the FBI, the CIA, and Army Intelligence all collected data on dissenters. Agents took photographs at demonstrations, checked license plate numbers of cars parked outside protest meetings, and opened files on persons who signed petitions against the Vietnam War. Speaking in 1971, Rehnquist posed a rhetorical question: "To what extent may law enforcement officials properly observe members of the citizenry in public places?" He answered critics who claimed that no person "ought to be subject to such surveillance unless there is 'probable cause' to believe that he is guilty of committing a crime. The imposition of such a standard, in my view, would be a virtually fatal blow to law enforcement."

His support for political surveillance brought the wrath of Senator Sam Ervin, who later chaired the Watergate Committee. Ervin called Rehnquist before his Judiciary Committee panel on constitutional rights. The two men debated the issue at length, and Ervin finally put this question: "Do you feel that there are any serious constitutional problems with respect to collecting data or keeping under surveillance, persons who are merely exercising their right of peaceful assembly or petition to redress a grievance?" Rehnquist was forthright. "My answer to your question is no, Mr. Chairman. I do not believe it raises a constitutional question."

During his time in the Justice Department, only once did Rehnquist take a public position at odds with his personal views. The issue was the proposed Equal Rights Amendment to the Constitution, which the Justice Department grudgingly endorsed and which Rehnquist personally opposed. He testified before the House Judiciary Committee in 1971 that "the Department supports the enactment" of the ERA. He added that "opponents of that amendment have raised significant questions" about its potential effect. Rehnquist doubted that "there is a national consensus for compelling all levels of government to treat men and women across the board as if they were identical human beings." He suggested that "laws which are adopted with the genuine purpose of protecting women, rather than as a disguise for discriminating against them," would be undermined by the ERA.

Rehnquist was certainly not effusive in supporting the ERA. Fifteen years later, during the debate over his confirmation as Chief Justice, a reporter dug up a nine-page "Brief in Opposition" to the ERA that Rehnquist had written in 1970. "I cannot help thinking," he had said, that the feminist movement harbored "a virtually fanatical desire to obscure not only legal differentiation between men and women, but insofar as possible, physical distinctions between the sexes." Adding the ERA to the Constitution would be "almost certain to have an adverse effect on the family unit as we have known it." Rehnquist argued that the ERA would open "traditional marriage vows and most religious teaching" on relations between spouses to judicial scrutiny and "turn 'holy wedlock' into 'holy deadlock.' "

For almost three years, William Rehnquist provided legal advice to an administration whose conservative policies he shared, and made articulate, forceful speeches around the country to defend those policies. Lawyers are advocates for their clients, and John Mitchell and Richard Nixon were besieged by vocal and sometimes violent critics. Rehnquist took some of the heat from the press, hostile audiences, and Congress. Defending the Nixon administration was not easy during these tumultuous years, but Rehnquist performed his job with conviction and enthusiasm. He relished the mix of law and politics, but nomination to the Supreme Court offered a greater challenge.

SENATOR JAMES EASTLAND called the Judiciary Committee to order on the morning of November 3, 1971, for a hearing on the Supreme Court nomination of William Rehnquist. The Mississippi Democrat, a Senate power broker and leader of his party's Dixiecrat wing, invariably supported President Nixon's judicial nominees, including the ill-fated Clement Haynsworth and G. Harrold Carswell. Rehnquist was flanked by Arizona's two Republican senators, Barry Goldwater and Paul Fannin, and a GOP representative, John Rhodes. Nan Rehnquist sat behind her husband in the front row of spectator seats.

Eastland first placed in the record a report of the ABA Standing Committee on the Federal Judiciary, which had recently scuttled the nominations of Herschel Friday and Mildred Lillie. Attorney General Mitchell had angrily severed official ties with the ABA group, but the panel went ahead with reports on Rehnquist and Lewis Powell. The ABA report on Rehnquist was based on interviews with more than 120 lawyers and judges in ten states. Virtually all commented on his conservative political views, but the vast majority gave him high marks for "professional competence, judicial temperament, and integrity."

The portrait of Rehnquist that emerged from the ABA report was that of a "brilliant," "articulate," "rational," and "forceful" advocate of conservative political and legal views. Several judges—none quoted by name—questioned his impartiality; one said Rehnquist had "such deep convictions on social and economic problems that he might be unduly and injudiciously influenced by those views in deciding cases." The ABA committee agreed that the nominee manifested "an extremely conservative position as to appropriate governmental action in certain areas of racial and religious discrimination." Nine of the twelve panel members agreed that Rehnquist "is one of the best persons available for appointment to the Supreme Court." Three felt "his qualifications do not establish his eligibility for the Committee's highest rating," but said they were "not opposed to his confirmation," a verdict that left the panel without dissenters.

Eastland put a stack of letters in the record, all supporting Rehnquist. A Stanford law professor, John Hurlbut, recalled his former student as "nothing short of brilliant, dogged in his determination to achieve excellence" and "forthright and courageous" in expressing views that were "always precisely formulated and precisely expressed." Robert Bork, then a Yale law professor and a former Justice Department colleague, said that Rehnquist "possesses a brilliant and analytical mind." He predicted that "in the decision of constitutional cases he will be guided not by his personal philosophy but by a commitment to the commands of the Constitution, interpreted in the light of its text and its history."

Once the testimonials were over, Rehnquist faced the sixteen members of the Judiciary Committee. Democrats began the questioning, proceeding by seniority. Senator John McClellan, a law-and-order conservative from Arkansas, used his time to denounce the Warren Court for imposing "on a helpless society new rights for the criminal defendant." McClellan noted that since 1960, the Court had reversed twenty-nine of its prior decisions in the field of criminal law, many by narrow, 5–4 margins, and that "26 of these 29 decisions were handed down in favor of a criminal defendant."

McClellan clearly hoped that Rehnquist would help to reverse Warren Court rulings in criminal law. He asked the nominee how much weight he would give to Supreme Court precedent. This was a crucial and delicate question, and Rehnquist approached it gingerly. "I feel that great weight should be given to precedent," he began. But he signaled his willingness to roll back the Warren Court legacy. "I think the Supreme Court has said many times," he added, that precedent is "entitled to perhaps less weight in the field of constitutional law than it is in other areas of the law." Having opened the door to reversal, Rehnquist pushed it wider. He would be more willing to overrule an earlier decision "if a court was 5 to 4 in handing down a decision" and if the case had not "stood for a very long time" as precedent. McClellan liked what he heard and leaned back in his chair.

Senator Sam Ervin liked to pose as a "simple country lawyer" from North Carolina. During his Justice Department years, Rehnquist had been one of many witnesses who encountered the sharp mind behind Ervin's slow drawl. They had clashed over wiretapping and surveillance of protesters, but Ervin did not harbor political grudges. "I do not hold the fact that a man reaches honest conclusions different from mine against him," he told Rehnquist. Praising his competence and integrity, Ervin drew laughter in concluding, "I am not going to ask you any question because I do not want to be shaken in my conviction."

In his folksy manner, Ervin lightened the mood in the hearing room. The atmosphere shifted quickly, as Rehnquist faced a grilling over the next four hours from four liberal Democrats who had led the successful campaigns against Haynsworth and Carswell. None questioned Rehnquist's legal competence, but they sharply probed his political and legal views. The four senators—Philip Hart of Michigan, Birch Bayh of Indiana, Edward Kennedy of Massachusetts, and John Tunney of California—had caucused before the hearing and divided the issues they would raise with Rehnquist. They were armed with copies of his speeches, articles, and testimony before Congress.

Following up on McClellan's questions, Hart asked if Rehnquist would try as a justice to "swing the pendulum" back to the government's side in criminal cases. Rehnquist admitted his belief "that the pendulum had been swung too far toward the accused not by virtue of a fair reading of the Constitution" but rather "the personal philosophy of one or more of the Justices."

This response gave Hart an opening to question Rehnquist about his 1957 article in *U.S. News & World Report*. Discussing his stint as law clerk to Justice Jackson, Rehnquist attacked the Warren Court as an "unconscious" tool of his fellow clerks, whom he labeled as "to the 'left' of either the nation or the Court." Rehnquist did not say what prompted his article, but he was most likely upset by four Warren Court decisions, handed down earlier that year, holding that state and federal officials had violated the rights of alleged Communists. The result of this "left" bias, Rehnquist wrote, was "extreme solicitude for the claims of Communists and other criminal defendants, expansion of federal power at the expense of state power, great sympathy toward any government regulation of business—in short, the political philosophy now espoused by the Court under Chief Justice Earl Warren." Rehnquist still believed, he told Hart, that "ideological" factors had driven the Warren Court to its decisions.

The liberal Democrats continued to press Rehnquist on his attitude toward reversing Supreme Court precedent. "What assurances can you tell us," Senator Kennedy inquired, "that you are not going to move back on what I would consider the march of progress during the period of the Warren Court?" Rehnquist limited his judicial deference to cases decided by unanimous vote and repeatedly affirmed by the Court. Decisions that were "handed down by a sharply divided court" or had "stood for a shorter period of time," he said, deserved "less weight as a precedent." He gave a similar answer to Senator Tunney, citing *Brown v. Board of Education* as "a decision that was handed down unanimously" and stands as "the established constitutional law of the land." Rehnquist would not give equal weight, he said, to cases decided "by a closely divided Court more recently" than *Brown*, handed down in 1954. The clear message was that later decisions by a divided Court, including virtually all the "Communist" and criminal law cases, were fair game for reversal.

Senator Birch Bayh had led the opposition to Haynsworth and Carswell, questioning the commitment of both men to racial equality. He left this touchy issue for the end of his questioning. He quoted from Rehnquist's testimony to the Phoenix City Council in 1964 opposing the city's public accommodations ordinance, and asked if the statement was "still an accurate reflection of your views now?" Rehnquist had changed his mind. "I think the ordinance really worked very well in Phoenix," he replied. "I have come to realize," he added, "the strong concern that minorities have for the recognition of these rights." Rehnquist did not, however, withdraw his earlier opposition to busing students to foster school integration.

Bayh finally got to the issue that posed the greatest obstacle to Rehnquist's nomination. He quoted a resolution of the Arizona NAACP, which claimed that Rehnquist had engaged in "harassment and intimidation of voters in 1968 during the Presidential election in precincts heavily populated by the poor." This charge, later broadened to elections as far back as 1958, stemmed from Rehnquist's role as a legal adviser to the Republican Party in Phoenix. Statements from NAACP members claimed that Rehnquist had appeared at polling places in heavily black and Hispanic areas, confronting minority voters with forceful demands that they read portions of the Arizona constitution as proof of literacy. According to these witnesses, he scared many of the challenged voters out of the polling place.

During the 1971 hearing, Bayh asked Rehnquist only three questions about the intimidation claims. The nominee denied he had ever personally challenged voters. "I had absolutely nothing to do with any sort of poll watching," he said. He simply gave "legal advice to persons who were challengers" for the Republicans in heavily Democratic precincts. Fifteen years later, several witnesses, including a former U.S. Attorney, provided the Senate committee with eyewitness testimony that Rehnquist had challenged and intimidated minority voters. But the issue died quickly in 1971, with no witness to counter Rehnquist's denial that he prevented any voter from casting a ballot.

None of the Republicans on the Judiciary Committee gave Rehnquist a hard time. After two days of questioning, he left the witness table with confirmation seemingly assured. Not one senator had voiced any criticism of his legal competence or personal integrity, and Rehnquist had deflected charges of racial bias and voter intimidation. Senator Eastland pressed for an early confirmation vote, but Senator Bayh persisted in a lengthy floor debate, which Republicans denounced as a filibuster. Bayh did not stand in the way of Lewis Powell, whose confirmation hearing had proceeded smoothly. On December 6, 1971, eighty-nine senators voted for confirmation; just one Democrat opposed Powell. The same day, a *Newsweek* reporter provided Bayh with new ammunition against Rehnquist. What the Indiana senator hoped would be a "smoking gun" to shoot down the nomination was a two-page, single-spaced document from the files of Justice Jackson.

Back in 1953, when the Supreme Court was considering the issue of school segregation in the *Brown* case, Rehnquist wrote a memorandum to Jackson entitled "A Random Thought on the Segregation Cases." His thoughts were anything but random. He canvassed the Court's decisions in cases that raised questions of individual rights since 1810, concluding that "it was not part of the judicial function to thwart public opinion except in extreme cases." Rehnquist felt that public opinion, at least in southern states, supported racial segregation in public schools. He suggested to Jackson that the Court was "being asked to read its own sociological views into the Constitution." As a Stanford undergraduate, Rehnquist had argued that "moral standards are incapable of being rationally demonstrated." He followed this line of argument in dismissing the claim of Linda Brown and other black students that the Supreme Court should consider "the moral wrongness of the treatment they are receiving."

In his memorandum, Rehnquist brushed aside the statement of NAACP lawyer Thurgood Marshall that "a majority may not deprive a minority of its constitutional right," countering that "in the long run it is the majority who will determine what the constitutional rights of the minority are." Rehnquist urged that Justice Jackson uphold the "separate but equal" ruling of the *Plessy* case, decided by the Court in 1896. "I realize that it is an unpopular and unhumanitarian position," Rehnquist confessed, "for which I have been excoriated by 'liberal' colleagues, but I think *Plessy v. Ferguson* was right and should be reaffirmed."

Two decades after he wrote this memo, Rehnquist was again excoriated, in the press and on the Senate floor. Bayh asked Senator Eastland to reopen the hearing and call Rehnquist to explain his memorandum, but the imperious chairman refused. Aware that his nomination was now in jeopardy, Rehnquist wrote Eastland a letter claiming that "the memorandum was prepared by me at Justice Jackson's request; it was intended as a rough draft of a statement of his own views at the conference of the Justices, rather than as a statement of my own views." Jackson could not dispute his former clerk's story; he died shortly after joining the unanimous vote in the *Brown* case, which reversed and repudiated the *Plessy* decision. Elsie Douglas, Jackson's longtime secretary, spoke for him; she challenged Rehnquist's account as "incredible on its face" and told the Washington *Post* that he had "smeared the reputation of a great Justice." Rehnquist consistently denied that the "Random Thoughts" over his initials were actually his. But the wording, style, and contents of the disputed memo closely match those of his writings over a span of more than two decades.

The uproar did not, however, derail the confirmation. Just before the final vote on December 10, 1971, Senator Bayh conceded that he was "about to be repudiated" by his colleagues. In a final question, he asked what the American public would think "when they see placed on the Court a man who testified against letting black people in drugstores and in schools, a man who has repeatedly urged the expansion of the power of the executive branch at the expense of the rights of individuals." The Senate answered with a resounding vote, approving the nomination by a margin of sixty-eight to twenty-six. All but four Republicans voted for Rehnquist, and a majority of Democrats supported his confirmation. He and Lewis Powell stood together in the Supreme Court chamber on January 10, 1972, and recited the oath of office. Because his confirmation followed Powell's, the youngest justice also became the "junior" in seniority.

WILLIAM REHNQUIST came to the bench with a clear, consistent political and legal philosophy, but without a judicial record that would show his philosophy in action. It took only a few years of votes and opinions to provide evidence that his judicial philosophy followed the path of his earlier positions. Speaking at the University of Texas Law School in 1976, he outlined his views in a speech entitled "The Notion of a Living Constitution." Of all his speeches, articles, and opinions, this address presents Rehnquist's jurisprudence in its most developed form.

In many ways, his Texas speech was simply an expanded version of the views expressed in Rehnquist's 1948 letter to the *Stanford Daily*, in which he argued that "one personal conviction is no better than another" and rejected "the implication that humanitarianism is desirable" as a moral value. His speech explicitly adopted the position of legal positivism, the notion that the legislative will is supreme and that the content of laws is not a proper concern of judges. If legislators follow the rules, they are constrained only by the explicit commands of the Constitution. The most extreme form of legal positivism—approached in the civil law system of continental Europe—does not allow for judicial review of legislation. The American form of positivism—articulated most forcefully by Robert

Bork—gives judges an independent but limited role in reviewing laws, constrained by precedent and the constitutional text. In both systems, judges are expected to show deference to the legislative will.

Rehnquist took as the text for his Texas speech an excerpt from a legal brief submitted to a federal judge on behalf of state prisoners who claimed that prison conditions violated their constitutional rights. He did not identify the case name or the prison, or provide any details of the prisoners' complaints. Rehnquist quoted from the brief: "This Court, as the voice and conscience of contemporary society, as the measure of the modern conception of human dignity, must declare that the [prison] and all it represents offends the Constitution of the United States and will not be tolerated." Rehnquist responded with scorn to these words. "Here we have a living Constitution with a vengeance," he said. The point of his speech, in fact, was to refute the notion of a "living Constitution" and the jurisprudence of "human dignity" it reflected.

Rehnquist admitted that "in exercising the very delicate responsibility of judicial review," judges had authority to strike down laws they "find to violate some provision of the Constitution." But he took a narrow view of this authority. The concept of judicial review, he said, "has basically antidemocratic and antimajoritarian facets that require some justification" in a system based on majority rule. The idea of a "living Constitution" struck Rehnquist as a negation of "the nature of political value judgments in a democratic society." He agreed that constitutional safeguards for individual liberty "take on a generalized moral rightness or goodness." But this goodness has no source outside the premise of majority rule, no basis in any "morality" that relies on personal conscience. Constitutional protections "assume a general social acceptance," Rehnquist asserted, "neither because of any intrinsic worth nor because of any unique origins in someone's idea of natural justice but instead simply because they have been incorporated in a constitution by the people."

The major theme of Rehnquist's speech was that political majorities are entitled to enact "positive law" and to impose their moral views on minorities. Laws "take on a form of moral goodness because they have been enacted into positive law," he argued. One complement of legal positivism is moral relativism, the notion that no moral value is inherently superior to another. Rehnquist took this position as a college student and stuck by it as a justice. "There is no conceivable way," he told his Texas audience, "in which I can logically demonstrate to you that the judgments of my conscience are superior to the judgments of your conscience, and vice versa." The "goodness" of any value is decided in the voting booth.

The bottom line of Rehnquist's jurisprudence is deference to majority rule and legislative will. Two legal scholars have tested this conclusion against the record of his judicial votes and opinions. Writing in 1976, four years after Rehnquist joined the Supreme Court, Harvard law professor David Shapiro examined the justice's votes in more than 1,200 cases and 164 signed opinions. Shapiro concluded that "his votes are guided by three basic propositions: (1) Conflicts between an individual and the government should, whenever possible, be resolved against the individual; (2) Conflicts between state and federal authority, whether on an executive, legislative or judicial level, should, wherever possible, be resolved in favor of the states; and (3) Questions of the exercise of federal jurisdiction, whether on the district court, appellate court or Supreme Court level, should, wherever possible, be resolved against such exercise." In only thirteen cases, less than 1 percent of the total, did Shapiro find that Rehnquist displayed "less of a commitment to these propositions" than any of his colleagues.

Another study of Rehnquist's votes between 1976 and 1981 put Shapiro's propositions to a statistical test. Professor Robert Riggs of Brigham Young University's law school found that Rehnquist sided with state governments in more than 80 percent of all cases, well above the 52 percent level of the Court's majority. He voted to uphold federal jurisdiction in only 35 percent of cases, while the majority was equally divided at 50 percent in these cases. Rehnquist also voted to uphold 88 percent of all criminal convictions, far above the 59 percent of the majority. And he sided with plaintiffs in only 16 percent of "freedom of expression" cases under the First Amendment, in contrast to 44 percent for the majority.

This record shows that Rehnquist is a principled political conservative. But is he also, as he describes himself, a judicial conservative? His philosophy of deference to legislative acts is not, by itself, either liberal or conservative. Laws can be "liberal" by granting rights to minorities, or "conservative" by placing burdens on them. For example, a legislature can pass laws that protect homosexuals from discrimination, or laws that make homosexual behavior a crime. However, in consistently voting to uphold criminal convictions, to deny First Amendment claims, and to reject the claims of racial minorities and women, Rehnquist has taken a "conservative" position on the political issues raised in these cases. He is equally *not* a conservative in the sense of displaying the respect for precedent shown by those who profess "judicial restraint" as a principle. His candid answers to questions at the 1971 Senate hearing foreshadowed a voting record to overturn precedent in dozens of cases. In this sense, Rehnquist is exactly the kind of judicial "activist" he has deplored in opinions and speeches.

One witness against Rehnquist's confirmation called him "an activist of the most amazing type." Joseph Rauh spent his legal career defending political dissenters and civil rights demonstrators. "If there ever was an activist, Mr. Rehnquist is it," Rauh told the Senate panel. "For President Nixon to call him a judicial conservative is 180 degrees wrong. This will be the most judicial radical for reaction that we have ever had." Rauh was just as much a liberal partisan as Rehnquist had been a conservative partisan in his politics. But his prediction was largely correct. Rehnquist agrees that he votes to apply his conservative principles. "I want to see that version of the law applied when the case comes up," he confessed in 1985. "If that makes me a partisan, certainly I'm a partisan. But I don't think that distinguishes me from most of my colleagues."

The jurisprudence of Justice Rehnquist does, in fact, distinguish him from *all* of his colleagues since he joined the Court. None has voted more consistently to uphold governmental actions, legislative and executive. And none has voted more consistently against the claims of dissenters and minorities. His "deference" principle stands in stark contrast to the "dignity" value of Justice Brennan. Their competing visions of the Constitution are rooted in historic struggles over American law and politics.

FOUR

"Beyond the Reach of Majorities"

Understanding the constitutional battles of Justices Brennan and Rehnquist requires some historical context. Much like ancient disputes between nations that erupt into warfare, conflicts within the Supreme Court are rooted in arguments that have lasted more than two centuries, between defenders of individual rights and partisans of state power. Many of the Court's decisions illustrate the continuing debate over these positions. One case, however, provides a clear view of the judicial skirmishes that still echo in the opinions of these two justices. Almost a century after the Court decided *Lochner v. New York* in 1905, its issues remain alive. This case involved laws designed to provide recent immigrants with decent working conditions. The origins of laborers in America's sweatshops have changed: Eastern and Southern Europeans have been replaced by Latin Americans and Asians. Political conflict over laws to protect these workers from exploitation has not changed, although the Court's response has shifted.

The facts of the *Lochner* case are simple. In 1901 the New York legislature passed a law that prohibited bakers from working more than ten hours a day and sixty hours a week. Joseph Lochner, who owned a Utica bakery, was fined fifty dollars for requiring Aman Schmitter to work more than sixty hours in one week. After the state's highest court upheld the law, the Supreme Court reversed the ruling by a 5–4 vote. Justice Rufus Peckham wrote for the majority that the statute "interferes with the right of contract" between workers and employers and deprived both of their "liberty" under the Due Process clause of the Fourteenth Amendment.

Since the Court's ruling, the *Lochner* decision has been attacked from both the right and the left. It is not surprising that judicial liberals have denounced Peckham's opinion. What *is* surprising, however, is that most professed judicial conservatives have repudiated a ruling that upheld a basic tenet of laissez-faire capitalism. During his first nomination hearing in 1971, Rehnquist was asked by Senator Edward Kennedy for his views on judges "superimposing their own political philosophy on the Constitution." Rehnquist disavowed any such intent on his part, and characterized the *Lochner* decision as "an intrusion of personal political philosophy which the Framers had never intended" in protecting personal "liberty" against governmental deprivation.

The *Lochner* case highlights the impact of economic conflict on individual rights, a recurring issue in American society. This case began with the Progressive and socialist movements of the 1890s, a time of real class conflict in America. Many states responded to populist pressures by enacting laws to protect workers, including women and children, by limiting hours of work and setting health and safety standards. Pressure for the New York law to limit the hours of bakers came from the Journeymen Bakers' Union, whose secretary, Henry Weismann, enlisted the support of the Church Association for the Advancement of Labor and other "social gospel" groups. Bakers worked long hours in hot, dusty workshops. One medical report noted the results: "The constant inhaling of flour dust causes inflammation of the lungs and of the bronchial tubes. The long hours of toil to which all bakers are subjected produce rheumatism, cramps and swollen legs."

One of the ironies of *Lochner* is that the man who lobbied for the law, Henry Weismann, later argued for its repeal by the Supreme Court. "When I was young," he explained, "I was fiery and full of ideals. Later I became a master baker, and, undergoing an intellectual revolution, saw where the law which I had succeeded as a journeyman baker in having passed was unjust to the employers." Weismann moved from baking and labor politics to law and the Republican Party. As counsel for the State Association of Master Bakers, he defended Joseph Lochner in his appeal to the Supreme Court.

When the case reached the Court in 1905, Weismann no longer voiced concern for the health of his former union members. He waxed poetic in his brief. "The average bakery of the present day is well ventilated, comfortable both summer and winter, and always sweet smelling." Weismann denied that limiting work hours had any relation to health or safety. The Constitution, he wrote, was not designed "to erect a government so paternal in its character that the treasured freedom of the individual and his right to the pursuit of life, liberty and happiness, should be swept away under the guise of the police power of the State." Weismann painted the American housewife in glowing words: "Here is the real artist in biscuits, cake and bread, not to mention the American pie. The housewife cannot bound her daily and weekly hours of labor. She must toil on, sometimes far into the night, to satisfy the wants of her growing family."

In contrast, the brief of New York's attorney general, Julius Mayer, was pedestrian. Unfortunately for Mayer, the "Brandeis brief" had not yet been invented. Three years after the *Lochner* decision, Louis Brandeis persuaded the Supreme Court to uphold—without dissent—an Oregon ten-hour law for women. Brandeis filed a brief in *Muller v. Oregon* that presented 113 pages of "social facts" and only two pages of legal argument. The justices were impressed by this compendium of expert data and testimony on health and safety issues. In the *Lochner* case, Mayer defended his state's law with a flat statement that "it was a proper exercise of the police power of the State." He also suggested that bakers were deficient in brains. "The State, in undertaking this regulation, has a right to safeguard the citizen against his own lack of knowledge."

The Supreme Court majority hardly concealed its contempt for Mayer's argument. "There is no contention," Justice Peckham wrote, "that bakers as a class are not equal in intelligence and capacity to men in other trades or manual occupations, or that they are not able to assert their rights and care for themselves without the protecting arm of the State interfering with their independence of judgment and of action. They are in no sense wards of the State." Peckham waved aside the state's health argument: "To the common understanding the trade of a baker has never been regarded as an unhealthy one." He insinuated that the law was passed to placate socialist and labor groups. "It is impossible for us to shut our eyes to the fact," he wrote, "that many of the laws of this character, while passed under what is claimed to be the police power for the purpose of protecting the public health or welfare, are, in reality, passed from other motives."

Peckham's lengthy opinion in *Lochner* was overshadowed by the very short dissent of Oliver Wendell Holmes, the Great Dissenter. Holmes had just one point to make, without mention of the majority opinion. He took no position on the necessity for the New York law, but summed up his judicial philosophy in these words: "I strongly believe that my agreement or disagreement has nothing to do with the right of a majority to embody their opinions in law." Justice Holmes spoke the language of judicial deference in this case, in words that would be echoed by an admiring successor, Justice Rehnquist, who later wrote that Holmes's dissent in *Lochner* "has been overwhelmingly vindicated by the passage of time."

Justices Brennan and Rehnquist agree that *Lochner* was wrongly decided. How does this case, then, illustrate their fundamental division over constitutional interpretation? Answering this question requires an exercise in reading judicial opinions through different lenses. Brennan focuses on the "social facts" that supported the New York law. Rehnquist looks instead to the doctrine of "substantive due process" the Court employed to strike down the law. Viewed through Brennan's eyes, the vice of the *Lochner* decision was the Court's dismissal of the factual record. Brennan objects to laws that favor employers over workers. From his perspective, Rehnquist rejects the Court's adoption of a standard that allows judicial review of legislation. Rehnquist objects to doctrines that favor judges over lawmakers.

Lochner lies at the heart of the debate between Brennan and Rehnquist. Speaking at the University of Texas in 1976, Rehnquist linked the *Lochner* case with the infamous *Dred Scott* decision that upheld the constitutionality of slavery. Both decisions, he said, reflected the evils of Brennan's vision of the "living Constitution," although he diplomatically refrained from criticizing his colleague by name.

Calling the *Dred Scott* decision the "apogee of the living Constitution doctrine," Rehnquist implicitly tarred Brennan and other judicial liberals with defending slavery. He derided their practice of placing "moral judgments" into the Constitution. Rehnquist quoted Abraham Lincoln, who said in his First Inaugural Address that if issues of public policy were "irrevocably fixed by decisions of the Supreme Court," then "the people will have ceased to be their own rulers" and will have "practically resigned their government" to the Court. It is hard to discern the relevance of Lincoln's comments—which sound like the complaints of those who defended segregation against the *Brown* decision a century later—to any notion of a "living Constitution," but no one has ever been criticized for denouncing the *Dred Scott* decision. Linking it with *Lochner*, another discredited case, is a clever rhetorical tactic. But there is, in fact, a constitutional chasm between the two decisions.

First, human slavery is certainly not comparable to labor regulation. Second, the Supreme Court decided the *Dred Scott* case in 1857 and fueled the political flames that ignited the Civil War. Following the Union victory, Congress enacted the Fourteenth Amendment to reverse *Dred Scott*. Rehnquist noted that the decision "was repealed in fact as a result of the Civil War and in law by the Civil War amendments" to the Constitution. But the Fourteenth Amendment did more than extend civil rights to the former slaves. It was explicitly written to protect "any person" from deprivation of "liberty" without "due process of law."

The hostility of judicial conservatives to the Fourteenth Amendment helps to explain why Rehnquist tried to link the *Dred Scott* and *Lochner* cases, and to tie them around Brennan's neck. For Rehnquist and other apostles of judicial deference, the vice of *Lochner* was its espousal of "substantive due process," the notion that the Due Process clause embodies substance as well as procedure. The *Lochner* majority found a substantive "right of contract" within the Fourteenth Amendment's protection of "liberty" against state deprivation. Rehnquist explained in his University of Texas speech the error of this notion, and why *Lochner* was an example of the "living Constitution" heresy. The Fourteenth Amendment, he noted, "said nothing about any freedom to make contracts." Justices who "subscribed to the general philosophy of social Darwinism" had substituted their personal views for the Framers' concept of "liberty" in the Constitution. Similarly, justices who supported the practice of slavery imported their personal views into the Constitution.

Rehnquist had an obvious purpose in linking the *Dred Scott* and *Lochner* cases. Both decisions reach outside the constitutional text for support, the former to a distorted reading of history and the latter to a distorted reading of sociology. Rehnquist correctly noted that the Fourteenth Amendment does not mention "freedom of contract" as a component of "liberty." Neither does it mention abortion, or education, or any number of "rights" that have been claimed under the Fourteenth Amendment. This helps to explain Rehnquist's critique of *Lochner* for adopting the notion of "substantive due process." Claims to rights of abortion and education rest on arguments that the Due Process clause *does* have substance, and that its reach should not be limited to protection of blacks and other racial minorities. These modern claims of rights are what trouble Rehnquist, and their adoption by some of his colleagues helps to explain why he picked up *Dred Scott* and *Lochner* as clubs to swing against them.

Rehnquist had another motive for linking the *Dred Scott* and *Lochner* decisions. In his Texas speech, he made clear his hostility to any "expansion of the protection accorded to individual liberties against the state or to the interest of 'discrete and insular' minorities" that cannot "be derived from the Constitution itself," a reference to textual literalism. Rehnquist disparaged those who would "go beyond even a generously fair reading of the language and intent of that document" to protect groups other than racial minorities. He mentioned prisoners as one such group. The arguments of Brennan and others who read the Fourteenth Amendment more broadly, Rehnquist said, "are not really distinguishable from those espoused in *Dred Scott* and *Lochner*." The real purpose of linking two unconnected cases becomes evident: those who espouse rights to abortion or the rights of prisoners, in Rehnquist's mind, rely on the discredited arguments of those who defended human slavery and wage slavery.

REHNQUIST'S REFERENCE to "discrete and insular" minorities introduces the second historic case that shapes his debate with Justice Brennan. Although *Lochner* has become a convenient punching bag, the Court's 1938 decision in *United States v. Carolene Products Co.* remains vital and controversial. The case itself was totally unremarkable; the Court upheld the "Filled Milk Act" of Congress against a challenge by the makers of Milnut, a compound of condensed milk and coconut oil. During the Depression, many poor people were tempted to buy cheap products that looked and tasted like real milk. Congress found that products like Milnut were "injurious to the public health" and constituted "a fraud upon the public." Writing for the Court, Justice Harlan Fiske Stone easily found a "rational basis" for the law in the protection of public health. Such decisions, he wrote, were "a matter for the legislative judgment and not that of courts."

The *Carolene Products* ruling could not upset defenders of judicial deference such as Justice Rehnquist. What did upset him, and what created a lasting conflict with Justice Brennan, was Footnote Four in Stone's opinion, the most famous footnote in the Court's history. Added as a *dictum*, a statement that is not necessary to the decision, Footnote Four outlined the "strict scrutiny" approach that has turned the Fourteenth Amendment into a constitutional shield for members of "discrete and insular minorities" against official discrimination.

In separate paragraphs, Footnote Four produced two branches of the "strict scrutiny" doctrine, directed at different types of laws. One paragraph suggested that "legislation which restricts those political processes which can ordinarily be expected to bring about repeal of undesirable legislation, is to be subjected to more exacting judicial scrutiny" under the Due Process clause of the Fourteenth Amendment. This branch of Footnote Four became known as the "preferred freedoms" doctrine. First Amendment rights of expression and assembly had a "preferred place" in the Constitution, and laws that were challenged as restricting these rights lost their normal presumption of constitutionality. Significantly, of the eleven Supreme Court cases that Stone cited in this paragraph, most dealt with Communists and anarchists, members of unpopular and "un-American" political groups.

The second branch of Footnote Four singled out members of "particular religious, or national, or racial minorities" for judicial protection against laws directed at them. Justice Stone also suggested that laws which displayed "prejudice against discrete and insular minorities" would "call for a correspondingly more searching judicial inquiry." His use of the words "discrete and insular" opened the door for groups other than religious, national, and racial minorities to employ the Equal Protection clause against official discrimination. This branch of Footnote Four became known as "suspect class" analysis; it was not the members of protected minorities who were "suspect," but the legislative classification that subjected them to "invidious" discrimination which became "suspect" of unconstitutionality. But the term, perhaps confusing to those who do not practice constitutional law, is revealing in a broader sense: members of unpopular minorities—gays and lesbians, for example—are "suspect" in the minds of many who belong to the "majority." This is precisely why, Justice Brennan has argued in many opinions, the Court should apply "suspect class" analysis to laws that display evidence of prejudice and stereotyping. Justice Rehnquist has answered that he cannot find "any constitutional authority for such a 'ward of the Court' approach to equal protection."

Like the *Lochner* case, *Carolene Products* was decided in a time of political and economic turmoil. The Great Depression of the 1930s shook the nation, which repudiated the laissez-faire economics of the *Lochner* era and swept Franklin D. Roosevelt into the White House with promises of a New Deal for the American people. Elected with a mandate for change, Roosevelt had no trouble in persuading Congress to enact his program for reviving an economic system on the verge of collapse. During the Hundred Days session of 1933, Congress passed and Roosevelt signed a dozen recovery laws. The two most important, and far-reaching, were the National Industrial Recovery Act and the Agricultural Adjustment Act. The first law set up a business-government partnership to draft "codes of fair competition" that allowed price-fixing, production quotas, and other business practices that would normally violate antitrust laws. The "Triple A" law was designed to raise farm income by imposing taxes on agricultural production that would be paid directly to farmers and growers, bypassing the national treasury.

Both recovery laws gave more benefits to the big business and big farm groups that dominated their administration. Congress turned a deaf ear to the small businessmen and farmers who complained of unfair competition. So they turned to the federal courts, firmly controlled by conservative judges to whom the *Lochner* case was constitutional gospel. When the New Deal cases reached the Supreme Court, the justices struck down almost every recovery law. Ruling in the *Schechter Poultry* case in 1935, the Court agreed without dissent that Congress exceeded its authority in the National Industrial Recovery Act by delegating legislative power to private groups. The next year, the Agricultural Adjustment Act met a similar fate in *United States v. Butler*.

The decisions in the *Schechter* and *Butler* cases provoked President Roosevelt to launch a political attack on the "Nine Old Men" of the Supreme Court and their "horse-and-buggy" approach to the Constitution. Roosevelt lost the political battle to "pack" the Court with sympathetic justices, but he won the war to break the conservative grip on the federal bench. That fascinating story is beyond the scope of this book, but the outcome of the "Constitutional Revolution" of 1937 is relevant to the genesis of Footnote Four in 1938.

During the reign of the "Nine Old Men," the Supreme Court struck down not only federal recovery laws but also a host of state laws to establish minimum wages and maximum hours of work. Ruling in 1936, the Court invalidated a New York minimum-wage law and looked to *Lochner* for precedent: "Freedom of contract is the general rule and restraint the exception," wrote Justice Pierce Butler in *Morehead v. Tipaldo*. He spoke for a bare majority of five. Justice Harlan Fiske Stone responded in a pointed dissent: "There is a grim irony in speaking of the freedom of contract of those who, because of their economic necessities, give their service for less than is needful to keep body and soul together."

The Court's decision in the *Morehead* case unleashed a barrage of criticism. Irving Brant, a respected newsman, had a caustic comment: "Because five is a larger number than four, and for no other reason, the law is unconstitutional." Even the Republican Party, facing a tough presidential campaign against Roosevelt, added to its 1936 platform a pledge to seek "the adoption of state laws" to regulate wages, hours, and working conditions. Roosevelt brushed aside the GOP challenge, and the Supreme Court read the election returns with the rest of the nation. Ruling in March 1937 in a case that was virtually identical to *Morehead*, the Court upheld a Washington state minimum-wage law in *West Coast Hotel v. Parrish.* The Court's opinion rested on "social facts" that it previously ignored. "We may take judicial notice of the unparalleled demands for relief which arose during the recent period of depression and still continue to an alarming extent," wrote Chief Justice Charles Evans Hughes. The only difference between the *Morehead* and *West Coast Hotel* cases was that Justice Owen Roberts switched from opposition to support of minimum-wage laws. After Roosevelt announced his "court-packing" plan in February 1937, Roberts's change of vote defused the plan and provoked quips about "the switch in time that saved nine." The facts are unclear, but most likely Roberts had switched his vote in December 1936 and was more influenced by Roosevelt's massive election victory. In any event, the Court clearly responded in the *West Coast Hotel* case to what Justice Holmes once called "the felt necessities of the time."

From a constitutional perspective, *West Coast Hotel* sounded the death knell of the *Lochner* era. The hotel's owners claimed the minimum-wage law deprived them of "freedom of contract" with their workers, including Elsie Parrish, who earned twenty-two cents an hour as a chambermaid. Chief Justice Hughes responded with scorn. "What is this freedom? The Constitution does not speak of freedom of contract. It speaks of liberty and prohibits the deprivation of liberty without due process of law." Hughes added that "the liberty safeguarded is liberty in a social organization which requires the protection of law against the evils which menace the health, safety, morals and welfare of the people." The "police powers" doctrine had emerged from its long sleep with renewed vigor.

Two weeks after its *West Coast Hotel* decision, the Supreme Court in 1937 upheld the National Labor Relations Act in the *Jones & Laughlin* case. The giant steel company's firing of several workers for union activities had violated the federal law passed in 1935 to protect the right of workers to organize and "bargain collectively" with employers. The Court based its decision on the "social facts" of labor strife and the power of Congress "to protect interstate commerce from the paralyzing consequences of industrial war." Chief Justice Hughes, again speaking for the Court, led a narrow majority in the final battle of the Constitutional Revolution that reshaped the American economy.

The *West Coast Hotel* and *Jones & Laughlin* decisions signaled Roosevelt's victory over the Supreme Court. Within months, conservative justices began to retire and were replaced by men whom Roosevelt considered—wrongly in some cases—to be staunch New Deal supporters. The Court's new majority quickly expanded the powers of federal and state lawmakers over virtually every business and industry, to the extent in 1942 of barring a farmer from growing wheat for his own cattle because it might affect interstate commerce. Such decisions, the Court ruled, "must proceed from political rather than judicial processes."

These decisions effectively removed judicial review of economic legislation from the Court's docket. But the Court adopted a new agenda after the Constitutional Revolution had ended, and Footnote Four of the *Carolene Products* case set that agenda. The political context of the time helps to explain its significance. During the Great Depression, groups that had been forced by repressive state laws into silence during the 1920s regained their voices and members. Organized labor renewed its militance and millions of workers signed union cards. Radical political groups, including the Communist Party, moved from street-corner agitation to Madison Square Garden rallies and electoral influence. And black Americans, who suffered more than any other group from poverty and prejudice, began to fight back against Jim Crow laws and the ultimate indignity, the "lynch law" of southern mobs.

It might seem odd that the author of Footnote Four, Justice Harlan Fiske Stone, a New England Republican, was placed on the Supreme Court by another Yankee Republican, President Calvin Coolidge. But his birthplace, in the Granite State of New Hampshire, and his Revolutionary forebears say much about Stone's granite integrity and stubborn independence. Stone never lost the values of his town-meeting background, but thirteen years in New York City as dean of Columbia Law School exposed him to legal scholarship and cosmopolitan urban life. His later service as a reformist U.S. Attorney General—the nominal superior of J. Edgar Hoover, who considered the Constitution an impediment to crime-busting—added an understanding of how governmental power can be abused.

Footnote Four was actually drafted by Stone's law clerk, Louis Lusky, but the Justice reviewed it carefully and added it to his 1938 *Carolene*

Products opinion with a conscious purpose. Stone wrote to his friend New York Judge Irving Lehman the day after the decision was announced. "I have been deeply concerned," he confessed, "about the increasing racial and religious intolerance which seems to bedevil the world, and which I greatly fear may be augmented in this country." Stone did not mention any incidents, but he was clearly aware of the Nazi program of anti-Semitism. The day the *Carolene Products* case was argued, Stone could read in the *New York Times* that under Nazi rule in Austria, "2,000 Jewish lawyers in Vienna will be excluded from the bar" and that "Jewish physicians and surgeons have been removed from all hospitals." The same week, *Time* magazine reported a speech of Hitler's minister for propaganda, Joseph Goebbels: "I know some say 'the Jew is also a human being.' Just the word 'also' is the best indication of what the Jew really is! Our racial theory is the sole basis for the correct solution of the Jewish problem."

Stone also knew that lynch law still pervaded the Deep South; the *New York Times* reported in April 1937 that Roosevelt Townes, accused of murder in Duck Hill, Mississippi, was tied to a tree, his "eyes were gouged out with an ice pick," and he was "tortured slowly to death with flames from a blow-torch." The week before *Carolene Products* was argued, Stone read about the death of the federal antilynching law at the hands of southern senators. Despite a huge Democratic majority of 76 to 16, President Roosevelt could not budge the Dixiecrats, whose racist diatribes rivaled those of Goebbels. Mississippi Senator Theodore Bilbo railed against "the Ethiopian who has inspired this proposed legislation" and "the lust and lasciviousness of the rape fiend in his diabolical effort to despoil the womanhood of the Caucasian race."

Justice Stone and Louis Lusky—a Jew from New York City—read these and similar accounts of racial and religious persecution with horror. The *Carolene Products* case gave them a convenient medium for their message: the Supreme Court was ready to shift its agenda from economic regulation to the rights of minorities. Their words were new, but they were not written on a totally blank slate. The Court had only recently begun to apply the Bill of Rights to the states, an essential step in protecting minorities against hostile lawmakers. Back in 1833, the Court had ruled in *Barron v. Baltimore* that the Bill of Rights restrained only federal action and was not "applicable to the states." But most laws that punished dissenters or minorities were enacted by local or state bodies, not by Congress. Almost a century passed before the Court shifted course and began the slow process of "incorporation," moving the Bill of Rights under the broader umbrella of the Fourteenth Amendment.

The Court took its first step toward incorporation in 1925, in a case that challenged a New York law against "criminal anarchy." Benjamin Gitlow, a Communist Party leader, was convicted for publishing a "Left Wing Manifesto" that urged a "proletariat revolution" and called workers to join "the final struggle" against capitalism. Breaking with *Barron v. Baltimore*, the Court's majority stated that "freedom of speech and of the press—which are protected by the First Amendment from abridgement by Congress—are among the fundamental personal rights and 'liberties' protected by the due process clause from impairment by the states." Ironically, the majority—including the newest member, Justice Stone —upheld the New York law as an "exercise of its police power" and sent Gitlow to prison over the dissent of Justices Holmes and Brandeis.

Twelve years later, in 1937, the Court took another step toward applying the Bill of Rights to the states. The question in *Palko v. Connecticut* was whether the Double Jeopardy clause of the Fifth Amendment prevented a second state prosecution for murder, after a state judge found serious errors in the first trial, which resulted in a life sentence. Going beyond this criminal law issue, Justice Benjamin Cardozo wrote that First Amendment rights were "implicit in the concept of ordered liberty, and thus, through the Fourteenth Amendment, become valid as against the states." Cardozo went further in stating that "even in the field of substantive rights and duties the legislative judgment, if oppressive and arbitrary, may be overridden by the courts." Cardozo had no intention of reviving *Lochner* after its recent demise; "economic" due process remained in its grave. But his opinion added "social and moral values" to the substance of the Fourteenth Amendment's "liberty" clause. Ironically, the Court refused to apply the Double Jeopardy clause to the states; after his second trial, Palko was sentenced to death.

Imposing the First Amendment on the states through its "incorporation" into the Fourteenth Amendment gave Justice Stone a strong basis in precedent for the "strict scrutiny" test of Footnote Four. In fact, several of the cases that Cardozo cited in *Palko* showed up in Stone's footnote. These cases had protected members of religious, racial, and radical minorities from laws that reflected the prejudices of political majorities. What Stone proposed in Footnote Four was to turn the "presumption of constitutionality" against such laws. Later decisions of the Supreme Court made the "strict scrutiny" test a daunting challenge for lawmakers. They are forced by Footnote Four to prove a "compelling state interest" when their laws deny "fundamental rights" to any person or create a "suspect class" for any minority group. Not only must their interest be "compelling," they must also show that no "less restrictive alternative" to the challenged law can be devised. Gerald Gunther, a noted legal scholar, did not exaggerate when he described Stone's constitutional test as "strict in theory, but fatal in fact."

THE "STRICT SCRUTINY" test was designed to protect members of unpopular and vulnerable minorities from the prejudice of hostile majorities, when that prejudice spills over from personal animus into official acts. Those who reject this test—like Robert Bork and Justice Rehnquist—argue that it undermines the democratic political system and the principle of majority rule. Bork writes, for example, that "in wide areas of life majorities are entitled to rule, if they wish, simply because they are majorities." But he admits that "there are some things majorities must not do to minorities, some areas of life in which the individual must be free of majority rule." This is the so-called Madisonian dilemma, the inherent tension between majority rule and minority rights in the Constitution.

Bork resolves this dilemma by confining judicial protection to clearly defined "religious, national, and racial minorities." He is suspicious of Footnote Four and the concept of "discrete and insular minorities." "What minorities," he asks, "could Stone be talking about?" Bork suspects they are groups, like homosexuals, "who cannot win their point in the political process because of 'prejudice' " on the part of majorities. That was, of course, exactly Stone's point in Footnote Four. Bork responds that "the Constitution does not prohibit laws based on prejudice *per se*," and claims that Footnote Four "means nothing more than that the Justices will read into the Constitution their own subjective sympathies and social preferences."

Justice Rehnquist also denies "that whenever the Court feels that a societal group is 'discrete and insular,' it has the constitutional mandate to prohibit legislation that somehow treats the group differently from some other group." He notes that American society, "consisting of over 200 million individuals of multitudinous origins, customs, tongues, beliefs, and cultures is, to say the least, diverse." Given this diversity, "it would hardly take extraordinary ingenuity for a lawyer to find 'insular

and discrete' minorities at every turn of the road." Rehnquist fears
that Footnote Four invites the Supreme Court to "choose a 'minority'
it 'feels' deserves 'solicitude' and thereafter prohibit the States from
classifying that 'minority' differently from the 'majority.'" He clearly
used the internal quotation marks in this sentence to disparage those—
like Justice Brennan—who display judicial "feeling" and "solicitude" for
minorities.

Bork and Rehnquist both criticize judges who replace the majoritarian
principle with personal "solicitude" for those who lose at the ballot box.
But is this charge true? Do those who apply the "strict scrutiny" test use
it to mask their own prejudices? Bork denounces judges who scoff at "the
community's morality" and see only "the community's bigotry" in laws
that proscribe behavior such as homosexual sodomy. He has another
question: "In any event, how is the Court to know whether a particular
minority lost in the legislature because of 'prejudice,' as opposed to morality, prudence, or any other legitimate reason?"

Bork's question lies at the heart of the conflict between Brennan and
Rehnquist, and demands an answer. And there *is* a persuasive answer,
found in a multitude of cases that provide evidence of overt prejudice—
sometimes violence—against members of unpopular minorities. Several
cases decided since the time of Footnote Four illustrate the Court's differing responses to prejudice. They have been chosen from hundreds that
could equally document the ubiquity and persistence of hostility to dissenters and minorities in small towns and big cities across America. And
each answers the question posed by Robert Bork with facts that belie any
"legitimate reason" for the official action being challenged.

The first case began in 1935 in a small Pennsylvania mining town.
The public schools in Minersville opened each day with the Pledge of
Allegiance and flag-salute ceremony; students faced the flag with the
raised-palm salute that had also been adopted by the German Nazi regime. Twelve-year-old Lillian Gobitis and her younger brother, William,
decided to stop saluting the flag because of persecution of Jehovah's
Witnesses, the Gobitis family's religion. Lillian and William took their
unpopular stand in solidarity with German Witnesses who were thrown
into concentration camps for refusing to salute the swastika flag and
emblem.

Years later, Lillian explained what had happened: "I loved school, and
I was actually kind of popular. I was class president in the seventh grade,
and I had good grades. And I felt that, oh, if I stop saluting the flag, I

will blow all this! And I did. I sat down and the whole room was aghast. After that, when I came to school, they would throw a hail of pebbles and yell things like, 'Here comes Jehovah!' " The school superintendent, Charles Roudabush, could not convince Lillian's father, Walter, to order his children to stand up and put their palms out. Roudabush also knew that neither state nor local law required participation in the flag salute or punished refusal to take part.

The Minersville school board decided to deal with the issue. Walter Gobitis and the mother of Edmund Wasliewski, another Witness objector, explained their positions to the hostile board members. "We are not desecrating the American flag," Gobitis said. "We show no disrespect for the flag, but we cannot salute it. The Bible tells us this, and we must obey." The board promptly passed a resolution making refusal to salute the flag "an act of insubordination," and Superintendent Roudabush immediately expelled the three young Witnesses from school.

This drumhead hearing was hardly a model of the legislative process, although it was typical of the response in many small towns to Jehovah's Witnesses and other unpopular groups. Walter Gobitis made good on his parting shot to the Minersville board: "I'm going to take you to court for this!" His suit came before Philadelphia federal judge Albert Maris, who belonged to another religious minority, the Quakers. The board's lawyers argued that the flag-salute law was adopted for the "reasonable" purpose of "inculcating patriotism" in students, and that the board had simply exercised its "police powers" to protect the "health, safety, welfare, and morals" of Minersville students. Judge Maris rejected this argument, ruling that Lillian and William Gobitis had "liberty" rights under the Fourteenth Amendment that outweighed the powers of the school board. He wrote that "the refusal of these two earnest Christian children to salute the flag cannot even remotely prejudice or imperil the safety, health, morals, property or personal rights of their fellows."

When the board's appeal reached the Supreme Court in 1940, war clouds loomed over two oceans, moving closer to American shores. Justice Felix Frankfurter, a fervent apostle of judicial deference, spoke for all but one justice in reversing Judge Maris. Frankfurter's opinion in *Minersville v. Gobitis* read like an Army recruiting poster. "National unity is the basis of national security," he wrote. "The ultimate foundation of a free society is the binding tie of cohesive sentiment." The refusal of the Gobitis children to salute the flag "might cast doubts in the minds of the other children" about "the kind of ordered society which is summarized by our flag." Frankfurter looked ahead to wartime, depicting the American flag as the symbol of "absolute safety for free institutions against foreign aggression."

Frankfurter's opinion went beyond judicial deference to lawmakers, coming close to judicial abdication. He ignored evidence of hasty action by the school board in passing its regulation. "The case before us must be viewed as though the legislature of Pennsylvania had itself formally directed the flag-salute for the children of Minersville," he wrote. Frankfurter made a quick bow toward the Supremacy clause of the Constitution: "Judicial review, itself a limitation of popular government, is a fundamental part of our constitutional scheme." But he refused to second-guess the Minersville officials. The Constitution gives to elected lawmakers "no less than to courts," Frankfurter wrote, "the guardianship of deeply cherished liberties." He ended his judicial sermon with these words for the Gobitis family: "To fight out the wise use of legislative authority in the forum of public opinion and before legislative assemblies, rather than to transfer such a contest to the judicial arena, serves to vindicate the self-confidence of a free people."

The only justice who dissented from this condescending civics lecture was Harlan Fiske Stone. "History teaches us that there have been but few infringements of personal liberty by the state," he reminded his colleagues, "which have not been directed, as they are now, at politically helpless minorities." Frankfurter had compelled the Gobitis children to choose between the flag salute and public schooling. Stone rejected such a forced choice. He denied that the Constitution allowed lawmakers to decide "whether the citizen shall be compelled to give public expression of such sentiments contrary to his religion." Stone did not cite his *Carolene Products* opinion, but he urged "careful scrutiny of legislative efforts to secure conformity of belief and opinion," and expressed his sympathy with "this small and helpless minority" in confronting state power. Stone answered the apostles of judicial deference with these words: "The Constitution expresses more than the conviction of the people that democratic processes must be preserved at all costs."

The Gobitis family and many other Witnesses paid the costs of defying the "democratic process." Within two weeks of the Court's opinion, federal officials later wrote, "hundreds of attacks upon the Witnesses were reported to the Department of Justice." In Kennebunk, Maine, the Kingdom Hall of Jehovah's Witnesses was burned to the ground. The police chief in Richwood, West Virginia, forced a group of Witnesses to drink large doses of castor oil and dragged them out of town behind a police car, tied together with rope. In Nebraska, a Witness was kidnapped, beaten, and castrated. Federal officials traced these terrorist attacks directly to Frankfurter's opinion. "In the two years following the opinion," they reported, "the files of the Department of Justice reflect an uninterrupted record of violence and persecution of the Witnesses. Almost without exception, the flag and the flag salute can be found as the percussion cap that sets off these acts." Lillian Gobitis never returned to public school. She completed her education in schools set up for expelled Witnesses, who numbered about 2,000.

The Supreme Court does not often retreat from its decisions. Faced with public hostility to decisions on school segregation and classroom prayer, the Court restated its opinions in even stronger language. But the violent reaction to the *Gobitis* decision forced the justices to look closely at the reality of prejudice. They voted in 1943 to review an almost identical case. The West Virginia legislature had enacted a flag-salute law that included wording from Frankfurter's opinion in the *Gobitis* case. School officials expelled several Witness children who refused to salute the flag.

The Court's decision in *West Virginia v. Barnette* exposed the constitutional faultline that divided the justices over the issue of judicial review. Justice Robert Jackson wrote for a majority of six in reversing the *Gobitis* decision. He pointed to "social facts" about the persecution of Jehovah's Witnesses. "Children of this faith have been expelled from school," Jackson noted, and their parents "threatened with prosecutions for causing delinquency." The cost of refusing to salute the American flag was high. "Officials threaten to send them to reformatories maintained for criminally inclined juveniles," Jackson said of the Witness children.

Jackson quoted Frankfurter's claim in his *Gobitis* opinion that minorities should "fight out" their battles with majorities "in the forum of public opinion and before legislative assemblies" rather than in court. He reminded Frankfurter that minorities were often powerless to fight off "village tyrants" who act "under color of law" and consider their power "beyond reach of the Constitution." Jackson pointed to ancient history and current events, from "the Roman drive to stamp out Christianity" to "the fast failing efforts of our totalitarian enemies." He drew a line from Minersville to Berlin: "Those who begin coercive elimination of dissent soon find themselves eliminating dissenters. Compulsory unification of opinion achieves only the unanimity of the graveyard."

No other Supreme Court opinion, before or since Jackson wrote, has more profoundly and eloquently captured the essence of the Constitution: "The very purpose of a Bill of Rights was to withdraw certain subjects from the vicissitudes of political controversy, to place them beyond the reach of majorities and officials and to establish them as legal principles to be applied by the courts. One's right to life, liberty, and property, to free speech, a free press, freedom of worship and assembly, and other fundamental rights may not be submitted to vote; they depend on the outcome of no elections."

Jackson ended with this ringing peroration: "If there is any fixed star in our constitutional constellation, it is that no official, high or petty, can prescribe what shall be orthodox in politics, nationalism, religion, or other matters of opinion or force citizens to confess by word or act their faith therein."

Just three years after the Court decided the *Gobitis* case, over the solitary dissent of Justice Stone, a new majority overruled that opinion. Three justices—William Douglas, Hugo Black, and Frank Murphy—had repented their votes in *Gobitis*, and two new justices—Robert Jackson and Wiley Rutledge—joined them and Harlan Stone, now the Chief Justice, to move Frankfurter into dissent with Owen Roberts and Stanley Reed. Frankfurter vented his ire at this "deciding shift of opinion" by asking whether the Constitution had become "the sport of shifting winds of doctrine?"

Frankfurter took the reversal as a personal rebuff, and responded in personal terms, with reference to his Jewish forebears. "One who belongs to the most vilified and persecuted minority in history is not likely to be insensible to the freedoms guaranteed by our Constitution." He noted his "personal attitude" that compulsory flag-salute laws were unwise. "But as judges we are neither Jew nor Gentile, neither Catholic nor agnostic." Frankfurter argued that judges had just one duty, that of deciding "whether legislators could in reason have enacted such a law." He expressed frustration at the "Jehovah's Witnesses cases" that prompted the new majority to "restrict the powers of democratic government." Frankfurter ended his dissent with an implicit rejection of Stone's "strict scrutiny" test: "Even though legislation relates to civil liberties," he wrote, "our duty of deference to those who have the responsibility for making the laws" demands an "attitude of judicial humility" toward lawmakers.

JUSTICE STONE took the lecture about judicial humility to heart in an opinion he issued just one week after the Court decided the *Barnette* case. This case also involved wartime fears and passions, and a "discrete and insular" minority that suffered from racial prejudice. The legislative villain in this case was not a small-town school board but the U.S. Congress. In February 1942, two months after the Japanese attack on Pearl Harbor, President Franklin Roosevelt signed an Executive Order authorizing the expulsion of "any or all persons" from military zones that encompassed the entire Pacific coast. Roosevelt's order subjected 110,000 Americans of Japanese ancestry—two-thirds of them native-born citizens—to curfew and exclusion orders that led to internment camps from the California deserts to the Mississippi Delta in Louisiana.

The legislative history of this mass evacuation is paltry. Roosevelt spent no more than an hour in considering the exclusion order that military officials had drafted. The declared purpose of the order was to protect West Coast military bases from "espionage and sabotage" by Japanese spies and sappers. The files of intelligence agencies—including the FBI, the Navy, and the Army—show that not one act of espionage or sabotage was ever linked to any Japanese American. The actual reason for the exclusion order was racism. General John DeWitt, the West Coast commander who pushed for the order, did not conceal his racial animus. "A Jap is a Jap," he told a congressional committee. "There isn't such a thing as a loyal Japanese." Regardless of American birth, DeWitt claimed, they belonged to an "enemy race" and were presumed to be disloyal.

After Roosevelt signed the order that DeWitt had drafted, Congress promptly passed a law to make violation of exclusion orders a federal criminal offense. Not a single witness appeared against the bill in brief hearings, and not a single member of Congress voted against the law in floor debate that took no more than ten minutes. Only "Mr. Republican," Ohio Senator Robert Taft, raised a skeptical voice on the floor: "I think this is probably the sloppiest criminal law I have ever read or seen anywhere," he said, before joining the unanimous vote.

The vast majority of Japanese Americans bowed to military edict and boarded the buses and trains that carried them to America's concentration camps. Only three young men—Gordon Hirabayashi, Minoru Yasui, and Fred Korematsu—had the courage to challenge the military orders in court. They were all convicted in perfunctory trials, and each appealed his sentence to the Supreme Court. Justice Stone wrote for a unanimous Court in *U.S. v. Hirabayashi*, which upheld the curfew orders in June 1943. His opinion made no mention of *Carolene Products* or the "strict scrutiny" test, although Stone admitted that "legislative classification or discrimination based on race alone has often been held to be a denial of equal protection." But Stone felt "the successful prosecution of the war" allowed Congress and the president to adopt "defense" measures that might "place citizens of one ancestry in a different category from others."

Stone relied on "social facts" in his opinion, but his "facts" blamed Japanese Americans for the prejudice they had endured for more than five decades. He noted that "large numbers of children of Japanese parentage are sent to Japanese language schools," and that some children "have been sent to Japan for all or a part of their education." He also observed that "state legislation has denied to alien Japanese the privilege of owning land" and that "federal legislation has denied to the Japanese citizenship by naturalization." Stone concluded from these "facts" that "social, economic and political" factors had prevented the assimilation of Japanese Americans "as an integral part of the white population."

Stone's comment about the "white population" exposes the link between racial stereotypes and judicial deference to lawmakers. Bowing to wartime pressures, Stone looked for guidance not to the "liberty" clauses of the Constitution but to tainted evidence that Japanese Americans had shown "relatively little social intercourse between them and the white population." He built upon this unproven—and entirely irrelevant— claim the conclusion that "in time of war residents having ethnic affiliations with an invading enemy may be a greater source of danger than those of a different ancestry." Stone cited no evidence for this assertion, although the only prior example in American history had been Tory support for the British invasion of 1812.

Eighteen months later, in December 1944, the Supreme Court ruled on the exclusion orders in *U.S. v. Korematsu*. With Allied forces nearing victory in the Pacific, the Court had less reason to defer to military judgment. Writing for the majority, Justice Hugo Black agreed with Chief Justice Stone that "all legal restrictions which curtail the civil rights of a single racial group are immediately suspect" and that "courts must subject them to the most rigid scrutiny."

Despite this nod to Footnote Four, Black wrote for a majority that upheld Fred Korematsu's criminal conviction. Like Stone in the *Hirabayashi* case, Black relied on "social facts" about Japanese Americans. Unlike Stone, who blamed this racial minority for reacting to prejudice that predated the war, Black blamed them for responding to prejudice after their forced evacuation. Government officials had imposed a "loyalty" oath on all camp inmates, forcing them to "forswear" an allegiance to the Japanese emperor that most never had. "Approximately five thousand American citizens of Japanese ancestry refused to swear unqualified allegiance to the United States," Black noted, "and several thousand evacuees requested repatriation to Japan."

Black did not charge Fred Korematsu—a shipyard welder who volunteered for military service—with disloyalty. But he heatedly denied that this was "a case involving the imprisonment of a loyal citizen in a concentration camp because of racial prejudice." Like Stone before him, Black placed his "confidence in this time of war in our military leaders" and their judgment that "all citizens of Japanese ancestry be segregated from the West Coast" during the war.

Three members of the Court dissented in the *Korematsu* case. The most vocal dissenter, Justice Frank Murphy, cited a voluminous record of prejudice against Japanese Americans. He charged Black with relying upon "questionable racial and sociological grounds not ordinarily within the realm of expert military judgment." Murphy cited a different set of "social facts," including evidence that Caucasian farmers in California supported the mass evacuation for economic reasons. He quoted a leading farm lobbyist: "We're charged with wanting to get rid of the Japs for selfish reasons. We do. It's a question of whether the white man lives on the Pacific Coast or the brown men." Murphy placed blame for exclusion on "people with racial and economic prejudices—the same people who have been among the foremost advocates of the evacuation."

Justice Black remained an advocate of the evacuation. His comments, more than twenty years later, illustrate the power and persistence of racial stereotypes. "People were rightly fearful of the Japanese," he explained, because "they all look alike to a person not a Jap." Fred Korematsu, who looks nothing like Gordon Hirabayashi, finally cleared his criminal record of the taint of racial disloyalty. Federal judge Marilyn Patel reversed his conviction in 1984, holding that government lawyers had lied to the Supreme Court in 1944 about charges of espionage against Japanese Americans. Judge Patel echoed the sentiments of Justice Jackson in the

Barnette case in writing that the *Korematsu* case "stands as a caution that in times of international hostility our institutions, legislative, executive, and judicial, must be prepared to protect all citizens from the petty fears and prejudices that are so easily aroused." But those prejudices cost Fred Korematsu the stigma of a criminal record.

MOST AMERICANS would recoil in horror at this record of prejudice against Jehovah's Witnesses and Japanese Americans. The harm done to Lillian Gobitis and Fred Korematsu has been partially redressed, but conflicts over religion and race continue to bedevil American society. These two cases vividly illustrate how "village tyrants" can turn the legislative process into star-chamber proceedings, from school boards to Congress. And they raise troubling questions for the defenders of judicial deference to lawmakers. Briefer accounts of five other cases show that lawmakers and officials—and even Supreme Court justices—have not heeded Justice Jackson's words in the *Barnette* opinion.

The next case involves probably the most feared and least popular group in American history: the Communist Party. The legislative crusade against the Party began the year it was formed, in 1919, and led to state sedition laws, "red flag" laws, and other efforts to stamp out the Red Menace. But the campaign became more serious in 1940, as war approached and Communists joined isolationists in opposing "preparedness" measures. Congress passed in that year the Smith Act, officially called the Alien Registration Act. This law was actually a classic "bill of attainder," directed against one man, Harry Bridges, who headed the West Coast longshoremen's union for many years. Federal officials tried for more than two decades to deport Bridges to his native Australia as a Communist, despite his continuing denials of Party membership.

The sponsors of the Smith Act made no bones about their aims: "It is my joy to announce," said the bill's House manager, Sam Hobbs of Alabama, "that in a perfectly legal and constitutional manner this bill changes the law so that the Department of Justice should now have little trouble in deporting Harry Bridges and all others of similar ilk." The bill was, in fact, flatly unconstitutional, and the Supreme Court ruled in 1945 that Bridges was entitled to American citizenship. With Bridges as its target, the Smith Act included a provision making it a federal crime to advocate the violent overthrow of the U.S. government. The entire debate on this provision consisted of the following colloquy between

Congressman Hobbs and John McCormack, a future House Speaker: McCormack: "Is this the Smith bill?" Hobbs: "Yes, sir, the conference report thereon." McCormack: "The gentleman will remember that I offered an amendment which the House adopted, making it a crime to knowingly and willfully advocate the overthrow of the Government by force and violence. Is that written into the bill?" Hobbs: "Of course it is, in substance." This was the entire debate over a law that produced hundreds of criminal prosecutions, sent scores of actual or alleged Reds to prison, and convulsed our political system for two decades with charges that Communists were conspiring to destroy the American Way of Life.

Once again, the Supreme Court spoke as if Congress had deliberated like the Greek solons. Upholding the convictions of Party leaders in 1951, the Court held in *Dennis v. United States* that the Free Speech clause of the First Amendment is not "above and beyond control of the legislature" when it decides "that certain kinds of speech are so undesirable as to warrant criminal sanction." Justice Felix Frankfurter pontificated in his concurrence that "there is ample justification for a legislative judgment that the conspiracy now before us is a substantial threat to national order and security." The legislative judgment to which Frankfurter deferred took roughly twenty seconds to make, from start to finish.

Another legislative body, the city council of Little Rock, Arkansas, met in October 1957. The councilors discussed an ordinance that was designed to force the state NAACP to turn over its membership records for public inspection and publication. The law was drafted by the state's attorney general, Bruce Bennett, who appeared before the council and admitted his purpose: "One of the troubles with the South," he complained, "is that we have been letting the Negroes run to federal courts while we don't use the state courts to attack them." Bennett's target was Daisy Bates, the young president of the Arkansas NAACP, who guided nine black students through the howling mobs that surrounded Central High School in Little Rock.

The NAACP was "scared of losing its followers" if their names became public, Bennett told the council. "Daisy Bates admits this in the NAACP suit in federal court." Alderman Bill Hood could not conceal his eagerness to send Daisy Bates and other black leaders to jail. "Let's pop 'em!" he urged. In this case, the Supreme Court refused to defer to official racism. The Court noted evidence that NAACP members "had been subjected to harassment and threats of bodily harm." One witness, Birdie Williams, testified that "they have throwed stones at my home" and "they threaten my life over the telephone." Daisy Bates was subjected not only to death threats but to dynamite bombs in her front yard.

Two cases from the 1960s illustrate the Court's differing responses to protest against the Vietnam War. Popular opposition to American policy prompted thousands of acts of civil disobedience, including the public burning of draft cards. Congress responded in 1965 with a law that made destruction of draft cards a federal crime. Senator Strom Thurmond of South Carolina called these acts "treason in time of war." Only two House members spoke on the floor about the bill. Congressman Charles Bray of Indiana denounced the "filthy, sleazy beatnik gang" who he said "would destroy American freedom." Congressman Mendel Rivers of South Carolina added that those who "thumb their noses at their own Government" should be "sent to prison" for burning draft cards. The House promptly approved the bill by a vote of 393–1.

David O'Brien and two other young men later burned their draft cards on the courthouse steps in South Boston, Massachusetts, a patriotic stronghold. They were beaten by a mob while police officers stood by and did nothing. O'Brien was convicted under the federal law and sentenced to a year in prison. Writing for the Supreme Court in 1968, Chief Justice Earl Warren admitted that O'Brien burned his card to protest the Vietnam War. But he defended the law as a legitimate effort to ensure "the smooth functioning of the Selective Service System." Warren took pains to prop up another shaky pillar of judicial deference, the refusal to examine the legislative record for evidence of hostility toward minorities or dissenters. He avoided any mention of the invective of Congressmen Bray and Rivers by falling back on "a familiar principle of constitutional law that this Court will not strike down an otherwise constitutional statute on the basis of an alleged illicit motive."

The Vietnam War produced another case with a different outcome. Just before Christmas in 1965, Mary Beth Tinker went to her eighth-grade class at Warren Harding Junior High in Des Moines, Iowa, wearing a black armband to protest American bombing of Vietnam and to support calls for a Christmas truce. The day before, having learned of Mary's plan, school officials had banned the wearing of armbands. The school-board president, Ora Niffenegger, explained that "our country's leaders have decided on a course of action and we should support them."

Mary Tinker explained what happened after she wore her armband to algebra class: "People threw red paint at our house, and we got lots of calls. We got all kinds of threats to our family, even death threats. They even threatened my little brothers and sisters, which was *really* sick. People called our house on Christmas Eve and said the house would be blown up by morning. I was leaving for school one morning and the phone rang and I picked it up. This woman said, 'Is this Mary Tinker?' And I said, 'yes.' And she said, 'I'm going to *kill* you!' "

School officials defended the ban on armbands in words that echoed Felix Frankfurter in the *Gobitis* case. One testified at trial that if Mary Tinker, who was only thirteen, "didn't like the way our elected officials were handling things," she should express her protest at "the ballot box and not in the halls of our public schools." Ruling in 1969, at the end of Earl Warren's tenure as Chief Justice, the Supreme Court issued a ringing defense of the First Amendment. Justice Abe Fortas looked to the facts of the case and found none that justified the suspension of Mary Tinker. He wrote for the majority that public schools "may not be enclaves of totalitarianism" and that students "are possessed of fundamental rights which the State must respect."

Justice Hugo Black, who had become crotchety in his eighties, dissented in *Tinker v. Des Moines.* Endorsing "the old-fashioned slogan that 'children are to be seen not heard,' " Black saw in Mary Tinker's armband "the beginning of a new revolutionary era of permissiveness in this country" that would end with "rioting, property seizures, and destruction." This was quite a burden to place on a junior high student. Mary Tinker later talked about her reaction to the Supreme Court decision. "I just wanted to put it out of my mind. I didn't want to be a big star, because I was a teenager. Teenagers never want to stand out in a crowd. They just want to blend in. It was kind of a rough time when it broke."

Just before he retired in 1971, Justice Black wrote for the Court in another case that examined legislative hostility toward minorities. This was now the Burger Court, with Warren Burger and Harry Blackmun in the seats of Earl Warren and Abe Fortas. The "Minnesota Twins," as the new justices were dubbed by the press, joined Black in upholding the right of Jackson, Mississippi, to close its public swimming pools to evade an integration order of a federal judge. The record in this case, *Palmer v. Thompson,* left no doubt that city officials were motivated by racism. Jackson's mayor, Allen Thompson, vowed that "we are not going to have any intermingling" of black and white swimmers in city pools.

Justice Black put on judicial blinders to shield his eyes from the reality of racism. "Some evidence in the record," he confessed, supported claims that Jackson closed its pools "because of ideological opposition to racial

integration in swimming pools." But he read the record differently, finding that "the pools were closed because the city council felt they could
not be operated safely and economically on an integrated basis." The
"rational basis" for Jackson's decision to close its pools rested on claims
that integration might cause fights or reduce the city's revenues. Neither
claim had any support in the case record. Black simply ignored this record.
His opinion cited *United States v. O'Brien* in rejecting arguments that
"illicit motivation" could support judicial nullification of laws that punished unpopular minorities. The Supreme Court had never held, Black
wrote, "that a legislative act may violate equal protection solely because
of the motivations of the men who voted for it."

Justice Black was wrong in this statement, and he ignored a historical
record that he clearly knew. Back in 1886, the Supreme Court struck
down a San Francisco ordinance that denied business licenses to every
Chinese laundry owner in the city. The legislative motivation for closing
the Chinese laundries was identical with that of Mississippi lawmakers in
closing swimming pools. The motive was racism, pure and simple. The
Supreme Court recognized the reality of racism in *Yick Wo v. Hopkins.*
"Though the law be fair on its face and impartial in appearance," the
Court held, "if it is applied and administered by public authority with
an evil eye and an unequal hand," it violates the Constitution.

The *Yick Wo* case is relevant, more than a century later, to the decisions
of Justices Brennan and Rehnquist. Without using the terms "strict scrutiny" or "rational basis," the Supreme Court looked at "social facts" and
challenged the motivations of lawmakers in discriminating against the
Chinese. "The fact of this discrimination is admitted," the Court noted.
"No reason for it is shown, and the conclusion cannot be resisted, that
no reason for it exists except hostility to the race and nationality to which
the petitioners belong, and which in the eye of the law is not justified."

In his ill-fated *Gobitis* opinion, Justice Frankfurter posed a crucial
question. How can judges decide, he asked, whether a law promotes
"some great common end" or exacts "a penalty for conduct which appears
dangerous to the general good?" Frankfurter answered with the principle
of judicial deference to majority rule. Justice Stone answered with an
appeal to the "constitutional liberty of religious and racial minorities."
More than five decades later, the Supreme Court remains divided on
Frankfurter's question. During their years together on the bench, Brennan
and Rehnquist almost never agreed on the answer.

FIVE

"The Greatest Dangers to Liberty"

AMERICANS ARE DEEPLY attached to "liberty" as a defining element of both personal and national identity. Fourth of July rhetoric about "the land of the free," and the promise in the Pledge of Allegiance of "liberty and justice for all," convey more than empty sentiment. Most people will agree they have a right to lead their lives with a minimum of governmental intrusion. Although few can articulate just what "liberty" encompasses, and even fewer can define the term "due process" with lawyerly precision, the majority of Americans share a conviction that they have rights against the government. At the same time, a majority believe that government has both the power and the duty to maintain "order" in society, protecting citizens against harm to their persons and property.

Striking the proper balance of liberty and order is difficult. Many people agree with the adage, reduced to basics, that "your rights end where my nose begins." We give legislators the job of putting that slogan into specific and enforceable terms, with laws that cover a wide range of activities, from criminal penalties for assault and theft, to civil codes that prohibit discrimination and pollution. Each area of legal regulation involves a balancing of personal right and governmental power. We give judges the task of deciding whether laws and official actions violate any provisions of the Constitution. Some of these are enumerated in fairly clear terms: the First Amendment protects freedom of religion, speech, press, and assembly from governmental restriction. Others are couched in very general—some would say vague—terms: perhaps the most important are the "liberty" clauses of the Fifth and Fourteenth amendments. Identical in wording, they prohibit federal and state officials from depriving any person of "life, liberty, or property, without due process of law."

The "liberty" clauses impose on judges their most difficult task of constitutional interpretation. The range of interests covered by this one word is virtually limitless, particularly in areas outside the scope of enumerated rights. Some claims of protected rights would strike many as trivial: Are prison inmates protected against "double-bunking" in cell blocks? Others raise profound questions of life and death: Do parents of an accident victim who "exists" in a vegetative state have a right to turn off her respirator and end their daughter's life? The Supreme Court has been asked many questions about the meaning of "liberty" over the years. Guidance comes partly from precedent, but in large measure each justice brings to the definition of this term a personal vision of the Constitution.

In looking at "liberty" cases that divided Justices Brennan and Rehnquist, it is helpful to envision the relations of citizens to the government as a circle. Our focus will move from the outside to the center, from being watched by officials without our knowledge to arguing with them in hospital rooms about whether our loved ones should live or die. In between are cases that involve police officers and citizens, some suspected but not charged with crimes, some charged but not convicted, and some imprisoned after conviction. Few of us have encountered all these situations, but we could face any one at any time. The chances of walking peacefully down the street and winding up in prison or an operating room may be small, but the consequences are certainly serious. And the "liberty" clauses of the Constitution may be all that protects us from those consequences.

FEW PEOPLE QUESTION the powers of officials to investigate crime and place suspected criminals under surveillance. But the Constitution limits these powers. Any "search or seizure" that is "unreasonable" is barred by the Fourth Amendment, and searches must be based upon "probable cause" to believe a crime has been committed or is about to happen. The First Amendment also protects rights of speech and assembly, and the right "to petition the government for a redress of grievances." During the Vietnam War, millions of Americans expressed their opposition to government policy by attending meetings, joining demonstrations, and signing petitions against the war.

Every president since Franklin Roosevelt has authorized the FBI to collect "political intelligence" on administration critics, but Richard Nixon unleashed the Army on his domestic opponents. Members of Army

Intelligence units conducted wide-ranging surveillance of antiwar groups. They took photographs at demonstrations, tapped phones, and put "tails" on activists. Some agents—especially those in Reserve units—objected to this domestic warfare, and leaked documents to the press. In 1970, several antiwar leaders filed suit against Defense Secretary Melvin Laird, with Arlo Tatum of the Central Committee for Conscientious Objectors as the lead plaintiff. They alleged that Army "surveillance of lawful and peaceful civilian political activity" cast a "chill" over their exercise of First Amendment rights.

In June 1972, the Supreme Court reversed the ruling of a federal appellate panel that the case raised substantial First Amendment issues and should go to trial. Chief Justice Burger wrote for a narrow 5–4 majority, including Justice Rehnquist. Burger denied that the plaintiffs had suffered any "present or immediately threatened injury resulting from unlawful governmental action." He also dismissed as "speculative" any claims that Vietnam War opponents could be "chilled" by Army surveillance in expressing their views. Justice William Douglas wrote a long and passionate dissent, comparing the Army's actions with KGB surveillance of Russian dissidents. "The Constitution was designed to keep government off the backs of the people," he said. "The Bill of Rights was designed to keep agents of government and official eavesdroppers away from assemblies of people." Justice Brennan added a short dissent, quoting the appellate opinion that the lawsuit alleged an "inhibition of lawful behavior and of First Amendment rights" and should be tried on the merits.

It is not surprising that Brennan and Rehnquist differed in *Laird v. Tatum*, given their conflicting views of individual rights and governmental powers. What *is* surprising is that Rehnquist voted at all, and did not recuse himself from the case. Appearing before a Senate committee in 1970 as a Justice Department official, he defended the Army's surveillance program and specifically discussed the *Laird* case, questioning whether "an action will lay by private citizens to enjoin the gathering of information" on their political activities. Rehnquist's decision to cast the deciding vote in the case raised eyebrows. One reporter noted that Justice Lewis Powell had recused himself from an antitrust suit against major-league baseball "because he owned stock in the beer company that owned the ball club that once owned plaintiff Curt Flood." The reporter posed a question: "How much has the judiciary actually learned about conflict of interest on the bench?"

Three months after the Court decided the *Laird* case, Rehnquist took the unprecedented step of publicly responding to the criticism. Lawyers for the losing plaintiffs had filed a motion that he disqualify himself, arguing that his "impartiality is clearly questionable" because of "his public statements about the lack of merit" in the plaintiffs' case. Rehnquist denied the motion, but admitted in his fifteen-page response that he had expressed opinions that were "contrary to the contentions of respondents in this case." But he said the bias allegations "make a great deal of very little." He had not appeared as a lawyer or witness in the case, which would have required disqualification. Rehnquist had no apologies for expressing opinions on the legal issues in the case. "Proof that a Justice's mind at the time he joined the Court was a complete *tabula rasa* in the area of constitutional adjudication," he wrote, "would be evidence of lack of qualification, not lack of bias." The aggressive tone of his response suggests that Rehnquist relished the conflict with his ideological foes.

Four years later, in 1976, Rehnquist expressed strong views on the "liberty" clauses in an opinion that further restricted claims against governmental power. Surveillance by government agents may "chill" the exercise of First Amendment rights, but finding one's picture on posters as an accused criminal must certainly be a chilling sight. In December 1972, the police in Louisville, Kentucky, printed a five-page flyer that alerted business owners to "active shoplifters" in the area. The flyer included mug shots and names of persons who had been arrested for shoplifting, and asked merchants to "inform your security personnel to watch for these subjects." It included the picture and name of Edward Davis III, a photographer for the Louisville *Courier Journal & Times*. He had been arrested in June 1971 for shoplifting, pleaded not guilty, and a judge later dismissed the charges for lack of evidence.

After spotting his mug shot on store walls around Louisville, Davis filed suit in federal court against the city's police chief, Edgar Paul. He claimed the flyer "defamed" his reputation and deprived him of "liberty" under the Fourteenth Amendment. Davis based his suit on a law, passed by Congress during the Reconstruction era, called the Ku Klux Klan Act. After the Civil War, white-sheeted Klansmen conducted a reign of terror against southern blacks who dared to vote in state and federal elections. Congress responded in 1871 with a law that protected "any citizen of the United States" from officials who acted "under color of law" to deny rights "secured by the Constitution" or federal law. The Klan Act was added to the federal statute books as Section 1983 of Title 42 in the U.S. Code. Federal officials failed to enforce this law for almost a century, until civil rights lawyers convinced the Warren Court to make it a potent weapon against official misconduct. Claims under Section 1983 now make up a substantial chunk of federal court dockets.

Edward Davis did not claim that Chief Paul was a hooded Klansman, bent on lynching him, but he relied on Section 1983 to force the chief into federal court. After a district judge dismissed the complaint, a federal appellate panel held that Paul's actions constituted "a denial of due process of law" and returned the case for trial. The chief's appeal struck a responsive chord with Justice Rehnquist, who wrote for five members of the Court in reversing the appellate court. Rehnquist admitted that Davis's complaint "would appear to state a classical claim for defamation actionable in the courts of virtually every state." He denied, however, that Section 1983 allowed recovery for this claim. Rehnquist argued that such claims would "result in every legally cognizable injury which may have been inflicted by a state official" to be found in violation of the Fourteenth Amendment. He found "no constitutional doctrine converting every defamation by a public official into a deprivation of liberty" under the Fourteenth Amendment. Rehnquist offered Davis no redress for the injury to his reputation.

Justice Brennan wrote an indignant dissent. The majority, he said, would allow police to "condemn innocent individuals as criminals and thereby brand them with one of the most stigmatizing and debilitating labels in our society." Without "constitutional restraints on such oppressive behavior," the rights given to criminal defendants "are rendered a sham." Removing any "personal interest in reputation" from the protection of the Fourteenth Amendment, he argued, would render "due process concerns *never* applicable to the official stigmatization" of citizens as criminals.

Brennan's dispute with Rehnquist was rooted in definitions of the "liberty" clauses. He denied that the interests of people like Edward Davis "are protected only if they are recognized under state law or protected by one of the specific guarantees of the Bill of Rights." Brennan argued that "the meaning of 'liberty' must be broad" and that "the enjoyment of one's good name and reputation" had been historically considered "as falling within the concept of personal 'liberty.' "

Brennan ended his dissent with a lecture to his younger colleague. "I have always thought," he wrote, "that one of this Court's most important roles is to provide a formidable bulwark against governmental violation of the constitutional safeguards securing in our free society the legitimate expectations of every person to innate human dignity and sense of worth." Brennan found it "a saddening denigration of our majestic Bill of Rights when the Court tolerates arbitrary and capricious official conduct branding an individual as a criminal without compliance with constitutional procedures designed to ensure the fair and impartial ascertainment of criminal culpability."

Rehnquist's narrow reading of the "liberty" clauses clearly upset Brennan, who feared the Court was tilting further to the right. With the retirement of William Douglas in 1975, only three justices remained from the Warren Court, and one of them—Byron White—increasingly sided with the conservatives. Only Thurgood Marshall shared Brennan's expansive vision of the Constitution. Just as Brennan had assumed the Court's intellectual leadership under Earl Warren, Rehnquist was moving into the same role under Warren Burger. If the Court continued its rightward move, ordinary citizens would find little judicial protection against "oppressive" actions by government officials.

Another case decided in 1976 showed that Brennan's fears had substance. It demonstrated again that Rehnquist had little sympathy for claims under Section 1983. The case came from the Constitution's birthplace, Philadelphia. The City of Brotherly Love had a police chief, Frank Rizzo, who was notorious for urging his officers to employ head-knocking policies, especially in black neighborhoods. Rizzo ignored complaints of police brutality, and city officials resisted calls for any kind of civilian review board. In 1970, a coalition of thirty-two community groups, from the NAACP to the Black Panther Party, filed suit under Section 1983 against Rizzo and Mayor James Tate. They alleged that Philadelphia police officers "are biased against Negroes and other minority groups, and habitually violate their legal and constitutional rights." The suit also charged Rizzo with "failing to take appropriate disciplinary action" against officers who were found guilty of brutality.

Federal district judge John Fullam, appointed by President Lyndon Johnson, conducted lengthy hearings, with testimony from some 250 witnesses. His opinion included graphic accounts of more than twenty incidents of police brutality. In one, police arrested a blind man, Bernard Sisco, accused of joining a gang rape. He put up a struggle and was subdued. After Sisco was handcuffed, he spit on an officer. For that offense, he was beaten and suffered a cerebral concussion. The rape charges against Sisco were later dismissed. Judge Fullam ruled that the police exceeded the amount of force "required to 'subdue' a prisoner who was, after all, both blind and handcuffed." He ordered city officials to submit "a comprehensive program for dealing adequately with civilian complaints alleging police misconduct." Section 1983 imposed on federal courts, he wrote, an obligation "to prevent recurring and otherwise predictable violations of the constitutional rights of citizens."

The city's appeal reached the Supreme Court with a voluminous record. Appellate judges normally accept the factual findings of trial judges. Writing for the majority in *Rizzo v. Goode*, Justice Rehnquist dismissed Fullam's findings as "somewhat of an overstatement," without discussing the details of any police brutality incidents. He agreed, however, that the record included sixteen cases "in which numbers of police officers violated citizens' constitutional rights." He also agreed that Section 1983 imposes liability on government officials who subject anyone "to a deprivation of a right secured by the Constitution and laws."

The case record in *Rizzo* seemingly compelled the Supreme Court to accept Judge Fullam's findings and approve the injunctive relief he granted the plaintiffs, who did not seek individual damages. The injunctive power allows judges to remedy constitutional violations with specific conditions of compliance. In school integration cases, for example, hundreds of injunctions across the country have spelled out district boundaries, teacher and student assignments, even bus routes and lunch hours. Judicial precedent does not require that every school principal or board member be a party to the case for an injunction to govern their actions.

Rehnquist, however, took a narrow view of injunctive relief in the *Rizzo* case. "Individual police officers *not named as parties to the action,*" he wrote with emphasis, "were found to have violated the constitutional rights of particular individuals, only a few of whom were parties plaintiff." Rehnquist shunted to a footnote the fact that this was a "class action" and that the individual plaintiffs legally represented "all residents of Philadelphia and an 'included' class of all black residents of that city."

Rehnquist also noted that Judge Fullam's injunction directed *future* action by city officials to establish disciplinary procedures for the police force. This is basic legal doctrine: injunctive relief can only operate prospectively. Judges cannot tell defendants to do something that occurred in the past, or not to do something that already happened. Rehnquist, however, labeled as "speculation and conjecture" any prediction of what "a small, unnamed minority of policemen" might do in the future to the named plaintiffs. This reasoning led him to conclude that the plaintiffs "lacked the requisite 'personal stake in the outcome' " of the case to justify the grant of injunctive relief.

The plaintiffs' case, Rehnquist wrote, rested on claims that, "given the citizenry's 'right' to be protected from unconstitutional exercises of police power," citizens have a right to judicial relief "when those in supervisory positions do not institute steps to reduce the incidence of unconstitutional police conduct." A large body of Supreme Court precedent supported both the premise and the conclusion of this statement. But Rehnquist found it a "novel claim" and reversed the grant of injunctive relief. In doing so, he distinguished the "long line of precedents" in school integration cases, going back to *Brown v. Board of Education* in 1954. The defendants in those cases, he argued, "were found by their *own* conduct" to have denied the rights of black students. In contrast, neither Chief Rizzo nor Mayor Tate had personally beaten any individual plaintiff or ordered an officer to do so. Of course, few school-board members had physically barred black students from classrooms in white schools. Under Rehnquist's theory, responsible officials are virtually immune from judicial orders to discipline subordinates who break the law.

Justice Harry Blackmun, who voted with Rehnquist in *Paul v. Davis*, dissented in the *Rizzo* case. Justices Brennan and Marshall joined his opinion, which took Rehnquist to task for his abrupt departure from precedent. "The Court today appears to assert that a state official is not subject" to Section 1983, Blackmun wrote, "unless he directs the deprivation of constitutional rights." This holding "ignores both the language of Section 1983 and the case law interpreting that language." The clear words of the statute reach "not only the acts of an official, but also the acts of subordinates for whom he is responsible." Blackmun accused Rehnquist of treating lower-court judges with contempt: "In rejecting the concept that the official may be responsible under Section 1983, the Court today casts aside reasoned conclusions to the contrary reached by the Courts of Appeals of 10 Circuits." He cited cases from every federal circuit but one. Telling all these judges they were wrong struck Blackmun as a deliberate slap at opinions they had "meticulously and thoughtfully" crafted to remedy denials of "constitutional rights that we cherish and hold dear."

PUBLIC SUPPORT for "liberty" as a concept seems to erode when those who claim violations of their constitutional rights are accused criminals. There is little doubt that many people treat the constitutional "presumption of innocence" with cynical dismissal. Even a former attorney general, Edwin Meese, argued that police don't arrest innocent people. And the members of one group—the Mafia—are widely considered guilty by definition. Even the legendary ability of Mafia boss John Gotti to fend off federal prosecution ended with a lengthy prison term. The Mafia was, in fact, a major target of a law passed by Congress in 1984, misnamed the Bail Reform Act. The real purpose was not to reform bail procedures but to subject accused Mafia members and "drug lords" to pretrial detention without bail.

The Fifth and Fourteenth amendments protect the liberties of "any person" against deprivation without due process. Carving out an exception for "some person" who is feared or detested by the public creates a serious constitutional question. The issue of pretrial detention without bail came before the Supreme Court in 1987, through an appeal by Anthony Salerno and Vincent Cafaro. The two men were not arrested because of mistaken identity. Federal prosecutors presented evidence at their bail hearing that Salerno was the "boss" of the Genovese crime family in New York City and that Cafaro was a "captain" in La Cosa Nostra. They were charged in a twenty-nine-count indictment of "racketeering" crimes that included fraud, extortion, and conspiracy to commit murder.

The question at a normal bail hearing is not whether the defendant is guilty of the charges, but whether he or she is likely to show up for trial. Prosecutors at the hearing for Salerno and Cafaro posed a different question. The Bail Reform Act allows pretrial detention if a judge finds that release on bail would threaten "the safety of any other person and the community" as a whole. Government lawyers introduced wiretap transcripts they claimed showed that the defendants "had participated in wide-ranging conspiracies to aid their illegitimate enterprises through violent means." Two witnesses testified that Salerno "personally participated in two murder conspiracies." None of these charges had been submitted to a jury, nor did the record include evidence the defendants were likely to flee before trial or would threaten the safety of anyone named by the government. But the law also permitted judges to consider "the nature and seriousness of the charges" as factors in bail decisions; Salerno and Cafaro were ordered into pretrial detention on this basis.

Justice Rehnquist wrote for six members of the Court in upholding the lower court. The case forced him to deal with the concept of "substantive due process." The Court had long held that "liberty" meant more than fairness in criminal and civil proceedings. The term has a substantive content that includes, at the very least, freedom from arbitrary physical restraints and restrictions on rights to travel. Rehnquist disputes any expansion of the Due Process clause beyond these narrow limits, but Supreme Court precedent forces him to consider broader "liberty" claims.

Rehnquist's opinion in *United States v. Salerno* dismissed the "so-called right" of substantive due process. But he did cite earlier rulings that government conduct which "shocks the conscience" or denies rights "implicit in the concept of ordered liberty" violates the Constitution. Rehnquist, in fact, believes these formulations of due process have no constitutional basis. His *Salerno* majority, however, included three moderates, Justices Blackmun, Powell, and O'Connor. Acknowledgment of "substantive due process" was the price he paid for their votes.

The rest of Rehnquist's opinion made up for this concession. He first addressed the argument that the Bail Reform Act "violates substantive due process because the pretrial detention it authorizes constitutes impermissible punishment before trial." Law is a Wonderland in which everything depends on the definition of words, and Rehnquist denied that detention without bail could be defined as punishment. The legislative history, he argued, "clearly indicates that Congress did not formulate the pretrial detention provisions as punishment for dangerous individuals." Rehnquist defined pretrial detention as "regulatory" and not "penal," despite the fact that jails are certainly penal institutions. Congress, he wrote, "perceived pretrial detention as a potential solution to a pressing societal problem." He admitted "no doubt that preventing danger to the community is a legitimate regulatory goal."

Justice Brennan joined a ferocious dissenting opinion by Thurgood Marshall. Laws permitting the detention of defendants on charges that "are legally presumed to be untrue" smacked of "the usages of tyranny and the excesses of what bitter experience teaches us to call the police state," Marshall wrote. The majority opinion, he added, "disregards basic principles of justice established centuries ago and enshrined beyond the reach of governmental interference in the Bill of Rights."

Marshall accused Rehnquist of a "disingenuous division" of questions about the purpose of bail. Questions about the danger posed by defendants were secondary in Marshall's mind to questions about their guilt or innocence. He pointedly noted that Rehnquist had not cited the provision of the Bail Reform Act that it "shall not be construed as modifying or limiting the presumption of innocence." But, Marshall wrote, "the very pith and purpose of this statute is an abhorrent limitation" of this presumption.

To underline his objections, Marshall quoted Justice Robert Jackson, whom Rehnquist had served as law clerk. Dissenting from the denial of bail to Communist Party leaders who had appealed their criminal convictions, Jackson wrote in 1950 that he found it "difficult to reconcile with traditional American law the jailing of persons by the courts because of anticipated but as yet uncommitted crimes." Joined by Brennan, Marshall accused the *Salerno* majority of "an ominous exercise in demolition" of the Due Process clauses: "Theirs is truly a decision which will go forth without authority, and come back without respect."

THE COURT FURTHER LIMITED the "liberty" interests of accused criminals in a 1979 decision. *Bell v. Wolfish* also dealt with defendants held before trial without bail. Rehnquist wrote for five justices, ruling that conditions in the Metropolitan Correctional Center—the federal jail in New York City—did not violate the Constitution. His opinion reversed the findings of a federal district judge, upheld by an appellate panel, that some twenty policies and practices of jail officials violated the constitutional and statutory rights of MCC inmates. These practices included "double-bunking" prisoners in cells designed for one person, limiting access to books and magazines, and conducting "strip searches" of all inmates when they returned from the visiting room.

The appellate decision in this case, filed against Attorney General Griffin Bell, imposed a "compelling necessity" standard on MCC policies that restricted inmate rights. Despite their inability to make bail, inmates enjoyed a "presumption of innocence" and had greater rights than convicted inmates. Rehnquist denied the applicability of this judicial standard. He agreed that the presumption of innocence "plays an important role in our criminal justice system." But he claimed it applied only during trials. The presumption did not affect "the rights of a pretrial detainee during confinement before his trial has even begun." This was truly a novel claim, for which the opinion failed to cite a single case as precedent.

Rehnquist phrased the issue of inmate rights as "the understandable desire to be as comfortable as possible" during confinement. Judged by this standard—as if the MCC were a Holiday Inn—he held that the constitutional rights of inmates do not "rise to the level of those fundamental liberty interests delineated in cases such as *Roe v. Wade*" and other historic "privacy" cases. These citations carry a whiff of hypocrisy: they have little relevance to questions of inmate rights, and Rehnquist has made clear his disagreement with their holdings.

The majority opinion hardly blinked at challenges to "double-bunking" and censorship of reading material. Rehnquist did pause briefly at the rule that MCC inmates "expose their body cavities" to guards after every visit with family, friends, or lawyers. He admitted that guards had only once found contraband after such a search. But he reversed the trial and appellate judges and ruled that "under the circumstances, we do not believe that these searches are unreasonable."

Rehnquist's bottom line was that prison officials "should be accorded wide-ranging deference" in adopting policies "that in their judgment are needed to preserve internal order and discipline and to maintain institutional security." The case record, however, failed to show that the challenged practices were necessary to secure these penal goals. The lower-court judges had ruled that these practices violated the rights of inmates who were presumed innocent of any crime. But Rehnquist adopted in the *Bell* case what he called a "hands-off" attitude, placing "judgment calls" on prison security in the hands of officials who should run prisons without judicial scrutiny.

Justice Thurgood Marshall wrote another outraged dissent. He disputed Rehnquist's claim that body-cavity searches were "reasonable" efforts to intercept contraband. Throwing one of Rehnquist's citations in his face, Marshall said the practice "is so unnecessarily degrading that it 'shocks the conscience.' " Justice Brennan joined the dissenting opinion of Justice John Paul Stevens, who argued that the MCC policies were "obnoxious to the concept of individual freedom protected by the Due Process Clause." Stevens wrote that the inmates were "innocent men and women who have been convicted of no crime" and that "any form of punishment at all is an unconstitutional deprivation of their liberty."

What most bothered Stevens and Brennan about Rehnquist's opinion was that it "mistakenly implied that the concept of liberty encompasses only those rights that are either created by statute or regulation or are protected by an express provision of the Bill of Rights." This argument, of course, is the basis of Rehnquist's objection to the concept of "substantive due process." He *would* limit constitutional rights to those enumerated in the first eight amendments, and construe them narrowly. In contrast, Stevens and Brennan would look to the "judgment and experience" of those who interpreted the clause in earlier opinions.

Stevens also disputed the "rational basis" test that Rehnquist applied to the challenged MCC policies. This test, he wrote, "effectively abdicates to correction officials the judicial responsibility to enforce the guarantees of due process." In addition, the test provides inmates "with virtually no protection against punishment." Almost *any* policy designed to enhance "security" would meet Rehnquist's minimal standard. "Under the test as the Court explains it today," Stevens wrote, "prison guards could make regular use of dungeons, chains, and shackles, since such practices would make it possible to maintain security with a smaller number of guards." Behind this hyperbole, the dissenters meant to expose the lack of standards in the "rational basis" test, which could exonerate virtually any official action.

Ever since Rehnquist joined the Court in 1972, Brennan had been on the losing side in most cases that raised claims outside the enumerated protections in the Bill of Rights. One reason was that "moderate" justices—a group that included Stewart, Blackmun, Powell, Stevens, and O'Connor over the years—were reluctant to venture beyond the clear words of the constitutional text. Adding substance to the "liberty" clauses made them nervous; they consequently sided most often with government officials whose actions were challenged. On occasion, however, Brennan could swing the moderates to his side in cases that demonstrated clear violation of official duties.

The Court decided one such case, *Carlson v. Green,* in 1980. Norman Carlson, director of the Federal Bureau of Prisons, was sued by the mother of Joseph Jones, an inmate of the federal penitentiary in Terre Haute, Indiana. Jones had a chronic asthmatic condition and suffered an attack in his cell. The trial record showed that prison officials failed to provide any medical treatment for more than eight hours, then gave Jones "contraindicated" drugs that made his condition worse. They also used a respirator "known to be inoperative," and failed to take him to an outside hospital after his breathing stopped. Jones died, and his mother alleged that prison staff "were deliberately indifferent" to his condition, and that "their indifference was in part attributable to racial prejudice." Jones was black, and many Terre Haute officers were known to harbor racist attitudes.

The problem that Jones's mother faced in seeking damages was that no statute allowed suits against federal officials for violating constitutional rights, although Section 1983 allowed suits against state officials. Without a law that provided a "cause of action" against prison officials, she had no legal recourse. Justice Brennan offered her a path around this legal barrier. He had written an important opinion in 1971 holding that the Constitution itself provided a cause of action for violations of protected rights. The case that this opinion addressed began with a nightmare for Webster Bivens and his family in Brooklyn, New York. Without any warning, six men broke down his apartment door, pointed guns at his head, threw him to the floor, shouted threats at his wife and children, tore up the apartment, and dragged him away in handcuffs. They took Bivens to the Brooklyn federal courthouse, grilled him without an attorney, booked him for narcotics violations, and threw him in a cell.

The whole episode was a mistake. Federal Bureau of Narcotics agents had the wrong address and broke down the wrong door. They offered no apologies for terrorizing Bivens and his family. He filed suit for damages, claiming the agents had violated his Fourth Amendment rights against unlawful "search and seizure." Government lawyers argued that the Constitution did not allow claims against federal officials. A federal appellate panel agreed and dismissed the suit.

Justice Brennan wrote the majority opinion in *Bivens v. Six Unknown Federal Narcotics Agents*. He reversed the appellate court, noting that the Fourth Amendment offers all citizens "the absolute right to be free from unreasonable searches and seizures carried out by virtue of federal authority." Brennan further ruled that providing damages against federal officials for violating this right "should hardly seem a surprising proposition. Historically, damages have been regarded as the ordinary remedy for an invasion of personal interests in liberty."

Brennan applied his *Bivens* opinion to the *Carlson* case, writing that "the victims of a constitutional violation by a federal agent have a right to recover damages against the official in federal court despite the absence of any statute conferring such a right." He went further, holding that the dead inmate's mother could seek "punitive damages" from prison officials. Such additional damages, intended to deter future violations, Brennan added, "are especially appropriate to redress the violation by a Government official of a citizen's constitutional rights."

The majority opinion in *Carlson* was relatively brief at ten pages. Writing in dissent, Justice Rehnquist devoted more than twenty pages to a ferocious attack on the "wrong turn" the Court had taken in the *Bivens* case. The Court had a duty to "exercise judicial restraint in attempting to attain a wise accommodation between liberty and order under the Constitution," Rehnquist wrote. He denounced the *Bivens* decision as having a "weak precedential and doctrinal foundation" and wrote that its use as precedent in *Carlson* made "almost all of the Court's opinion" nothing more than "dicta." Rehnquist normally preached judicial deference to legislators, but he rebuked Congress for passing a 1974 law to allow *Bivens* claims against federal officials.

It seems odd that Rehnquist would deny any legislative body the right to pass any laws it pleased. But his *Carlson* dissent argued that the Supreme Court should not permit "Congress to displace this Court in fashioning a constitutional common law of its choosing merely by indicating that it intends to do so." Behind these confusing words is a firm belief that lawmakers and judges alike have no business creating a constitutional "cause of action" against federal officials. Brennan's opinions in *Bivens* and *Carlson* struck Rehnquist as the worst kind of judicial lawmaking, and he responded with scorn.

Brennan's opinion in the *Carlson* case marked the virtual end of judicial concern for the rights of prison inmates. Since that decision, the Supreme Court has rejected almost every damage claim by prisoners who were beaten by guards or fellow inmates. Writing in 1986, Rehnquist rolled back the protections of Section 1983 against prison officials. In this case, *Davidson v. Cannon*, an inmate in the New Jersey State Prison inflicted serious injuries on another inmate. Before the attack, the injured prisoner had written a note to a guard, appealing for protection from his attacker. The record showed the guard knew of conflict between the two inmates but "left the note on his desk unread."

The trial judge found that prison officials were liable under Section 1983 because they "negligently failed to take reasonable steps to protect" the injured inmate. Federal and state law normally allow damages for negligent action that causes physical injury. But Section 1983 does not define a standard for liability. Writing for the majority, Rehnquist held in *Davidson* that "where a government official is merely negligent in causing the injury, no procedure for compensation is constitutionally required." Although he agreed the attack "implicated a recognized liberty interest," Rehnquist argued that only "deliberate or callous indifference" to threats of injury could meet the requirements of Section 1983.

Justice Brennan wrote a brief dissent in this case. He read the case record as indicating that the guard's action "was reckless and not merely negligent," which would allow recovery under Section 1983. Brennan's opinion struck a note of resignation. He had lost three justices—White, Powell, and Stevens—from his *Carlson* decision. The political situation had changed significantly between 1980 and 1986. The Reagan administration preached "law and order" and built more prisons. Judicial opinions rarely discuss such factors, but they certainly exert an influence, however elusive and subtle. By 1986, the Court had narrowed its view of "liberty" to the point of virtual invisibility. Rehnquist became Chief Justice that year and President Reagan nominated Antonin Scalia to the vacant seat. The retirement of Justice Lewis Powell in 1987, and his replacement by Anthony Kennedy, turned the Court even further to the right.

THE FULL EXTENT of the Court's aversion to "liberty" claims became evident in a case decided in 1989, *DeShaney v. Winnebago County Department of Social Services*. This appeal came not from Mafia dons or convicted criminals, but from a child who had been brutally beaten and turned into a human vegetable. Joshua DeShaney was born in Wyoming in 1979. His parents, Randy and Melody, were divorced the next year. Randy gained custody and took his son to Winnebago County, Wisconsin. He married again and was again divorced in 1982. His second wife complained to Department of Social Services (DSS) officials that Randy "hit the boy causing marks and [was] a prime case for child abuse." County social workers interviewed Randy but he denied hitting Joshua and there was no further action.

The Supreme Court opinion of Justice Rehnquist traced the unfolding tragedy. "In January 1983, Joshua was admitted to a local hospital with multiple bruises and abrasions. The examining physician suspected child abuse and notified DSS, which immediately obtained an order from a Wisconsin juvenile court placing Joshua in the temporary custody of the hospital." Three days later, the county's Child Protection Team "decided that there was insufficient evidence of child abuse to retain Joshua" and returned him to Randy. "A month later, emergency room personnel called the DSS caseworker handling Joshua's case to report that he had once again been treated for suspicious injuries. The caseworker concluded that there was no basis for action." During home visits over the next six months, the caseworker "observed a number of suspicious injuries on Joshua's head," and "dutifully recorded these incidents in her files, along with her continuing suspicions that someone in the DeShaney household was physically abusing Joshua, but she did nothing more."

Rehnquist continued the gruesome story. "In March 1984, Randy DeShaney beat four-year-old Joshua so severely that he fell into a life-threatening coma. Emergency brain surgery revealed a series of hemorrhages caused by traumatic injuries to the head inflicted over a long period of time. Joshua did not die, but he suffered brain damage so severe that he is expected to spend the rest of his life confined to an institution for the profoundly retarded. Randy DeShaney was subsequently tried and convicted of child abuse."

The question before the Court was not Randy's guilt, but the county's liability for the failure of officials to protect Joshua from his father more effectively. Melody DeShaney brought a federal suit under Section 1983, alleging that caseworkers knew of Joshua's repeated abuse, and that their continued inaction went beyond negligence to the level of "reckless" indifference to their duties. She claimed that Joshua had a "liberty" right to protection against a known danger to his health and safety. The case never went to trial; the district judge granted the county's motion to dismiss the suit for lack of a "cause of action" under Section 1983. The Supreme Court agreed to review Melody's case after an appellate panel affirmed the dismissal.

The Court went out of its way to decide the *DeShaney* case. Full review was not needed to affirm the suit's dismissal; denying the certiorari petition would have upheld the appellate ruling. Rehnquist's majority opinion in the case suggests that he wanted to send a message to federal judges whose rulings in similar cases had imposed on officials "an affirmative constitutional duty to provide adequate protection" to children they knew were in danger of abuse.

Rehnquist wrote for six justices, including the most recent Reagan appointees, Scalia and Kennedy. He admitted the tragedy of Joshua's plight. "Judges and lawyers, like other humans, are moved by natural sympathy in a case like this to find a way for Joshua and his mother to receive adequate compensation for the grievous harm inflicted upon them." But sympathy is not a legal cause of action. Rehnquist cautioned that, "before yielding to that impulse, it is well to remember once again that the harm was inflicted not by the State of Wisconsin, but by Joshua's father. The most that can be said of the state functionaries in this case is that they stood by and did nothing when suspicious circumstances dictated a more active role for them."

Rehnquist again expressed his disdain for "substantive due process." He wrote that Joshua had no affirmative right to official protection. The "liberty" clauses, Rehnquist wrote, "is phrased as a limitation on the State's power to act, not as a guarantee of certain minimal levels of safety and security." Although he essentially viewed government as a police officer, Rehnquist did not want it to intervene in "private" disputes. The purpose of the Due Process clause, he wrote, "was to protect the people from the State, not to ensure that the State protected them from each other. The Framers were content to leave the extent of governmental obligation in the latter area to the democratic political processes."

Having delivered a civics lecture to Melody DeShaney, Rehnquist evaded the fact that Wisconsin law *did* impose legal obligations on case-workers in child abuse cases, a point that did not escape the dissenters. Justice Brennan, writing also for Marshall and Blackmun, accused Rehnquist of telling "only part of the story" and of asking the wrong legal questions. He agreed that "the Due Process Clause as construed by our prior cases creates no general right to basic governmental services." Brennan had dissented from many of those decisions but he accepted them as precedent. But that proposition "is not the question presented here," he wrote. Melody DeShaney had not asked the Court "to proclaim that, as a general matter, the Constitution safeguards positive as well as negative liberties."

Rehnquist claimed that Joshua had no affirmative right to official protection, and that consequently the caseworkers violated no legal duty they owed him. Brennan turned the question around. "I would focus first on the action that Wisconsin *has* taken with respect to Joshua and children like him, rather than on actions that the State failed to take." He noted that Wisconsin "has established a child-welfare system specif-ically designed to help children like Joshua," and that state law imposes on caseworkers "a duty to investigate reported instances of child abuse." The case record showed many reports—from Randy DeShaney's second wife, emergency room personnel, the police, and the caseworker—that Joshua was repeatedly abused. But "that information stayed within the Department—chronicled by the social worker in detail that seems almost eerie in light of her failure to act upon it." Brennan quoted the caseworker's own premonition: "I just knew the phone would ring some day and Joshua would be dead." His fate was perhaps worse than death.

"It simply belies reality," Brennan chided Rehnquist, "to contend that the State 'stood by and did nothing' with respect to Joshua. Through its child-protection program, the State actively intervened in Joshua's life and, by virtue of this intervention, acquired ever more certain knowledge that Joshua was in grave danger." Brennan denied that the Due Process clause allowed the state "to displace private sources of protection and then, at the critical moment, to shrug its shoulders and turn away from the harm that it has promised to prevent. Because I cannot agree that our Constitution is indifferent to such indifference, I respectfully dissent." Brennan actually felt no respect for the majority opinion he disputed on both facts and law.

THE LAST IMPORTANT "liberty" case decided before Justice Brennan retired from the Court raised a profound question: Does the Constitution protect a right to "die with dignity"? The Court had rebuffed Melody DeShaney's claim that state officials were obligated to protect her son's life. The parents of Nancy Cruzan asked the Court to rule that state officials were required to let them *end* their daughter's life. The claims in the two cases were very different, but they both stemmed from the competing interests of parents and state officials over the welfare of children.

Justice Rehnquist again recounted a tragic story. "On the night of January 11, 1983, Nancy Cruzan lost control of her car as she traveled down Elm Road in Jasper County, Missouri. The vehicle overturned, and Cruzan was discovered lying face down in a ditch without detectable respiratory or cardiac function. Paramedics were able to restore her breathing and heartbeat at the accident site, and she was transported to a hospital in an unconscious state." Nancy's brain had been deprived of oxygen for at least twelve minutes. She suffered permanent brain damage, could not speak, and was kept alive by a tube in her stomach that provided food and water. "She now lives in a Missouri state hospital in what is commonly referred to as a persistent vegetative state," Rehnquist continued, "a condition in which a person exhibits motor reflexes but evinces no indications of significant cognitive function." In short, Nancy Cruzan was brain-dead.

Four years after Nancy's accident, Lester and Joyce Cruzan asked hospital officials to remove her food-and-water tube. She had no feelings, and would not suffer as the rest of her body died. The officials refused to act without court approval, which a state judge granted. He ruled that Nancy's parents, acting as her guardians, had a "fundamental right" under state and federal constitutions to direct the withdrawal of "death prolonging procedures." The judge also found that Nancy had expressed thoughts before her accident "in somewhat serious conversation with a household friend that if sick or injured she would not wish to continue her life unless she could live at least halfway normally," which he considered sufficient evidence of her wishes.

The Missouri Supreme Court reversed the trial judge by a one-vote margin. The majority denied that the "liberty" clauses in the state and federal constitutions supported "the right of a person to refuse medical treatment in every circumstance," and further ruled that Nancy's statements to her roommate were "unreliable for the purpose of determining her intent" in this situation. The judges held that the Missouri Living Will statute imposed a standard of "informed consent" to the removal of life-sustaining procedures that Nancy had not met before her accident.

Rehnquist again spoke for six justices in denying a "liberty" claim against state officials. "This is the first case," he wrote, "in which we have been squarely presented with the issue of whether the United States Constitution grants what is in common parlance referred to as a 'right to die.' " The legal principle "that a competent person has a constitutionally protected liberty interest in refusing unwanted medical treatment may be inferred from our prior decisions," he admitted. But Nancy Cruzan was not legally competent to make *any* decisions, and Missouri "requires that evidence of the incompetent's wishes be proved by clear and convincing evidence." The trial record showed that Nancy had told her roommate she would not wish to live as a "vegetable" if she were injured. Rehnquist held that her statement "did not deal in terms with withdrawal of medical treatment or of hydration and nutrition" and did not meet the state's legal test.

Rehnquist admitted the case raised "a perplexing question with unusually strong moral and ethical overtones." But he denies that judges should answer such questions. Nancy's parents had asked the Court to substitute its judgment for that of Missouri lawmakers. "But constitutional law does not work that way," he chided. Rehnquist's opinion left Nancy Cruzan in a persistent vegetative state that doctors said could last for thirty years.

Justice Brennan was again joined in dissent by Marshall and Blackmun. In this case, however, he agreed with Rehnquist on the basic legal question. "The starting point for our legal analysis," Brennan wrote, "must be whether a competent person has a constitutional right to avoid unwanted medical care." But the two justices differed on the answer. Brennan argued that "Nancy Cruzan has a fundamental right to be free of unwanted artificial nutrition and hydration."

His path to this conclusion proceeded through four steps. First, decisions that involve "the basic civil rights of man" are entitled to constitutional protection. Brennan cited for this proposition a 1942 case that barred the sterilization of criminals. Second, rights that are "deeply rooted in this Nation's history and tradition" are included among these protected liberties. He cited a decision that allowed "extended families" to live together. His third proposition, that the right "to determine what shall be done with one's own body, *is* deeply rooted in this Nation's traditions," came directly from Rehnquist's opinion. Finally, Brennan noted that guardians have the legal right to make decisions for persons who lack the competence to choose for themselves.

Putting these propositions together, Brennan argued for application of the "fundamental right" standard in the *Cruzan* case, which would have imposed the "strict scrutiny" test on Missouri officials. Brennan felt they should identify the "important state interests" in keeping Nancy Cruzan alive, and show that their laws are "closely tailored to effectuate only those interests." He did not believe the state could meet this test. "The only state interest asserted here is a general interest in the preservation of life. But the State has no legitimate general interest in someone's life," Brennan added, "that could outweigh the person's choice to avoid medical treatment." He quoted testimony by Nancy's roommate that she would not want to live in a vegetative state, "because if she was going to live, she wanted to be able to live, not to just lay in a bed and not be able to move because you can't do anything for yourself."

Brennan argued that the Constitution gave Nancy Cruzan the choice to "die with dignity." He said the Court's majority had "discarded evidence of her will, ignored her values, and deprived her of the right to a decision as closely approximating her own choice as humanly possible." In a pointed conclusion to his last opinion as a justice, Brennan quoted one of his judicial heroes, Louis Brandeis: "The greatest dangers to liberty lurk in insidious encroachments by men of zeal, well meaning but without understanding." He did not say—nor did he need to—who he thought lacked understanding of Nancy Cruzan's plight, or of the Constitution's "liberty" clauses.

The *Cruzan* case did not end with the Supreme Court ruling. Two months later, Nancy's parents returned to Missouri courts with additional testimony that she had clearly expressed her wish to avoid medical treatment if she were so badly injured. The state's lawyers withdrew their opposition, and a judge found "clear and convincing" evidence of Nancy's wishes after an emotional hearing. He ruled on December 14, 1990, that Joyce and Lester Cruzan could require hospital officials to remove their daughter's feeding tube, and doctors complied. The case aroused strong feelings on both sides. Police arrested twenty-five protesters who tried to invade Nancy's hospital room and reconnect her tube. One minister who led the protesters accused the Cruzans of murdering their daughter. Other religious leaders supported their position. "Caring for the sick is indeed a work of mercy commanded by the Gospel," wrote a Catholic leader; "robbing the hopelessly ill of their deaths by prolonging their dying is not." Nancy Cruzan died on the day after Christmas, nearly eight years after her brain ceased to function.

These cases, ranging from political dissenters to Mafia bosses to comatose patients, demonstrate that the boundaries of the "liberty" clauses are hard to define. It is not surprising that Justices Brennan and Rehnquist rarely agreed on these issues. Cases that raise issues of life and death cannot be decided simply by citing precedent or pointing to the constitutional text. Political and judicial philosophy, personal values, and the Court's shifting balance are all factors that affect the liberties of Americans as diverse as Anthony Salerno and Nancy Cruzan.

SIX

"This Is a Christian Nation"

SPEAKING FOR A UNANIMOUS Supreme Court in 1892, Justice Joseph Brewer confidently declared that "this is a Christian nation." He professed tolerance, and quoted the esteemed Chancellor Kent on the necessity for the "undisturbed enjoyment of religious opinion, whatever it may be." Brewer did not, however, envision a nation that welcomed the adherents of all faiths, or those who belonged to no church. The Constitution did not protect those who challenged the Christian faith. Brewer agreed with Kent that the First Amendment did not bar laws designed to "punish" followers of "Mahomet" or the "Grand Lama" and to proscribe "the doctrines or worship of those imposters." And he supported laws that would force public officials to confess belief in the Trinity.

A century after Brewer's opinion, a federal judge in San Diego, California, ordered the removal of a forty-three-foot-high "Easter Cross" from a public park. This decision sparked a political campaign to "Save Our Cross." The city council voted unanimously for a ballot proposition to sell the cross to a private group that sponsored annual Easter services around its base. Campaigning for this measure, San Diego's mayor claimed the First Amendment was written to protect the majority from "religious intolerance that masquerades as civil liberties." Voters approved the proposition by a majority of 76 percent. Supporters of the Easter Cross flooded the newspapers with comment. Liz Odinga of La Jolla addressed a letter to Howard Kreisner, an atheist activist who sued to remove the cross. "This is a God-fearing, Christian country," she wrote, "tolerant to a fault, and if you don't appreciate it, get out, we shall not miss you."

The battles between Justices Brennan and Rehnquist over the religion clauses of the First Amendment are rooted in the fact that Justice Brewer and Liz Odinga are both correct. The United States *is* a Christian nation, in the sense that most Americans profess the Christian faith. Members of this sectarian majority value their right to the "free exercise" of religion. They are often reluctant, however, to grant the same right to religious minorities, such as Jews and Muslims, or to adherents of "exotic" sects like Santeria. And, like other majority groups, Christians have used the ballot box to "establish" their faith through such practices as school prayer and municipal nativity scenes. For more than a century, contending groups of "separationists" and "accommodationists" have brought religious disputes to the Supreme Court. During their service together, Brennan and Rehnquist adopted these respective positions, and differed in almost every religion case.

The context of their conflict lies in religious practice and history. A national census in 1989 showed that more than five of every six Americans identify themselves as Christian. There are two Protestants for each Roman Catholic, 56 percent to 28 percent. However, the Catholic Church is by far the largest denomination, with 55 million members. Protestants are splintered into hundreds of groups; the recent census listed some sixty-six churches that claimed more than 50,000 members each. Outside the Christian fold, Jews make up 2 percent, while 4 percent belong to "other" religions, such as Buddhism and Spiritualism. Significantly, those who answered "none" in the religious census have increased fivefold since 1967, from 2 to 10 percent. It is also notable that members of all religions have organized almost 300,000 congregations, but fewer than half attend services regularly.

Observers have long noted this disparity of religious profession and practice. Alexis de Tocqueville wrote in 1835 that "there is no country in the whole world in which the Christian religion retains a greater influence over the souls of men than in America," but he added that "a certain number of Americans pursue a peculiar form of worship, from habit more than conviction." Tocqueville also recognized the close ties of religion and politics. He noted that "religious zeal is perpetually stimulated in the United States by the duties of patriotism," and remarked that in conversing with "missionaries of Christian civilization," he was struck that "you meet with a politician where you expected to find a priest."

Tocqueville did not name the pastoral politicians he met, but his description fit latter-day leaders such as the Reverend Jerry Falwell, who said that the major task of the "religious right" was "getting people to participate in politics." The most strident political sermon in recent years came from Patrick Buchanan, who, at the 1992 Republican National Convention, called for a "religious war" at the ballot box. He later charged the Supreme Court with responsibility for the "barbarians" who rioted in Los Angeles after the Rodney King verdict. The rioters and looters, he said, "came out of public schools where God and the Ten Commandments and the Bible were long ago expelled."

Religious conflicts are deeply rooted in American history, and have exposed the Supreme Court to the crossfire of battles over Church and State. The "religious wars" that have spilled from church pulpits into polling places go back to the Pilgrims who founded the Plymouth colony in 1620 and who proclaimed the "Advancement of the Christian Faith" as their goal. The Pilgrims fled the orthodoxy of the Anglican Church, but the Puritans who followed them imposed their own orthodoxy. Puritan laws were explicitly based on biblical commands, and "marginal references to book, chapter and verse were supplied to guide further action." One historian reports that "a literal construction of Bible mandates was carried so far that children were actually put to death for striking their parents." The Massachusetts constitution authorized the taxation of all residents "for the support and maintenance of public Protestant teachers of piety, religion and morality."

After the first wave of migration, Catholics, Baptists, Quakers, and others—even Jews—joined the Puritans in Massachusetts. They were not welcomed. Members of these religions faced persecution, banishment, even death as heretics. But as the colonies grew in number and diversity, the preservation of religious orthodoxy proved impossible. Before the Revolution, advocates of religious tolerance moved in two areas to protect dissenters: first, to "disestablish" the established religions; and second, to allow dissenters to "freely exercise" their beliefs. James Madison of Virginia led his colony's drive for religious liberty and advocated a "perfect separation" of Church and State. After the Revolution, he argued for the inclusion of these principles in the Constitution. Madison failed to win approval of a Bill of Rights in the charter that was ratified in 1787. But he forced the Constitution's backers to agree to amendments that limited governmental powers over individuals. Ratification of the Bill of Rights in 1791 incorporated Madison's goals in the First Amendment: "Congress shall make no law respecting an establishment of religion, or prohibiting the free exercise thereof," it began.

FOR MORE THAN a century after adoption of the First Amendment, the Supreme Court faced just a handful of religion cases. Only federal laws fell within its reach, and Congress generally stayed out of this field. The one major exception reached the Court in 1879, from the Territory of Utah. The Mormons who settled Utah established a theocracy, much like Puritan Massachusetts. Relations of Church and State collided over the Mormon practice of polygamy, which required men to have more than one wife under pain of "damnation in the life to come."

When Mormon leaders sought recognition as a federal territory, Congress agreed on the condition that polygamy be outlawed. Church leaders grudgingly revised their theology, but many members resisted this new edict. George Reynolds, who lived with two wives, offered to test the polygamy law. His challenge rested on the Free Exercise clause of the First Amendment. Federal officials had trouble finding jurors who were not polygamists, but they finally secured Reynolds's conviction, which the Supreme Court upheld without dissent in *Reynolds v. United States.*

This first opinion in a First Amendment case, written by Chief Justice Morrison Waite, is significant in three respects. First, Waite noted that "the word 'religion' is not defined in the Constitution." He looked for the meaning of this term in "the history of the times" in which it was adopted. Waite wrote that in colonial times "people were taxed, against their will, for the support of religion," and that some were punished "for entertaining heretical opinions." He also recognized the "determined opposition" to established religion and Madison's role in drafting the First Amendment.

Waite's opinion also quoted approvingly from Thomas Jefferson's famous letter to the Danbury Baptist Association, which described the First Amendment as "building a wall of separation between church and State." The Court deferred to this "authoritative declaration of the scope and effect of the amendment thus secured" by the efforts of Madison and Jefferson. Few abstract concepts have been painted with such metaphoric power as Jefferson's "wall of separation." All subsequent debate in religion cases has revolved around this evocative phrase. Jefferson clearly meant his "wall" to keep established religions out of public life. Did he also intend to bar any regulation of religious practice?

Jefferson's answer to this question in his Danbury letter opened a door for the Supreme Court to rule against George Reynolds. The "natural rights" of mankind, Jefferson wrote, included "rights of conscience" in matters of religious belief. But he did not concede to the citizen any "natural right in opposition to his social duties." Chief Justice Waite opened the door even further to include "actions which were in violation of social duties or subversive of good order." He again looked to history for support: "Polygamy has always been odious among the northern and western nations of Europe, and, until the establishment of the Mormon Church, was almost exclusively a feature of the life of Asiatic and of African people."

Having dismissed the Mormons as religious Hottentots, Waite portrayed monogamous marriage as the institution from which all "social obligations and duties" arise, and on which "the government of the people, to a greater or less extent, rests." For evidence that polygamy was socially harmful, the Court looked to Chancellor Kent, who claimed that prohibitions were "founded on the precepts of Christianity" and that plural marriage was "incompatible with civilization, refinement, and domestic felicity."

The sincerity of Reynolds's belief in polygamy did not concern Waite. Making "the professed doctrines of religious belief superior to the law of the land," he wrote, would "permit every citizen to become a law unto himself." Waite's opinion employed a favorite lawyers' device, the slippery slope. "Suppose one believed that human sacrifices were a necessary part of religious worship," he asked; would government be powerless to prevent the loss of life? What if "a wife religiously believed it was her duty to burn herself upon the funeral pile of her dead husband?" Simply posing these questions provided the obvious answer: "Laws are made for the government of actions, and while they cannot interfere with mere religious belief and opinion, they may with practices."

The *Reynolds* decision had little impact outside Utah, although Mormon fundamentalists continue to practice polygamy in rural areas. Its importance rested in the Court's search for the historical "intent" of those who framed the First Amendment's religion clauses, its embrace of Jefferson's "wall of separation" metaphor, and the "belief-action" distinction that allowed regulation of religious practices in "free exercise" cases. But these principles lay dormant for another sixty years, until the Court applied the First Amendment to state laws through its "incorporation" into the Fourteenth Amendment.

The Court's return to the religion clauses in the 1940s stemmed from the growth of two very dissimilar—and mutually hostile—denominations, Jehovah's Witnesses and Roman Catholics. In different ways, each reflected a challenge to America's conventional Protestant majority. The Witnesses preach an apocalyptic vision of Armageddon that thrives on bad news of economic hardship and warfare. The Great Depression and World War II spurred them to spread their message with aggressive evangelism. And the message, which vigorously attacked the Catholic Church, prompted dozens of cities and towns to muzzle the Witnesses. Some enacted ordinances that required licenses to distribute literature; others used existing laws against disturbing the peace or littering.

During the 1940s, the Supreme Court decided more than a dozen "free exercise" cases brought by Witnesses. The first important case involved the arrest of Newton Cantwell in New Haven, Connecticut. He set up a phonograph in a heavily Catholic area, played a record that denounced the Pope, and offered Witness pamphlets for sale. Angry residents called the police, and Cantwell was charged with violating a state law that prohibited "soliciting money for any cause" without a license.

Ruling in 1940, the Court unanimously reversed his conviction, holding that state officials could not impose a "prior restraint" on the exercise of religious beliefs they found offensive. But the justices also supported legitimate efforts to "safeguard the peace, good order and comfort of the community" from disruption. Reaching back to the *Reynolds* decision, they agreed that the First Amendment "embraces two concepts—freedom to believe and freedom to act. The first is absolute but, in the nature of things, the second cannot be. Conduct remains subject to regulation for the protection of society." Having restated the "belief-action" test, the Court sided with the Witnesses in almost every subsequent case that challenged their religious conduct.

The second round of religion cases involved the Catholic Church and the Establishment clause. The baby boom years after World War II brought dramatic growth in the numbers and influence of Catholics, as well as financial pressure on those who sent their children to burgeoning parochial schools. A number of states responded with programs to aid religious schools. Some gave direct benefits to schools, such as textbooks and teacher salaries; others made it easier for parents to afford private schools. New Jersey, for example, reimbursed parents for their children's travel expenses, mostly bus fares.

The Supreme Court picked a narrow path in these cases. Ruling in 1947, the Court narrowly upheld the New Jersey law in *Everson v. Board of Education*. Justice Hugo Black quoted Jefferson's "wall of separation" letter in his majority opinion, and canvassed the history of religious persecution in America. He admitted that New Jersey helped Catholic children "get to church schools." But the state also helped children get to public schools, benefiting "all its citizens without regard to their religious belief." The Establishment clause, Black wrote, "requires the state to be neutral in its relations with groups of religious believers and nonbelievers; it does not require the state to be their adversary."

The *Everson* decision upheld an indirect benefit to religion. A year later, in 1948, the Court struck down an Illinois program that brought Catholic, Protestant, and Jewish instructors into schools. Parents chose between religion classes for their children and secular courses during the "released-time" program. Justice Black again wrote for the Court, holding in *McCollum v. Illinois* that tax-supported schools were "used for the dissemination of religious doctrine." This direct benefit to religion breached the "wall of separation" between Church and State. Later decisions tried to sort out the "direct-indirect" benefit distinction, but failed to provide a clear-cut standard in religion cases. While the Court looked for a middle road, conflict between "separationists" and "accommodationists" mounted during the 1950s. John F. Kennedy's election in 1960 as the first Catholic president brought simmering religious disputes to a political boil. The Court finally caught the heat over the emotional issue of school prayer.

"ALMIGHTY GOD, we acknowledge our dependence upon Thee, and we beg Thy blessings upon us, our parents, our teachers and our country." This prayer was adopted in the 1950s by the New York State Regents, who control the state's education system. It would be hard to imagine more innocuous words. Who could object to their children reciting this prayer? Many people would be genuinely puzzled at this question. But some are offended by even this generic prayer. Atheists would reject any reference to "God," agnostics would be doubtful, and some devout believers—of many faiths—feel that vocal prayer should be confined to home and church, and not be imposed on children in public schools.

Steven Engel and nine other parents in the Long Island suburb of New Hyde Park, New York, challenged the "Regents' prayer" in a suit against

William Vitale, the school-board president. Ruling in 1962, the Supreme Court struck down the daily religious practice. Justice Black again wrote for the Court in *Engel v. Vitale*, and again cited "the constitutional wall of separation between the Church and State." He wrote that the Establishment clause "must at least mean that in this country it is no part of the official business of government to compose official prayers for any group of the American people to recite as part of a religious program carried out by government."

Reaction to the *Engel* decision revealed the volatile nature of religion as a political issue. Catholic and Protestant leaders denounced the Court, joined by members of both parties in Congress. Cardinal McIntyre of Los Angeles called the decision "positively shocking and scandalizing to one of American blood and principles." Evangelist Billy Graham was "shocked and disappointed." Alabama Representative George Andrews complained that the Court "put the Negroes in the schools, and now they've driven God out."

The following year, the Court struck down another devotional ritual in *Abington Township v. Schempp*. This ruling went beyond *Engel* in banishing the Lord's Prayer and the Bible from classroom recital. The parents of Roger and Donna Schempp filed suit against school officials in their Philadelphia suburb. The Schempps attended a Unitarian church, whose members reject the Christian Trinity. Perhaps hoping to deflect further criticism, Chief Justice Warren assigned the opinion to Tom Clark, a conservative Texan. Drawing on Black's prior opinions, Clark reviewed America's history as a "religious people" and its record of sectarian persecution. The positive and negative aspects of this historical record, Clark wrote, prompted the inclusion in the First Amendment of both the Free Exercise and Establishment clauses. He proposed a judicial standard for laws that affected religious belief or practice: "The test may be stated as follows: What are the purpose and the primary effect of the enactment? If either is the inhibition or advancement of religion then the enactment exceeds the scope of legislative power" under the First Amendment. Judged by this test, Bible reading and recital of the Lord's Prayer were "religious exercises" that had both the purpose and the effect of advancing the Christian faith.

With all but one justice—Potter Stewart—behind the prayer decisions, the Warren Court had raised Jefferson's "wall of separation" to new heights. Clark's opinion in *Schempp* had fashioned a more precise judicial standard for religion cases. The Court knowingly went against the grain of public opinion. Thirty years later, the prayer decisions are widely disobeyed in schools across the country, and lawmakers from rural hamlets to the nation's capital still try to fashion laws that will "return God" to classrooms.

JUSTICE BRENNAN had no quarrel with Clark's opinion in the *Schempp* case. But he had been thinking about the full range of Church and State issues, and expressed his views in a concurring opinion, at seventy-four pages, three times longer than Clark's. Beginning with John Locke's "Letter Concerning Toleration," Brennan ranged widely over history, law, and politics, citing more than a hundred books, articles, and cases. He confessed that "the line which separates the secular from the sectarian in American life is elusive. The difficulty of defining the boundary with precision inheres in a paradox central to our scheme of liberty. While our institutions reflect a firm conviction that we are a religious people, those institutions by solemn constitutional injunction may not officially involve religion in such a way as to prefer, discriminate against, or oppress, a particular sect or religion."

His thorough canvass of history persuaded Brennan that the religion clauses were designed "to prevent those official involvements of religion which would tend to foster or discourage religious belief or worship." But "an awareness of history and an appreciation of the aims of the Founding Fathers do not always resolve concrete problems." Brennan cautioned that a "too literal quest" for the Framers' intent "seems to me futile and misdirected," because "the historical record is at best ambiguous, and statements can readily be found to support either side" of a contested issue.

Writing only for himself, Brennan looked ahead to religious issues that might reach the Court. These included the role of military and prison chaplains, prayer in legislative bodies, Sunday-closing laws, and "In God We Trust" as a motto on currency. He distinguished these practices from classroom prayer, which imposed coercive pressure on impressionable children. Outside the school setting, he was willing to accept religious practices that were woven "so deeply into the fabric of our civil polity" they had become traditional and "no longer have a religious purpose or meaning." Brennan concluded from his survey of these "forms of accommodation" between Church and State that "the First Amendment commands not official hostility toward religion, but only a strict neutrality in matters of religion."

American society changed dramatically in the two decades after the *Schempp* decision. One enduring feature, however, was the persistence of religion as a divisive political factor. After the Court's leadership moved from Earl Warren to Warren Burger in 1969, the justices decided several important Church-State cases. Burger surprised many observers by taking the "separationist" side in cases that challenged government aid to churches. His opinion in *Lemon v. Kurtzman*, decided in 1971, set out a standard for judging statutes under the religion clauses. This case involved a Pennsylvania law providing for payment of secular teaching in private schools; of $5 million in tax funds, 96 percent went to religious schools, mostly Catholic.

Burger distilled from earlier decisions a three-part test: "First, the statute must have a secular legislative purpose; second, its principal or primary effect must be one that neither advances nor inhibits religion; finally, the statute must not foster 'an excessive government entanglement with religion.' " What became known as the *Lemon* test has remained as the judicial standard in religion cases. Although Burger did not use the term "strict scrutiny" in his opinion, the test does shift the burden of persuasion from plaintiffs to the state, which must satisfy all three "prongs" to prevail. For example, the Pennsylvania law at issue in *Lemon* satisfied the "purpose" and "effect" prongs, but failed the third. The administrative burden of assuring that state funds went only for "secular" programs, Burger wrote, "involves excessive entanglement between government and religion."

Justice Brennan embraced the *Lemon* test and defended it from attacks by the Court's accommodationists, led by Justice Rehnquist. In the process, Brennan moved firmly to the separationist camp. He wrote in 1983 that, "after much reflection, I have come to the conclusion that I was wrong" in approving those "forms of accommodation" he surveyed in his *Schempp* concurrence. Dissenting from a decision that upheld the practice of legislative prayer, Brennan pointed to another factor in religion cases. The main purpose of the "wall of separation," he wrote, was to "assure that essentially religious issues, precisely because of their importance and sensitivity, not become the occasion for battle in the political arena." Brennan was distressed by the "religious wars" that followed the Court's school-prayer decisions. He recognized that "there will be winners and losers in the political battle" over most issues, and that losers retain "the right to fight the battle again another day." But those who challenge government aid to religion face the risk of social excommunication. Brennan felt strongly that "no American should at any point feel alienated from his government" because of religious disputes. Only "a strict separation of religion and state," he argued, can prevent further casualties in battles that divide many American communities.

CONSISTENT WITH his philosophy of judicial deference to official action, Rehnquist made clear his accommodationist views in his first opinion as a justice. "I would apply the rule of deference to administrative discretion," he wrote in 1972. Rehnquist was alone in this case, dissenting from a decision that granted a judicial hearing to a prisoner who claimed he was prevented from practicing his Buddhist faith. Dissenting in another case, he supported government aid to religious schools and wrote that "these decisions are quite rightly hammered out on the legislative anvil."

With few exceptions, Rehnquist has supported the state against challenges from individuals, in both Free Exercise and Establishment clause cases. This is a "statist" position, not one of "libertarian" principles. His approach places Rehnquist in most cases on the side of religious majorities—generally Christian—and against religious minorities. He rarely sides with Jews, Buddhists, Muslims, and the secular humanists who bedevil the Religious Right. This is less a matter of theological bias than a reflection of the "loser" status of these groups in sectarian battles. Religious minorities are often caught between the hammer and the anvil in the legislative process, and suffer political beatings that often leave personal bruises.

Despite their differences, Brennan and Rehnquist share an interest in history. Both have applied the tools of history—citation to primary sources, analysis of salient factors, and reference to the studies of specialists—in their opinions on many issues. Both have searched the historical record for the "intent" of those who framed and ratified the First Amendment's religion clauses. Their reading of this record has produced diametrically opposed conclusions. Brennan found the Framers' intent in Madison's advocacy of the "perfect separation" of Church and State and Jefferson's call for a "wall of separation."

Writing in 1985, Rehnquist challenged Brennan's history. Dissenting in a school-prayer case, *Wallace v. Jaffree*, Rehnquist concluded that the

Establishment clause "did not require government neutrality between religion and irreligion nor did it prohibit the Federal Government from providing nondiscriminatory aid to religion." He also examined the roles of Madison and Jefferson in framing the religion clauses. He admitted that Madison had advocated "strict separation" in pressing the Virginia Statute of Religious Liberty in 1786. But he denied that Madison "carried these views" into the congressional debate on the Bill of Rights in 1789. Rehnquist based this claim on Madison's motion that the committee draft of the First Amendment, which read that "no religion should be established by law," should be amended "by inserting the word 'national' in front of the word 'religion.'" From this record, Rehnquist argued that Madison designed the First Amendment only "to prohibit the establishment of a national religion, and perhaps to prevent discrimination among sects."

Moving his target from Madison to Jefferson, Rehnquist turned up his rhetoric. "The 'wall of separation between church and State' is a metaphor based on bad history," he wrote, "a metaphor which has proved useless as a guide to judging. It should be frankly and explicitly abandoned." Rehnquist based his criticism of this "misleading metaphor" on two facts. He first noted that Jefferson was out of the country, serving as ambassador to France, when Congress adopted the Bill of Rights. Second, he stressed that Jefferson wrote his "wall of separation" letter in 1802, "14 years after the Amendments were passed by Congress." Rehnquist concluded that Jefferson "would seem to any detached observer as a less than ideal source" on the meaning of the religion clauses.

What made the "wall theory" shaky, Rehnquist argued, was that it "has proved all but useless as a guide to sound constitutional adjudication." He showed no more respect to Chief Justice Burger than he did to Thomas Jefferson. Admitting that the *Lemon* test had "initially provided helpful assistance" in religion cases, he groused that it "has no more grounding in the history of the First Amendment than does the wall theory upon which it rests."

Rehnquist urged the Court to reject the "unprincipled results" of the *Lemon* test and to apply the "true meaning of the Establishment Clause" in religion cases. That meaning, he wrote, is limited to the prohibition of laws that grant "a preference for one religious denomination or sect over others." But he has no quarrel with laws that "aid all religions evenhandedly," even if nonbelievers are taxed for their support. Rehnquist wrote a twenty-four-page opinion in the *Jaffree* case, his longest discussion of the religion clauses, but he suggested no alternative to the *Lemon* test. This is not surprising, since the "strict scrutiny" test was designed to force government officials to justify their actions. The principle of judicial deference to legislative decision would only test laws under the religion clauses to see if one denomination is clearly preferred over others. His voting record shows that few laws have failed Rehnquist's minimal test.

GOVERNMENTAL AID to religious schools poses the sternest test of the Establishment clause, because such programs transfer public funds to church groups or their members. Most children attend public schools, but government does not have a monopoly on education; the Supreme Court ruled in 1925 that parents may send their children to private schools. More than 4 million children—out of 45 million in primary and secondary grades—attend schools run by religious groups; Roman Catholic parochial schools enroll almost 3 million students. The parents of these children face a double financial burden; they pay taxes for public schools, and tuition for the church school. Political pressure to ease this burden has resulted in many laws, which are invariably challenged by "separationist" groups.

Since 1971, every law designed to aid church schools has faced the *Lemon* test, and most have failed. The reason is obvious: the purpose and effect of such laws is clearly to support schools that teach a particular religious doctrine, and government officials become "entangled" in their administration.

The first school-aid case in which Justices Brennan and Rehnquist both voted came before the Court in 1973. The facts in this case, *Committee for Public Education and Religious Liberty v. Nyquist*, were fairly typical. The New York legislature had established three financial-aid programs for private schools. The first offered direct money grants for maintenance and repair to schools with a high concentration of students from low-income families, the second provided tuition grants to low-income parents, and the third offered state-tax relief to families who did not qualify for tuition grants. Also typical were the contending parties: a "separationist" group against the state education commissioner. A lower court struck down the first two programs but upheld the third. Both sides appealed this split decision to the Supreme Court.

Most likely, the justices voted to hear the *Nyquist* case because of the lower court's division. Justice Lewis Powell, a former school-board member, wrote for a majority that included Justice Brennan. Powell confessed that religion cases "have presented some of the most perplexing questions to come before this Court." But the "thorough and thoughtful scholarship" of earlier justices had answered many of these questions. "Indeed, the controlling constitutional standards have become firmly rooted and the broad contours of our inquiry are now well defined," Powell wrote. This combination of scholarship and precedent made *Nyquist* an easy case for Powell. All three New York programs failed the second prong of the *Lemon* test, he said, because each had "the impermissible effect of advancing the sectarian activities of religious schools."

Justice Rehnquist did not agree that *Nyquist* was an easy case. "Differences of opinion are undoubtedly to be expected when the Court turns to the task of interpreting the meaning of the Religion Clauses," he wrote in dissent. Rehnquist traced these differences to the *Lemon* test, which he dismissed as a departure from the "benevolent neutrality" of the *Everson* decision. He compared the reimbursement of bus fares for parochial students to the *Nyquist* programs. The benefits in each case, Rehnquist wrote, "go to the parents rather than to the institutions." He sympathized with parents who were "compelled to support public school services unused by them and to pay for their own children's education." These parents, he added, "are rendering the State a service by decreasing the costs of public education and by physically relieving an already overburdened public school system." Rehnquist ended his *Nyquist* dissent by accusing the Court's majority of abandoning "constitutional limits" on judicial powers for an "exercise of legislative powers which transgresses those limits."

Justices Brennan and Rehnquist differed in every school-aid case the Court decided after *Nyquist*. In 1975, the Court struck down Pennsylvania laws that provided religious schools with instructional materials such as films and projectors, and "auxiliary services" such as counseling, testing, and speech therapy. Brennan wrote a concurrence in *Meek v. Pittenger* to stress the importance of a "significant fourth factor" that Chief Justice Burger discussed in the *Lemon* opinion but did not include in his three-part Establishment clause test. Burger had noted "the divisive political potential of these state programs." Religion became an electoral issue. "Partisans of parochial schools, understandably concerned with rising costs," Burger wrote, "will inevitably champion this cause and promote political action to achieve their goals." Brennan italicized this warning from Burger's opinion: *"political division along religious lines was one of the principal evils which the First Amendment was intended to protect."*

Rehnquist expressed a different concern in the *Meek* case. "I am disturbed as much by the overtones of the Court's opinion as by its actual holding," he wrote in dissent. "The Court apparently believes that the Establishment Clause of the First Amendment not only mandates religious neutrality on the part of government but also requires that this Court go further and throw its weight on the side of those who believe that our society as a whole should be a purely secular one." Rehnquist offered no evidence for this claim, other than the Court's rulings in church-aid cases. But he made a point of quoting a statement of Justice William Douglas: "We are a religious people whose institutions presuppose a Supreme Being." Rehnquist was clearly distressed by what he perceived as judicial hostility to religious believers. And he did not share Brennan's concern with the political divisiveness of religious conflicts.

The two justices also differed in a pair of school-aid cases decided in 1985. The issues were similar and familiar. Officials in Grand Rapids, Michigan, and New York City used public funds to pay teachers in religious schools. The classes in both programs were secular in content, designed to supplement the regular curriculum. The Supreme Court could have declined to hear the appeals from lower-court rulings that both programs violated the Establishment clause. But these cases fit the conservative political agenda of the Reagan administration, and the Justice Department was involved in both, directly in the New York case and as "friend of the Court" in the other. It seems likely that Justice Brennan urged that the two cases be heard. He learned to count votes at his father's knee, and knew he had a majority in religion cases. As the senior justice in the majority, Brennan assigned both opinions to himself, and used them to rebuke those who continued to pass laws that aided religious schools.

In his lengthy opinion in the Michigan case, *Grand Rapids School District v. Ball*, Brennan reviewed the Court's holdings since *Everson* in 1947. The Court's only Catholic justice at that time also preached a sermon on the relations of Church, State, and schools. "Providing for the education of schoolchildren is surely a praiseworthy purpose," he began. "But our cases have consistently recognized that even such a praiseworthy, secular purpose cannot validate government aid to parochial schools when the aid has the effect of promoting a single religion or religion generally or when the aid unduly entangles the government in matters religious."

Brennan looked at both the personal and public aspects of religion. "For just as religion throughout history has provided spiritual comfort, guidance, and inspiration to many, it can also serve powerfully to divide societies and to exclude those whose beliefs are not in accord with particular religions or sects that have from time to time achieved dominance." The Framers of the First Amendment took account of both aspects, inserting both the Free Exercise and Establishment clauses "to guard the right of every individual to worship according to the dictates of conscience while requiring the government to maintain a course of neutrality among religions, and between religion and non-religion."

Turning to the facts of the *Grand Rapids* case, Brennan noted the "pervasively sectarian" character of the religious schools. He quoted the parent handbook of one Catholic school, which stressed its mission of giving students "knowledge of the Catholic faith, its traditions, teachings and theology." The Protestant schools stated that "the word of God must be an all-pervading force in the educational program." Brennan worried that teachers in these programs "may become involved in intentionally or inadvertently inculcating particular religious tenets or beliefs." He also noted that "the programs may provide a crucial symbolic link between government and religion, thereby enlisting—at least in the eyes of impressionable youngsters—the powers of government to the support of the religious denominations operating the schools."

Justice Rehnquist confined his *Grand Rapids* dissent to three paragraphs. He faulted Brennan for relying on "the faulty 'wall' premise" of the *Everson* decision. "In doing so the Court blinds itself to the first 150 years' history of the Establishment Clause," he chided. Rehnquist also wrote that Brennan's opinion "impugns the integrity of public school teachers." The record showed, however, that most teachers in the Grand Rapids programs were employed by religious schools. Rehnquist nonetheless charged Brennan with assuming they would act as "eager inculcators of religious dogma" in the public-school programs.

Brennan based his opinion in the New York case, *Aguilar v. Felton*, on the entanglement prong of the *Lemon* test. City officials were assigned to monitor the content of classes taught by public-school teachers for low-income children in religious schools. "The numerous judgments that must be made by agents of the city," Brennan wrote, "concern matters that may be subtle and controversial, yet may be of deep religious significance to the controlling denominations." He restated his basic concern: "As government agents must make these judgments, the dangers of political divisiveness along religious lines increase."

In a one-paragraph dissent, Rehnquist also restated *his* concern, the provision of "sorely needed assistance" to low-income students in religious schools. He charged that the Court had "traveled far afield from the concerns which prompted the adoption of the First Amendment when we rely on gossamer abstractions to invalidate a law which obviously meets an entirely secular need."

Commentary on the Court's opinions in the school-aid cases reflected their political overtones. Edd Doerr, director of a leading separationist group, Americans for Religious Liberty, hailed the decisions as "serious setbacks for the Reagan–Moral Majoritarian campaign to wreck the First Amendment." He praised the Court for blocking the most "intensely pursued goal of the largest and most powerful sectarian special interests." Writing in a Catholic journal, David Carlin suggested with sarcasm that "something over and above the transparent constitutional merits of the case led to the decision." Carlin found the culprit in the concept of "negative liberty," which he said has replaced freedom *of* religion with "freedom *from* religion."

THE POLITICAL NATURE of governmental aid to church schools is matched—perhaps exceeded—by conflicts over religion inside the public schools. Since the *Engel* and *Schempp* decisions in the 1960s, the Supreme Court has consistently ruled against classroom prayer and other religious displays. In many schools, especially in southern and mountain states, these rulings are simply ignored. In others, evangelical Christian groups have tried to devise ways to "return God" to public schools. School-board members and principals often share their aims, or bow to organized pressure. But the Supreme Court—over the dissents of Justice Rehnquist—has refused to overturn the Warren Court precedent in this area.

Rehnquist sees nothing wrong with classroom religion. He dissented from a 1980 ruling that struck down a Kentucky law mandating the posting of the Ten Commandments on every classroom wall. Lawmakers did, however, require the addition in small print of this disclaimer: "The secular application of the Ten Commandments is clearly seen in its adoption as the fundamental legal code of Western Civilization and the

Common Law of the United States." The Court did not tarry long over
Stone v. Graham. Deciding the case without oral argument, the justices
cited the *Engel* and *Schempp* decisions, and applied the *Lemon* test. The
law's purpose was "plainly religious in nature," and "no legislative rec-
itation of a supposed secular purpose can blind us to that fact."

The law's drafters obviously had read the *Lemon* opinion and carefully
wrapped a secular purpose around the Commandments. Rehnquist counseled the Court to give "such pronouncements the deference they are
due." He did not dispute the Court's holding that the Decalogue is
"undeniably a sacred text." But he found it "equally undeniable" that
the Commandments "have had a significant impact on the development
of secular legal codes of the Western World." Although he rejected the
Lemon test, Rehnquist would read it to uphold laws that make *any* claim
of secular purpose, however subordinate to religious aims.

The *Engel* and *Schempp* decisions made clear—at least to the Court—
that public-school teachers may not lead students in vocal prayer. Does
the Establishment clause also prohibit laws that mandate a period of
silence for the purpose of meditation or voluntary prayer by students?
The Court faced this unresolved question in *Wallace v. Jaffree,* which
came from Mobile, Alabama. The suit was filed by Ishmael Jaffree, an
agnostic lawyer with three children in elementary school. Their teachers
were all "born-again" Christians who led students in the Lord's Prayer
and other classroom devotions. State law allowed teachers to devote one
minute to silent "meditation," but vocal prayer was not permitted. Jaffree's lawsuit, filed after school officials ignored his objections, prompted
state lawmakers to enact an official school prayer, which acknowledged
"Almighty God" as "the Creator and Supreme Judge of the world."
Conscious of the prayer's legal infirmities, they also provided for silent
meditation or prayer.

The *Jaffree* case featured the ruling of a maverick federal district judge,
Brevard Hand, that the First Amendment did not prohibit Alabama lawmakers from establishing a state religion. The Supreme Court did not
need to review his decision, which had been reversed by an appellate
panel. But the justices granted the state's appeal in 1984, striking down
the oral prayer without argument and rebuking Judge Hand for presuming
to overrule their decisions. The next year, the Court turned to the "narrow
question" of the period of silent meditation or prayer. The case record
included statements by the law's principal sponsor, State Senator Donald

Holmes, that "Alabama was founded by people who believe in God" and that his bill would "accomplish the return of voluntary prayer in our public schools and return to the basic moral fiber." During the trial Judge Hand asked Holmes if the bill had any other purpose. His answer twisted grammar but made his meaning clear: "No, I did not have no other purpose in mind."

Writing for the majority, Justice John Paul Stevens focused on the term "prayer" in the Alabama law. He quoted Senator Holmes in holding that the law "was not motivated by any clearly secular purpose—indeed the statute had *no* secular purpose." The Court's opinion left open the question of whether a moment of silence, with no mention of prayer, could satisfy the Establishment clause. Justice Brennan joined the decision without a separate opinion.

Justice Rehnquist did not remain silent in the *Jaffree* case, devoting most of his lengthy dissent to attacking Jefferson's "wall of separation" as a "misleading metaphor" based on "bad history." He made clear his sympathy with Judge Hand's reading of the Establishment clause, which denied that the First Amendment applied to the states. Rehnquist was reluctant, however, to stake out a lonely position on this issue. He grudgingly agreed that precedent established the incorporation of the Establishment clause into the Fourteenth Amendment and prohibited states from establishing a religion. But he denied that states were barred from employing "sectarian means" to accomplish "secular ends."

Rehnquist left the Alabama law for the last two paragraphs of his *Jaffree* opinion. He professed "shock" at the Court's ruling, noting that "George Washington himself" had proclaimed a day of public thanksgiving and prayer to "Almighty God." And he asked whether "it was the Father of his Country in 1789, or a majority of the Court today, which has strayed from the meaning of the Establishment Clause." Rehnquist answered that he saw no constitutional barrier to any "generalized 'endorsement' of prayer" in public schools.

Another southern state senator prompted a replay in the 1980s of the famous "monkey trial" that riveted the nation in 1925. Biology teacher John Scopes had challenged a Tennessee law that barred him from teaching Darwin's theory of evolution. His trial featured a classic duel between two famous lawyers, Clarence Darrow and William Jennings Bryan. The Scopes case never reached the Supreme Court, but in 1968 the justices struck down a similar law in *Epperson v. Arkansas*. Justice Abe Fortas wrote that evolution theory could not be banned from schools because of a "fundamentalist sectarian conviction" that it conflicted with the Genesis account of creation.

After a decade of relative silence, opponents of evolution resumed their crusade after the election of President Ronald Reagan, who endorsed their position. Activists of the Christian Right shifted tactics, pressing for laws that would grant "equal time" to evolution and "creation science" in biology classes. Blocked from a direct assault on Darwin, "creationist" lawyers drafted statutes that carefully avoided religious terms. But the legislators who debated them were not so careful. Louisiana Senator Bill Keith told his colleagues in 1981 that "a creator was responsible for everything that is in this world." He equated the theory of evolution with something he called "atheistism." The lawyer who drafted the Louisiana statute told Keith that "I view this whole battle as one between God and anti-God forces."

Don Aguillard, a high school biology teacher, challenged the law in a suit against Louisiana governor Edwin Edwards. Relying on the *Epperson* case for precedent, the Supreme Court had no trouble in deciding *Edwards v. Aguillard* in 1987. With Chief Justice Rehnquist in dissent, Justice Brennan took the opinion for himself. He applied the *Lemon* test to the "creationism" law and gave it a failing grade. Although he agreed that "the Court is normally deferential to a State's articulation of a secular purpose," Brennan stressed that "it is required that the statement of such purpose be sincere and not a sham." He found that the law's ostensible purpose of advancing "academic freedom" was a cover for its real purpose, "to restructure the science curriculum to conform with a particular religious viewpoint." Brennan concluded that Louisiana lawmakers "passed the Act to give preference to those religious groups which have as one of their tenets the creation of humankind by a divine creator."

Rehnquist stayed aloof from the rhetorical battle over the *Aguillard* case. But he joined the acidic opinion of Justice Antonin Scalia, who professed to be "astonished" at Brennan's supposed conclusion that "no one could be gullible enough" to believe in creationism. Suggesting with sarcasm that "the legislation's stated purpose must be a lie," Scalia proposed that a Louisiana lawmaker "may have been intoxicated" or "mad at his wife" rather than motivated by a desire to "foster religion or because he wanted to improve education." He also argued that Christian fundamentalists are entitled "to have whatever scientific evidence there may be against evolution presented in their schools," if they can win political battles over the biology curriculum. Rehnquist agreed with Scalia's proposal that the Court should revise "our embarrassing Establishment Clause jurisprudence" and his suggestion that abandoning the *Lemon* test "would be a good place to start."

Commentary on the *Aguillard* case reflected its political stakes. James Wall, editor of *Christian Century*, a liberal Protestant journal, deplored the fact that "the fundamentalists, the aggressive members of the religious community these days, have taken their constricted religious views to a public forum." Nathan Glazer, a leading Jewish neoconservative, answered that "about 95 percent of the country is Christian" and that the Court should not undermine "the ability of the small communities that make up the great Republic to maintain their values and their cultures." Catholics, who mostly accept evolution, stayed out of this fight.

The retirements of Justices Brennan and Marshall raised fears in the liberal camp that the "wall of separation" would soon crumble. The Court had divided 6–3 in the *Jaffree* case, the last prayer decision before their departures. By the time of the next prayer case, three members of the *Jaffree* majority had been replaced by supposed conservatives. Anthony Kennedy took the seat of Justice Lewis Powell, followed by David Souter and Clarence Thomas. Leaders of the Religious Right were confident that "accommodationists" now controlled the Court. They were surprised and chagrined when Kennedy and Souter voted in 1992 against religious devotions at school graduation ceremonies.

There was an odd twist to *Lee v. Weisman*, which came from the only state with a Catholic majority, Rhode Island. This case featured a Jewish parent against a Jewish rabbi. Their conflict was started in 1989 by a Christian school principal who had, in previous years, invited priests and ministers to lead graduation prayers. Daniel Weisman, whose daughter Deborah was graduating from Nathan Bishop Middle School, objected to any religious ceremony. Principal Robert E. Lee responded by inviting Rabbi Leslie Gutterman to lead the prayers. Although Deborah and her family attended the ceremony, they continued their suit against graduation prayers.

Justice Kennedy flexed the muscles of the emerging "centrist" group in the Court's majority opinion. He relied on "settled rules" in prayer cases, citing precedent that began with *Everson* and concluded with *Jaffree*. "No holding by this Court," he wrote, "suggests that a school can persuade or compel a student to participate in a religious exercise." Kennedy looked to Justice Brennan in noting the "potential for divisiveness" of the prayer ceremonies.

Chief Justice Rehnquist assigned the dissent to Justice Scalia, who produced another acerbic opinion. Scalia accused the new "separationist" majority of running a "bulldozer" over school prayer in pursuit of "social engineering." He disputed Kennedy's suggestion that any student would feel "psychological coercion" in being asked to join in prayer. Scalia urged Deborah Weisman, when she graduates from high school, to endure the "minimal inconvenience" of standing while her classmates pray "to the God whom they all worship and seek." He did not, however, cite any evidence for his assertion that every other student believed in God.

JUSTICE BRENNAN did not prevail in all religion cases. He was on the losing side in several decisions that upheld religious practices outside the public schools. Brennan could not persuade most "centrist" justices that "ceremonial deism" violated the Establishment clause.

One such case dealt with the practice of legislative prayer. Both houses of Congress and many states employ chaplains, and hundreds of local bodies ask ministers to bless their deliberations. Beginning in 1965, the Reverend Robert Palmer, a Presbyterian minister, served as chaplain of Nebraska's unicameral legislature. Not surprisingly, his prayers were often explicitly Christian, but he removed all references to Christ after a Jewish member complained in 1980. This change did not satisfy another member, Ernest Chambers, who sued State Treasurer Frank Marsh to end the paid chaplaincy altogether.

Ruling in 1983, the Supreme Court reversed a federal appellate decision that the practice violated all three prongs of the *Lemon* test. Chief Justice Burger wrote for a 6–3 majority in *Marsh v. Chambers*. He ignored his own *Lemon* test and looked instead to "history and tradition" for precedent. Even the history of legislative prayer offered a mixed record; Burger admitted that sessions of the Constitutional Convention were not opened with prayer, but suggested "this may simply have been an oversight." Burger, who was deeply conventional in belief and habits, brushed aside the contrary evidence. "In light of the unambiguous and unbroken history of more than 200 years," he wrote, "there can be no doubt that the practice of opening legislative sessions with prayer has become part of the fabric of our society."

Justice Brennan delivered a history lecture to the Chief in his lengthy dissent. Much of his opinion reviewed the history of the religion clauses, but he also looked closely at the Nebraska case. Brennan chided Burger for making "no pretense" of applying the *Lemon* test, noting that the Reverend Palmer had stated his purpose as providing lawmakers with "divine wisdom" in their deliberations. Brennan argued that legislative prayer "is nothing but a religious act." He also noted that controversy over legislative prayer had "led to serious political divisiveness" in several states; a California legislator who objected to Christian prayers was denounced as "an irreverent and godless man." Brennan urged that the prospect of political conflict over religion should be added as a fourth prong of the *Lemon* test, but his opinion failed to carry the "centrist" group of Justices Blackmun, Powell, and O'Connor, who sided with him in school-prayer cases.

The next year, Brennan won Blackmun's vote in another religion case, but he still lost by one vote. *Lynch v. Donnelly* involved the annual Christmas display in Pawtucket, Rhode Island, which city workers had erected in a downtown park for many years. As the Court noted, it was much like those "in hundreds of towns or cities across the Nation," with a life-size Nativity crêche of Jesus, Mary, and Joseph in a manger, surrounded by a Christmas tree, colored lights, carolers, and Santa's sled with reindeer. Above the entire scene was a large banner that read "Season's Greetings." Applying the *Lemon* test, a lower federal court ruled that the crêche had the "effect" of endorsing the Christian religion and violated the Establishment clause.

Chief Justice Burger wrote for the majority in reversing the lower court. He did not ignore the *Lemon* test in this case; he just swept it under the constitutional rug. Burger proclaimed the Court's "unwillingness to be confined to any single test or criterion in this sensitive area." He cited his opinion in the legislative-prayer case to argue that *Lemon* was not "relevant" to the Nativity case, and another of his opinions as evidence that the Supreme Court "consistently has declined to take a rigid, absolutist view of the Establishment Clause."

Burger devoted much of his *Lynch* opinion to refuting Brennan's dissent, a sign of judicial insecurity. "The dissent asserts," he wrote, "that the city has aligned itself with the Christian faith" in sponsoring the Nativity scene. Admitting that the display "advances religion in a sense," Burger replied that "our precedents plainly contemplate that on occasion some advancement of religion will result from governmental action."

Ironically, he cited for this proposition a decision from which he dissented, striking down state aid to religious schools.

The Chief Justice faced the task of explaining away the clear sectarian nature of the Nativity scene. He did not dispute Brennan's description of the display as "the heart of the Christian faith." And he admitted that "the crêche is identified with one religious faith" and has a "special meaning" to Christians. Visitors to the display could not "fail to be aware of its religious implications." Burger's answer to Brennan simply removed the case from its sectarian context: "The display engenders a friendly community spirit of goodwill in keeping with the season." By seeming to take Christ out of Christmas, Burger opened himself to Brennan's reply that he equated the Bethlehem manger with Santa's house. "Of course this is not true," Burger huffed, without explaining *why* it was not true.

In his dissent, Justice Brennan tried to explain why Burger had tried so hard to please everyone. He knew the Chief loved the trappings of Christmas, from trees in the Court's rotunda to caroling in the hallways. "After reviewing the Court's opinion," he wrote, "I am convinced that this case appears hard not because the principles of decision are obscure, but because the Christmas holiday seems so familiar and agreeable." Brennan concluded that the public display "of a symbol as distinctively sectarian as a creche simply cannot be squared with our prior cases."

Brennan revealed his frustration in denouncing the Court's "careless decision" as a departure from its normal reliance "upon concrete, specific historical evidence" in religion cases. "Without that guiding principle and the intellectual discipline it imposes," he wrote, "the Court is at sea, free to select random elements of America's varied history solely to suit the views of five Members of this Court."

It is hard to imagine a closer judicial division than five to four. But in the next religion case, decided in 1989, the justices divided into nine separate groups, with no faction in control. This case did not even produce majority and minority opinions. Justice Harry Blackmun announced the "judgment of the Court," but he was alone in this position. None of his colleagues agreed with every part of his opinion; some joined three of its five sections, others two or one. Five justices concurred in the judgment, but seven dissented from all or part of Blackmun's opinion. The result was like nine Christmas carolers, each singing a different song.

The reason for judicial discordance in this case, *Allegheny County v. ACLU*, was that it mixed Christian and Jewish symbols, and secular and sectarian displays. The facts were relatively simple in this case from

Pittsburgh, Pennsylvania. Since 1981, officials allowed the Holy Name Society, a Catholic group, to display a Nativity crêche in the county courthouse during the Christmas season. Over the crêche was a banner that read "Gloria in Excelsis Deo." A block away, outside the city building, a Jewish group erected an eighteen-foot menorah to celebrate the Chanukah holiday. The menorah stood near a forty-five-foot Christmas tree. The American Civil Liberties Union filed suit against both religious displays. After a federal appellate court ruled that display of the crêche and the menorah violated the Establishment clause, the Supreme Court agreed to review the case.

The outcome of the *Allegheny* case rested on Justice Sandra O'Connor, who had joined the majority in the *Lynch* decision. In voting that the menorah could stay but the crêche must go, she agreed with Brennan that "political divisiveness" should be considered in religion cases. But she also proposed replacing the purpose and effect prongs of the *Lemon* test with a more stringent "endorsement" test. This test looked to the perception of a challenged practice by members of the general public. Applying this test, O'Connor found the Christmas crêche sent a "message to Christians that they are favored members of the political community." On the other hand, displaying a menorah near a Christmas tree "did not endorse Judaism or religion in general, but rather conveyed a message of pluralism and freedom of belief during the holiday season."

Justice Brennan devoted his opinion to the menorah. He disputed O'Connor's assumption that placing a Jewish symbol next to a Christian symbol would somehow turn both into secular objects and foster "religious pluralism." He argued that "this attempt to take the 'Christmas' out of the Christmas tree is unconvincing," and restated his position that the Establishment clause was designed "to require neutrality, not just among religions, but between religion and nonreligion."

Four justices voted to approve both the crêche and the menorah displays. The Court's junior member, Anthony Kennedy, spoke for this group, which also included Rehnquist, White, and Scalia. Kennedy took issue with the majority that struck down the crêche. He did not dispute its religious nature, but argued that "the Establishment Clause permits government some latitude in recognizing and accommodating the central role religion plays in our society."

The real target of Kennedy's opinion was the *Lemon* test, which he claimed "reflects an unjustified hostility toward religion, a hostility inconsistent with our history and our precedents" in religion cases. Kennedy expressed the frustration of the Court's "accommodationists." They knew that as long as Blackmun and O'Connor deferred to *Lemon*, the "separationists" would prevail in close decisions. Only the addition to the Court of a more conservative justice would shift the balance. Perhaps looking ahead, Kennedy proposed replacing the *Lemon* test with a new, less stringent "coercion" test. "Barring all attempts to aid religion through government coercion" would satisfy the Establishment clause, he wrote.

Kennedy gave one example of a practice that would fail his test. "I doubt not," he wrote, "that the Clause forbids a city to permit the permanent erection of a large Latin cross on the roof of city hall." Such an "obtrusive year-round religious display would place the government's weight behind an obvious effort to proselytize on behalf of a particular religion." Kennedy did not object to the religious message of the cross, but to its permanence. Presumably, erecting a cross in a park during the Easter holiday would not violate the "coercion" test. "Passersby who disagree with the message," he wrote, could simply "turn their backs, just as they are free to do when they disagree with any other form of religious speech." This vision of America, as a nation in which religious dissenters stand in public places with backs turned to their fellow citizens, is at odds with that of an inclusive, tolerant society.

Having weathered the assault of the Court's "accommodationists," Jefferson's "wall of separation" faces another charge by religious crusaders. Following their electoral defeat in 1992, leaders of the religious right urged supporters of a "Christian nation" to redouble their efforts. "The less we emphasize the Christian religion," Mississippi governor Kirk Fordice warned, "the further we fall into the abyss of poor character and chaos in the United States of America." Although his remarks were roundly criticized, they underscore the political volatility of religion in American society. This fact ensures another round of Establishment clause cases. And the justices, most likely, will remain divided in their decisions.

VIRTUALLY ALL the uproar over the Court's religion decisions has followed Establishment clause rulings. In contrast, hardly anyone gets exercised over Free Exercise cases. The reasons for this difference are obvious. Telling the Christian majority that children can't pray in school upsets millions of voters. Decisions in cases brought by religious minorities, such as Orthodox Jews or Muslims, affect a relative handful of people, who generally lack political clout. Recognizing this fact, Justice Harlan Stone devised the "strict scrutiny" test to redress this disparity between religious majorities and minorities.

During the years they served together, Justices Brennan and Rehnquist differed in almost every Free Exercise case. Brennan set the judicial standard in 1963, writing for the Court in *Sherbert v. Verner*. This case was brought by Adell Sherbert, who worked for thirty-five years as a spool tender in a South Carolina textile factory. She joined the Seventh-Day Adventist Church in 1957. Two years later, she was assigned to work on Saturdays, which conflicted with her religious beliefs. When she declined, the company fired her. State officials denied her claim for unemployment compensation, although she offered to take any job that did not require Saturday work. When she appealed this ruling, state judges ruled for the company.

Speaking for the Supreme Court, Justice Brennan sympathized with Sherbert. "The door of the Free Exercise Clause stands tightly closed against any governmental regulation of religious *beliefs* as such," he wrote. Citing the nineteenth-century Mormon polygamy case, Brennan admitted that laws can prohibit conduct, based on religious belief, which poses "some substantial threat to public safety, peace, or order." But this was a case of belief, not of conduct. Adell Sherbert had not injured the state in any way. Brennan applied the "strict scrutiny" test and asked whether "some compelling state interest" justified the denial of jobless benefits. Not even "a rational relationship to some colorable state interest would suffice," he wrote. Because state officials admitted her religious sincerity, and did not argue that she submitted a fraudulent claim, Brennan ruled that South Carolina had placed a "burden" on Adell Sherbert's free exercise of religion.

Eighteen years later, in 1979, the Court decided a virtually identical case. This suit was brought by Eddie Thomas, a Jehovah's Witness who worked for an Indiana company that made steel products. After his transfer from the roll foundry to a department that produced turrets for military tanks, he learned that all the available jobs involved weapons production. He told company officials that his religious beliefs prohibited military work. When they denied his request for a layoff, he quit his job. And when state officials denied his request for jobless benefits, he sued them.

Most likely, the justices accepted *Thomas v. Review Board* to rebuke the Indiana Supreme Court for ignoring the *Sherbert* decision. Chief Justice Burger, who normally sided with government in religion cases, wrote for the Court. The state judges had ruled that Eddie Thomas did not have "good cause" for leaving his job. "A similar argument was made and rejected in *Sherbert*," Burger noted. The "coercive impact" of the state law on Thomas "is indistinguishable from *Sherbert*," he added. This was an easy decision for every justice but one.

Justice Rehnquist filed a solo dissent. He ignored Burger and leveled his guns at Brennan's opinion in the *Sherbert* case. Denying that *Sherbert* "was correctly decided," Rehnquist claimed that it construed the Free Exercise clause "more broadly than is warranted." His opinion did not mention the *Lemon* test, which applied primarily to Establishment clause cases. But he argued that if the "purpose and effect" of a state law advanced "secular goals," the Free Exercise clause did not "require the State to conform that statute to the dictates of religious conscience of any group." Rehnquist predicted that the Court's decision would tempt Indiana workers to "quit their jobs, assert they did so for personal reasons, and collect unemployment insurance." During the next five years, however, not a single person filed for jobless benefits on religious grounds.

Brennan and Rehnquist also differed in *Hobbie v. Florida*, decided in 1987. Paula Hobbie, who worked in a jewelry store, joined the Seventh-Day Adventist church in 1984 and arranged a schedule with her supervisor that avoided Saturday work. For reasons he never explained, the company's general manager objected and fired her. He also opposed her claim for jobless benefits, claiming her refusal to work on Saturdays constituted "misconduct" under company rules. The Florida Supreme Court refused to follow the *Sherbert* and *Thomas* decisions and ruled for the company.

Once again, the justices accepted a Free Exercise case to rebuke state judges. Justice Brennan again spoke for the Court. The *Sherbert* and *Thomas* cases, he wrote, made clear that restrictions on religious belief "must be subjected to strict scrutiny and could be justified only by proof by the State of a compelling interest." Florida officials argued that Paula Hobbie had changed her religious affiliation during her employment and was thus "responsible for the consequences of the conflict between her job and her religious beliefs." Brennan rejected this claim, ruling that the Free Exercise clause protects workers who "convert from one faith to another after they are hired." Once again, Rehnquist filed a solo dissent, based on his *Thomas* opinion.

Brennan did not prevail in all the Free Exercise cases. He lost to Rehnquist in a case that pitted a Jewish rabbi against military rule. Simcha Goldman, an Orthodox rabbi, received financial support for several years in the Armed Forces Health Professions program. After completing a Ph.D. in psychology, Rabbi Goldman entered active service in the Air Force. His problems began in 1981, when he testified as a defense witness in a military court-martial. Instead of his service cap, Rabbi Goldman wore a Jewish yarmulke on his head. The military prosecutor complained to Goldman's superior, who charged him with violating a regulation that prohibited the wearing of any "headgear" indoors except by "armed security police in the performance of their duties."

After threats of court-martial for refusing to remove his yarmulke, Rabbi Goldman sued the Secretary of Defense, Caspar Weinberger. Justice Rehnquist, who had served in the Army Air Corps, wrote for the majority in *Goldman* v. *Weinberger*. He stood up and saluted the military brass. "Our review of military regulations challenged on First Amendment grounds," Rehnquist wrote, "is far more deferential than constitutional review of similar laws or regulations designed for civilian society." Rehnquist indicated his approval of any military regulation that was designed to "foster instinctive obedience, unity, commitment, and esprit de corps."

Justice Brennan dissented from this rebuff to the most important religious obligation of an Orthodox Jew, "to cover his head before an omnipresent God." The Air Force regulation, he wrote, required Rabbi Goldman "to violate the tenets of his faith virtually every minute of every workday." Brennan noted that military regulations allowed Mormons to wear "temple garments" under their uniforms and Catholics to wear crosses and scapulars outside theirs. Citing the Air Force regulation, Brennan asked what was "so extreme, so unusual, or so faddish" about Dr. Goldman's yarmulke that hindered his ability to perform his duties.

Brennan ended his dissent with a lecture to his fellow Americans. "Through our Bill of Rights," he wrote, "we pledged ourselves to attain a level of human freedom and dignity that has no parallel in history. Our constitutional commitment to religious freedom and to acceptance of religious pluralism is one of our greatest achievements in that noble endeavor." Speaking for Rabbi Goldman, Brennan voiced his own basic values. "A critical function of the Religion Clauses of the First Amendment," he wrote, "is to protect the rights of members of minority religions against quiet erosion by majoritarian social institutions that dismiss minority beliefs and practices as unimportant, because unfamiliar." Moving outside his judicial role, Brennan asked Congress to "correct this wrong" to Rabbi Goldman. Congress listened, and passed a law in 1986 that allowed military personnel to wear yarmulkes and other religious headgear.

For more than forty years, the Court's decisions in religion cases have provoked debate, even disobedience. The lesson of these disparate cases is that no institution, however prestigious or powerful, can impose its will on people who are deeply divided on questions of faith. Jefferson's "wall of separation" has thus far kept religious factions apart, and spared Americans the sectarian wars that have torn other societies apart.

SEVEN

" 'No Law' Does *Not* Mean No Law"

Most Americans are proud of their rights to free expression, and will eagerly voice their support for the First Amendment's guarantees of speech, press, and assembly. Compared with other countries, the United States is virtually alone in granting constitutional protection to vocal dissenters. Even in wartime, critics of government policies can picket the White House, hand out leaflets on street corners, and denounce the nation's leaders in the most personal terms. During the Vietnam War, protesters chanted, "Hey, hey, LBJ, how many kids did you kill today!" The Supreme Court has even granted First Amendment protection to groups such as Nazis and Klansmen, with records of violence against Jews and blacks. Legal toleration of those who preach and practice intolerance provides the ultimate test of an open society and its commitment to the "marketplace of ideas."

The most obvious explanation for this record of toleration is the wording of the First Amendment itself: "Congress shall make no law," the Framers wrote, "abridging the freedom of speech, or of the press; or the right of the people peaceably to assemble, and to petition the Government for a redress of grievances." This flat prohibition of laws that restrict expression seemingly allows no exceptions. Justice Hugo Black became known as a First Amendment "absolutist" because of his admonition, repeated time and again, that " 'no law' *means* no law." During argument of the 1971 Pentagon Papers case, a dramatic showdown between the press and the government, Solicitor General Erwin Griswold spoke directly to Black: "You say that 'no law' means no law, and that should be obvious. To me, it is equally obvious that 'no law' does *not* mean no law."

Black joined the Court's majority in holding that the government could not restrain publication of the Pentagon Papers. But only one justice,

William Douglas, joined his "absolutist" opinion. Even Black's staunch First Amendment ally, William Brennan, suggested that different circumstances in a later case might require a different outcome. Government suppression of "information that would set in motion a nuclear holocaust" might justify a "prior restraint" on publication, Brennan wrote. Not even Justice Black, in fact, has taken a consistently "absolutist" position in First Amendment cases. For example, he dissented loudly from a 1969 ruling that high school students could wear black armbands to protest the Vietnam War.

Despite his apparent disregard of logic, Solicitor General Griswold was right. Every justice has agreed that the "no law" command has exceptions that are required by greater needs, especially the demands of public safety. Justice Oliver Wendell Holmes framed the example that almost everyone knows: "The most stringent protection of free speech would not protect a man in falsely shouting fire in a theater and causing a panic." Most people have an intuitive understanding of why the First Amendment should not protect the malicious creation of panic or the instigation of nuclear holocaust. The real test of the "no law" rule, however, lies in conflicts that begin in America's schools and street corners. For every momentous clash like the Pentagon Papers case, the Supreme Court faces dozens of disputes over issues such as saying "chicken-shit" in court. It is these relatively mundane cases that test the limits of free expression, and that distinguish the First Amendment jurisprudence of Justices Brennan and Rehnquist.

Viewed from the marble steps of the Supreme Court, looking at the demonstrators who periodically crowd the sidewalk below, the First Amendment seems remarkably vibrant and resilient. Its vitality is best measured, however, not in the nation's capital but in small towns across the country. Local and state officials, even those in federal agencies, are often ignorant or contemptuous of judicial decisions. It is their actions that the First Amendment governs with the "no law" command. The Supreme Court requires the "exhaustion of remedies" before it will hear a case, and imposes substantial filing fees on those who are not exhausted by the quest for justice. Faced with these obstacles, few people are willing to risk their jobs or expulsion from school to defend the First Amendment. But some have the gumption to speak out, even if their cases never reach the Supreme Court. A sampling of small-town cases in recent years shows the range of conflict between outspoken citizens and censorious officials.

Jesse Ethredge is one such citizen. He has worked for twenty-five years as an aircraft mechanic at Robins Air Force Base in Georgia. Ethredge is an old-fashioned, "yellow dog" Democrat. Back in 1984, he put a bumper sticker on his pickup truck that read "To Hell with Reagan." Military officials grumbled but took no action. In 1992, he placed a new sign on his truck that read "Read My Lips: To Hell with Geo. Bush." This time, military officials ordered Ethredge to keep his truck off the base, claiming his stickers "have a negative impact on the good order and discipline" of military personnel. Ethredge refused to back down and contacted the American Civil Liberties Union. "If you don't stand up for your rights, you won't have no rights," he said. "I'm the kind of fella that whenever I know I'm right, I'm going to fight you until I'm shot down." Air Force officials finally decided against a legal shoot-out with Ethredge and his volunteer lawyers.

Officials in Hancock County, West Virginia, took more direct action against a sign that criticized the state's governor, Gaston Caperton. Pam and Vito Riggi felt the state highway department had mishandled the repair of the road that fronted their property. Whenever it rained, they said, the road turned into a mudslide. Highway officials ignored their complaints, so the Riggis erected a six-by-twelve-foot sign on their property that read "Governor, You Call This Road Progress. We Call It Incompetence." Sam DeCapio, the county highway superintendent, noticed the sign and promptly pulled it down. Pam Riggi asked what authority he had to remove a sign from private property. "He said he didn't have to talk to me and he left." The Riggis asked the West Virginia Civil Liberties Union for help. "We are still a democracy and you can't push people around because you have a government position," Pam Riggi told a reporter.

Another First Amendment defender is Lindsey Jones. While a senior at Meridian High School in Idaho, she arranged a visit by a lesbian couple to a program on parenting skills. The lesbians talked about their experiences as parents to classes on sociology, government, and English. After an offended parent complained to the school superintendent, Bob Haley, he suspended the teachers of all three classes. Some five hundred students held a lunchtime rally to support the teachers. "Most of the seniors here are old enough to vote for a president of the United States," Jones said, "but we're not old enough to know whether we should listen to homosexuals." Katie Jolly, who worked with Jones on the parenting program, added that "our community is very conservative, and a small minority dictates what the rest of us learn." Superintendent Haley answered as a parent and an official. "I am concerned about what my children are exposed to in the schools," he told a reporter, "and it is certainly not a part of the curriculum to bring lesbians in to discuss their lifestyle."

Jason Roth, a college freshman, grew up on a farm near Albert Lea, Minnesota, and was active in the 4-H Club. He won prizes at the Freeborn County Fair for livestock, but his passion was sculpture. Roth won a grand champion award in 1991 for his entry, *Lost in Bondage*, a memorial to the prisoners and missing soldiers in the Vietnam War. His 1992 entry, however, stirred up controversy. Roth produced an eight-foot-tall depiction of a blindfolded goddess of justice, with imitation blood flowing from her mouth and from spikes that nailed her wrists and ankles to a cross. He called the sculpture *Pro-Choice*. A few hours after Roth took his entry to the 4-H exhibit, the fair board voted to ban it from public display. Fair manager Howard Reckner said that some children had seen the sculpture and "it made them feel bad." Roth replied that "the purpose of all the artwork I do is to arouse emotions in people. The more powerful I make it, the more clear-cut those choices within them become." He called on the American Civil Liberties Union for legal assistance. Marjorie Heins, who directs the ACLU's national arts censorship project, visited Minnesota to help Roth. "This is a good piece of art," she said. "When you see a teenager concerned about something other than sex, drugs, and rock 'n' roll, you ought to applaud him, not censor him."

First Amendment protection of the right "peaceably to assemble" is not limited to political rallies. People can assemble for any lawful reason, even to "hang out" on street corners. Many communities, however, impose curfews on teenagers, ostensibly to curb gang activity. Speaking to the Marysville, California, city council, Meika Cooper and Gina Caselli urged the repeal of the town's curfew ordinance. The two seventeen-year-olds said the law was "extremely unconstitutional" and had been enforced against many teenagers who were out after 11 p.m. for legitimate reasons. "A lot of parents we have talked to," Cooper told the councilors, "feel the law infringes on their right to raise their children the way they see fit." Juvenile court judge Jack Feldman, who said he normally imposed twenty-dollar fines on curfew violators, defended the law. "There will always be protests but it is an issue of safety," he responded. Marysville police chief Jack Simpson said the curfew was designed to stop teenagers from "going down to cruise" the streets, a traditional practice of kids in small towns across America.

Even those who are not yet teenagers have stood up for the right to express themselves. Jimmy Hines, a fifth-grader at Caston Elementary School in Fulton County, Indiana, was sent home in September 1992 when he refused to remove a diamond stud from his left ear. The school board voted unanimously to remove him from school for violating the district's dress code, which allows only girls to wear earrings. Jimmy's father, who also wears an earring, spoke against the policy at the board meeting. James Hines said the issue went beyond his son's diamond stud. "I don't care if he takes it out tomorrow," he said. "I want the rule changed for the other kids." Paul Baker, the school superintendent, answered for the board. "When you buy into the community," he said, "you buy into that community's standards."

None of these cases is likely to reach the Supreme Court. Most conflicts over the First Amendment never reach the newspapers, let alone the courts. Almost every day, teachers order students to conform to dress codes, principals censor articles in school papers, and police officers tell groups of teenagers to "break it up." Backed with the power of law, officials have little fear of rebuke. In many cases, it takes the intervention of groups like the American Civil Liberties Union to force officials to think twice and consult with lawyers. The First Amendment is not posted on the walls of most government offices. Even judges wink at the Constitution. Maryellen Hicks, a state district judge in Fort Worth, Texas, defended a teenage curfew law. "It's unconstitutional," she confessed. "No doubt about it. But any tool we can employ to stop violence in our community, I support."

THE CLAIM of a child to wear a diamond stud in his ear may seem to trivialize the historic purpose of the First Amendment. The primary object of the Framers was to protect dissidents who aimed broadsides at government officials from the wrath of their targets. Both in England and in colonial America, authors and publishers were subject to laws that made "seditious libel" a capital crime. These laws were closely related to statutes that punished "blasphemy" with death or imprisonment. Because the monarch was divinely appointed to impose God's ordinances on earth, criticism of the King was a slander on the Almighty. English judges ruled that any publication tending to foster an "ill opinion of the government" could be punished, regardless of its truth. In 1663, William Twyn printed a book that endorsed the right of revolution; for this crime, he was "sentenced to be hanged, cut down while still alive, and then emasculated, disembowled, quartered, and beheaded—the standard punishment for treason."

British prosecutors filed hundreds of "seditious libel" charges, and dozens of offending writers and publishers followed Twyn to the gallows. In the Colonies, however, only a handful of cases reached trial. The most notorious trial ended with the acquittal of John Peter Zenger in 1735. His *New York Weekly Journal* had accused the royal governor, William Cosby, of misdeeds that included jury rigging and election fraud. Zenger's lawyer argued that his charges were true. Even worse than falsehood, replied the royal prosecutor: "The law says their being true is an aggravation of the crime." He reasoned that proof of official misconduct would create even more public outrage than false charges. Governor Cosby could not rig Zenger's jury, and his acquittal encouraged other publishers to denounce British rule openly, with little fear of prosecution.

The historical record makes clear that the Framers of the First Amendment did not intend to remove *all* restrictions on speech, press, and assembly. Their primary target was the system of "prior restraint" on the press, imposed through licensing statutes and "Crown censors" who read every publication before it went to press. They retained the common-law crime of seditious libel, amending it only to allow "truth" as a defense. James Wilson, a major figure among the Framers, argued in 1787 that "every author is responsible when he attacks the security or welfare of the government, or the safety, character and property of the individual." The rule became "publish at your peril," subject to the ebb and flow of political tides. During the presidency of John Adams, Congress passed a Sedition Act in 1798 that outlawed "any false, scandalous and malicious writing" that might bring either the president or Congress "into contempt or disrepute." The law was aimed at supporters of Adams's political rival Thomas Jefferson. Its first victim was Vermont Congressman Matthew Lyon, a member of Jefferson's Republican Party who was sentenced to prison for writing that President Adams had "an unbounded thirst for ridiculous pomp, foolish adulation, and selfish avarice." Lyon was punished, not for the alleged falsity of his statements but for his low opinion of a thin-skinned president. Supportive constituents returned him to Congress during his four months in prison.

The first Sedition Act expired in 1801 and was never tested before the Supreme Court. Chief Justice John Marshall had been appointed by Adams and most likely would have upheld the law. Ironically, even Jefferson wanted to punish his press critics for their "lying" articles about him. After his election as president, Jefferson wrote to a friend that "a few prosecutions of the most eminent offenders would have a wholesome effect in restoring the integrity of the presses." Asserting a federal common law of seditious libel, prosecutors charged several of Jefferson's political enemies. None of the cases reached trial, perhaps because some of the offending articles had a substantial basis in fact. One charged Jefferson with attempting to seduce a friend's wife; after reading the article he ordered "an immediate dismission of the prosecution."

Another century passed before Congress enacted another sedition act and government critics again went to jail. During the intervening years, however, the press was under constant siege. The bitter national conflict over slavery produced state laws like one in Virginia that imposed prison terms on anyone who "by speaking or writing maintains that owners have no right of property in slaves." The crusade against slavery cost one crusading editor his life. Elijah Lovejoy, publisher of *The Observer* in Alton, Illinois, was shot to death in 1837 after he rejected demands that he stop printing attacks on slavery.

The First Amendment survived the Civil War only because the Supreme Court had no concern with private violence or with state and local restrictions on free expression. World War I, however, produced another federal assault on critics of the war effort. Congress passed a second sedition law, part of the Espionage Act, in 1918 that imposed criminal penalties on "disloyal" speech or writing. More than 2,000 people were prosecuted under this law, which equated dissent with treason. The most prominent victim was Socialist Party leader Eugene Debs, sentenced to twenty years in prison for denouncing the "capitalist" war. Debs ran for president in 1920 from his Atlanta Penitentiary cell and received more than a million votes.

Another Socialist agitator, Charles Schenck, provoked the first Supreme Court test of the new sedition law. Many Americans are unaware of the widespread opposition to U.S. participation in World War I. Congress imposed a military draft to raise troops, but more than half a million men failed to register. As the Socialist Party secretary in Philadelphia, Schenck printed 15,000 leaflets for a mailing to draft-age men. One side of the leaflet quoted the Thirteenth Amendment and equated conscription with slavery. The other side denounced the war and urged young men to "assert your opposition to the draft." Schenck was careful not to advocate, in direct terms, refusal to register for the draft. He was not careful enough, however, to escape criminal prosecution.

Justice Oliver Wendell Holmes wrote for a unanimous Court in upholding Schenk's conviction. Holmes had been gravely wounded in the Civil War, and had no sympathy for "shirkers" in the Great War to save democracy. His bellicose opinion had the tone of a recruiting poster. "When a nation is at war many things that might be said in times of peace are such a hindrance to its effort that their utterance will not be endured so long as men fight," Holmes wrote.

The Court's first opinion in a free-speech case stated a doctrine that has endured decades of criticism. Holmes asked in *Schenck v. United States* if the challenged words might "create a clear and present danger that they will bring about the substantive evils that Congress has a right to prevent." Under this test, prosecutors did not have to prove that Schenck's leaflets actually induced anyone to resist the draft. They need only show, Holmes wrote, that the "tendency of this circular" might interfere with recruitment. Schenk had no chance to avoid prison under this test, and received a five-year prison sentence.

Holmes wrote his *Schenck* opinion in April 1919. Eight months later, he dissented from the Court's ruling in another sedition case. The defendants in *Abrams v. United States* were Russian anarchists who opposed American military intervention against the Bolshevik Revolution. They were arrested for dropping leaflets from tenement windows in New York City, urging a general strike by munitions workers. Their leaflet actually supported the Allied war against Germany, but the five defendants were convicted and sentenced to ten-year prison terms. Holmes was appalled by the Court's use of his "clear and present danger" test to punish what he called the "poor and puny anonymities" of the anarchists. He proposed a more stringent First Amendment test, allowing only the punishment of words that "so imminently threaten immediate interference with the lawful and pressing purposes of the law that an immediate check is required to save the country." But the Court continued to apply the "clear and present danger" test over the dissent of its author.

DURING THE FOUR DECADES after the *Schenk* and *Abrams* decisions, the Supreme Court looked to political currents in deciding First Amendment cases. Free expression remained hostage to fear of communism. The Court upheld in 1925 the conviction of Communist Party leader Benjamin Gitlow for "criminal anarchy" under New York law. Gitlow was charged with no act of revolution, but simply with signing the Party's "Left Wing Manifesto." With Holmes again in dissent, the Court stretched the "clear and present danger" test past its wartime limits. Even if "the effect of a given utterance cannot be accurately foreseen," Justice Edward Sanford wrote, any call for revolution involves "danger to the public peace and to the security of the State." Gitlow went to prison, hardly comforted by the Court's ruling that First Amendment rights were "protected by the due process clause of the Fourteenth Amendment from impairment by the States."

The First Amendment survived World War II with hardly a scratch. Two major factors explain why free speech did not again become a wartime casualty. Most important, the campaign against the Axis was popular. The relatively few men who refused to fight on religious grounds were allowed to perform "alternative service." The attitude of federal officials also made a difference. Attorney General Francis Biddle belonged to the American Civil Liberties Union, and he restrained most efforts to punish war critics. Biddle did, however, approve a prosecution under a third sedition law, passed by Congress in 1940. Known as the Smith Act for its sponsor, this law imposed criminal penalties on anyone who "advocates" the overthrow of the government "by force or violence." The law was aimed at the Communist Party, which at the time vigorously opposed the "imperialist" war in Europe. Ironically, Biddle used the Smith Act against the Socialist Workers Party, a Trotskyist group that was a thorn in the paw of the Soviet bear. After the German invasion of Russia, American Communists waved the flag and cheered the prosecution of their critics. But the Supreme Court declined in 1943 to review the convictions and prison terms of eighteen Trotskyist leaders.

Within a year of the Allied victory in 1945, an Iron Curtain separated the United States and the Soviet Union. Ironically, the First Amendment became the first casualty of the Cold War between the recent allies. The congressional elections of 1946 sent to Washington "anti-Communist" zealots like Richard Nixon, who painted their liberal opponents with a "Red" brush. Nixon joined the House Committee on Un-American Activities, which pursued Communists from Harvard to Hollywood. Federal officials joined the hunt for spies and subversives. The ultimate irony for the Communist Party was the Smith Act indictment in 1948 of twelve

Party officials, the same people who supported the jailing of their Trotskyist opponents during the war.

Irony abounded in the Smith Act cases. Attorney General Tom Clark, a conservative Texan, opposed the prosecutions on First Amendment grounds. But legal issues gave way to politics in a presidential election year. Clark was overruled by Truman administration "liberals" who urged the president to campaign against Joseph Stalin. Truman won the election, and the Communist officials went to prison. Upholding the Smith Act convictions, the Supreme Court rejected claims that the First Amendment protected calls for revolution, however abstract or remote. Chief Justice Fred Vinson, a Truman crony, wrote that prevention of revolution, "even though doomed from the outset because of inadequate numbers or power of the revolutionists, is a sufficient evil for Congress to prevent." Vinson did not look to the First Amendment for guidance, but quoted newspaper headlines that in his opinion trumpeted "world crisis after crisis" in the conflict between East and West.

The irony of the Smith Act was compounded by passage in 1950 of the Internal Security Act. Hoping to blunt the "Red hunt" of Senator Joseph McCarthy, liberals such as Hubert Humphrey and Paul Douglas voted for a law that required the Communist Party to register with federal officials as a "subversive" group. Congress passed the law over Truman's veto, but the Supreme Court finally ruled that Party members could not be prosecuted for their revolutionary opinions. Reversing the conviction of Oleta Yates in 1957, Justice John Harlan wrote that the Smith Act "was aimed at the advocacy and teaching of concrete action for the forcible overthrow of the Government, and not of principles divorced from action."

Well before the Soviet Union surrendered in the Cold War, the Supreme Court voted to shield political dissidents from the "chilling effect" of First Amendment restrictions. The most important case involved one of the most hated groups in American history, the Ku Klux Klan. Clarence Brandenberg, an Ohio Klan leader, invited television reporters to a rally at which he vowed "revengeance" against advocates of racial integration. His hooded followers waved their guns at the cameras. Standing before a burning cross, Brandenberg urged that "the nigger should be returned to Africa, the Jew returned to Israel."

Ruling in 1969, the Court unanimously reversed Brandenberg's conviction under the state Criminal Syndicalism Act. The justices dusted off the "clear and present danger" test and gave it the meaning Holmes had intended when he framed it fifty years earlier. The Court affirmed in *Brandenberg v. Ohio* "the principle that the constitutional guarantees of free speech and free press do not permit a State to forbid or proscribe advocacy of the use of force or of law violation except where such advocacy is directed to inciting or producing imminent lawless action and is likely to incite or produce such action." The phrases do not ring with Holmes's clarity, but they got the message across.

IF THE FIRST AMENDMENT protects even speech that advocates violence and lawless acts, can there be any lesser limits on free expression? The Court's *Brandenberg* opinion seems to say no. But the answer is clearly yes, at least to most justices. The Court has erected three different kinds of barriers in First Amendment cases. The first is based on the "police powers" doctrine, which protects public health, safety, and welfare from danger and disruption. Regulation of the "time, place, and manner" of speech and assembly is permitted as long as the restriction is reasonable and fairly applied. For example, the Court in 1949 upheld a local ordinance that barred "loud and raucous" sound amplifiers. But officials cannot single out certain kinds of expression for approval or prohibition on the basis of the message alone.

The most famous—or infamous—example is the Skokie case of 1977, in which a Chicago suburb with a large Jewish population (including about 1,200 Holocaust survivors) tried to block a demonstration by a small Nazi group. Many people with strong opinions on this case have forgotten—or never knew—its facts. About fifty Nazis planned to parade before Skokie City Hall for thirty minutes on a Sunday, wearing khaki uniforms with swastika emblems and carrying placards, but staying on the sidewalk and making no speeches. The city council quickly banned "military style" uniforms and "symbols offensive to the community." The ensuing uproar and national press coverage gained the ragtag Nazis more free publicity than a short march on Sunday ever could. At the cost of several thousand outraged members, the American Civil Liberties Union defended the Nazis' right to demonstrate in Skokie. After a lengthy court battle, the Supreme Court declined to review a federal appellate decision that struck down the city's ordinances. Having won their point, the Nazis never showed up in Skokie. But the case dramatically illustrates the principle that "time, place, and manner" restrictions must be "content-neutral" and punish no message, however hateful.

A second limit to free expression, related to the first, is based on the "speech-action" distinction. The problem lies in the fact that even "pure speech," such as quietly holding a placard in a park, has elements of "action" that might legitimately be regulated. Protest against the Vietnam War provided several examples of "symbolic speech," on both sides of a very fuzzy line. The most extreme case is the use of violence to make a statement; one protester blew up a University of Wisconsin building that housed an Army research unit, killing an innocent graduate student. The bombing conveyed a political message, but the First Amendment did not protect the bomber from homicide charges.

The Supreme Court treated two forms of "symbolic speech" differently during the Vietnam War. It upheld in 1968 a federal law that imposed criminal penalties for burning draft cards. Chief Justice Earl Warren wrote for the majority, which included Justice Brennan, that "when 'speech' and 'nonspeech' elements are combined in the same course of conduct, a sufficiently important governmental interest in regulating the nonspeech element can justify incidental limitations on First Amendment freedoms." The government has a "vital interest" in punishing acts that might disrupt "the smooth and proper functioning" of the draft law, Warren argued in the *O'Brien* case. The next year, however, the Court struck down a ban on black armbands in the Des Moines, Iowa, schools. Mary Beth Tinker had been suspended for her symbolic protest of the war. Justice Abe Fortas called her act "closely akin to 'pure speech' which, we have repeatedly held, is entitled to comprehensive protection under the First Amendment." The distinctions between *O'Brien* and *Tinker* are unclear, but wartime is obviously not a good time to burn government property.

A third barrier to free expression is the practice of shrinking the boundaries of the First Amendment, and placing certain kinds of speech outside the circle of protection. The Court listed the categories of nonprotected speech in a case that began on a New Hampshire street corner in 1940. Walter Chaplinsky, a Jehovah's Witness, was offering religious tracts for sale. A hostile crowd gathered, words grew heated, and Chaplinsky was attacked. When the police arrived, they handcuffed him. Chaplinsky demanded to know why *he* was being arrested and not his attackers. An officer replied, "Shut up, you damn bastard," and Chaplinsky responded by calling the cop a "damn fascist and a God damned racketeer." He was convicted under a state law prohibiting the use of "any offensive, derisive, or annoying word to any other person" in a public place.

Justice Frank Murphy, who normally defended the rights of dissidents, articulated the "nonspeech" doctrine in his opinion for a unanimous Court in 1942. "There are certain well-defined and narrowly limited classes of speech," he wrote, "the prevention and punishment of which have never been thought to raise any Constitutional problem. These include the lewd and obscene, the profane, the libelous, and the insulting or 'fighting' words—those which by their very utterance inflict injury or tend to incite an immediate breach of the peace." Murphy defended the exclusion of these categories of speech from First Amendment protection. "It has been well observed that such utterances are no essential part of any exposition of ideas, and are of such slight social value as a step to truth that any benefit that may be derived from them is clearly outweighed by the social interest in order and morality." In this case, the "police powers" doctrine trumped the First Amendment.

The *Chaplinsky v. New Hampshire* decision was unanimous; even First Amendment stalwarts like Hugo Black, William Douglas, and Harlan Stone joined Murphy's opinion. But over the past five decades the Court has been sharply divided in many First Amendment cases, especially challenges to laws against obscenity, libel, "fighting words," and acts of symbolic speech. The reasons for division include personal and philosophical differences, as the opinions of Justices Brennan and Rehnquist illustrate.

DURING THE FIRST two years they served together, from 1972 to 1974, Brennan and Rehnquist voted on more than a dozen First Amendment cases, and differed on all but one. These were run-of-the-mill cases; all but two were appeals from decisions that upheld actions of local and state officials. The Court decided several cases without argument and with short, unsigned *per curiam* opinions, a slap on the wrist of lower-court judges. These relatively minor cases show the Court as a high school civics teacher, using a red pencil to underline the flagrant errors of dull students.

The two justices brought to this task very different approaches to the First Amendment. Brennan had written, in 1964, the most stirring defense of free expression since the time of Holmes and Brandeis. His opinion in *New York Times v. Sullivan* dealt with Alabama's libel law, but the issues were national and fundamental. In March 1960, shortly after black students launched a "sit-in" movement against segregation, a support group of prominent black entertainers and white liberals placed a full-page appeal for funds in the *New York Times*. One paragraph of the lengthy text focused on Montgomery, Alabama, charging that "truckloads of police armed with shotguns and tear-gas ringed the Alabama State College Campus." Although the ad contained several minor factual errors, it did not name any city official or make charges of unlawful conduct. Nonetheless, Montgomery's police commissioner, L. B. Sullivan, sued the *Times* for libel, and won a half-million-dollar judgment from an all-white jury.

Brennan wrote for a unanimous Court in reversing the libel award. He surveyed the history of the First Amendment, quoting James Madison's claim that "the censorial power is in the people over the Government, and not in the Government over the people." Reaching back two centuries, he struck down the Sedition Act of 1798, holding that "the restraint it imposed upon criticism of government and public officials, was inconsistent with the First Amendment." The justices were conscious of the potentially crippling effect of libel judgments against civil rights leaders. The case was decided, Brennan wrote, "against the background of a profound national commitment to the principle that debate on public issues should be uninhibited, robust, and wide-open, and that it may well include vehement, caustic, and sometimes unpleasantly sharp attacks on government and public officials." The *Sullivan* case became the standard for the Court's First Amendment jurisprudence.

Justice Rehnquist came to the Court without an articulated First Amendment philosophy, although his statements as a Justice Department official expressed hostility to political dissidents. His first opinion in free-speech cases involved the kind of "caustic" language that Brennan was willing to protect. Ruling jointly on three cases in 1972, the Court reversed state court decisions without argument. Each case involved a criminal conviction for using the term "motherfucker" in public. The Court relied on two recent opinions, which held that uttering the vulgar term—and the word "fuck" as well—could not be punished without a showing of "imminent" violence.

Dissenting from this denial of review, Rehnquist revealed a disdain for precedent, even cases decided the previous year. He dismissed the earlier opinions as examples of "a verbal game of logic-chopping" and argued that states should be able "to punish language of the sort used here by appropriate legislation." Rehnquist looked back thirty years for precedent, arguing that the term "motherfucker" was "lewd and obscene" and also "profane," and thus "clearly falls within the class of punishable utterances described in *Chaplinsky*."

The late 1960s and early 1970s produced a rash of "motherfucker" cases; Chief Justice Burger sniffed about "a disquieting deterioration in standards of taste and civility in speech." Brennan and Rehnquist disagreed in another such case, involving a newspaper that made caustic attacks on government officials. The offending paper, however, was not the august *New York Times* but *New Left Notes*, published by the radical Students for a Democratic Society. Barbara Papish, a University of Missouri journalism student, was expelled in 1969 for distributing SDS papers that included a cartoon depicting policemen raping the Statue of Liberty and an article with the headline "Motherfucker Acquitted," reporting the clearing on assault charges of an SDS member who belonged to an offshoot group called "Up Against the Wall, Motherfucker." School officials charged Papish with "indecent speech," and a lower court held that the paper was "obscene." Six justices summarily reversed the expulsion order in 1973, holding that "neither the political cartoon nor the headline story involved in this case can be labeled as constitutionally obscene or otherwise unprotected."

Justice Rehnquist wrote for three dissenters in *Papish v. Board of Curators*. He considered this a "fighting words" case, and turned again to *Chaplinsky* for precedent. Arguing that "the public use of the word 'M——f——' is 'lewd and obscene,' " he quoted Murphy's opinion that "such utterances are no essential part of any exposition of ideas," a statement Rehnquist said "applies with compelling force" to the *Papish* case. The *Chaplinsky* decision was limited to spoken, face-to-face epithets, and there was no evidence that the SDS paper incited "an immediate breach of the peace." Rehnquist, however, was clearly offended by its graphic vulgarity. He also deplored the fact that Papish "hawked her newspaper" near a memorial tower "dedicated to the memory of those students who died in the Armed Services in World Wars I and II," although the record showed that this was the central gathering spot on the campus.

These short but revealing dissents show that Rehnquist valued civility over free speech, and would reach the result he wanted by sweeping recent precedent from his path. After remand to a state court, one of the "motherfucker" cases returned for argument, and Brennan addressed the issue of vulgarity. The defendant in this Louisiana case, a black woman named Mallie Lewis, was convicted of using "obscene and opprobrious language" toward a white police officer who arrested her son. Brennan held that the statutory term "opprobrious" was overbroad and vague, and could be used to punish language that did not fall within the "fighting words" doctrine. Rehnquist joined the dissent of Justice Harry Blackmun, who complained that the overbreadth and vagueness doctrines "have become result-oriented rubberstamps" in the hands of the Court's liberals. The opinions in the "motherfucker" cases show that both sides could manipulate precedent to reach a desired result.

Rehnquist did prevail in one free-speech case with political impact. Captain Howard Levy, an Army doctor at Fort Jackson, South Carolina, was ordered in 1966 to train Special Forces troops in dermatology, his medical specialty. Levy was perhaps the Army's least suited officer. He went straight from medical school to service with virtually no military training, and he belonged to a radical political group that opposed the war. Instead of training the troops, he urged them to refuse service in Vietnam and said that "Special Forces personnel are liars and thieves and killers of peasants and murderers of women and children." He was charged under Article 134 of the Code of Military Justice of acting "to the prejudice of good order and discipline in the armed forces" and sentenced to three years at hard labor.

After losing ten court battles for review, including two rebuffs by the Supreme Court, Levy won a federal appellate decision that Article 134 was "void for vagueness." Ironically, the judges relied on the Supreme Court's "motherfucker" decisions for precedent. Rehnquist wrote for five justices who reversed the lower court in *Parker v. Levy*. His normal deference to civilian officials became a crisp military salute. "This Court has long recognized that the military is, by necessity, a specialized society separate from civilian society." Justice Holmes had written in *Schenck* that different standards applied to speech in wartime and peacetime. Rehnquist stretched this claim, arguing that the Army's "fundamental necessity for obedience, and the consequent necessity for imposition of discipline, may render permissible within the military that which would be constitutionally impermissible outside it." He thus sidestepped the troubling fact that Vietnam was not a declared war and Levy was not subject to wartime laws.

Under Rehnquist's command, the Court would not impose its vagueness doctrine on the military. In its place, he applied "the standard which applies to criminal statutes regulating economic affairs." He quoted an opinion dealing with the dairy industry, offering a standard "which supports the constitutionality of legislation" against vagueness challenges. Under this standard, Captain Levy "could have had no reasonable doubt that his public statements urging Negro enlisted men not to go to Vietnam" would prejudice "good order and discipline."

Three justices dissented from this bizarre application of dairy cases to military justice. Brennan joined the opinion of Justice Potter Stewart, who suggested that Rehnquist engaged "in an act of judicial fantasy." Stewart considered it unreasonable to assume that Levy, with virtually no military training, could have understood the meaning of Article 134, "even assuming that *anybody* could *ever* acquire such expertise." But the dissenters could not release Captain Levy, now cashiered from service, from Lewisburg Penitentiary.

FAR MORE PEOPLE use vulgar language, or denounce government policies, than deface or burn the American flag. But each is a form of expression, and the First Amendment plays no favorites. Measured by public reaction, however, flag desecration ranks near—or even above— such crimes as child abuse in provoking outrage. The reasons are obvious. Justice Holmes observed that "we live by symbols," and no symbol has more potency than the American flag. Many thousands of citizens have given their lives to defend the flag and the values it embodies. Suggesting that the First Amendment protects those who treat the flag with contempt strikes most Americans as a perversion of free speech.

Only the most foolhardy—or principled—lawmaker would vote against a flag-desecration bill. The legislatures of all but two states, in fact, have passed such laws. Much to their discomfort, unelected judges have been forced to decide challenges to these laws, most often when someone has been sentenced to jail for an act of flag abuse. During their years of service together, Justices Brennan and Rehnquist voted on four flag cases, and differed in each one.

The first two cases began in 1970 and were decided in 1974. They had very different facts, but the same outcome. One came from Leominster, Massachusetts, a working-class town with a large French Canadian population. Valarie Goguen was standing on a street corner, talking with friends, when a policeman walked by and noticed an American flag, about four by six inches, sewn to the seat of his blue jeans. The officer swore out a complaint that the young man had violated state law by treating "contemptuously the flag of the United States." Goguen was convicted by a jury and sentenced to six months in jail. There was no evidence he had any political motivation in sewing the flag to his pants. It seems clear that Goguen showed "contempt" by wearing the flag on the wrong part of his anatomy; wearing it over his heart would not likely have prompted his arrest.

The Supreme Court affirmed the ruling of a federal judge that the state law was both vague and overbroad. Justice Lewis Powell, who rarely strayed from the Court's center, avoided the First Amendment question and rested his majority opinion in *Smith v. Goguen* on the "vagueness" doctrine. He stressed the difficulty of defining "contempt" with enough precision to alert Goguen to the consequences of his act. Laws are vague, Powell noted, when they do not draw a clear line between lawful and unlawful behavior. A law against wearing flags on blue jeans may—and does—violate the First Amendment, but it is certainly not vague. Making "contempt" of the flag a crime, however, leaves to conjecture "what conduct may subject the actor to criminal prosecution."

Writing in dissent, Rehnquist brushed aside the vagueness issue and eagerly attacked the First Amendment defense. He faced two hurdles: the facts that Goguen owned the flag on his pants and that states normally cannot tell people how to dispose of private property. His creative search for precedent turned up laws dealing with land use, drug possession, firearms, and billboards. The government's interest in regulating such forms of private property, Rehnquist argued, outweighed the owners' "traditional property interest." If a state may regulate other forms of property, Rehnquist saw no reason why it may not "create a similar governmental interest in the flag by prohibiting even those who have purchased the physical object from impairing its physical integrity."

First Amendment doctrine requires that states show a "compelling interest" in regulating speech. These interests are normally limited to protection of public health and safety. Rehnquist raised the flag above the Court's "highly abstract, scholastic interpretation of the First Amendment." The flag's significance, he wrote, lies in "the deep emotional feelings it arouses in a large part of our citizenry" and its historic role as a symbol of national unity. To illustrate the "special place" of the flag in American history, he quoted Ralph Waldo Emerson and cited John Greenleaf Whittier, John Philip Sousa, and Francis Scott Key. He also noted "the photographs of the members of the United States Marine Corps raising the United States flag" on Iwo Jima in World War II.

The *Goguen* case allowed Rehnquist to ignore political issues and focus on preserving the "physical integrity of the flag." The next case, *Spence v. Washington*, forced an entirely different response. Harold Spence, a college student in Seattle, responded in May 1970 to the American invasion of Cambodia and the killing of four students at Kent State University by hanging a large American flag from his apartment window. He put a peace symbol on the flag with removable black tape. Three policemen saw the flag and arrested Spence under a state law that prohibited placing any "figure" or "design" on the flag. He told the jury that "I wanted people to know that I thought America stood for peace," but he was convicted nonetheless and sentenced to a suspended jail term.

This was an easy case for the six justices who reversed Spence's conviction in a *per curiam* opinion. His protest was clearly political and obviously an act of "symbolic speech." He had not damaged or desecrated his flag, and the state law clearly violated the First Amendment. But this was a tough case for Justice Rehnquist, who wrote for Chief Justice Burger and Justice White in dissent. He skipped the citations to Emerson and Whittier. He also ignored the political message on Spence's flag, blandly noting that "some forms of expression are not entitled to any protection at all under the First Amendment," citing an obscenity case. Forced to rummage for precedent, Rehnquist found a 1907 ruling that "Nebraska could prevent use of a flag representation on beer bottles," a case he admitted was decided without reference to the First Amendment. That case, he argued, held that flags could "not be turned into a common background for an endless variety of superimposed messages." Rehnquist was concerned with "the character, not the cloth, of the flag which the State seeks to protect." The flag, he said in both the *Goguen* and *Spence* dissents, was a "unique national symbol" and could not be touched by the First Amendment.

FIFTEEN YEARS PASSED before the Court faced another flag case. Passions aroused by Vietnam had cooled, but new targets of protest abounded. The right-wing policies of President Ronald Reagan provoked a new generation of protesters. Critics accused him of waging a "war on the poor" at home and arming death squads in Central America. One bumper sticker read "El Salvador is Spanish for Vietnam." The prospect of Reagan's reelection in 1984 attracted hundreds of demonstrators to Dallas, site of the Republican convention. They espoused many causes, and most were content to picket and distribute leaflets.

One small group, however, the Revolutionary Communist Youth Brigade, marched through downtown Dallas, chanting slogans and spray-painting the walls of corporate buildings. One marcher pulled an American flag from its pole outside a bank and handed it to Gregory Lee Johnson, who led the noisy band to City Hall. Closely watched by Dallas police, Johnson unfurled the flag, doused it with kerosene, and flicked a cigarette lighter. While the flag burned, the protesters chanted, "America, the red, white, and blue, we spit on you." No fights broke out, and the police did not intervene. One spectator, Daniel Walker, gathered the burned remains and buried them in his backyard. Police later arrested Johnson under a Texas law that punishes anyone who "desecrates" a flag with knowledge the act will "seriously offend" an observer. Walker told a jury he was offended by the flag burning, and Johnson received a one-year jail term.

A panel of state judges reversed the conviction, citing the *Goguen* and *Spence* decisions and holding that Johnson's act "was clearly 'speech' contemplated by the First Amendment." The Supreme Court accepted the state's appeal for review. Its ruling in *Texas v. Johnson*, issued in June 1989, surprised many people, probably Gregory Johnson the most. Since the 1974 flag cases, four reputed conservatives had joined the Court, now led by Chief Justice Rehnquist. The judicial balance had shifted to the right, but two newcomers—Antonin Scalia and Anthony Kennedy—confounded those who assumed they would line up with Rehnquist. They voted with the Court's remaining liberals—Brennan, Marshall, and Blackmun—to strike down the Texas law.

As the senior majority justice, Brennan assigned the Court's opinion to himself. A quarter century after his historic opinion in *New York Times v. Sullivan*, he reaffirmed the constitutional primacy of the First Amendment. Because "fundamental rights" of free expression were at stake, Brennan applied the *Carolene Products* test, requiring "the most exacting scrutiny" of challenged laws; only "compelling" state interests can pass this test. The state conceded that flag burning was symbolic speech, but asserted two "compelling" interests: preventing breaches of the peace and protecting the flag as a symbol of national unity. Brennan quickly disposed of the first claim. Johnson was not charged with breaching the peace, and states may not "ban the expression of certain disagreeable ideas on the unsupported presumption that their very disagreeableness will provoke violence."

Brennan addressed the "national unity" claim with a nod to Rehnquist, echoing the words of his *Goguen* dissent that accorded the flag a "special place" in public sentiment. But he argued that Gregory Johnson's act "will not endanger the special role played by our flag or the feelings it inspires." Paraphrasing the *Abrams* dissent of Justice Holmes seventy years earlier, Brennan wrote that "nobody can suppose that this one gesture of an unknown man will change our Nation's attitude toward its flag." He summarized his views in one sentence: "If there is a bedrock principle underlying the First Amendment, it is that the government may not prohibit the expression of an idea simply because society finds the idea itself offensive or disagreeable."

Brennan had no need to charm or cajole Scalia into the majority. Scalia has a "libertarian" streak that conflicts with Rehnquist's "statist" position in some—but not all—First Amendment cases. It is more likely that Brennan, the senior justice, lobbied for the vote of Kennedy, the junior justice. In a brief concurrence, Kennedy agreed with Brennan that "we are presented with a clear and simple statute to be judged against a pure command of the Constitution." But he confessed the personal toll the case exacted from him. "The hard fact is that sometimes we must make decisions we do not like," Kennedy wrote. "We make them because they are right, right in the sense that the law and the Constitution, as we see them, compel the result."

In his impassioned dissent, Rehnquist responded as if the Court were personally responsible for the death of the marines who died on Iwo Jima, fighting "hand to hand against thousands of Japanese." Rehnquist, who reportedly glared at Brennan when he read portions of his majority opinion from the bench, accused the senior justice in his dissent of giving a "patronizing civics lesson" to the Court. But the Chief Justice delivered his own civics lecture, devoting six pages to quotations from patriotic literature and poems, spanning American history from the Revolution to the Vietnam War. He again quoted Emerson's tribute to the "embattled farmers" who stood at the Concord bridge and "their flag to April's breeze unfurled." He sang the first verse of "The Star-Spangled Banner," and recited all sixty lines of John Greenleaf Whittier's epic poem, "Barbara Frietchie," including her immortal—and apocryphal—words, "Shoot, if you must, this old gray head, But spare your country's flag."

Rehnquist evaded the "strict scrutiny" test in his dissent, denying that it applied to *any* case. Without using the term, he argued that the state's compelling interest lay in the "unique position" of the flag in American history, which "justifies a governmental prohibition against flag burning" to protect the nation's symbol. Without citing the case record, Rehnquist also argued that Johnson's act "had a tendency to incite a breach of the peace." Searching for precedent, he cited three state cases holding that flag burning "is so inherently inflammatory that it may cause a breach of public order." But these cases were decided before *Goguen* and *Spence* and did not bind the Supreme Court.

Rehnquist dismissed the First Amendment claim by equating flag burning with "fighting words." Walter Chaplinsky, however, aimed his words at a particular policeman. Rehnquist admitted that Gregory Johnson meant to convey a "bitter dislike of his country." He was troubled that insults to one person could be punished, but not those addressed to millions. But he made clear his deference to elected officials, even in First Amendment cases. "Surely one of the high purposes of a democratic society," he wrote, "is to legislate against conduct that is regarded as evil and profoundly offensive to the majority of people—whether it be murder, embezzlement, pollution, or flag burning." In Rehnquist's mind, Johnson had murdered the American flag and deserved a prison term for his "evil" act.

Not since the school-prayer rulings of the early 1960s had the Supreme Court ignited such a firestorm of public outrage. Newspapers printed thousands of heated letters, and hundreds were reprinted in the *Congressional Record*. George Bush, whose 1988 campaign featured the flag, proposed a constitutional amendment to protect it. The House of Representatives passed a resolution condemning the decision without one dissenting vote. In the Senate, the leaders of both parties sponsored a similar resolution. "The Court's decision is wrong and should be corrected," said George Mitchell, the majority leader. Minority leader Robert Dole added that "there has been a lot of talk lately about how the Supreme Court has tilted right. Well, yesterday, the Court did not tilt right—it tilted wrong. Dead wrong." Only three senators voted no.

The campaign to amend the First Amendment ran out of steam after the speeches ended and second thoughts began. Nebraska Senator Bob Kerrey, who lost a leg in Vietnam and won a Medal of Honor, dampened the rhetorical flames with a dramatic speech against a constitutional amendment. "At first I was outraged by the Supreme Court's opinion," he said. Later, during the Fourth of July recess, he read the opinions. "I was surprised to discover that I found the majority argument to be reasonable, understandable and consistent with those values that I believe make America so wonderful." Kerrey responded to the "disappointing dissent" of Chief Justice Rehnquist with his own civics lecture. Recalling "the smell of my own burning flesh" on the battleground, he said that "I don't remember giving the safety of our flag anywhere near the thought that I gave the safety of my men."

By a slim margin, the Senate refused to amend the Constitution. Congress did, however, pass a Flag Protection Law that made it a federal crime to "knowingly mutilate, deface, physically defile, burn, maintain on the floor or ground, or trample upon any flag of the United States." Gregory Johnson promptly burned another flag, this time on the Capitol steps. But a group of Seattle radicals won the race to the Supreme Court in 1990. Justice Brennan wrote for the same majority of five in *United States v. Eichman,* striking down the federal law. By this time, even Rehnquist seemed tired of the issue. "Surely there are not many people who burn flags in this country," he told a lawyers' group after the decision. Now that "it has finally been established it is legal, there will be far fewer." He was right; protesters against the Gulf War in 1991 did not burn flags but waved them under the banner "Support Our Troops— Bring Them Home." Forms of protest change, but the First Amendment endures.

EIGHT

"UTTERLY WITHOUT REDEEMING SOCIAL IMPORTANCE"

WELL BEFORE the First Amendment was adopted, Benjamin Franklin wrote a spicy essay, "Advice to a Young Man on the Choice of a Mistress." The Founding Fathers were not a group of prudish Puritans in matters of sex, and many savored erotic literature. James Madison was known for "Rabelaisian anecdotes," and Thomas Jefferson denounced proposals that any book, even one considered obscene, "can become a subject of inquiry, and of criminal inquiry too." But the Puritan mentality has endured in American politics. In 1872, Congress passed a federal obscenity law "as a result of the efforts of that feverish Puritan, Anthony Comstock." This label was applied by lawyers for Samuel Roth, a New York publisher who was arrested by latter-day Comstocks for reprinting and selling copies of Benjamin Franklin's erotic writings.

Roth escaped a prison term after a judge dismissed the charges. He was convicted, however, in 1956 for offering to sell "obscene, indecent and filthy matter" to federal postal inspectors who used false names to order copies of *American Aphrodite* and other magazines with photographs of naked women. The prosecutor told the jurors that "if you want me and the post office inspectors to continue to work and fight to stop this kind of thing," they should convict Roth "as quickly as you possibly can." If Roth was acquitted, the prosecutor warned, "I can assure you that the sewers will open." The jury acted quickly and the judge sentenced Roth to five years in prison.

Roth's appeal to the Supreme Court tested the outer limits of the First Amendment. This case also tested the tolerance of Justice William Brennan. He supported the rights of political dissidents to speak and write against the government, even to advocate its violent overthrow. Brennan applied a stringent version of the "clear and present danger" test to political speech. But questions remained. Should this test be applied to pornography, expressed in words or pictures? Did erotic literature even qualify as "speech" under the First Amendment?

Brennan addressed these questions in *Roth v. United States,* writing in 1957 to uphold the conviction. It is unknown whether he was drafted by Chief Justice Warren, or volunteered for this opinion. In either case, he faced hostile fire on both sides. Solicitor General J. Lee Rankin supported the New York law for the federal government, while Abe Fortas and Morris Ernst filed briefs on behalf of publishers against the law. Politicians had already jumped on the issue. Tennessee Senator Estes Kefauver submitted a committee report in 1956 on "Pornographic Literature and Juvenile Delinquency." He decried "the deleterious effect that obscene and pornographic literature has on the minds of our young people." Kefauver expressed pleasure that postal inspectors had helped "to eradicate this menace to our youth" by legal action against purveyors of pornography.

Faced with unsettled questions, Brennan picked a careful path through a legal minefield. The First Amendment was fashioned, he wrote, "to assure unfettered interchange of ideas for the bringing about of political and social changes desired by the people." He agreed that "all ideas having even the slightest redeeming social importance" were protected from censorship. But this conception of the Constitution imposed a limiting condition on free expression. With little support from precedent, Brennan grounded his opinion on legislative history. He noted the "universal judgment" of every state and more than fifty nations that "obscenity should be restrained" by law. And he found "implicit in the history of the First Amendment" an agreement that obscenity was "utterly without redeeming social importance." Brennan concluded that "obscenity is not within the area of constitutionally protected speech or press."

Brennan could not ignore the argument of Roth's lawyers that obscenity, however defined, did not pose a "clear and present danger" to society. They quoted the judge who sentenced Roth to prison, who told jurors they could convict him for selling books that had "a tendency to excite lustful thoughts." Brennan answered this claim by citing two earlier Supreme Court opinions that dealt with "fighting words" and public disturbances. The *Chaplinsky* case held that "the social interest in order and morality" could justify restrictions on obscenity. And the Court ruled in *Beauharnais v. Illinois,* decided in 1952, that it was "unnecessary" to consider issues of "clear and present danger" in libel cases. Brennan was not bothered that both statements were *dicta,* with no force as precedent.

Holding that obscenity was "in the same class" as libel, he stitched the two opinions together and evaded arguments that prosecutors had shown no connection between "lustful thoughts" and antisocial actions in the Roth case.

Brennan faced another hard question in this case. Could the Supreme Court define "obscenity" with enough precision to tell jurors and judges who should go to prison? He framed his definition as a question: "whether to the average person, applying contemporary community standards, the dominant theme of the material taken as a whole appeals to prurient interest." These twenty-three words included five separate terms, each undefined, that gave jurors little help in deciding particular cases. Brennan admitted that "different juries may reach different results" in applying his test, but he considered that "one of the consequences we accept under our jury system." The first consequence of his opinion was that Samuel Roth went to prison for five years.

Both sides of the Court criticized Brennan's effort to define the indefinable. Justice John Harlan, a judicial conservative, wrote that Brennan painted "with such a broad brush" that judges could not decide what constituted obscenity in any particular case. Harlan did not understand how the Court could decide obscenity cases without "facing up to the tough individual problems of constitutional judgment involved in every obscenity case." From the liberal side, Justice William Douglas, joined by Hugo Black, objected to *any* restraint on free expression. Douglas said he could "understand the motives of the Anthony Comstocks who would impose Victorian standards on the community." He argued that any test of obscenity "that turns on what is offensive to the community's standards is too loose, too capricious, too destructive of freedom of expression to be squared with the First Amendment." Douglas predicted that juries would find obscene almost any work that aroused a "lustful thought" and that the Court would face an "endless" parade of obscenity cases.

Douglas was right. Pornography became an enticing political target in the Eisenhower years. Prosecutors found it easy to win convictions, and the Court was flooded with appeals. Justice Brennan found himself stuck to the tar baby of obscenity, as Chief Justice Warren continued to assign opinions to him. It was a thankless job, one he did not relish. He referred in one opinion to the Court's reviewing function as "a difficult, recurring, and unpleasant task." And he complained privately to a law clerk that "I'm sick and tired of seeing this goddamn shit." In practice, the justices became a national board of censorship. They even outfitted a screening room and set aside a "movie day" to watch films that had been judged obscene. This led to much tittering among the clerks, who rarely missed a showing. Justice Douglas, who never voted to uphold an obscenity conviction, refused on principle to attend. Brennan, however, argued that "whether a particular work is obscene necessarily implicates an issue of constitutional law. Such an issue, we think, must ultimately be decided by this Court."

So Brennan sat in the dark to watch films such as *The Lovers*, a French import that offended jurors in Cleveland Heights, Ohio. Nico Jacobellis was convicted and fined for showing the film at his theater. Writing for a unanimous Court in 1964, Brennan provided this review: " 'The Lovers' involves a woman bored with her life and marriage who abandons her husband and family for a young archaeologist with whom she has suddenly fallen in love. There is an explicit love scene in the last reel of the film, and the State's objections are based almost entirely upon that scene." The justices "have viewed the film," Brennan wrote, "and we conclude that it is not obscene" under the *Roth* test.

But if juries found films like *The Lovers* obscene, Brennan recognized that Harlan was correct in writing that *Roth* was phrased too broadly. He tried again, aiming his *Jacobellis v. Ohio* opinion at prosecutors and judges. He reminded them that "material dealing with sex in a manner that advocates ideas, or that has literary or scientific or artistic value or any other form of social importance, may not be branded as obscenity and denied the constitutional protection." Brennan also denied that "the standards of the particular local community" should govern in obscenity cases. "This is an incorrect reading of *Roth*," he wrote. The proper reading was that juries must apply "a national standard" to challenged works. "We have applied that standard to the motion picture in question," he wrote, noting that *The Lovers* had been "rated by at least two critics of national stature" as one of the best films of the year.

Brennan used the term "we" rather broadly, since only Justice Arthur Goldberg joined his *Jacobellis* opinion. The case showed, in fact, the difficulty in framing an obscenity test that could satisfy more than two people, to say nothing of defining a national standard. Even Goldberg wrote a separate opinion to express his distaste for censorship crusades. Justices Black and Douglas stated they would not uphold the conviction of anyone for showing *any* film. Justice Potter Stewart sympathized with Brennan's effort "to define what may be undefinable." He put the difficulty of defining "hard-core pornography" into a famous line: "I know it when I see it, and the motion picture involved in this case is not that."

After this honest if unartful opinion, Stewart became the butt of jokes. Irreverent law clerks, protected by darkness, would call out at "movie day" screenings, "That's it, I know it when I see it." Academic critics also poked fun at Stewart, but none has yet devised a test that avoids the trap of subjective judgment. The *Jacobellis* decision inflamed conservatives, who blamed the Warren Court for every social ill, and who demanded Warren's impeachment. Louisiana Representative Joe Waggoner called it "a banner day at the Court for sellers and traders in obscenities and pornography." The only litigants who "enjoy complete success before the present Court," he sniped, "are atheists, Communists, pornographers, and members of diverse, subversive groups."

The *Roth* test and its refinement in *Jacobellis* failed to stem the flood of obscenity cases. Brennan tried again in 1966, writing to reverse the decision of a Boston judge who banned the book *Memoirs of a Woman of Pleasure* (commonly known as *Fanny Hill*) from Massachusetts. *Fanny Hill* was written in 1750, and had been read by Bostonians for two centuries before the state attorney general—pressured by Citizens for Decent Literature—brought suit against the book itself. Brennan reviewed the trial testimony of five English professors, who agreed the bawdy book was a minor "work of art" with modest literary merit. He added to the *Roth* test this stringent requirement: "A book cannot be proscribed unless it is found to be *utterly* without redeeming social value." He felt the italics would make his message crystal clear.

However clear its new obscenity test, Brennan's opinion in *Memoirs v. Massachusetts* contained a loophole that opened a wide door for prosecutors. If books like *Fanny Hill* were "commercially exploited for the sake of prurient appeal," he wrote, this "might justify the conclusion that the book was utterly without redeeming social importance." How a book's advertising could determine its obscenity was a question Brennan evaded in the *Memoirs* case. But on the same day, he wrote for the Court in upholding the five-year prison sentence of Ralph Ginzburg for advertising a magazine called *Eros* and other erotic publications. Federal prosecutors stipulated that the circulars were not themselves obscene, and Brennan made no decision on this issue. He based his opinion on their "editorial formats" and Ginzburg's choice of cities for mailing circulars—he applied for postal permits in the Pennsylvania towns of Blue Ball and Intercourse. (Presumably, residents of these towns could not be prosecuted for their postmarks.) Holding that the "leer of the sensualist" permeated Ginzburg's advertising, Brennan held that nonobscene material could become obscene if "titillation" was employed to sell it.

Brennan did not escape a scolding from Justice Hugo Black, who wrote in dissent that Ginzburg had been "condemned to serve five years in prison for distributing printed matter about sex which neither Ginzburg nor anyone else could possibly have known to be criminal." The more troubling aspect of Brennan's opinion was that he referred to the one issue of *Eros* that prosecutors singled out in their indictment. This issue included erotic, but definitely not obscene, photographs of a nude couple embracing and kissing—the woman was white and the man was black. The combination of race and sex remained a potent issue in American society. Ralph Ginzburg really went to prison for breaking an ancient taboo.

DURING THE 1960s, pornography gave way as a political issue to civil rights and Vietnam. The justices had tired of watching dirty movies. They reversed most obscenity convictions without argument, even those for producing the kind of "hard-core" films that are shot in motel rooms. President Richard Nixon, however, exhorted Congress in 1969 to stop "the barrages of the filth peddlers" with stronger federal laws against "the flood of sex-oriented materials moving through the mails." Nixon's Justice Department also encouraged local prosecutors to revive the crusade against "smut peddlers." By the time William Rehnquist joined the Court in 1972, its docket included several obscenity cases. The new justice had no record on this issue, but he quickly joined the emerging conservative majority, led by Chief Justice Warren Burger, who epitomized the new Puritanism.

During his first year, Rehnquist agreed to write for the Court in a "nude dancing" case, *California v. LaRue*. The case involved state regulations designed to stamp out "sexual conduct between dancers and customers" in bars and clubs that were licensed to serve alcohol. Rehnquist reviewed the record in graphic detail, including testimony of "oral copulation" and "public masturbation in clubs," and of customers placing rolled-up bills "directly into the vagina of a female entertainer" while she danced. The lower court held that the regulations, which outlawed nudity and even "simulated" sexual acts, failed the *Roth* test and violated the First Amendment. California officials based their Supreme Court argument on the Twenty-first Amendment, which repealed Prohibition in 1933. On its face, this amendment simply allowed states to retain Prohibition or to permit "local option." But it granted the states no regulatory power over activities in licensed bars and clubs.

Conceding that the regulations banned conduct "that would not be found obscene" under the *Roth* test, Rehnquist took a detour around the First Amendment. The "broad sweep" of the Twenty-first, he wrote, conferred "something more than the normal state authority over public health, welfare, and morals." For Rehnquist, that "something more" included power to prohibit "the sort of bacchanalian revelries" that flourished in bottomless bars. He cited for authority his favorite case, *Williamson v. Lee Optical*, which dealt with regulation of the eyeglass industry. The "sordid" nature of the "gross sexuality" in the bars was clear to his eyes.

Justice Brennan, who dissented with Douglas and Marshall, made three points in his brief rebuttal. First, the state law "clearly applies to some speech protected by the First Amendment," as Rehnquist conceded. Second, "by requiring the owner of a nightclub to forgo the exercise" of these rights, "the State has imposed an unconstitutional condition on the grant of a license." And third, nothing in the language or history of the Twenty-first Amendment authorizes states to use their licensing power to ban "protected, even if distasteful, forms of expression."

With Burger at the helm, the conservative majority softened the *Roth* test in 1973 to help prosecutors win convictions. Writing for the Court in *Miller v. California*, the Chief Justice rejected the standard that material must be "utterly without redeeming social importance" to be found obscene. He fashioned a new three-part test: those works are obscene "which, taken as a whole, appeal to the prurient interest in sex, which portray sexual conduct in a patently offensive way, and which, taken as a whole, do not have serious literary, artistic, political, or scientific value." Although he disclaimed any intention "to propose regulatory schemes for the States," Burger drafted a model obscenity law to guide lawmakers. An example of "what a state statute could define" as criminal, he wrote, were "patently offensive representations or descriptions of ultimate sexual acts, normal or perverted, actual or simulated." He also replaced the "national community" standard of obscenity, which Brennan adopted in his *Jacobellis* opinion, with a "statewide" standard. Burger did not see why "the people of Maine or Mississippi" must accept "conduct found tolerable in Las Vegas, or New York City." He omitted his home state of Minnesota, perhaps to avoid any hint of bias.

Justice Brennan and other critics of the new *Miller* test argued that it would impose the sexual tastes and values of small-town jurors on the entire nation. As Brennan predicted, the Court soon faced a barrage of cases that raised issues of "community" standards on sex. Two cases, decided on the same day in June 1974, illustrate the complexity of the judicial burden. Rehnquist wrote for the Court in both cases. In one, Billy Jenkins was convicted in the small town of Albany, Georgia, for showing the film *Carnal Knowledge* in his movie theater. This was not a "motel movie," but a big-budget Hollywood film starring Jack Nicholson and Ann-Margret.

Seeing the film on "movie day" convinced even Burger to join the unanimous opinion in *Jenkins v. Georgia*, reversing the conviction. The film included the simulation of intercourse, but Rehnquist tactfully wrote that "the camera does not focus on the bodies of the actors at such times." His opinion sounded like Brennan's in *Jacobellis*, noting that the film appeared on many "Ten Best" lists and that Ann-Margret won an Academy Award nomination for her role. "Our own viewing of the film satisfies us that 'Carnal Knowledge' could not be found under the *Miller* standards to depict sexual conduct in a patently offensive way," he wrote. Brennan could not resist the temptation to point out in concurrence that the outcome depended on whether "at least five members of this Court" considered the film obscene under "inevitably obscure standards." This was hardly the way, he felt, to decide constitutional questions.

The First Amendment protects Hollywood films with simulated intercourse, but not pictures that show actual intercourse. That was the Court's holding in the second case, *Hamling v. United States*. This case followed Nixon's call for federal prosecutors to use the post office as an ally. William Hamling, along with several co-defendants, was convicted for mailing copies of the *Illustrated Presidential Report of the Commission on Obscenity and Pornography* to a post office box in San Diego, California. Ironically, this government report had concluded that pornography was *not* linked to criminal behavior such as rape and child molestation. Hamling had added to the dry text a set of explicit pictures of sexual acts, "as examples of the type of subject matter discussed" by the commissioners. Federal prosecutors did not indict Hamling in Los Angeles, where he mailed his books; they carefully picked San Diego as a conservative bastion, and excluded anyone under twenty-five from the jury.

Rehnquist wrote for a bare majority in *Hamling*, holding that the book's illustrations were "patently offensive" to San Diego residents. This was a strange opinion in several ways. The trial judge had instructed jurors to apply a "national standard," while Rehnquist argued for a "San Diego" standard. He simply inserted his own set of instructions. "A juror is entitled to draw on his own knowledge of the views of the average person in the community or vicinage from which he comes," he wrote, in deciding what is obscene. Rehnquist stretched the *Miller* standard on another issue. Some pictures in the *Illustrated Report* depicted homosexual acts; jurors were instructed to consider whether these pictures appealed to the "prurient interest of a specifically defined deviant group" such as homosexuals. How members of an admittedly "average" group could define the prurient interests of homosexuals, free of prejudice or stereotype, was a question Rehnquist evaded. In fact, he quoted from *Miller* a holding that "community standards" did *not* apply to material "aimed at a deviant group" by its publishers. He simply ignored this discrepancy between the two opinions.

Brennan aimed his *Hamling* dissent at the "community standards" issue. "National distributors choosing to send their products in interstate travels," he wrote, "will be forced to cope with the community standards of every hamlet into which their goods may wander." Although he argued for a "national standard" on obscenity, Brennan switched sides to criticize the trial judge for excluding from evidence a survey of San Diego residents showing that "a substantial majority of the 718 persons interviewed" did not object to Hamling's book. The judge told Hamling's lawyer he must "stay with your national standard." Rehnquist upheld this ruling in his opinion. Brennan attacked the "palpable absurdity" of calling for a "community standard" and rejecting evidence about community opinion on the material in question. He accused Rehnquist of judicial sleight of hand. "It is abundantly clear," he wrote, "that petitioners' convictions are sustained upon a charge wholly different from that upon which they were tried."

The *Jenkins* case showed that virtually any depiction of sex will offend someone. And *Hamling* revealed the Court's deep split over definitions of obscenity. Together, they promised an unending stream of petitions. Between 1974 and 1990, when Justice Brennan retired, the Court issued more than thirty opinions in obscenity cases. Two cases illustrate the continuing differences of Brennan and Rehnquist. One involved a road version of the Broadway rock musical *Hair*. This tribute to the "Age of Aquarius" included nudity and acts of simulated sex. It had played without legal reaction in more than 140 cities, including Memphis and Nashville in Tennessee. But the directors of the Chattanooga municipal theater banned the musical in 1971. The New York producers of *Hair* sued the theater board, whose chairman explained to a federal judge that only "productions which are clean and healthful and culturally uplifting" could appear on the public stage. The judge empaneled an "advisory jury," which concluded that *Hair* was obscene.

Justice Harry Blackmun wrote for the Court in *Southeastern Promotions v. Conrad*, reversing the lower court in 1975. He avoided the obscenity issue, basing his opinion on the "narrow ground" that the board's action constituted a "prior restraint" and did not offer the producers even "minimal procedural safeguards" against censorship. Joined in dissent by Justice Byron White, Rehnquist supported the power of Chattanooga officials to reserve the city theater "as a place for entertaining the whole family." It was not "unreasonable" to ban productions that might "offend any substantial number of potential theatergoers," he added. Rehnquist tried to have his cake and eat it too. He disclaimed any opinion as to whether *Hair* was obscene, but he also accused the majority of "the rather novel feat of elevating obscene productions to a preferred position under the First Amendment."

Since the Supreme Court adopted the *Miller* test in 1973, the national "war on pornography" has shifted to local skirmishes. The most important factor has been the shift in public opinion from revulsion to tolerance of sexually explicit materials. Most people simply don't care what their neighbors watch on VCRs. At the same time, they want to keep "adult stores" out of residential neighborhoods, much as they oppose halfway houses for criminals and mental patients. "Family values" are linked to "property values" in all these cases.

Many cities have used their zoning powers to segregate the sex industry from any "family dwelling, church, park, or school," to quote the ordinance adopted in 1980 by Renton, Washington. This law, requiring that "adult theaters" be located at least 1,000 feet from these protected areas, confined them to 5 percent of the city's acreage. A federal appellate court, which struck down the law, found that "practically none" of this land was available for sale or lease and that no "commercially viable" sites existed for adult theaters in Renton. The city was sued in 1982 by Playtime Theaters, which had been denied a licence to operate in downtown Renton.

Justice Rehnquist had been one of two dissenters in *Southeastern Pro-*

motions. But he commanded a majority of seven in *Renton v. Playtime Theaters*. His opinion rejected charges the city had acted to suppress the "content" of sexually explicit films. Rehnquist wrote that the ordinance was aimed "at the *secondary effects* of such theaters on the surrounding community." He cited no evidence of what those effects might be, other than quoting an opinion of the Washington Supreme Court that adult theaters "contribute to neighborhood blight." The theater owners had argued that the law allowed massage parlors and adult bookstores to operate in downtown Renton, while they were relegated to the outskirts. Shedding his judicial robe, Rehnquist suggested to Renton lawmakers that the city might "amend its ordinance to include other kinds of adult businesses that have been shown to produce the same kinds of secondary effects as adult theaters." Again, he offered no evidence of these effects. He simply cited his favorite case, *Williamson v. Lee Optical*, which allowed him to disregard the lack of evidence. What mattered to Rehnquist was not the First Amendment but the power of cities to protect "the quality of life in the community at large" from pornography.

In his last major obscenity opinion, Brennan noted that adult bookstores were not affected by the ban on movie theaters. This distinction, he wrote, showed that the law "was aimed at the *content* of the films shown in adult movie theaters." Brennan dismissed Rehnquist's citation to the *Williamson* case, which applied only to "social and economic legislation." When the First Amendment was involved, he wrote, "this one-step-at-a-time analysis is wholly inappropriate." Brennan also disparaged the "findings" of the Renton city council on the "secondary effects" of adult theaters. He noted that city officials were "unable to recount any testimony as to how adult movie theaters" affected residential areas. He concluded that "the ordinance is patently unconstitutional."

With this opinion, Brennan left the issue with a weary sigh. Unlike Douglas and Black, he had never taken an "absolutist" stand. He argued from beginning to end that obscenity was not protected by the First Amendment. This position forced Brennan, as a conscientious justice, to attempt a definition of obscenity that could draw a line between *Carnal Knowledge* and *Debbie Does Dallas*. His ultimate failure is no reflection on his skill. No other justice has ever succeeded at this Procrustean task.

THE FIRST AMENDMENT protects both freedom of speech and that of the press from official restriction. The line between verbal and written expression is often fuzzy. A newspaper article is simply another kind of speech. Indeed, newspaper articles most often repeat the words of people who say something newsworthy. And television has become part of "the press," even though it transmits words directly. But the Framers provided special protection to the press for a reason: its role in educating the citizenry about public issues. "When the press is free, and every man is able to read, all is safe," Thomas Jefferson assured his countrymen in 1816. Two decades later, Alexis de Tocqueville reported that not a single American "has as yet dared to propose any restrictions to the liberty of the press."

Jefferson substituted wishes for reality, and Tocqueville was simply wrong, having ignored the Sedition Act of 1798. Over the past two centuries, the press has been restricted in many ways, from "prior restraints" on publication to punishment for libelous statements. During the Warren Court era, however, the Supreme Court shielded the press from the cross-fire of political battles over civil rights and other explosive issues. The high-water mark of press protection came in 1964, with Justice Brennan's opinion in *New York Times v. Sullivan*. Holding that "neither factual error nor defamatory content suffices to remove the constitutional shield from criticism of official conduct," Brennan erected what he hoped was an impregnable barrier to assaults on the press.

Time showed that he was mistaken. Ruling in 1974, the Court decided that the John Birch Society had libeled a Chicago lawyer, Elmer Gertz, by falsely accusing him of Communist ties. Writing for a bare majority in upholding a substantial damage award to Gertz, Justice Lewis Powell held that he was not a "public figure" and that the *Sullivan* decision was "inapplicable" to cases involving private individuals. Brennan objected to this judicial surgery on his opinion, which he considered applicable to *every* libel case. The decision in *Gertz v. Welch* had an odd alignment of justices. Thurgood Marshall voted with Rehnquist in the majority, while Chief Justice Burger joined Brennan in dissent. The most likely explanation for this unlikely pairing is that Marshall had often been denounced as a radical and sympathized with Gertz, and that Burger felt there was some substance to the charges.

Two years later, Rehnquist spoke for the Court in extending the *Gertz* decision to reporting on court proceedings. The facts in *Time v. Firestone* were spicy, to say the least. Mary Alice Sullivan and Russell Firestone were married in 1961 and separated in 1964. Russell was heir to the Firestone tire fortune, and the couple lived in luxury in Palm Beach,

Florida. Their divorce battle attracted reporters like flies to honey. In his opinion, the trial judge recounted testimony that Mary Alice's extramarital affairs "would have made Dr. Freud's hair curl." He also held that Russell "was guilty of bounding from one bedpartner to another with the erotic zest of a satyr."

In a one-paragraph "Milestones" item, *Time* magazine reported that the divorce was granted "on grounds of extreme cruelty and adultery." This was not quite true, since the judge decided the case without making any findings on this issue. The *Time* report left unclear which spouse had been accused of these acts. Mary Alice Firestone, however, claimed that *Time* had libeled her; a jury agreed and awarded her one hundred thousand dollars in damages. Rehnquist wrote for the Court in holding that the jurors "properly could have found the 'Milestones' item to be false." Because Ms. Firestone was not a "public figure" under the *Gertz* standard, the jury was entitled to award her damages. Rehnquist concluded that no "blanket privilege for reports of judicial proceedings is to be found in the Constitution."

Brennan concealed his outrage with judicious language. "At stake in the present case," he wrote, "is the ability of the press to report to the citizenry the events transpiring in the Nation's judicial system." Brennan admitted "the probability of inadvertent error" in such reporting. But the First Amendment, he wrote, "insulates from defamation liability a margin for error sufficient to ensure the avoidance of crippling press self-censorship in the field of reporting public judicial affairs." In truth, nobody could say for sure whether *Time* had libeled *either* of the Firestones.

Another press issue that divided Brennan and Rehnquist involved a judge's decision to close a murder trial in Richmond, Virginia, to the public. This was the fourth trial of the defendant, accused of a gruesome murder. The first trial ended in conviction, but an appellate court held that procedural errors required a retrial, which ended with a hung jury, as did the third trial. Concerned that extensive publicity could hinder jury selection, both the defense lawyer and prosecutor asked the judge to bar the public from the courtroom. The Richmond newspapers sued the state, arguing that the press has a First Amendment right of access to all judicial proceedings. Seven justices agreed in 1980 with the newspapers—Lewis Powell, a Richmond native, did not vote—but they could not agree on the proper approach. *Richmond Newspapers v. Vir-*

ginia wound up with eight separate opinions, including Rehnquist's solo dissent.

Chief Justice Burger, who was no fan of the press, sounded like John Peter Zenger in upholding "the media claim of functioning as surrogates for the public" in reporting on trials. Citing an "unbroken, uncontradicted history," Burger wrote that "a presumption of openness inheres in the very nature of a criminal trial under our system of justice." His opinion even dusted off the Ninth Amendment, which adds to the Constitution's enumerated rights "others retained by the people." Brennan used his concurrence to argue that the First Amendment, standing alone, "secures the public an independent right of access to trial proceedings." Unlike Burger, he did not believe the Free Press clause needed help from any other amendments.

The year before this decision, Rehnquist had stated his conviction that *none* of the amendments, separately or jointly, grant a right of public access to judicial proceedings. "And I most certainly do not believe that the Ninth Amendment confers upon us any such power to review orders of state trial judges closing trials," he added in his *Richmond Newspapers* dissent, just in case anyone might doubt his position. He also delivered a sermon on the virtue of federalism and the vice of judicial interference with states' rights. Accusing his colleagues of arrogating to themselves "the ultimate decisionmaking power" over the states, he wrote that "it is basically unhealthy to have so much authority concentrated in a small group of lawyers who have been appointed to the Supreme Court and enjoy virtual life tenure." He suggested that the Court had sinned ever since 1803, when Chief Justice John Marshall defended judicial review in *Marbury v. Madison*. Nothing in that historic opinion, Rehnquist wrote, "requires that this Court through ever-broadening use of the Supremacy Clause smother a healthy pluralism which would ordinarily exist in a national government embracing 50 States." He did not say what prompted his sermon. Perhaps he was responding to Burger's apostasy in writing that "certain unarticulated rights are implicit in enumerated guarantees" of the Constitution, including a "privacy" right that Rehnquist denied could be found anywhere in that document.

THE FIRST AMENDMENT was designed to protect authors and publishers from official censorship. But does it confer on the public a corollary right to read those works, free of censorship? This is a harder question, since libraries cannot possibly carry every book and magazine. Choices must be made, especially in school libraries, and librarians and teachers make their decisions fully aware that some works are controversial. The American Library Association compiles lists of hundreds of book-banning efforts each year in public schools. Most are prompted by conservatives who object to "indecent" language, but even liberals have objected to classics like *Huckleberry Finn* because Mark Twain used the word "nigger."

The Supreme Court faced one typical case in 1982, from the New York town of Island Trees on Long Island. Professed conservatives dominated the school board, and in 1975 the board president, Richard Ahrens, picked up at a political meeting a list of "objectionable" books. A search revealed that the high school library contained nine of the listed books, including works by Kurt Vonnegut, Langston Hughes, Richard Wright, and Bernard Malamud. Ahrens ordered the books removed from library shelves, over the school superintendent's warning of "the public furor" that would certainly result. He was right; someone—probably a librarian—alerted the press and the town was quickly aflame with debate. The board issued a press release that called the banned books "anti-American, anti-Christian, anti-Semitic, and just plain filthy." Steven Pico, an Island Trees high school student, contacted the American Civil Liberties Union and placed his name on a lawsuit against the board.

Without holding a trial, a federal district judge ruled that the board was entitled to act on "its conservative educational philosophy" in removing books it considered "vulgar, immoral, and in bad taste" from the library. An appellate panel reversed and remanded the case for a trial. The Supreme Court normally avoids cases without a trial record, but the briefs in *Island Trees v. Pico* included affidavits by Ahrens and other board members, and excerpts from the banned books. Justice Brennan, writing for the Court, posed the "narrow" questions before the justices: "Does the First Amendment impose *any* limitations" on the board's power to remove books from school libraries? If so, does the record show the board "might have exceeded those limitations"?

Brennan stressed the Court's historic deference to school officials in shaping curriculum and inculcating students with "community values." But his opinion soon widened into an expansive reading of the First Amendment as a guarantee of the right to receive information and ideas. He grounded this "inherent corollary of the rights of free speech and

press" on two propositions. "First, the right to receive ideas follows in-
eluctably from the *sender's* First Amendment right to send them," he
wrote. "More importantly, the right to receive ideas is a necessary pred-
icate to the *recipient's* meaningful exercise" of these rights. And for students, the "school library is the principal locus of such freedom."

Having granted Steven Pico the right to look for ideas in the school
library, Brennan considered whether the board had abridged that right.
He focused on admissions that books were banned for "anti-American"
sentiments; Richard Ahrens cited as evidence a book "which notes at one
point that George Washington was a slaveholder." The board also ignored
the district's book-selection procedures. This combination of suspect motives and "highly irregular" process convinced Brennan that the case
should return to the district court for trial. He could not, however,
persuade a majority to join his broad opinion. Justice Byron White added
a fifth vote to the remand order but disputed the need to discuss First
Amendment issues before trial.

One former school-board president, Justice Lewis Powell, chided Brennan for allowing "a debilitating encroachment upon the institutions of a
free people." What really bothered Powell was the language in the banned
books. He appended to his dissent seven pages of excerpts, including
dozens of uses of "fuck" and its cousins. Chief Justice Burger, another
dissenter, finally ended his crusade to keep that word from the pages of
the Court's opinions.

Justice Rehnquist did not conceal his scorn for Brennan's effort to
constitutionalize a "right to read." To him, this was the height of judicial
lawmaking. Rehnquist was satisfied that the banned books "contained
demonstrable amounts of vulgarity and profanity" and that the board
could remove them from the library. He denounced the plurality opinion
as "analytically unsound and internally inconsistent," and as a "confusing, discursive exegesis" on constitutional issues. And he went after Brennan personally. Rehnquist objected to "Justice Brennan's combing
through the record" for "bits and snatches of dispute" in the case. "I
entirely disagree with Justice Brennan's treatment of the constitutional
issue," he wrote, and "I also disagree with his opinion for the entirely
separate reason that it is not remotely tailored to the facts presented by
this case." Rehnquist called Brennan's opinion "wholly fatuous" and
"supported neither by logic nor authority" in its reliance on "transparently
thin" precedent. The personal tone of the dissent revealed Rehnquist's
frustration that Brennan had once again defeated the Court's conserva-

tives, and had again expanded a Constitution they were determined to shrink.

Brennan's failure to find a majority in *Island Trees* returned to haunt him in 1988. The Court faced another high school First Amendment case, this one from the St. Louis suburb of Hazelwood, Missouri. Students in the journalism class at Hazelwood East High School put out a weekly paper called *Spectrum*. In May 1983, the journalism teacher delivered page proofs of the next issue to Robert Reynolds, the school's principal. Reynolds looked them over and ordered that two articles be removed. One described the experiences of three Hazelwood students with pregnancy; the other discussed the impact of divorce on students. Both articles included quotes from students, but neither used real names.

After *Spectrum* was published with two blank pages, Kathy Kuhlmeier and two other editors contacted the American Civil Liberties Union. Like Steven Pico, Kathy wound up with her name on a lawsuit against the school board. But unlike the *Island Trees* case, this suit was tried and resulted in an appellate decision that found "no evidence in the record" that the censored articles "would have materially disrupted classwork or given rise to substantial disorder in the school." The appellate judges relied on the Supreme Court's 1969 decision in *Tinker v. Des Moines*, holding that "students are entitled to freedom of expression of their views" on controversial issues. That case supported the right of students to wear black armbands to protest the Vietnam War.

The Supreme Court reversed the appellate panel by a 5–3 vote; Justice Powell had recently retired. Justice Byron White wrote for the majority. He had concurred with the Court's judgment in the *Island Trees* case, and had earlier joined the *Tinker* opinion, which drew a vehement dissent from Justice Hugo Black. Almost two decades later, White quoted approvingly in his *Hazelwood v. Kuhlmeier* opinion from Black's dissent. Nothing in the Constitution compelled officials to "surrender control of the American public school system" to students, Black had written. That statement was "equally relevant to the instant case," White said.

Rehnquist—now the Chief Justice—joined White's opinion, which distinguished *Tinker* from *Hazelwood*. Whether schools must "tolerate particular student speech" was a different question, White wrote, than "whether the First Amendment requires a school affirmatively to promote particular student speech." White found the distinction in faculty supervision of the Hazelwood journalism class that produced *Spectrum*.

The *Tinker* decision, however, gave White some trouble. Hazelwood school officials had adopted a statement that "only speech that 'materially and substantially interferes with the requirements of appropriate discipline' can be found unacceptable" for publication in *Spectrum*. The internal quotation came directly from the *Tinker* decision. White dodged the issue by holding that "school officials never intended to designate *Spectrum* as a public forum" and were not bound by their statement. He concluded that public schools are entitled to insist on "high standards for the student speech that is disseminated under its auspices" and to censor speech that officials consider "biased or prejudiced, vulgar or profane, or unsuitable for immature audiences." And judges, he argued, should give "substantial deference" to school officials and stay out of classrooms unless the First Amendment is "directly and sharply" in peril.

Justice John Stevens also shifted sides from *Island Trees* to *Hazelwood*, leaving Brennan to write for only Marshall and Blackmun in dissent. His opinion avoided personal references, but did not conceal strong feelings. The students in Hazelwood's journalism class, he wrote, "expected a civics lesson" in learning to report on their school's activities. Their expectations were based on a promise by school officials to honor the *Tinker* standard in their paper. But their hopes had been dashed. "In my view the principal broke more than a promise," Brennan wrote. "He violated the First Amendment's prohibitions against censorship of any student expression that neither disrupts classwork nor invades the rights of others," he added.

Brennan strenuously disagreed with White's treatment of *Tinker*. "The Court does not, for it cannot, purport to discern from our precedents the distinction it creates" between student-initiated and school-sponsored expression. Citing the examples White offered, Brennan agreed that school officials could reject bad writing. "But we need not abandon *Tinker* to reach that conclusion; we need only apply it." In his *Island Trees* dissent, Rehnquist had accused Brennan of combing the record for "bits and snatches" of evidence for his argument. Brennan turned the tables in *Hazelwood*, accusing White of relying on "bits of testimony" to claim that Reynolds gave the students a "pedagogical lesson" in good journalism. In Brennan's view, Reynolds acted as chief of the school's "thought police" in censoring articles he considered inappropriate for students. He ended his dissent with a reprimand: "The young men and women of

Hazelwood East expected a civics lesson, but not the one the Court teaches them today."

Between them, the *Island Trees* and *Hazelwood* cases illustrate the root of the conflict between Brennan and Rehnquist over the Constitution. Put simply, Brennan exalts the individual and Rehnquist defers to the state. One further press case shows that the two justices could agree when "state action" was not a factor in the First Amendment equation. Libel actions generally involve private parties, but the antagonists in *Hustler Magazine v. Falwell* were noted—even notorious—public figures. This lawsuit pitted Larry Flynt, publisher of a raunchy sex magazine, against the Reverend Jerry Falwell, head of the Moral Majority. It began when *Hustler*, copying the format of advertisements for Campari liqueur, printed a "parody ad" that portrayed Falwell engaging in sex with his mother in an outhouse. The trial judge dismissed Falwell's libel claim, ruling that no reader could possibly interpret the ad as anything but parody. However, a Virginia jury awarded Falwell two hundred thousand dollars for the "intentional infliction of emotional distress" imposed on him by Flynt.

Brennan and Rehnquist became judicial bedfellows in this case. Exercising his prerogative as Chief Justice in this unanimous decision, Rehnquist assigned the opinion to himself. The *Carnal Knowledge* case had demonstrated his tolerance of ribald humor. Nonetheless, in twenty earlier libel and invasion-of-privacy cases, Rehnquist had voted against the press in each one. Two factors seem to explain his vote in this case. One is that Rehnquist loves practical jokes and laughs easily, in contrast to his prudish predecessor, Warren Burger. Second, he appreciates political satire and caricature, ranging back to depictions of George Washington as an ass. His opinion quoted one scholar's statement that political cartoons are "as unwelcome as a bee sting" to their victims. Jerry Falwell was certainly stung, but the culprit was just a cartoon.

Rehnquist sounded almost like Brennan in his *Hustler* opinion. "At the heart of the First Amendment," he wrote, "is the recognition of the fundamental importance of the free flow of ideas and opinions on matters of public interest and concern." He went out of his way to quote Brennan's opinion in *New York Times v. Sullivan* and lauded the role of "robust political debate" in American society. Many commentators responded to Rehnquist's opinion with raised eyebrows. Were his expressions sincere or cynical? Was this opinion a harbinger of a "new Rehnquist" or just an aberration? Most likely, the *Hustler* opinion reflected only his appreciation for a good joke. But on one day, at least, Rehnquist and Brennan signed the same opinion.

THE AMERICAN TRADITION of "robust political debate" is not confined to speeches and articles. It often spills into the streets, with the message on a placard. People march and picket to promote their causes. The First Amendment extends its protection to "the right of the people peaceably to assemble, and to petition the government for a redress of grievances." That right, however, has always been subject to the government's duty to protect the public safety and welfare. The Supreme Court has long upheld "reasonable" regulations of the "time, place, and manner" of public assemblies. But it has struck down efforts to censor the content of messages expressed by picketers and leafleters. In 1963, the Court reversed the convictions of civil rights protesters who carried signs that read "I Am Proud to Be a Negro." The justices have also upheld the right of Klansmen to parade with signs that say "Niggers Go Back to Africa." The doctrine of "content neutrality" applies, the Court has said many times, not only to "pure" speech but to public assembly as well.

Most of the Court's "right of assembly" cases arose from the civil rights movement of the 1960s. By the time Justice Rehnquist arrived in 1972, precedent was firm, and later cases involved leftover issues. Nonetheless, he ruled for the government in most of these cases. One came from the dying embers of Martin Luther King's futile campaign in 1966 to break the grip of housing and school segregation on Chicago. A decade after King left the city in despair, a militant group called the Committee Against Racism picketed the home of Mayor Michael Bilandic, carrying placards that protested his refusal to support busing as a means of school integration. The demonstration was peaceful, but Roy Brown and other marchers were arrested under a state law that banned picketing "before or about the residence or dwelling of any person." The law, however, exempted picketing in labor disputes. A federal appellate panel ruled that it violated the First Amendment, and the Cook County attorney, Bernard Carey, appealed to the Supreme Court.

Justice Brennan considered this a simple case. His majority opinion in *Carey v. Brown*, issued in 1980, noted that "this is not the first instance" the Court faced a law that banned picketing "on the basis of the placard's message." He cited a 1972 decision in a similar case, also from Chicago, striking down a law that barred picketing at schools except in labor disputes. Both laws, he wrote, adopted a "content-based distinction" between the motives of picketers and thus violated the Fourteenth Amendment's Equal Protection clause. The state claimed, however, that privacy in the home deserved special protection. Brennan rejected this argument. By allowing labor picketing, even of homes, the state undermined its asserted "interest in maintaining domestic tranquility." The First Amendment did not shield a public official, even in his home, from "a challenge to his views on significant issues of social and economic policy," Brennan concluded.

Writing for three dissenters, Rehnquist argued that Brennan had placed states in a Catch-22 dilemma. They must either ban all residential picketing or bar none. Rehnquist felt strongly that homes deserved more protection than schools and other public buildings. The First Amendment did not stand in the way. "Time after time," he wrote, "the States have been assured that they may properly promote residential privacy even though free expression must be reduced."

Eight years after this decision, the Court had changed and Brennan lost his majority in a similar case. This dispute arose in the Milwaukee suburb of Brookfield, close to Rehnquist's hometown. The case reflected the growing tensions of the abortion controversy. Dr. Benjamin Victoria performed abortions, and members of "pro-life" groups began picketing his home in April 1985. They carried placards that read "Abortion Is Legal Murder" and warned children to stay away from the "baby killer." The protesters shouted slogans and once blocked access to the doctor's house, although they were not arrested for harassment or trespassing. The town council quickly adopted an ordinance that banned all residential picketing. Threatened with arrest, Sandra Schultz and fellow protesters filed suit against Russell Frisby, the council president, and other town officials. A federal district judge and an appellate panel both ruled against the ordinance on First Amendment grounds.

The Supreme Court reversed these rulings in *Frisby v. Schultz*, decided in 1988. Chief Justice Rehnquist joined the opinion of Justice Sandra O'Connor, who admitted that the ordinance affected "the core of the First Amendment" by banning picketing "on an issue of public concern." But "the protection of residential privacy" outweighed the rights of protesters. "There simply is no right to force speech into the home of an unwilling listener," O'Connor argued. She quoted Rehnquist's *Carey* dissent on the values of "family privacy and truly domestic tranquillity." And she rejected claims that the picketers had directed their message to the public.

Their goal was not "to disseminate a message to the general public, but to intrude upon the targeted resident, and to do so in an especially offensive way." The opinion focused less on the picketers' disruptive tactics—covered by other laws—than on objections of "the unwilling residential listener" to their message.

Although he wrote in dissent, Justice Brennan professed to find only one flaw in the majority opinion. He agreed with O'Connor that Brookfield residents had a right "to be left alone in their homes." And he agreed that the First Amendment did not allow protesters "to imprison a person in his or her own house merely because they shout slogans or carry signs." Brennan would approve an ordinance that was "narrowly tailored" to specify the number of picketers allowed, the hours of picketing, and noise levels. Such a "time, place, and manner" regulation could satisfy the First Amendment. He objected, however, to the blanket prohibition on picketing in the Brookfield ordinance. Brennan took issue with O'Connor's assumption that the picketers aimed their message only at Dr. Victoria. The case record showed they sought also to reach his neighbors and the general public. Brennan argued that making one person "uncomfortable" provided no warrant for banning picketing entirely.

The Court shifted ground in a final picketing case, decided in 1988, with the site moving from suburban Milwaukee to Washington, D.C. Congress had forbidden groups to "congregate" within five hundred feet of an embassy or to "display" signs that might cast "public odium" on its government. Michael Boos and other members of the Young Conservative Alliance were blocked by police from picketing the Soviet embassy with placards that read "Release Sakharov." They sued the city's mayor, Marion Barry. An appellate panel upheld the law, but ruled that police could enforce the "congregation" clause only when "a threat to the security or peace of the embassy is present."

The *amicus* groups in *Boos v. Barry* included an odd couple: the liberal American Civil Liberties Union and the conservative Washington Legal Foundation both urged the Supreme Court to strike down the District ordinance. The Court's lineup in the case featured other odd couples: Justice Brennan joined Antonin Scalia on one issue, while Chief Justice Rehnquist was paired with Harry Blackmun on another. The matchmaker in this judicial farrago was Sandra O'Connor, whose five-part opinion divided her colleagues into five separate factions.

Justice O'Connor persuaded both Brennan and Rehnquist to uphold the "congregation" clause, as narrowed by the appellate court. But she displeased both in her treatment of the "display" clause. O'Connor tried hard to placate Brennan on this issue, citing his opinions in *New York Times v. Sullivan* and *Carey v. Brown*. Because the law prohibited only signs "critical of foreign governments," she wrote, it was an impermissible "content-based" regulation. Brennan was not pleased, however, by O'Connor's citation of the *Renton* case, which upheld zoning laws against adult theaters and allowed regulation of such "secondary effects" of picketing as congestion or visual clutter. Brennan expressed his displeasure in a concurring opinion, in which he deplored this extension of the *Renton* doctrine to political speech. He warned that O'Connor's "ominous dictum" could "lead to the evisceration of First Amendment freedoms" in later cases.

Justice Rehnquist confined his dissent to a single paragraph. "For the reasons stated by Judge Bork in his majority opinion below," he would uphold the "display" clause of the District ordinance. Rehnquist rarely named lower-court judges in his opinions, but there was a personal reason for this exception. Six months earlier, the Senate had rejected Robert Bork's nomination to the Supreme Court. The two men shared not only a personal friendship but also a "statist" approach to the Constitution. Rehnquist agreed with Bork that Congress had the power to prevent "affronts to the dignity of foreign governments and their diplomatic personnel" by hostile picketers. One reason that Rehnquist found himself in the minority in *Boos v. Barry* was that Bork's former colleague, Antonin Scalia, looked at this case as a libertarian and rejected the "statist" position on First Amendment issues.

This case, the last First Amendment case in which Brennan and Rehnquist both voted, puts into focus *all* the cases decided over the years they served together. The decision in *Boos v. Barry* reflects the Court's divisions over issues of religion, speech, press, and assembly. But its outcome also shows that the Court has rarely wavered in protecting the core values of the First Amendment from serious infringement. Brennan's defense of free expression in *New York Times v. Sullivan* has endured for three decades, spanning some of the most tumultuous years in American history. Justice O'Connor's citation of this opinion in *Boos v. Barry* was a tribute to the continuing power of Brennan's vision of a free society. He did not prevail in every case, and there has been some erosion as the tides of public opinion have shifted the Court. But debate on public issues remains amazingly "uninhibited, robust, and wide-open," for which Justice Brennan deserves much credit.

NINE

"You Are Under Arrest"

"You are under arrest. You have the right to remain silent. Anything you say can be used against you in court. You have the right to consult a lawyer before we question you. If you cannot afford a lawyer and want one, a lawyer will be provided for you." These words are probably as widely known as the Pledge of Allegiance, and are recited thousands of times every day. We know them as the "Miranda warning," named after Ernest Miranda, a convicted rapist who was granted a new trial in 1966 because the police failed to advise him of his rights to remain silent and consult a lawyer. Miranda's signed confession, the Supreme Court ruled, was not "truly the product of free choice" and should not have been admitted by the trial judge.

Even the prestige of Chief Justice Earl Warren, who wrote the opinion in *Miranda v. Arizona*, could not shield the Court from criticism by those who feared the ruling would "handcuff" the police. Some predicted that sharp lawyers would exploit police mistakes to return killers and rapists to the streets. Few critics admitted that reversal of convictions did not mean freedom for criminals in most cases, only a new trial. Ernest Miranda did not leave prison; a retrial without his tainted confession resulted in a second conviction and a twenty-year sentence. But these facts did not deter those who exploited the *Miranda* decision for political gain. More than any other, this case illustrates the link between the politics of the Constitution and the politics of crime.

No politician has played on the public's fear of crime with more skill—and success—than Richard Nixon. Running for president in 1968, he charged that courts "have gone too far in weakening the peace forces as against the criminal forces in this country." Nixon did not directly attack Chief Justice Warren, but his campaign message was clear: the

Supreme Court was soft on crime. New justices were needed to strengthen the forces of law and order. After his election, Nixon wasted little time in reshaping the Court. Warren's retirement in 1969 prompted the nomination of Warren Burger, a federal appellate judge whose hard-line criminal opinions had impressed the new president. The selection of William Rehnquist in 1971 was clearly a law-and-order choice. Campaigning for a second term in 1972, Nixon reminded voters of his pledge to appoint judges who shared his views on crime.

This issue worked for Nixon because he understood the public's real and legitimate fear of crime. But that fear is often directed against the poor and members of racial minorities, especially young males who live in urban ghettos. More in this group are now enrolled in the criminal justice system than in college. Nixon felt compelled to deny that "law and order is the code word for racism," but police officers routinely employ rough tactics against black and Latino suspects. They are more likely to be stopped on the streets, frisked and searched, arrested for "suspicion," charged with multiple crimes, and held under prohibitive bail. They are, in short, people much like Ernest Miranda, who was poor, Latino, uneducated, and mentally deficient. They are certainly not a fair match for the police and prosecutors who control the criminal justice system.

The Supreme Court's opinions in criminal cases rarely mention the factors of poverty and race. But these "social facts" are relevant, and help to explain the divided votes of Justices Brennan and Rehnquist. During the years they served together, the two men showed a differing sensitivity to these factors in criminal cases. Applying his "dignity" principle to defendants who were largely poor and black or brown, Brennan followed the lead of Chief Justice Warren, who wrote that the police treatment of Ernest Miranda was "destructive of human dignity." In contrast, Rehnquist's "deference" principle rules out consideration of "social facts" that might tilt the scales of justice toward defendants.

Many people are unaware that the Bill of Rights includes a detailed code of criminal procedure. Four of the first ten amendments deal with this subject. The Fourth Amendment protects our "persons, houses, papers, and effects, against unreasonable searches and seizures," and imposes a "probable cause" standard on the judicial issuance of search warrants. The Fifth Amendment requires a grand jury indictment for serious crimes, bans multiple prosecutions with a double-jeopardy clause, and protects defendants against self-incrimination. Most important, this amendment guards every person against deprivation of "life, liberty, or property, without due process of law," a phrase that encapsulates the principle of fair treatment of all persons. The Sixth Amendment outlines the elements of fair trial, including an "impartial jury" and the "assistance of counsel" for defense. Finally, the Eighth Amendment prohibits "excessive bail" before trial and the imposition of "cruel and unusual punishments" after conviction. Each provision has provoked debate within the Court and outside its walls, as courts are flooded with defendants and prisons are crowded with inmates.

THE FIRST ENCOUNTER most people have with the police begins with a stop. The purpose is normally interrogatory. "Can I ask you a few questions? Where have you been? What were you doing?" The Constitution does not prohibit the police from asking such questions of anyone. But it does place limits on a "seizure," in which the person stopped for questioning is not free to leave without restraint. And it restricts the officer's power to "search" anyone, before or after questioning. The Fourth Amendment prohibits only *unreasonable* searches and seizures, and imposes a "probable cause" standard on the police. Definitions of these imprecise terms depend on the facts of each case, and elude the Court's best efforts to paint a "bright line" that allows the police to separate the guilty and innocent.

The facts of one Fourth Amendment case illustrate this problem. Officer Martin McFadden, a plainclothes officer in Cleveland, Ohio, was patrolling a downtown area when he noticed two black men walking back and forth in front of a jewelry store. He decided they were "casing" the store for a robbery and ordered them to stop. He "frisked" the suspects and found pistols inside their coat pockets. The question before the Supreme Court in *Terry v. Ohio* was whether McFadden had probable cause to "seize" John Terry and search him for weapons. Chief Justice Earl Warren, writing for the Court in 1968, held that it would have been "poor police work" to ignore Terry's suspicious behavior and that McFadden's search of his overcoat was "reasonably designed to discover" weapons that might have been used against the officer. Under these facts, the "stop and frisk" was lawful.

Justice William Douglas was the only dissenter in the *Terry* case. Brennan joined the majority, but he wrote privately to Chief Justice Warren that the "stop and frisk" rule might "aggravate the already white heat resentment of ghetto Negroes against the police—and the Court will become the scapegoat." Brennan knew that confrontations of police and ghetto residents had sparked dozens of urban riots from Newark to Los Angeles. He felt strongly that the police must have more than mere "suspicion" to stop and search a criminal suspect.

Justices Brennan and Rehnquist have expressed very different views on the Fourth Amendment. "We cannot allow our zeal for effective law enforcement to blind us to the peril to our free society," Brennan warned in 1983, "that lies in this Court's disregard of the protections afforded by the Fourth Amendment." Rehnquist objects strenuously to judicial oversight of police conduct. "The ultimate standard set forth in the Fourth Amendment is reasonableness," he wrote in 1973, based on the subjective views of police officers.

The case in which Brennan wrote the above words illustrates these differences. Mark Royer, a college student, was arrested in 1978 at the Miami airport by detectives who observed him buying a ticket and felt he fit a "drug courier profile." They testified that Royer was young, carried two suitcases that seemed heavy, "appeared pale and nervous," and paid cash for his ticket. The detectives approached Royer, identified themselves, and asked if he had a "moment" to speak with them. He agreed, and produced his ticket and driver's license, which had a different name than his baggage tags. Royer complied with a request that he accompany the detectives to a small room off the airport concourse, while they held his ticket. One detective retrieved the luggage from the airline and asked to look inside. Royer opened the bag, the detectives found a large package of marijuana, and they arrested him.

The relevant facts were clear. The detectives questioned Royer without "probable cause" to know his bags contained drugs. They detained him for some fifteen minutes while the bags were retrieved. And they searched the bags without a judicial warrant. The trial judge denied Royer's motion to suppress the evidence, and he was convicted. The question before the Supreme Court was the "reasonableness" of the stop-and-search. Five members voted to reverse the conviction. Justice Byron White, normally a hard-liner in criminal cases, wrote for a plurality of four justices. They agreed that the detectives had a "reasonable suspicion" that Royer might be carrying drugs and that the initial stop was lawful. But they also held that "the limits of a Terry-stop" were exceeded. The fifteen minutes Royer was held after his ticket was confiscated made the difference to the plurality.

Justice Brennan wrote separately to make two points. He first disagreed that the initial stop was lawful. The facts of the case, he wrote, "are perfectly consistent with innocent behavior" on Royer's part. Brennan also rejected "any suggestion that the *Terry* reasonable-suspicion standard justifies anything but the briefest of detentions or the most limited of searches" by the police. Admitting that "traffic in illicit drugs is a matter of pressing national concern," Brennan was unwilling to "excuse this Court from exercising its unflagging duty to strike down official activity that exceeds the confines of the Constitution."

In his dissent, Rehnquist recited the same facts as Brennan, but he viewed them from a police officer's perspective. He quoted extensively from manuals on "drug courier profiles" and cited statistics that about half of the suspects who fit a profile were found to carry drugs. Rehnquist concluded that "in this case the 'profile' proved effective." He berated the plurality for "its total indifference to the legitimate needs of law enforcement agents seeking to curb trafficking in dangerous drugs."

Rehnquist also unleashed a barrage of sarcasm. The plurality opinion "betrays a mind-set more useful to those who officiate at shuffleboard games" than to officers who confront drug smugglers. Suggestions that detectives could employ other procedures, such as drug-sniffing dogs, were "little more than saying that if my aunt were a man, she would be my uncle." If the opinion were "judged by standards appropriate to Impressionist paintings, it would perhaps receive a high grade, but the same cannot be said if it is to be judged by the standards of a judicial opinion." One suspects that Rehnquist felt particularly betrayed by Justice White, usually his ally in criminal cases.

Most Fourth Amendment cases, like the *Royer* case, involve a motion to suppress evidence that was allegedly seized illegally. The Supreme Court has fashioned an "exclusionary rule" to bar such evidence at trials. This rule initially applied only to federal cases. The Court ruled in 1961 that state judges must also exclude illegally obtained evidence. The case began with a police raid in Cleveland, Ohio, on the home of Dollree Mapp, a black woman suspected of harboring a fugitive. She refused to let the police in without a warrant, but they broke down the door and searched the house. They did not find the fugitive, but the search turned up some allegedly obscene pictures. Mapp was sentenced to prison for possessing this material. Justice Tom Clark, a criminal law hard-liner, wrote for the Court that "all evidence obtained by searches and seizures in violation of the Constitution" must be excluded in all courts. "Nothing can destroy a government more quickly than its failure to observe its own laws," Clark admonished in *Mapp v. Ohio.*

Law-and-order politicians have lined up to denounce the exclusionary rule. President Ronald Reagan told a police convention in 1981 that the rule "rests on the absurd proposition that a law enforcement error, no matter how technical, can be used to justify throwing an entire case out of court, no matter how guilty the defendant or how heinous the crime." He charged that "the criminal goes free, the officer receives no effective reprimand, and the only ones who really suffer are the people of the community."

The exclusionary rule has judicial critics as well. Justice Rehnquist has led the crusade, writing in 1981 that it impedes "the efforts of the national, state, and local governments to apprehend and convict those who have violated their laws." But he has failed to persuade a majority to overrule the *Mapp* decision. Rehnquist has succeeded, however, in broadening numerous exceptions to the rule. The biggest loophole is wide enough to drive a police car through. Many Fourth Amendment cases begin with stops of automobiles. Almost single-handedly, Rehnquist has moved the Court to recognize an "automobile exception" to the Fourth Amendment's warrant requirement. His rationale is that cars, unlike houses, are "ambulatory" and that suspects could drive away if police were forced to secure a warrant.

Rehnquist won an initial victory in a case that involved a police officer. Ironically, this officer had appealed a murder conviction that relied on evidence found in a warrantless search of his car. Chester Dombrowski, a Chicago policeman, was arrested for drunken driving in Wisconsin after his car smashed into a bridge abutment. Several hours after the car was towed to a private garage, a Wisconsin officer searched it looking for Dombrowski's service revolver. He did not find the gun, but he discovered several items covered with blood, including a police nightstick. Confronted with this evidence, Dombrowski told the police they could find a body on his brother's farm. The victim had been beaten and shot. The police never found the revolver, but the victim's blood matched the type found on Dombrowski's nightstick.

Writing in 1973 for a bare majority in *Cady v. Dombrowski*, Rehnquist admitted the conviction "was based wholly on circumstantial evidence." All the state's evidence came from the warrantless search of Dombrowski's car, conducted while he was in a hospital bed. Rehnquist justified the search on two grounds. First, the car had been towed because it was disabled and "constituted a nuisance along the highway." Second, the private garage "was vulnerable to intrusion by vandals" and the search for a gun was reasonable under the circumstances. Rehnquist ignored the question of whether the Wisconsin officers could have obtained a warrant to search for the missing gun.

Writing for the four dissenters, Brennan accused the majority of creating a new exception to the warrant requirement with no support in precedent. The facts of *Dombrowski* did not fit any existing exception, he argued. The car was wrecked and could not be driven away. It was not searched "incident to arrest," as Dombrowski was hospitalized at the time. And the "plain view" exception did not apply to items that were locked in a car's trunk. "The police knew what they were looking for and had ample opportunity to obtain a warrant," Brennan wrote. The majority had made "a serious departure from established Fourth Amendment principles."

More than other areas of law, search-and-seizure cases depend on particular fact situations and elude the bright-line standards—rules that easily distinguish cases—that lawyers and judges prefer. Decisions often turn on what might appear to be trivial questions. Was a jacket pocket open or zipped shut? Was a container opaque or translucent? In one case, Brennan complained that the Court's search for bright-line rules simply invited the police to rummage through anything they pleased, at any time or place. This case, *New York v. Belton*, involved a search of a car whose occupants were outside and could not reach in. An officer opened a zipped pocket of a jacket inside the car and found cocaine. Prior cases held that police could lawfully search items "within reach of the arrestee" for weapons, as a protective measure. The Court broadened this rule in *Belton* to include items located in areas where a suspect had recently been.

This was too much for Brennan, who noted that Belton could not possibly have reached the jacket, even if it contained a weapon. He posed a series of hypothetical questions. Would a search be valid "if conducted five minutes after the suspect left his car? Thirty minutes? Three hours?" His point was that "courts should carefully consider the facts and circumstances of each search and seizure, focusing on the reasons supporting the exception rather than on any bright-line rule of general application."

None of this concerned Rehnquist. He would not bother with warrants in the first place. "It is often forgotten," he wrote in 1981, "that nothing in the Fourth Amendment itself requires that searches be conducted pursuant to warrants." He answered Brennan's focus on facts by arguing that "one need *not* demonstrate that a *particular* automobile was capable of being moved, but that automobiles *as a class* are inherently mobile," regardless of whether the driver is inside or miles away. Rehnquist would "hold that a warrant should not be required to seize and search any personal property in an automobile" that was stopped for any lawful reason. "I would not abandon this reasonably 'bright line' in search of another," he wrote.

The basic issue dividing Brennan and Rehnquist in Fourth Amendment cases boils down to one question: Should the police, or judges, decide what is "reasonable" in conducting a search or seizure? Rehnquist stated his position in these words: "If the purpose of the exclusionary rule is to deter unlawful police conduct then evidence obtained from a search should be suppressed only if it can be said that the law enforcement officer had knowledge, or may properly be charged with knowledge, that the search was unconstitutional under the Fourth Amendment." In other words, the "good faith" belief of the officer that he or she was acting lawfully should prevail.

Brennan found this a chilling prospect, especially since Rehnquist wrote for the Court's majority. He warned that this "entirely new" approach to the Fourth Amendment "removes the very foundation of the exclusionary rule as it has been expressed in countless decisions." The heart of that rule "has been that suppression is necessarily the sanction to be applied when it is determined that the evidence was in fact illegally acquired." The "good faith" exception would swallow the rule. It would be hard to find an officer who does not believe her actions are lawful. Brennan leveled a challenge: "If a majority of my colleagues are determined to discard the exclusionary rule in Fourth Amendment cases, they should forthrightly do so, and be done with it. This business of slow strangulation of the rule," he wrote, "demeans the adjudicatory function, and the institutional integrity of this Court." The exclusionary rule has survived, but growing exceptions—like vines around a tree—are squeezing out its vitality. Rehnquist has not abandoned his goal of overruling *Mapp* if he secures the votes.

THE CRIMINAL LAW amendments in the Bill of Rights roughly track the steps from police inquiry to arrest, and from trial to imprisonment of those convicted. The provisions of the Fifth and Sixth amendments are designed to ensure fair trials of the accused. Backing up these specific guarantees, the Due Process clause serves as a trump card in the Constitution. It protects, Justice John Harlan wrote in 1884, "the fundamental principles of liberty and justice" that we inherited from English common law and its roots in the Magna Carta. Stating those broad principles is easy. But applying them to the unique facts of criminal cases has proven a difficult task. Every case—however mundane—requires a new look at these ancient precepts.

No principle is more fundamental to the notion of a fair trial than the presumption of innocence. But the Constitution says nothing about this; it is a judicial construct, often negated by other burdens on defendants. One case that divided Justices Brennan and Rehnquist in 1973 provides an example. Hugh Naughton was tried and convicted in an Oregon court of armed robbery. Two witnesses identified him as the robber, and two police officers added corroborating testimony. Naughton did not take the stand or call any witnesses on his behalf. The trial judge charged the jury that Naughton was presumed innocent "until guilt is proved beyond a reasonable doubt." He added another instruction: "Every witness is presumed to speak the truth." This presumption could be overcome by contrary evidence, the judge said, but none was presented in Naughton's trial. A federal appellate court granted a *habeas corpus* petition and ordered a new trial. The judges felt the challenged instruction placed "the burden on Naughton to prove his innocence" and was "offensive to any fair notion of due process of law."

Justice Rehnquist wrote for the Court in *Cupp v. Naughton*, reversing the appellate panel. He admitted that instructing jurors to believe the prosecution's witnesses might prejudice a defendant who does not controvert their testimony or take the stand. But the instruction was designed, he wrote, "to get the jury off dead center and to give it some guidance by which to evaluate the frequently confusing and conflicting testimony which it has heard." Rehnquist concluded that whatever harm was imposed on Naughton "is not of constitutional dimension."

Justice Brennan wrote for three dissenters. The jurors, he argued, were "directed in effect to ignore certain doubts they may have entertained concerning the credibility of the prosecution's witnesses." Brennan cited cases from every federal appellate circuit that had disapproved of similar presumption-of-truthfulness instructions. One opinion, in fact, had been written by Chief Justice Burger, who was hardly soft on crime. Rehnquist answered that none of these cases "dealt with review of a *state* court proceeding," and that federal courts should not interfere with state judges unless their actions clearly violated the Due Process clause. Brennan replied that the violation was clear to him. But he did not prevail in this contest with Rehnquist.

Eight years later, the Court decided another presumption-of-innocence case, this time for the defendant. Five justices who voted with Rehnquist in the *Naughton* case switched sides, leaving him the sole dissenter in *Carter v. Kentucky*. This case involved a store burglary and the testimony of two police officers, one of whom arrested Lonnie Joe Carter after chasing a suspect for several blocks. Carter declined to take the stand after being warned that his testimony could be impeached with evidence of several earlier felony convictions. But the judge refused his lawyer's request to instruct the jury that Carter "is not compelled to testify and the fact that he does not cannot be used as an inference of guilt and should not prejudice him in any way." The majority of states, and the federal courts, required such an instruction at the defendant's request.

Justice Potter Stewart wrote for the Court, holding that the requested instruction was necessary to prevent jurors from speculating about "incriminating inferences from a defendant's silence." In his solo dissent, Rehnquist accused the majority of "Thomistic reasoning" in converting a negative right *not* to testify into a positive demand on the court. The Court's decision, he complained, "allows a criminal defendant in a state proceeding virtually to take from the trial judge any control over the instructions" to the jury. Again, the majority relied on federal court precedent. Rehnquist again argued that federal cases were of "no relevance" to state proceedings. He added a cavil at "the mysterious process of transmogrification" by which the Court had applied the Bill of Rights to the states. His words were long but his point was clear: states should be free to conduct trials any way they saw fit.

A crucial question in every criminal case is whether the defendant is competent to stand trial. The insanity defense is widely criticized but is actually quite rare, being raised in fewer than 1 percent of all trials. One question the Supreme Court did not decide until 1985 was whether states must provide indigent defendants with "access to the psychiatric examination and assistance necessary to prepare an effective defense" on insanity grounds. This case involved a defendant, Glen Ake, who was arrested in 1979 for murdering a minister and his wife and shooting their two children. His behavior at arraignment and in jail was "so bizarre" that the judge ordered a psychiatric exam. The doctor reported that Ake was "delusional" and claimed "to be the 'sword of vengeance' of the Lord and that he will sit at the left hand of God in heaven." After a competency hearing, the judge found Ake to be "a mentally ill person" and incompetent to stand trial. He was committed to a state mental hospital.

Six weeks later, the state's doctors reported an amazing recovery. Huge doses of Thorazine, an antipsychotic drug, had restored Ake to competency. He was quickly placed on trial. His lawyer asked the judge to appoint an outside psychiatrist to determine if Ake was insane when the murders occurred, but this motion was denied. Jurors were instructed to presume that Ake was sane at the time of the crime, unless *he* presented evidence to raise a reasonable doubt about his sanity. He did not, and he was convicted and sentenced to death. Justice Thurgood Marshall wrote for eight members of the Court in *Ake v. Oklahoma* that "a defense may be devastated" if a defendant has no psychiatrist to counter the state's doctors. The Court ordered a new trial for Glen Ake.

Justice Rehnquist wrote another solo dissent. He admitted that the state's doctors had diagnosed Ake as psychotic in the hospital, but added that none could say he was insane at the time of the murders. Rehnquist stressed that Oklahoma law placed the burden of proving insanity on Ake and that he "failed to carry the initial burden." That statement, of course, begged the question, since Ake had no psychiatrist to testify on that issue. That was the only issue in the case. Rehnquist offered his own diagnosis, concluding that the "evidence of the brutal murders" did not "raise any question of sanity unless one were to adopt the dubious doctrine that no one in his right mind would commit a murder." He concluded that "I do not think due process is violated merely because an indigent lacks sufficient funds to pursue a state-law defense as thoroughly as he would like." The fact that Ake was poor was irrelevant to Rehnquist.

ONE FACT OF LIFE in criminal law is that many defense lawyers make mistakes. Some are grossly incompetent, particularly those who scratch out a living as court-appointed counsel. Others, including many public defenders, have adequate training but are overwhelmed with cases and often go to trial with little preparation. And many mistakes result from confusing and highly technical state court rules. Some rules literally force lawyers to jump from their seats and make an objection on the spot, or lose the chance to raise the issue on appeal. Appellate judges often spend months reviewing a lawyer's error that was made in seconds. The person who pays for the mistake is the helpless defendant, who is behind bars and often dependent on inmate "writ writers" for legal help. Only in rare cases will an experienced criminal appellate lawyer offer to pursue what seems to be a hopeless case.

The judicial pursuit of justice often begins in tangled thickets of state law. The case of Leon Chambers provides an example. One Saturday night in 1969, two police officers in the small town of Woodville, Mississippi, entered a bar with an arrest warrant for C. C. Jackson. The suspect resisted, a hostile crowd wrestled him from custody, and officer "Sonny" Liberty was shot and killed during the melee. Before he died, Liberty fired two blasts from his twelve-gauge shotgun and hit Leon Chambers in the head. Three men, including Gable McDonald, took Chambers to the hospital, where he was arrested for Liberty's murder. At the trial, a deputy sheriff testified that he saw Chambers shoot the officer. Two other witnesses, however, said they saw McDonald shoot Liberty. McDonald, in fact, had signed—and later retracted—a sworn confession and had told three friends he was the killer. Chambers's lawyer called McDonald as a witness, but the trial judge refused to allow him to cross-examine McDonald as an "adverse" witness. Mississippi court rules required that each side "vouch" for its witnesses and not attack their credibility in cross-examination. Chambers was convicted and sentenced to life in prison.

The Supreme Court ruled in 1973 that Chambers had been denied "a fair opportunity to defend against the State's accusations." The right to cross-examine hostile witnesses, Justice Lewis Powell wrote, "is more than a desirable rule of trial procedure." Forcing Chambers to vouch for the testimony of McDonald that he was not the killer blocked any effort to cast doubt on Chambers's guilt. The voucher rule denied Chambers "a trial in accord with traditional and fundamental standards of due process," Powell concluded.

Only one justice dissented from this holding. Rehnquist disagreed with the Court's "constitutionalization of the intricacies of the common law of evidence." Having admitted the law was intricate, he went on to blame Chambers's lawyer for getting tangled in its snares. The lawyer made two mistakes, according to Rehnquist. First, he violated the state's "contemporaneous objection" rule by not objecting to the trial judge's rulings in proper language. It was "perfectly true," Rehnquist conceded, that the lawyer "objected during trial to each of the court's rulings." But the objections were not phrased explicitly in constitutional terms. Therefore,

Chambers's appeal did not raise a "substantial federal question" and should be dismissed.

Second, Rehnquist wrote, even if the Court gave "some extraordinarily lenient construction" to the trial objections, the formal appeal filed by the lawyer claimed only that "the Court erred" in refusing to allow cross-examination of Gable McDonald. Rehnquist noted that the appeal *did* include a claim that Chambers's trial "was not in accord with fundamental fairness guaranteed by the Fourteenth Amendment" of the Constitution. But the two claims were not in the same paragraph. It would take "an extraordinarily perceptive" judge, Rehnquist argued, to figure out that the claims of trial error were related to "the generalized assertion of the violation of due process contained in a separately stated point." Of course, the other eight justices figured this out without much trouble.

Many criminal cases reach the Supreme Court through the back door of federal *habeas corpus.* Congress has allowed state prisoners to ask federal judges for relief if their conviction was obtained "in violation of the Constitution." Justice Rehnquist has never concealed his opposition to this remedy, which he considers an intrusion on states' rights. Justice Brennan, in contrast, views the federal courts as refuges for victims of legal misconduct in state courts. The case of *Wainwright v. Sykes* illustrates their conflict over *habeas corpus.*

In 1972, John Sykes was convicted of murder in DeSoto County, Florida. His wife had called the police, who found the body of Willie Gilbert a few feet from their trailer home. Sykes approached the officers and volunteered that he had shot Gilbert. He was immediately arrested, taken to the police station, and read his *Miranda* rights. He declined the offer of counsel and made a statement about the shooting. Several witnesses testified that Sykes had been drinking heavily, and the officers said that he appeared intoxicated when they first saw him, but his lawyer made no objection to his statement to the police. Only after his conviction did Sykes claim that he had not understood the *Miranda* warning and that his statement was involuntary. From his state prison cell, he drafted a *habeas* petition as a *pro se* litigant and filed it with the state courts. The Florida judges rejected the claim and Sykes then filed his petition in federal court.

The Supreme Court reviewed the case in 1977 after two federal courts had ruled that Sykes was entitled to a hearing on the voluntariness of his confession. Florida court rules required that motions to suppress confessions "be made prior to trial" unless the defendant was unaware of the grounds for the motion. The lower courts held that this "contemporaneous objection" rule did not apply where the confession might be involuntary and thus violate basic due process rights. The Supreme Court had earlier ruled that "a state decision resting on an adequate foundation of state substantive law is immune from review in the federal courts." The question in *Wainwright v. Sykes* was whether this policy applied to state court decisions on procedural rules as well. If the Florida rule did not violate the Constitution, federal judges had no power to review the case.

Justice Rehnquist used the *Sykes* opinion to expound his objections to federal *habeas* review in general. A state criminal trial should be a "decisive and portentous event," he wrote. "Society's resources have been concentrated at that time and place in order to decide, within the limits of human fallibility, the question of guilt or innocence of one of its citizens." He portrayed the trial as a great drama: "the accused is in the courthouse, the jury is in the box, the judge is on the bench, and the witnesses, having been subpoenaed and duly sworn, await their turn to testify." Experienced criminal lawyers might suggest that Rehnquist, who never practiced criminal law, looked at trial courts with rose-colored glasses. Working solely from a paper record, it is hard to see a judge's raised eyebrows, a prosecutor's sneer, or a defense lawyer's stumble.

Rehnquist did not dispute the need for some *habeas* protection, but he argued that federal courts should entertain challenges to state convictions only when a defendant "will be the victim of a miscarriage of justice" without federal review. Because Sykes "advanced no explanation whatever for his failure to object at trial," he was not prejudiced by admission of his confession. Rehnquist likened defense lawyers to gamblers, suggesting that some decide to "take their chances on a verdict of not guilty in a state trial with the intent to raise their constitutional claims in a federal habeas court if their initial gamble does not pay off." They would be gambling, of course, with their clients' lives. Sykes's lawyer should have objected to the confession before trial, Rehnquist suggested, to "force the prosecution to take a hard look at its hole card" and perhaps throw in the state's hand if the confession was tainted.

Writing for himself and Justice Marshall in dissent, Justice Brennan rejected this depiction of defense lawyers as card sharks. The only former state trial judge on the Supreme Court bench, Brennan asked his colleagues a question: "How should the federal habeas court treat a procedural default in a state court that is attributable purely and simply to the error or negligence of a defendant's trial counsel?" The fact that Sykes offered no explanation for his lawyer's failure to object to the confession before trial did not puzzle Brennan. He looked at "the real world" and argued that "any realistic system of federal habeas corpus jurisdiction must be premised on the reality that the ordinary procedural default is born of the inadvertence, negligence, inexperience, or incompetence of trial counsel." The case record does not identify Sykes's trial lawyer, but he was certainly no Cool Hand Luke. Brennan could have noted, but did not, that the Supreme Court had appointed an experienced criminal lawyer to argue the appeal.

The majority opinion in this case did not mention that John Sykes was poor, uneducated, and black. These "social facts" are buried in the case record and are supposedly irrelevant to the Court's decision. But they are part of the "real world" that Brennan tried to bring into the Court's marble chamber. He pointed out that "many indigent defendants are without any realistic choice in selecting who ultimately represents them at trial," and that courts "traditionally have resisted any realistic inquiry into the competency of trial counsel." In the *Sykes* case, he concluded that "any realistic reading of the record demonstrates that we are faced here with a lawyer's simple error." Whether intentional or not, this repeated use of the term "realistic" underscored Brennan's dismissal of Rehnquist's "comfortable fiction that all lawyers are skilled or even competent craftsmen in representing the fundamental rights of their clients." It is unfair, Brennan argued, that people like John Sykes must pay the penalty for the incompetence of their lawyers. The reality is that federal *habeas corpus* remains the only recourse for many victims of legal malpractice. Justice Rehnquist has tried to slam the courthouse door, but it remains open just a crack.

THE SUPREME COURT decided in 1963 that Clarence Gideon was not a good lawyer. In fact, he was not a lawyer at all, but a poorly educated criminal defendant who was forced to defend himself against a charge of breaking into a pool room in Panama City, Florida. The trial judge rejected Gideon's claim that the Sixth Amendment guaranteed every defendant "the assistance of counsel for his defense," as its words clearly state. That provision did not apply to the states, the judge explained.

Forced to proceed without a lawyer, Gideon did his best, even examining himself on the stand. But he was no match for the prosecutor and he wound up in state prison with a five-year sentence.

From his prison cell, Gideon sent a handwritten petition to the Supreme Court restating his Sixth Amendment claim. The Court accepts fewer than 1 percent of prisoners' petitions, but the justices were eager to review a 1942 precedent that had rejected a similar claim. They appointed a noted lawyer, Abe Fortas, to argue for Gideon. There was no doubt about the outcome of *Gideon v. Wainwright*. Justice Hugo Black, a former state judge, wrote for a unanimous Court that "in our adversary system of criminal justice, any person haled into court, who is too poor to hire a lawyer, cannot be assured a fair trial unless counsel is provided for him. This seems to us to be an obvious truth." Granted a new trial, this time with a real lawyer to defend him, Gideon won an acquittal and release from prison. The *Gideon* case has been hailed as proof that the legal system works for even the poor and powerless. But its real lesson has been overlooked: it took an Abe Fortas and a sympathetic Supreme Court to reach into the Florida trial courts and make sure that one defendant got a fair shake.

The *Gideon* decision has become almost sacrosanct. Even Justice Rehnquist, who disputes the "incorporation" doctrine that imposed the Bill of Rights on the states, has not proposed overturning this landmark case. He has, however, voted consistently to restrict its reach. One case, which may seem trivial to many, illustrates the differences of Rehnquist and Brennan on Sixth Amendment issues. Aubrey Scott was charged in Illinois with theft, which carries a one-year maximum jail sentence. He asked for a lawyer, but the prosecutor said he would not ask for a jail term if Scott was convicted, and the judge denied the request. Scott defended himself, was convicted, and fined fifty dollars. He avoided jail, but now had a criminal record, which could be used against him in later trials and which might cost him jobs or licenses.

Rehnquist wrote for a bare majority in *Scott v. Illinois*, upholding the judge's ruling in 1979. He dismissed the clear intent of the Framers who wrote the Sixth Amendment. They applied its protections to "all criminal prosecutions," regardless of the penalty imposed. Rehnquist was less concerned with the constitutional text than with public funds. Extending the *Gideon* rule to all trials, he wrote, would "impose unpredictable, but necessarily substantial, costs on fifty quite diverse States." A defendant has a right to counsel only if "actual imprisonment" is imposed after conviction, he concluded.

In his dissent, Brennan accused Rehnquist of ignoring both "the plain wording of the Sixth Amendment" and the "basic principles of prior decisions" on the right to counsel. The *Gideon* rule was a "categorical requirement" in all criminal trials and was not limited to felony cases. Rehnquist referred in his opinion to theft as a "petty" crime; Brennan replied that "a theft conviction implies dishonesty" and that Scott could be barred from twenty-three occupations licensed by the city of Chicago. With a touch of sarcasm, he proposed that states which objected to "the expense of meeting the requirements of the Constitution" might decide to remove jail terms for minor offenses. What most concerned Brennan, however, was not money but the Court's willingness to make "an abrupt break with its own well-considered precedents." The *Scott* case illustrates how "original intent" can become a judicial sword that cuts both ways.

Every state grants a criminal defendant an automatic right of appeal from a conviction. The exercise of this right obviously requires the assistance of counsel. Rules of appellate procedure are highly technical and formal, and the possibility of error is high. The Supreme Court has wrestled in several cases with questions about the application of the Sixth Amendment to criminal appeals. Justices Brennan and Rehnquist disagreed almost every time. Their differences on this issue are illustrated in three cases decided between 1974 and 1985. The first presents the recurring question of whether a defendant must pay for a lawyer's mistake.

Keith Lucey was convicted in 1976 of a drug offense in Kentucky. His lawyer then filed a "notice of appeal" with the state appellate court. Although it included all the information required by the court, this document did not conform to rules that required lawyers to specify the facts of the case in minute detail. At worst, this was a minor oversight by Lucey's lawyer. The appellate judges, however, granted the state's motion to dismiss the appeal for this technical violation. Lucey's case turned into a lawyer's nightmare. His appeal went through ten separate court decisions while he spent seven years in prison. A federal appellate panel finally granted a *habeas corpus* petition and ordered a new trial.

Justice Brennan wrote for the Court in *Evitts v. Lucey*, decided in 1985. Lucey's claim, he said, "arises at the intersection" of two constitutional provisions. The Sixth Amendment "comprehends the right to effective assistance of counsel" in criminal cases. And the Fourteenth

Amendment guarantees the right of appeal in state courts. Putting the two principles together, Brennan said the question in *Lucey* was whether "the appellate-level right to counsel also comprehends the right to effective assistance of counsel."

This was an easy question for Brennan, who first noted that Kentucky law provided Lucey with an "appeal of right" from his conviction. He also noted that Lucey's trial lawyer had been disciplined for his mistake in framing the appeal. Brennan concluded from these facts that Lucey deserved a new trial. "A first appeal as of right," he wrote, does not conform "with due process of law if the appellant does not have the effective assistance of an attorney." Brennan rested his opinion on the Due Process clause of the Fourteenth Amendment.

Two justices had a harder time with this case. Justice Rehnquist, joined by Chief Justice Burger, took an odd tack in his dissent. He first denied that either the Constitution or the Court's precedents "establish a right to effective assistance of counsel on appeal." Even granting this proposition, he disputed Brennan's reliance on the Due Process clause. Rehnquist suggested that the case should have been decided on equal protection grounds. Considering his general hostility toward this provision, Rehnquist had to explain his position. He took a backdoor route to his unfamiliar destination. He first cited rulings that states must give lawyers to indigent defendants "so that they stand on equal footings with non-indigents in seeking to upset their convictions." Under this argument, Keith Lucey would be entitled to a competent lawyer. Rehnquist then removed this right with a single sentence. "There is no constitutional requirement that a State provide an appeal at all," he wrote. Given this proposition, "there cannot be derived a constitutional right to *effective assistance of counsel* on appeal." Rehnquist obviously intended his italics to emphasize his complaint that Brennan's opinion would "indiscriminately free litigants from the consequence of their attorneys' neglect or malpractice."

The Court has also considered the related question of whether an indigent defendant can challenge his lawyer's competence after his time for appeal has expired. Rehnquist prevailed on this issue in *United States v. MacCollum*, decided in 1976. He turned his equal protection argument on its head in this case. Colin MacCollum was convicted by a federal jury in Washington State of passing forged currency, but did not appeal his sentence of ten years in prison. MacCollum later filed a motion for a new trial and asked for a transcript of his original trial, arguing that he needed one to show that he had been denied the "effective assistance of counsel." His appeal to the Supreme Court relied upon both the Due Process and Equal Protection clauses. The latter claim rested on the fact that MacCollum, as an indigent, had been denied a transcript he could have purchased if he had had the funds. After a federal district judge dismissed the new trial motion, an appellate panel reversed and ordered that MacCollum receive the transcript. Fearing an avalanche of similar motions if MacCollum prevailed, the government appealed to the Supreme Court.

Writing for the Court, Justice Rehnquist admitted that the federal rules "place an indigent in a somewhat less advantageous position than a person of means." This did not bother him in the least. All that mattered was that MacCollum had passed up his right to an initial appeal, and with it the right to a free trial transcript. He conceded that a transcript might help to show that MacCollum's lawyer had been ineffective in representing him. But he brushed this argument aside. MacCollum's motion "made only a naked allegation of ineffective assistance of counsel," he stated. Without proof of wrongdoing, MacCollum could not prevail. Because any discussions with his lawyer about his appeal would have been confidential, Rehnquist wrote, any evidence of the lawyer's errors were not likely to be "cured by a transcript."

Writing in dissent, Justice Brennan pointed out the Catch-22 nature of Rehnquist's opinion, which described MacCollum's claim as "frivolous." Brennan noted that MacCollum had been "denied a transcript for making an unsubstantiated allegation, an allegation that obviously cannot be made without a transcript." Any claim that MacCollum had received inadequate counsel at trial would necessarily require substantiation, which would be "virtually impossible without the aid of a trial transcript." It struck Brennan as "particularly egregious" that Rehnquist had effectively decided the issue without reference to the missing transcript.

Rehnquist dismissed the equal protection claim with the observation that giving MacCollum a free transcript might place him "in a more favorable position" than a prisoner with some funds, who would presumably deliberate carefully before spending them to pursue a motion that might be dismissed as frivolous. This kind of calculus, based entirely on speculation, offended Brennan's sense of fairness. Any discrimination among defendants on the basis of wealth, he wrote, "must necessarily be constitutionally intolerable where the stakes are no less than the constitutionality of a criminal conviction."

Brennan and Rehnquist also divided in a Sixth Amendment case that addresses the right to counsel at the end of the legal trail: an appeal to the Supreme Court. Claude Moffitt was convicted of passing bad checks by two separate North Carolina courts. His court-appointed lawyers filed appeals in each case and both were denied. Moffitt then filed federal *habeas corpus* petitions, asking that counsel be appointed to challenge both convictions, one in the state supreme court and the other before the Supreme Court in Washington. A federal appellate panel granted the petitions, ruling that the "concepts of fairness and equality, which require counsel in a first appeal of right, require counsel in other and subsequent discretionary appeals." Because other appellate courts took an opposing position, the justices decided to resolve this conflict.

Justice Rehnquist wrote for the majority in *Ross v. Moffitt*, decided in 1974. He agreed that states must provide lawyers at trial as a "shield" against unfair prosecution. But he saw no reason the state must pay for a lawyer to act "as a sword to upset the prior determination of guilt." Rehnquist admitted that "a skilled lawyer, particularly one trained in the somewhat arcane art of preparing petitions for discretionary review," would be helpful to a convict like Moffitt. Without a lawyer, he would be "somewhat handicapped in comparison with a wealthy defendant who has counsel assisting him in every conceivable manner at every stage in the proceeding." Rehnquist again argued, however, that the Constitution did not require states to "provide any appeal at all." So any provision of counsel for appeals was "a matter of legislative choice" and not subject to judicial review. But he offered the imprisoned defendant a suggestion. From the trial record and the first appellate brief, Moffitt could put together a petition that would give the court "an adequate basis for its decision to grant or deny review." Rehnquist did not send a bill for this free legal advice.

Along with Thurgood Marshall, Brennan joined the dissent of Justice William Douglas, who thought Rehnquist's advice was worth exactly what he charged. Moffitt would "draw little assistance" from his lawyer's first brief, since its arguments had already failed. An indigent defendant is at a "substantial disadvantage" when he is "forced to fend for himself" in preparing highly technical legal papers. Douglas argued that when states provide for appeals, they cannot discriminate between poor and wealthy defendants. "The right to seek discretionary review is a substantial one," he wrote, "and one where a lawyer can be of significant assistance to an indigent defendant." But this argument failed to gain a majority. Taken as a whole, the Sixth Amendment cases that divided Brennan and Rehnquist display a reluctance to extend the *Gideon* rule much further than a courtroom in Panama City, Florida.

THE POLITICS OF CRIME has one sure crowd-pleaser: calls for longer prison sentences. Judges in the United States impose the stiffest terms in the Western world, despite the lack of evidence that long sentences have any deterrent effect on crime rates. Voters believe, however, that putting criminals away protects them from what President Reagan called "human predators." Over the past three decades, sentences have steadily increased, pushing the prison population to the quarter-million mark in 1993. At any time, more than two and a half million people are in jail or prison, or under parole and probation supervision. The replacement of parole with mandatory minimum sentences, which limits judicial flexibility in sentencing, and the recent rash of "three strikes and you're out" laws both reflect political reaction to public pressure.

The only constitutional barrier to lengthy sentences is the "cruel and unusual punishment" clause of the Eighth Amendment. That clause is often invoked in capital punishment cases, but the Supreme Court rarely hears appeals from other types of sentencing decisions of state and federal judges. Two cases, decided in 1980 and 1982, were the first since 1910 that raised serious challenges to lengthy sentences imposed for relatively minor crimes. Not surprisingly, Justices Brennan and Rehnquist disagreed in both cases.

One case involved a grand total of $229.11 in bad checks. If William Rummel had passed just one check for that amount, he would have faced a maximum term of ten years. He made the mistake, however, of writing three bad checks and getting caught each time. At the conclusion of his third trial in 1973, the judge cited the Texas "recidivist statute" and sentenced Rummel to life imprisonment, with parole eligibility after twelve years. Designed to deter career criminals, the law applied to every defendant with three felony convictions; forgery of any amount over fifty dollars is a felony in Texas. Rummel filed a federal *habeas corpus* petition, arguing that his sentence was "grossly disproportionate" to the crimes he committed. Although two federal courts rejected his claim, the Supreme Court agreed to review the case, which spurred hope among prison reformers who felt that such crushing sentences violated the Constitution. Their hopes were dashed by the margin of one vote.

Justice Rehnquist wrote for the majority in *Rummel v. Estelle*. He first addressed the claim that Rummel's sentence was disproportionate to his crimes, noting that "successful challenges to the proportionality of particular sentences have been exceedingly rare." The Court, in fact, had not struck down a sentence on this ground since 1910. The defendant in that case, *Weems v. United States*, was convicted in the Philippines of falsifying a public record and sentenced to "confinement in a penal institution for twelve years and one day, a chain at the ankle and wrist of the offender, hard and painful labor," and lifetime deprivation of rights. This was too much for the Supreme Court to stomach, and the justices unanimously reduced the sentence. The decision was not based, however, on its length but on the conditions of hard labor and the triviality of the offense.

Rehnquist did not consider *Weems* relevant to Rummel's case. He pointed out that Texas had classified all three crimes as felonies, and that Rummel had been "graphically informed of the consequences of lawlessness and given an opportunity to reform, all to no avail." Rummel was not exactly Jesse James, but he was a repeat offender who took other people's money. The Constitution did not bar states from "dealing in a harsher manner with those who by repeated criminal acts have shown that they are simply incapable of conforming to the norms of society," Rehnquist admonished. Decisions on sentencing are "properly within the province of legislatures, not courts." The most he conceded to the disproportionality argument was a footnote stating that lawmakers could not make "overtime parking a felony punishable by life imprisonment." But he did not explain *why* a three-time loser at the parking meter should not go to prison for life.

Justice Brennan did not write a separate dissent in *Rummel*, but he joined the opinion of Justice Lewis Powell, who normally supported the states in criminal cases. Powell, however, mixed compassion with his conservative views, and he objected strongly to Rehnquist's dismissal of precedent on the disproportionality issue. He noted that the principle "is rooted deeply in English constitutional law" and that the Magna Carta limited punishment for a crime "according to its gravity." Powell concluded with words that sounded much like Brennan. "We are construing a living Constitution. The sentence imposed upon the petitioner would be viewed as grossly unjust by virtually every layman and lawyer. In my view, objective criteria clearly establish that a mandatory life sentence for defrauding persons of about $230 crosses any rationally drawn line separating punishment that lawfully may be imposed from that which is proscribed by the Eighth Amendment."

Two years later, Brennan did answer Rehnquist, again in dissent. Roger Davis was sentenced by a Virginia judge in 1973 to forty years in prison for possession and sale of nine ounces of marijuana. The case raised the same disproportionality issue that *Rummel* had, and the Court voted to consider it because a federal appellate panel had decided that *Rummel* did not apply. The Court did not even hear argument in *Hutto v. Davis*, reversing the appellate panel with a scolding for not following precedent. Justice Powell voted to uphold the sentence in this case, largely because Davis was a drug dealer with a prior record.

Justice Brennan did not conceal his outrage at the Court's "profoundly disturbing" action. He accused the majority of having "misused precedent" and of the "serious and improper expansion of *Rummel*" in the case of Roger Davis. Joined by Thurgood Marshall and John Stevens, he noted the "increasingly alarming penchant of the Court inappropriately to invoke its power of summary disposition" in deciding cases without full briefing or argument. Brennan pointed out the differences between the two cases. First, Rummel was convicted under a recidivist statute and Davis was not. Second, the Virginia legislature had recently reduced the maximum penalty for Davis's crimes from forty years to ten. Third, even the prosecutor admitted that the sentence was "grossly unjust" in view of the "extremely light" sentences imposed in similar cases, which averaged only three years. This was sufficient evidence to Brennan that Davis had been subjected to "cruel and unusual punishment."

Brennan ended with a harsh statement: "I dissent from this patent abuse of our judicial power." These words expressed more than dismay and anger. They also capture Brennan's feeling about the Court's rulings in most of its criminal law decisions. Whether the issue was that of search and seizure, police interrogation, the right to counsel, or sentencing, the Court most often viewed those accused of crime as persons who should be segregated "from the rest of society for an extended period of time," as Rehnquist wrote about William Rummel. Criminals have few champions, and Brennan was acutely conscious of the politics of crime. But he still felt sympathy for those who must "suffer the pains of the Court's insensitivity" to the Constitution, as he wrote about Roger Davis.

TEN

"Cruel and Unusual Punishment"

"ADHERING TO OUR VIEWS that the death penalty is in all circumstances cruel and unusual punishment prohibited by the Eighth and Fourteenth Amendments, we would grant the application for stay and a petition for writ of certiorari and would vacate the death sentence in this case."

Under the heading "Justice Brennan and Justice Marshall, dissenting," this sentence appeared several hundred times in the *United States Reports* between 1976 and 1990, when Brennan retired. It was generally relegated to the list of cases the Supreme Court declined to review. Each death penalty case raised the last-ditch arguments of a prisoner condemned to die. In virtually every one, Brennan and Marshall stood alone. Their long crusade against capital punishment was largely bereft of victories. They failed to persuade a single colleague to agree that the death penalty violated the Constitution. But they did slow down—and even stopped for eight years—the pace of executions. Once they retired, however, the Court turned an increasingly deaf ear to appeals from the crowded death rows in the nation's prisons. And no justice has voted more consistently to uphold death sentences than William Rehnquist.

There are several reasons that Brennan and Marshall had so little success. Every factor in the judicial equation—with one exception—supports the advocates of capital punishment. The historical record, the constitutional text, legislative decisions, and public opinion—all agree that death is an appropriate punishment for the most heinous crimes. The only contrary argument, stated forcefully by Justice Brennan, is that "evolving standards of decency" in American society have supplanted the Framers' acceptance of the death penalty. Brennan's principle of "human dignity" collides with Rehnquist's demand for "judicial deference" to legislative will. These incompatible standards raise a fundamental question: How can the justices choose between them?

The answer from history is clear. Capital punishment has existed for thousands of years, in societies around the world. It has deep roots in the biblical soil of the "Judeo-Christian" world. The Puritan settlers of Massachusetts Bay adopted a code of "Capital Lawes" that imposed the death penalty on fifteen crimes, each tied to specific Bible verses. The first ordered that any person who "shall have or worship any other God, but the LORD GOD he shall be put to death." Not until the fourth clause did the Puritans order that anyone who committed "any wilfull MURTHER" shall be "putt to death." They found other capital crimes in the Bible, including homosexuality, adultery, and children who "curse or smite" their parents.

The first person executed in Massachusetts was John Billington, hanged in 1630 for the murder of "his companion John New-Comin." Fifteen years later, an unnamed young woman "married an old man out of pique and then received the attentions of a young man of eighteen. They both were hanged." The Boston *Evening Post* reported in 1755 that "Mark, a Negro man, and Phillis, a Negro woman," were executed in Cambridge for poisoning their master, Captain John Codman. Mark was hanged and Phillis was "burned at a stake about ten yards distant from the gallows." Mark's body was "afterwards suspended in chains besides the Charlestown highway where it remained for nearly twenty years."

The Constitution reflects the Framers' acceptance of capital punishment, subject only to three limitations in the Fifth Amendment. One requires a grand jury indictment for "capital" crimes, a second protects defendants against being "twice put in jeopardy of life or limb," and the third provides that no person shall be "deprived of life, liberty, or property, without due process of law." This last provision, duplicated in the Fourteenth Amendment, imposes on both federal and state governments a standard of fair treatment of every person who faces the death penalty. In addition, the Eighth Amendment bars the imposition of "cruel and unusual punishments" on those convicted of crime. The Framers did not intend this amendment to ban capital punishment, but only barbaric methods of execution, such as burning at the stake.

The legislative record is equally clear. The federal government and most states carried over death penalty statutes from colonial times, and all but fourteen states enacted new laws after the Supreme Court ruled in 1972 that those laws in most states violated the Constitution. Lawmakers have responded to the voters, who support the death penalty by large—and increasing—majorities. Only during the early 1960s, by narrow margins, did the public oppose capital punishment. According to the Gallup Poll, between 1975 and 1989 support increased from 64 to 78 percent. Elderly white males are the most supportive—close to 90 percent—but a majority of every group, including blacks, endorses the death penalty.

Support of capital punishment has become a political necessity. From the time of Franklin Roosevelt, not a single president has spoken against it. Some have turned the issue to partisan advantage. Ronald Reagan urged that anyone who kills a police officer "should give up his life as his punishment." George Bush urged Congress in 1991 to impose "an enforceable Federal death penalty for the most heinous crimes," including drug offenses. Candidates who are liberal on most issues take a conservative stand on capital punishment. Running against President Bush in 1992, Bill Clinton left the campaign trail to sign the death warrant of Rickey Ray Rector, who was executed for killing a police officer. Rector had shot himself as well, destroying part of his brain and becoming, his lawyer said, a "zombie" who did not understand what death is. "It's just awful. Just terrible, terrible," Clinton told a friend the night of Rector's execution. But he was determined not to repeat the mistake of Michael Dukakis, who opposed capital punishment and was tarred by Bush as "soft on crime."

Politicians try to avoid discussion of two issues that lie under the surface of debates over the death penalty. These are the troubling questions of race and rape, which are closely related. More than half—53 percent—of the 4,002 persons who were executed between 1930 and 1990 were black. Before the Supreme Court struck down the death penalty for rape in 1977, almost 90 percent of those executed for this crime were black, and virtually all were sentenced to die for raping white women. There is also a strong regional bias in capital punishment, tilted toward the South. Between 1980 and 1993, more than two-thirds of all executions took place in four states: Florida, Georgia, Louisiana, and Texas.

Most Americans base their support for capital punishment on beliefs that homicide rates have steadily increased over the years. Statistics show just the opposite. The murder rate has not increased in sixty years, and is affected most of all by unemployment rates. During the depths of the Great Depression in 1933, the homicide rate jumped to 9.7 for every 100,000 persons. During the boom years of the 1950s, the rate fell by more than half, to a low of 4.5 in 1958. It climbed to a high of 10.2 in 1980, during a serious recession, then fell to 7.9 in 1985 before another climb to 9.4 in 1990. Just as hard times are harder on African Americans than on most whites, murder takes a much greater toll. The homicide rate for black males in 1989 was 61.1, almost eight times that for white males. Murder is now the leading cause of death among young black men. Whether the death penalty will cure this epidemic is a question with no simple answer.

THE SUPREME COURT heard argument in three capital punishment cases on January 17, 1972, one week after William Rehnquist took his seat on the bench. The lawyers in each case had been asked to address just one question: "Does the imposition and carrying out of the death penalty in [these cases] constitute cruel and unusual punishment in violation of the Eighth and Fourteenth Amendments?" The cases came from Georgia and Texas, and all the men sentenced to die were black. One defendant, William Furman of Georgia, accidentally shot and killed a white man during a house burglary. Lucious Jackson of Georgia and Elmer Branch of Texas were sentenced to death for raping white women, the most ancient taboo of the antebellum slave codes.

These cases had not been randomly selected from the Court's lengthy docket of death penalty appeals. They were carefully chosen by lawyers for the NAACP Legal Defense and Education Fund, because they raised the issues of race and rape, and claims of prejudice by southern jurors and judges. Each defendant had been convicted by all-white juries, and judges in each case had dismissed claims of racial bias. The lawyers who argued the cases included two law professors, one on each side. Anthony Amsterdam of Stanford Law School, who represented William Furman, had devised the NAACP attack on capital punishment as a legacy of slavery and the Jim Crow system. Charles Alan Wright of the University of Texas—who later defended Richard Nixon before the Supreme Court—supported the death penalty imposed on Elmer Branch.

Amsterdam noted in his argument that twenty-six of thirty-three inmates on Georgia's death row were black, and claimed that juries were influenced by "the color of the defendant's skin and the ugliness of his person." He also stated that "the death penalty is virtually unanimously repudiated and condemned by the conscience of contemporary society." Wright replied that juries represented "contemporary community values" and were "consistently, steadily, and even increasingly" imposing the death sentence. He responded to Amsterdam that many religious leaders supported capital punishment and that polls "show a majority of our population in favor of it."

Under the caption of *Furman v. Georgia*, the Court's decision was announced on June 29, 1972. Five justices voted to spare the lives of Furman, Jackson, and Branch. All the majority agreed upon was a one-paragraph, unsigned opinion, restating the question posed to the lawyers as a conclusion: "The Court holds that the imposition and carrying out of the death penalty in these cases constitute cruel and unusual punishment in violation of the Eighth and Fourteenth Amendments." Following that brief statement, each justice issued a separate opinion, a rare event in the Court's history. The issue compelled each justice to plumb the depths of his conscience. Harry Blackmun, who admitted his "abhorrence" of capital punishment but voted to uphold the death sentences, confessed to "an excruciating agony of the spirit" in deciding these cases.

The nine opinions filled 231 pages of the *United States Reports*, a revealing judicial symposium on a question of national concern. The Court's majority rested on two conservative justices, Byron White and Potter Stewart. They supported capital punishment but objected to laws that gave jurors and judges absolute discretion in deciding who should live or die. Stewart noted that many convicted murderers or rapists, "just as reprehensible as these," had been spared from execution. What bothered him most was that the death penalty had been "so wantonly and so freakishly imposed" by jurors who had no standards to follow.

Justice Brennan wrote the longest of the concurring opinions. In more than sixty pages, he canvassed the issues raised by the "cruel and unusual punishments" clause of the Eighth Amendment. He began with the historical record, admitting that it provoked "very little debate" in the Congress that adopted the Bill of Rights. Brennan concluded that "we cannot now know exactly what the Framers thought 'cruel and unusual punishments' were." He then constructed an ingenious argument to infer their intent. The congressional debate, however brief, showed that the Framers "intended to ban torturous punishments," he wrote. One representative, however, objected that the clause should not bar such "necessary" punishments as whipping and ear cropping. Brennan then noted that no member "rose to reply that the Clause was intended merely to prohibit torture." From this silence, he inferred that the Framers did not "intend simply to forbid punishments considered 'cruel and unusual' at the time." Later generations might consider the death penalty equally barbaric as torture and mutilation.

Brennan urged his colleagues to apply contemporary values to the constitutional text. "We must not," he wrote, "in the guise of 'judicial restraint,' abdicate our fundamental responsibility to enforce the Bill of Rights." He brought to this self-imposed task his favorite case, *Trop v. Dulles*, which dealt with a sad-sack Army private who served in North Africa during World War II. Albert Trop had walked away from a military stockade in Casablanca, where he had been confined for a minor breach of discipline. The next day, he changed his mind and started walking back to his base. An Army truck stopped, Trop got in, and he wound up with three years of hard labor and a dishonorable discharge for his "desertion" from duty. When he sought a passport in 1952, a federal judge applied a Civil War law which provided that any soldier convicted of desertion "shall lose his nationality." Trop became a man without a country.

Writing in 1958 for a bare majority, Chief Justice Earl Warren relied on the Eighth Amendment in restoring Trop's citizenship. Trop had already served a harsh sentence, and the added punishment of denaturalization far outweighed his crime. Warren traced the prohibition of "cruel and unusual punishments" to the Magna Carta. "The basic concept underlying the Eighth Amendment is nothing less than the dignity of man," he wrote. Warren added a prophetic sentence to his opinion: "The Amendment must draw its meaning from the evolving standards of decency that mark the progress of a maturing society."

Justice Brennan adopted Warren's words as his judicial credo, and quoted them in dozens of opinions. He put them to the ultimate test in the *Furman* case, which dealt with a far greater punishment than loss of citizenship. The Eighth Amendment, he wrote, "prohibits the infliction of uncivilized and inhuman punishments." It demands that states treat all citizens "with respect for their intrinsic worth as human beings." A punishment is "cruel and unusual," Brennan wrote, "if it does not comport with human dignity." This formulation, he admitted, "does not of itself yield principles for assessing the constitutional validity of particular punishments."

Brennan then listed four principles he considered relevant to capital punishment. "The primary principle is that a punishment must not be so severe as to be degrading to the dignity of human beings." The infliction of physical pain was not the only measure of severity. Punishments offended the Eighth Amendment, Brennan wrote, if they "treat members of the human race as nonhumans, as objects to be toyed with and discarded." The fundamental premise of the Constitution is that "even the vilest criminal remains a human being possessed of common human dignity."

Building on this principle, Brennan next argued that states "must not arbitrarily inflict a severe punishment" on those convicted of crime. In the context of capital punishment, a death sentence is arbitrary if jurors impose it on some criminals while others—equally guilty—are spared. Brennan rested this second principle on the fact that only a relative handful of capital defendants received the ultimate penalty. He saw "scant danger" that capital punishment would ever be "widely applied."

Brennan found "inherent" in the Eighth Amendment a third principle, that "a severe punishment must not be unacceptable to contemporary society." He acknowledged the "danger of subjective judgment" in allowing unelected judges to decide this question. Brennan professed confidence, however, that he could find "objective indicators" of "society's present practices" and attitudes toward capital punishment. Legislative acceptance of the death penalty, he quickly added, was not a relevant factor. "The acceptability of a severe punishment is measured," he wrote, "not by its availability, for it might become so offensive to society as never to be inflicted, but by its use."

The final principle in Brennan's explication of the Eighth Amendment was that "a severe punishment must not be excessive." He defined a penalty as excessive if "there is a significantly less severe punishment adequate to achieve the purposes" for which it is inflicted. Life in prison ensured that murderers would not be able to repeat their crimes.

Having stated these four principles, Brennan conceded his inability to show that capital punishment "is fatally offensive under any one principle." States were not inflicting torture on criminals. The death penalty was not imposed in "a reign of blind terror." Lawmakers had not authorized methods of execution that were "clearly and totally rejected" by society. And states would not enact criminal penalties with "no reason whatever for doing so." Brennan's concessions were tactical moves, designed to disarm his opponents. He launched his assault on the death penalty with an argument that relied upon the "convergence" of his four principles. He stated it in one sentence: "If a punishment is unusually severe, if there is a strong probability that it is inflicted arbitrarily, if it is substantially rejected by contemporary society, and if there is no reason to believe that it serves any penal purpose more effectively than some less severe punishment," then the penalty violates the Eighth Amendment.

From this "convergence" position, Brennan deployed an army of facts against capital punishment. The death penalty, he claimed, was unusual "in its pain, in its finality, and in its enormity." In a later opinion, Brennan reported the gruesome details of executions in which "the stench of burning flesh" from electrocution caused witnesses to vomit. In the Georgia execution of Alpha Stephens in 1983, the first electric charge "failed to kill him, and he struggled to breathe for eight minutes before a second charge carried out his death sentence," Brennan wrote. He also recounted executions in which prisoners' eyes popped out and witnesses heard sounds "like bacon frying" on a grill.

Brennan next marshaled statistics to show that capital punishment had become increasingly rare, from a yearly average of 167 executions in the 1930s to only one in 1966. If the death penalty is imposed so rarely, he argued, "it smacks of little more than a lottery system" and is thus arbitrary in its infliction. These statistics persuaded Brennan that "contemporary society views this punishment with substantial doubt." He also cited studies which showed that "the threat of death has no greater deterrent effect than the threat of imprisonment" for life on murder rates. His reading of the facts convinced Brennan that "the punishment of death is inconsistent with all four principles" in his constitutional equation. His basic question was whether capital punishment met the standard of human dignity. Brennan's answer was clear: "Death, quite simply, does not."

His position on this issue has exposed Brennan to much criticism. Even those who consider him a great justice have questioned his reading of the Eighth Amendment. Leonard Levy, a noted constitutional scholar who has literally destroyed the "original intent" argument, has charged that on this question "Brennan's humanistic activism runs amok and he evinces an arrogance beyond belief." Levy notes that the Framers accepted the legitimacy of capital punishment without question. "No one has a right to veto the Constitution because his moral reasoning leads him to disagree with it in so clear a case," he wrote. "Brennan and Marshall corrupt the judicial process and discredit it."

Answering these charges, Brennan has admitted that capital punishment has majority support and that many people see in his position "a refusal to abide by the principle of stare decisis, obedience to precedent." He responded in a 1985 speech, leveling his own charge that the Court had departed from the "essential meaning" of the Eighth Amendment, which cannot be found in the "anachronistic views of long-gone generations." Brennan argued that he was bound "by a larger constitutional duty to the community, to expose the departure and point toward a different path. On this issue, the death penalty, I hope to embody a community, although perhaps not yet arrived, striving for human dignity for all."

WRITING IN HIS FIRST death penalty case, Justice Rehnquist declined to debate either the morality of capital punishment or the meaning of the Eighth Amendment. He responded to the majority in *Furman* with the shortest dissenting opinion, just six pages long, which did not address any facts of the cases before the Court or even cite the Eighth Amendment. He wrote, instead, an essay in political philosophy, much like his student papers at Stanford and Harvard. Rehnquist posed this basic question: "How can government by the elected representatives of the people co-exist with the power of the federal judiciary, whose members are constitutionally insulated from responsiveness to the popular will, to declare invalid laws duly enacted by the popular branches of government?"

Rehnquist called on Alexander Hamilton and John Marshall to answer his question. At first glance, this seems an odd couple. Writing in the *Federalist* papers, Hamilton denied any Supreme Court power to strike down acts of Congress. With equal firmness, Marshall asserted that power in *Marbury v. Madison*. Rehnquist argued, however, that the two men agreed on the question that mattered to him. He began with a premise: "Sovereignty resides ultimately in the people as a whole." Exercising their sovereignty, the people adopted a Constitution that granted certain powers to government and denied others. Inherent in this theory of the Constitution is the conclusion that "its commands are superior to those of the legislature, which is merely an agent of the people."

Thus far in his argument, Rehnquist sounded much like Brennan in granting primacy to the Constitution as the basic charter of rights. But he abruptly shifted course, calling on Hamilton and Marshall for support. Although they differed on many issues, the two men denied the power of the Supreme Court to strike down state laws. Hamilton argued in *Federalist No. 78*, cited by Rehnquist, that the Court's power of judicial review was designed solely to prevent Congress from usurping the rights of states to legislate as they saw fit. And in *Marbury*, Marshall limited the "judicial power" to cases "arising under the laws of the United States," making no mention of state legislation. Writing later in *Barron v. Baltimore*, Marshall ruled that states were not bound by the Bill of Rights.

Determined to relegate the Supreme Court to a toothless role in reviewing state laws, Rehnquist ignored dozens of decisions which asserted that power. Instead, he chided his new colleagues for "imposing their own views of goodness, truth, and justice upon others." Echoing the words of Justice Oliver Wendell Holmes, he denied "that this Court has been granted a roving commission" by the Framers "to strike down laws that are based upon notions of policy or morality suddenly found unacceptable by a majority of this Court." Rehnquist shuddered at the thought of "a mistaken upholding of an individual's constitutional claim against the validity of a legislative enactment," which he said would "impose upon the Nation the judicial fiat of a majority of a court of judges whose connection with the popular will is remote at best." The Court was mistaken, he felt, in sparing William Furman from the electric chair.

Rehnquist's opinion in *Furman* said nothing about capital punishment. It could have been written in any case, from antitrust laws to zoning regulations. Perhaps he felt the need, early in his judicial career, to articulate his "deference" principle in response to what he considered "judicial overreaching" in this case. And perhaps the senior members of the minority, in their separate dissenting opinions, spoke for him in defense of capital punishment. At any rate, Rehnquist held his tongue on the issue for another four years, until the justices took another trip to Death Row.

BECAUSE THE *Furman* DECISION wiped out every state capital punishment law, it also erased the death sentences of more than a thousand inmates, who were in effect resentenced to life imprisonment. The political uproar over this mass clemency was deafening. The loudest voice came from the White House, where President Richard Nixon was preparing a reelection campaign against a Democrat, Senator George McGovern, who opposed the death penalty. Only hours after the *Furman* decision, Nixon told a televised press conference that he believed "capital punishment is a necessary deterrent for capital crimes." McGovern said nothing about the decision and later suffered a crushing defeat. The *Furman* case did not swing the election, but it allowed a skilled politician to exploit the issue.

State legislators followed Nixon's lead and quickly drafted laws to reinstate capital punishment. They read the *Furman* decision and tried to satisfy the Court's demand for "individualized determinations" in capital cases. Within two years, thirty-five states had passed new laws, most of which listed "aggravating" and "mitigating" factors that jurors must consider in deciding whether to impose the death penalty. By 1976, judges had sentenced 487 men—and one woman—to die for crimes that included murder, rape, robbery, and kidnapping. The pattern of sentences remained intact: more than half were imposed in Deep South states, and more than half of those condemned to die were black. Virtually all were poor and were defended by appointed lawyers, who usually received minimal compensation and no funds for investigation. Only a few states, such as California, required any formal training for lawyers who defended capital cases. In many states, lawyers were picked at random—often from the courthouse corridors—to defend someone on trial for his life.

Four years after *Furman*, the Supreme Court decided to review the new state laws for compliance with its mandate. From a crowded Death Row docket, the justices picked Troy Lee Gregg for the dubious distinction of placing his name on the next test of capital punishment. He was one of six inmates, from five states, whose sentences the Court agreed to review. Once again, NAACP lawyers guided these cases to the Court, with Anthony Amsterdam as the master strategist. Gregg was not the most appealing client. The trial evidence showed that he and a companion were hitchhiking north in Florida in 1973 when they were picked up by two men, Fred Simmons and Bob Moore. During a stop in Georgia, Gregg decided to rob his benefactors and steal their car. He ordered Simmons and Moore into a ditch and shot them both in the head. He was arrested in North Carolina in the stolen car, with a gun in his pocket that was shown to be the murder weapon. Gregg was returned to Georgia, where a jury applied the new law, found an "aggravating factor" in the robbery charge, and imposed the death penalty.

The question before the Supreme Court in *Gregg v. Georgia* was not the defendant's guilt, which was conceded, but whether his penalty met the *Furman* standard. Seven justices voted in 1976 to uphold Gregg's death sentence. The crucial votes were cast by Potter Stewart and Byron White, who both shifted from the *Furman* case to join a new majority.

But no more than three justices could agree on a single opinion. Stewart, the classical judicial centrist, announced the "judgment of the Court" in an opinion that spoke only for his fellow centrists, Lewis Powell and John Paul Stevens.

Stewart had objected in *Furman* to the Georgia law that gave juries complete discretion in capital cases, which he feared would be "freakishly" imposed. The new Georgia law satisfied his objections. His opinion considered the arguments of both sides in the capital punishment debate. Stewart first cited Chief Justice Warren's opinion in *Trop v. Dulles* and its concerns with "evolving standards of decency" in "a maturing society." Based on this principle, he wrote, "an assessment of contemporary values concerning the infliction of a challenged sanction is relevant to the application of the Eighth Amendment." In assessing these values, however, judges must look to legislative judgments and not intervene "so long as the penalty selected is not cruelly inhumane or disproportionate to the crime involved."

Addressing claims that "standards of decency" had shifted since the *Furman* decision, Stewart cited the actions of Congress and thirty-five states in passing new laws to conform with the Court's revised standards. These laws, he wrote, "make clear that capital punishment itself has not been rejected by the elected representatives of the people." In his *Furman* opinion, Stewart had cited the small number of death sentences as evidence of the "freakish" nature of the penalty. But he wrote in *Gregg* that "the reluctance of juries in many cases to impose the sentence may well reflect the humane feeling that this most irrevocable of sanctions should be reserved for a small number of extreme cases." He thus turned the rarity of the death penalty from an argument against its imposition to its defense.

Stewart also paid attention to measures of public opinion on capital punishment, citing state referenda in California, Massachusetts, and Illinois that endorsed the death penalty, and a 1972 Gallup Poll that showed 57 percent support across the nation. These facts, and the actions of juries in imposing death sentences, convinced Stewart of "the continued utility and necessity of capital punishment in appropriate cases." He then moved to the question of deciding "whether Georgia may impose the death penalty on the petitioner in this case." Over some twenty pages, Stewart discussed the Georgia statute in abstract terms but said nothing about the facts of Troy Gregg's case or his sentence. He endorsed Georgia's requirement that a jury must "identify at least one statutory aggravating factor before it may impose a penalty of death." The jury found this factor in the robbery charge. The bottom line of Stewart's opinion was that Troy Gregg should die, not for shooting Fred Simmons and Bob Moore, but for the crime of stealing their wallets and car. If Gregg had simply walked away from their bodies, he would have faced only a life sentence in Georgia's prisons.

Justice Brennan now spoke about capital punishment as a dissenter. The change in laws had not changed his mind. His *Gregg* opinion restated his position in the *Furman* case. Advancements in "moral concepts" about punishment, Brennan wrote, "require us to hold that the law has progressed to the point where we should declare that the punishment of death, like punishments on the rack, the screw, and the wheel, is no longer morally tolerable in our civilized society." He countered Stewart's public opinion polls with an article from the *Notre Dame Lawyer*. Although Brennan did not quote this argument by a Catholic scholar, the author concluded that *Furman* showed "the futility of the utilitarian debate" over capital punishment and that legislators are "ill-equipped to announce and elaborate on first moral principles." He suggested that the Supreme Court was the "most fit" among the institutions of government "to solve the problem on moral grounds in the context of the Constitution." Brennan found this an appealing buttress to his claim that the "primary moral principle" embodied in the Eighth Amendment is that capital punishment is inherently "degrading to human dignity."

Justice Rehnquist did not write separately in *Gregg*, but he joined the concurring opinion of Byron White, who defended capital punishment with more fervor than did Potter Stewart. Speaking also for Chief Justice Burger, White turned the *Furman* decision on its head. The flaw in Georgia's "standardless" law before *Furman*, he wrote, was that juries imposed the death penalty so infrequently that it was applied "freakishly" and violated the rule against "arbitrary" punishment. White had dissented in *Furman*, and did not consider the new Georgia law an improvement. But he did support any law that would allow jurors, whatever the standard given them, to "impose the death penalty in a substantial portion" of capital cases. The more persons sentenced to death, White reasoned, the less "freakish" and arbitrary the penalty would become. Charges that jurors might be swayed by other factors, such as race, did not bother White. "Mistakes will be made and discriminations will occur which will be difficult to explain," he admitted. But he did not find in these problems "an indictment of our entire system of justice."

The Court decided four other cases along with *Gregg*. One involved a North Carolina law that mandated the death penalty for every person convicted of first-degree murder. This law included defendants who had not killed anyone but were charged under a "felony murder" statute. Most states make every participant in a felony—such as robbery—responsible for a homicide committed by any other participant. The Supreme Court had long upheld felony murder laws, on the principle of "vicarious responsibility" for criminal acts, but the mandatory nature of the North Carolina law—similar to those of nine other states—conflicted with the "individualized determination" holding of the *Furman* decision. Five justices, including Brennan, voted to strike down such laws in *Woodson v. North Carolina*.

James Tyrone Woodson had been sentenced to die for a murder committed by Luby Waxton. Both men were black, poor, and illiterate. Woodson was also drunk during the crime, sitting in a car as a lookout while Waxton robbed a convenience store and fatally shot the clerk, Shirley Butler, a white woman and mother. But it would not have mattered if Woodson had been the state's governor; the statute mandated the death penalty for *any* accomplice to felony murder. Writing for the Court, Justice Stewart cited Brennan's *Furman* concurrence in holding that mandatory death sentences violated "civilized standards" and had been rejected by most states as "unduly harsh and unworkably rigid."

Justice Rehnquist chose the *Woodson* case to make his first head-on defense of the death penalty. He began with the "original proposition" in the Constitution that "the infliction of capital punishment is not in itself violative of the Cruel and Unusual Punishments Clause." As a firm believer in the "original intent" approach to constitutional interpretation, Rehnquist dismissed the argument, rooted in the *Trop* decision, that "evolving standards of decency" were relevant to this issue. He conceded, however, the relevance of legislative decisions about capital punishment, and agreed that many states had moved from mandatory to discretionary capital sentencing laws. But he denied that this change "evidences societal rejection of mandatory death penalties." Rehnquist cited no evidence for this assertion, relying on his own reading of legislators' minds that there would be "roughly the same number of capital convictions" under either mandatory or discretionary death penalty laws.

What appealed most to Rehnquist about laws such as North Carolina's was that "there can be no separate appellate review of the factual basis for the sentencing decision in a mandatory system." He denied, in fact, that the Constitution provided *any* "right to appellate review of a criminal sentence," although he was forced to reach back to 1894 for precedent. Conceding the power of states to allow appeals of criminal sentences, Rehnquist would limit review to questions of whether defendants received a "fairly conducted trial" before their sentencing. James Woodson had not contested the fairness of his trial, and Rehnquist felt the jury had no obligation to consider such "mitigating" factors as his drunken state—or that he had not killed anyone—in imposing the death penalty.

Rehnquist has a penchant for arcane language. He expressed his disdain for the Court's decision in the *Woodson* case with the term "glossolalial," from a word which means "incomprehensible speech in an imaginary language, sometimes occurring in a trance state." Considering that a human life was at stake, Rehnquist flirted with callousness in suggesting that his colleagues were deluded on the issue of capital punishment. He admitted no doubt that states could use any system they wished to impose the death penalty, including mandatory sentences in felony murder cases. But he fell one vote short of sending James Woodson to North Carolina's gas chamber.

DESPITE ITS RULING that the Eighth Amendment allows capital punishment, the Court did not close the door to further Death Row appeals. Following the *Gregg* and *Woodson* decisions, cases piled up on the Court's docket. The justices selected a handful for review that raised new and disputed legal questions. Two of these cases, argued together in March 1977, raised very different questions. One asked the Court to decide if killing a police officer demanded the death penalty. The other asked if death was an appropriate punishment for rape. In both cases, Justice Brennan answered no and Justice Rehnquist said yes.

The first case involved a Louisiana law, enacted after the *Furman* decision, requiring the death penalty for anyone who killed "a peace officer who was engaged in the performance of his lawful duties." During Mardi Gras festivities in 1974, a party in New Orleans became violent and Harry Roberts shot and killed a police officer, Dennis McInerney. Five justices voted to reverse the death sentence in *Roberts v. Louisiana* in a brief, unsigned opinion. Agreeing that killing a police officer might be an "aggravating circumstance" under a law that satisfied the *Furman* and *Gregg* standards, the majority held that it was "incorrect to suppose that no mitigating circumstances can exist" in such cases. Mandatory sentences of any kind, for any reason, violated the Eighth Amendment.

Justice Rehnquist wrote an angry dissent in the *Roberts* case. He expressed outrage that states could not protect "the foot soldiers of an ordered society" with mandatory death penalty laws. Even accepting the requirement for "individualized consideration" in other capital cases, he found the arguments for imposing the death sentence on Harry Roberts "far stronger than in the case of an ordinary homicide." Rehnquist faced the problem in *Roberts* of a recent Supreme Court decision—less than a year old—ruling directly against his position on mandatory death sentences. He simply waved aside the principle of *stare decisis*, the judicial respect for precedent, finding it a "meager basis" for deciding "large questions of how men shall be governed, and how liberty and order should be balanced in a civilized society." In this respect, Justice Rehnquist and Justice Brennan both read their own standards into the Eighth Amendment. Disregard for precedent by one justice, and disregard for the constitutional text by the other, turned both justices into "activists" on this issue.

The execution in 1977 of Gary Gilmore by a firing squad in Utah ended a ten-year hiatus in the carrying out of death sentences. By that year, close to five hundred inmates were confined on Death Rows, and virtually all had filed appeals that moved slowly through state and federal courts. Every state that allowed the death penalty required appellate review of capital sentences, and most cases raised issues of trial fairness, such as the exclusion or admission of evidence, incompetence of counsel, or jury instructions. Others raised more basic questions the Supreme Court had not addressed since the *Gregg* decision. One such case, again from Georgia, tested the death sentence imposed on Ehrlich Coker, who escaped from prison while serving three life sentences for murder, rape, and kidnapping. Hours after his escape, Coker broke into the home of Allen and Elnita Carver, tied up Allen, and then raped his sixteen-year-old wife at knifepoint. He then drove off in their car with her and was captured shortly after Allen Carver freed himself and called the police. Coker was again convicted of rape and kidnapping, and sentenced to death for the rape.

In passing new capital punishment laws after the *Gregg* decision, only four states—all southern—made rape a capital crime. The appeal in *Coker v. Georgia* claimed that the state's law violated the Eighth Amendment; the Supreme Court agreed in a 1977 opinion by Justice White, who normally voted to uphold capital sentences. He recognized that rape "is without doubt deserving of serious punishment; but in terms of moral depravity and of the injury to the person and to the public, it does not compare with murder, which does involve the unjustified taking of human life." One factor that influenced White was "the climate of international opinion" on this issue; he cited *Trop v. Dulles* and noted that only three "major nations" allowed the death penalty for rape—South Africa and the Soviet Union were two.

Chief Justice Burger spoke for himself and Justice Rehnquist in dissent. Citing the "lasting injury suffered by rape victims," Burger chided White for writing that Elnita Carver was "unharmed" when the police rescued her from Coker. The major point of Burger's opinion was that the Eighth Amendment "does not give the Members of this Court license to engraft their conceptions of proper public policy onto the considered legislative judgments of the States." Burger also feared that if capital punishment could be imposed only for crimes resulting in death, crimes such as airplane hijacking, kidnapping, and "mass terrorist activity" might not be adequately deterred. Burger and Rehnquist argued that federal and state lawmakers should be free to make any crime that threatened "grave bodily harm" a capital offense.

Burger and Rehnquist parted company the next year on an issue that affected several capital laws. Sandra Lockett, a young black woman, was sentenced to die under Ohio's felony murder statute as an accomplice in the death of a pawnbroker during a robbery. Because she knew the victim, Lockett had been assigned to act as lookout and driver of the getaway car. She did a poor job, leaving the car to eat during the robbery, which ended when the pawnbroker grabbed the gun and was shot as he grappled with Al Parker. In an ironic twist, Parker agreed after his arrest to testify against Sandra Lockett and two other defendants and bargained with the prosecutor for a life sentence. The killer was spared and the one person not in the pawnshop was sentenced to death.

The question in *Lockett v. Ohio* stemmed from the requirement that the trial judge impose the death penalty unless he found one of three factors: that the victim had "induced or facilitated" the crime that resulted in his death; that Lockett was "under duress" to participate in the robbery; or that she was suffering from "psychosis or mental deficiency." Because none of these factors existed, the judge had "no alternative" but to sentence Lockett to die, which he did reluctantly. Lockett's appeal claimed that the Ohio law effectively precluded the judge from considering such "mitigating" factors as her recovery from drug addiction and reports of court-appointed psychologists that her prognosis for rehabilitation was favorable. Anthony Amsterdam returned to the Supreme Court chamber to argue for Sandra Lockett on behalf of the NAACP Legal Defense Fund.

Chief Justice Burger wrote for the Court in reversing the death sentence. The Eighth Amendment, he said, required that judges "not be precluded from considering, *as a mitigating factor*, any aspect of a defendant's character or record and any of the circumstances of the offense that the defendant proffers as the basis for a sentence less than death." Ohio had passed a law that in effect made capital punishment mandatory in all but a few cases, violating the command of *Gregg* and *Woodson* that "an individualized decision is essential in capital cases."

Only one justice supported the Ohio law and its result in this case. Rehnquist admitted that "a sense of judicial responsibility" counseled that justices "bow to the authority" of earlier cases in most circumstances. But he again refused to accept the recent precedent—just two years old—that Burger cited as controlling in the *Lockett* case. Rehnquist opposed any judicial constraints on the states in deciding which crimes to punish with death and devising procedures for imposing that sentence. He complained that Burger's opinion told judges they "must receive in evidence whatever the defense attorney wishes them to hear" as mitigating evidence in capital cases. Rehnquist stood alone in claiming that "the Constitution is not offended by the State's refusal to consider mitigating factors at all" in passing sentence.

BETWEEN 1980 AND 1984, homicides in the United States declined by almost 20 percent, from 24,278 to 19,796. But the population of Death Row, America, grew during those years from 697 to 1,420 residents, an increase of more than 100 percent. That number did not include the thirty-two inmates who had been executed, twenty-one in 1984 alone. Every day in that year, more than forty persons pleaded guilty or were convicted of homicide, ranging from manslaughter to capital murder. Every second day, one of this group was sentenced to death. But just one of every eighty convicted murderers received the death penalty.

The sharp disparity between homicide convictions and capital sentences in these figures persuaded the Court to tackle another hard question: Does the Eighth Amendment require a "proportionality" review in each capital case? In other words, must judges look at sentences imposed in similar crimes before sending anyone to Death Row? To answer this question, the justices picked from their death penalty docket a particularly gruesome case, *Pulley v. Harris*. Robert Harris and his brother decided in 1978 to rob a bank in San Diego, California. First they stole a getaway car, picking one in which two teenage boys were sitting and eating hamburgers. Harris forced them at gunpoint to drive to a secluded park, where they tried to escape. He tracked them down, shot them both, and then calmly ate the rest of their burgers. The Harris brothers proceeded to rob the bank and were quickly apprehended in the stolen car.

After a jury convicted Robert Harris on two counts of first-degree murder, the jurors heard evidence at a separate penalty hearing, at which the state's lawyers introduced such "aggravating" factors as Harris's earlier manslaughter conviction and his rape of another prison inmate. Harris took the stand and told the jurors that he had a terrible childhood, that his father beat him regularly and had been convicted of sexually molesting his sisters. He also blamed his brother—who testified against him in exchange for a life sentence—for the shootings. This "mitigating" evidence did not impress the jury, which sentenced Harris to die in the San Quentin gas chamber. Many Californians had turned against capital punishment after the long and bitter struggle over the execution of Caryl Chessman for kidnapping in 1960. The *Harris* case changed many minds on this issue. News stories invariably reminded people that Harris had eaten his victims' hamburgers, as if that were a statutory aggravating factor.

Although several states required a proportionality review of capital sentences, California did not, and the state supreme court rejected Harris's claim that he had been denied "due process of law" under the Fourteenth Amendment. The U.S. Supreme Court declined to review this ruling in 1981. Harris then filed a *habeas corpus* petition in federal court and finally won an order from an appellate panel that the state court must compare his sentence with those imposed for similar crimes. This time, the Supreme Court accepted the state's appeal from the federal ruling. Once again, Anthony Amsterdam argued for the defendant.

"We take statutes as we find them," Justice White wrote for the Court in reversing the appellate ruling in 1984. He meant that the Constitution did not require states to provide proportionality review in capital cases; the fact that some did was not binding on all. White acknowledged that California juries may have spared other murderers whose crimes were as vicious as those of Robert Harris. "Any capital sentencing scheme may occasionally produce aberrational outcomes," he conceded. But Harris had received a fair trial and was sentenced under a law that met the

Court's new standards. Justice Rehnquist joined White's opinion without comment.

Justice Brennan railed against the majority in a dissent that spoke also for Thurgood Marshall. "I am convinced that the Court is simply deluding itself, and also the American public," he wrote, "when it insists that those defendants who have already been executed or are today condemned to death have been selected on a basis that is neither arbitrary nor capricious, under any meaningful definition of those terms." States were required by the Constitution and the Court's earlier rulings, he argued, to make every effort to eliminate "the irrationality that currently surrounds the imposition of the death penalty."

Brennan was particularly concerned by charges that racial discrimination had infected the system of capital punishment. At the time the Court decided the *Harris* case, 42 percent of those sentenced to death were black, four times their proportion in the American population. Robert Harris was Caucasian, but his appeal raised this issue and the federal appellate judges had ordered an examination of the available evidence on racial disparities in capital sentencing. The Supreme Court's decision wiped out this order, but Brennan listed a dozen academic studies and summarized their findings as "relatively clear" evidence that among the significant factors in death sentences were "the race of the defendant and the race of the victim." Brennan admitted that the question of racial disparities in sentencing "has not been properly presented to the Court and is not at issue in this case." Looking ahead to a better case, he wrote that "a rapidly expanding body of literature" was being produced on this issue; death penalty opponents took the hint and began searching for a proper case.

Brennan also noted in his *Harris* dissent that twelve years had passed since he wrote in *Furman* that capital punishment violated the Eighth Amendment. "Nothing that has occurred during the past 12 years has given me any reason to change these views," he wrote; "if anything, I am more persuaded of the unconstitutionality of the death penalty than ever before." Brennan pleaded with his colleagues. "As executions occur with more frequency," he wrote, "the time is fast approaching for the Court to reexamine the death penalty" and to root out "the irrationality prohibited by our decision in *Furman*." Underneath his crusading words, a note of resignation pervaded Brennan's dissent. Time was running out for more and more Death Row inmates. Before the Supreme Court decided the issue of racial disparities in capital sentencing in 1986, the

Death Row population increased to more than 1,700, and fifty inmates were executed.

Robert Harris and his lawyers kept on appealing after the Supreme Court decision, raising new claims that Harris had been prevented from presenting evidence of childhood brain damage and that execution by cyanide gas was "cruel and unusual punishment." His time ran out on April 21, 1992, eight years after the Court's ruling. One reporter described the "all-night legal free-for-all" that kept dozens of federal judges and all nine Supreme Court justices awake. Four times that day, the Court overturned lower-court orders to delay the execution to consider last-ditch motions. Even after Harris was strapped into the gas chamber, a telephone call by an appellate judge kept him waiting in the chair for twelve minutes without knowing the reason for delay. "Let's pull it," he said impatiently, nodding toward the lever that released the cyanide pellets. But guards hauled Harris out for another two-hour wait, until the Supreme Court rejected the last stay order at 6 a.m. with its own brusque order that it would consider no more stays for any reason.

Harris's last words, mouthed silently through a thick glass window to the father of one boy he shot, were "I'm sorry." He then "gasped and gagged several times" after the cyanide hit the pan of sulphuric acid under his chair, one reporter wrote. "Saliva drooled from his mouth, and his head jerked back and forth for about ten more minutes" before he was pronounced dead. "I knew it wouldn't be pretty," the reporter said. "I just didn't know it would be that ugly."

EVEN BEFORE the Court decided the *Harris* case, the justices had twice denied review to a Georgia inmate named Warren McCleskey. He was a poor candidate for judicial sympathy. During an armed robbery of a furniture store in Marietta, Georgia, police officer Frank Schlatt answered a silent alarm, entered the store, and was fatally shot in the face. Several weeks later, McCleskey was arrested for an unrelated offense. During interrogation, he confessed to participating in the robbery but denied killing Officer Schlatt. He refused a bargain to plead guilty in exchange for a life sentence. The trial evidence against McCleskey was entirely circumstantial, but two witnesses—including a prison cellmate—testified they heard McCleskey admit to the shooting. He was convicted of murder and the jury found two aggravating factors in the crime—killing an officer in the course of a robbery. McCleskey's court-appointed lawyer offered no mitigating evidence. The death sentence was hardly a surprise, and the state courts found no flaw in the trial or penalty hearing.

During the round of futile appeals, McCleskey's lawyer was approached by John Charles Boger, who directed the NAACP Legal Defense Fund campaign against the death penalty and worked closely with Anthony Amsterdam. The Fund had hired an Iowa University law professor, David Baldus, to conduct a detailed study of capital punishment in Georgia, which produced the largest crop of Supreme Court death penalty cases. Baldus had directed law and social science programs for the National Science Foundation, and was skilled in statistical analysis. He examined all 2,484 Georgia homicides between 1974 and 1979 in which a suspect was arrested. He identified 230 separate factors in each case—whether a gun was used, the defendant's prior record, and the race of the killer and victim, among others. Baldus then subjected this mountain of data to a powerful statistical tool, called multivariate regression analysis, which measured the relative impact of each factor on the outcome of each case, which was the sentence imposed on the defendant. The Baldus report, in fact, had been the first study Brennan cited in his *Harris* dissent, in urging the Court to review sentencing disparities.

John Boger received the initial version of the Baldus study in early 1982. He began shopping for federal judges who might admit the data as evidence in *habeas corpus* proceedings brought by Death Row inmates. Boger was not choosy in looking for cases, and attached the study to thirty different *habeas* petitions. He finally found a judge, Owen Forrester in Georgia, who agreed to consider this evidence. Recently appointed by Ronald Reagan, Forrester had been presented a petition by Warren McCleskey's lawyer that raised eighteen separate claims of constitutional violations in his trial and penalty hearing.

Forrester issued a sixty-page opinion in 1984, after a lengthy evidentiary hearing. He gave short shrift to most of McCleskey's claims, which had already been dismissed by state judges. The bulk of the opinion discussed the Baldus study, whose author testified for many hours. Although his report included thousands of figures, Baldus pointed the judge to one simple chart, called a "two-by-two box." Statisticians use these charts to show the connections of two variables, in this case the race of the killer and that of the victim. The figures showed huge disparities. When both killer and victim were black, juries sent only 1 percent of defendants to Death Row. When both were white, 8 percent of defendants received a death sentence, while only 3 percent of whites who killed blacks received this penalty. But in homicides with a black killer and a white victim, the death penalty was imposed in 22 percent of all cases. In other words, blacks who killed whites were twenty-two times more likely to be sentenced to death than if they killed another black. The most relevant factor in this case was that Warren McCleskey was black and Officer Schlatt was white.

Judge Forrester listened closely to Professor Baldus, but his opinion reflected the adage that "a little learning is a dangerous thing." Baldus had explained that a model showing a perfect connection of variables and outcomes would have a statistical value of 1.0; one that showed no relation between them would have a value of zero. In the most complex model that Baldus employed, with 230 variables, he found a value of 0.46. Forrester concluded that the model "does not predict the outcome in half of the cases." The judge completely missed the point of the Baldus study. What he ignored, or failed to understand, was that for a model with 230 variables, the figure of 0.46 has a very high predictive value. In more graphic terms, it showed that if a million Georgia juries had been asked to decide Warren McCleskey's fate, just *one* would not have imposed the death sentence. With these odds, his fate was sealed by his skin color.

After a federal appellate panel upheld Judge Forrester's decision in 1985, John Boger filed an appeal with the Supreme Court. He claimed to be surprised when the justices voted to hear the case. "It was such a clear-cut challenge to the death penalty that I thought they would duck it," he told a reporter. An unwritten Supreme Court rule allows the votes of four justices to grant review, although votes are normally not revealed. Justices Brennan and Marshall probably convinced two others—most likely Harry Blackmun and John Paul Stevens—to apply the "rule of four" to Warren McCleskey's appeal. Win or lose, the stakes were high. "I think everyone saw *McCleskey* as the biggest case of the year," one of the Court's law clerks said. The outcome depended on a single vote, not one of a million but one of nine. These were still poor odds for McCleskey.

During the oral argument on October 15, 1986, John Boger looked to Justice Lewis Powell for a possible fifth vote to spare McCleskey from the electric chair. Powell asked one distressing question: "What were the aggravating circumstances in this case?" Boger confessed that McCleskey had been convicted of killing Officer Schlatt. "So this defendant was guilty of shooting a police officer while he was in the process of committing a felony," Powell responded. This brief exchange dashed Boger's meager hopes of finding the fifth vote.

At the Court's conference, Powell joined a majority of five to uphold the death sentence in *McCleskey v. Kemp*. In one of his first opinion assignments as Chief Justice, Rehnquist asked Powell to write for the Court. Some felt this was a calculated move to put the name of a moderate justice on a hard-line opinion. Whatever the motivation, Powell did the job. Unlike Judge Forrester, he accepted the basic validity of the Baldus study and its findings of racial disparity in Georgia's death cases. But Powell distrusted statistics, however compelling, and refused to look beyond the courtroom in Marietta, Georgia. He wrote that "McCleskey must prove that the decisionmakers in *his* case acted with discriminatory purpose." From this premise, the conclusion was simple. McCleskey presented "no evidence specific to his own case," Powell wrote, "that would support an inference that racial considerations played a part in his sentence."

Powell looked at only one tree in the statistical forest. The Baldus study was premised on the fact that jurors in individual cases cannot be questioned about their motivations, beyond general inquiries during jury selection about race prejudice, to which few will confess. If McCleskey could have shown bias in his particular case, the Baldus study would have been superfluous. It was precisely because he and other black defendants could *not* make an individualized showing of prejudice that evidence of a systematic bias became relevant. Powell admitted that the Court "has accepted statistics as proof of intent to discriminate in certain limited contexts," citing cases involving selection of jury pools, bias in housing sales and rentals, and voting discrimination. But he declined to apply these precedents to capital punishment. "Because discretion is essential to the criminal justice system," Powell wrote, "we would demand exceptionally clear proof before we would infer that the discretion has been abused." He did not suggest what kind of proof might satisfy the Court.

Justice Powell, a humane and courtly man, knew that Brennan was crushed by the *McCleskey* decision, having lost by one vote his last real chance to halt or even slow down executions. In a footnote, Powell acknowledged Brennan's "eloquent dissent" and wrote that his views "are principled and entitled to respect." These gracious words hardly salved the wound. Brennan accepted the commiseration for himself, but suggested that his colleagues imagine "what is said on death row" as lawyers explained the Court's decision to condemned black inmates. He felt that "these painful conversations will serve as the most eloquent dissents of all."

Brennan imagined a conversation between McCleskey and his lawyer, prior to entering a plea, as if the Court's final decision was known to them. "At some point in this case," he wrote, "Warren McCleskey doubtless asked his lawyer whether a jury was likely to sentence him to die. A candid reply to this question would have been disturbing." The lawyer would have to admit that nothing was "more important than the fact that his victim was white." The lawyer "would feel bound to tell McCleskey that defendants charged with killing white victims in Georgia are 4.3 times as likely to be sentenced to death" as those charged with killing blacks. "The story could be told in a variety of ways," Brennan said, "but McCleskey could not fail to grasp its essential narrative line: there was a significant chance that race would play a prominent role in determining if he lived or died." The unstated conclusion was that McCleskey would weigh the odds and give up his right to trial, accepting a life sentence to avoid the risk of dying in the electric chair.

This imagined conversation illustrates Brennan's concern for the human story behind the briefs on the Court's mahogany conference table. His dissent also reflected his concern for the broader story that began with slavery and ended in McCleskey's death sentence. A fuller "understanding of history and human experience" would place the Baldus study in proper context, Brennan suggested. He traced the history of Georgia's "race-conscious criminal justice system" back to the slave era. "During the colonial period, black slaves who killed whites in Georgia, regardless of whether in self-defense or in defense of another, were automatically executed." He quoted the pioneering study of race relations in the 1940s, An American Dilemma. "For offenses which involve any actual or potential danger to whites," wrote Gunnar Myrdal, "Negroes are punished more severely than whites."

Brennan noted that the Supreme Court did not strike down racial segregation in Georgia and other southern states until the 1960s. He placed the issue of capital punishment against this historical backdrop. "Warren McCleskey's evidence confronts us with the subtle and persistent influence of the past," he wrote. "His message is a disturbing one to a society that has formally repudiated racism, and a frustrating one to a

Nation accustomed to regarding its destiny as the product of its own will. Nonetheless, we ignore him at our peril, for we remain imprisoned by the past as long as we deny its influence in the present."

Brennan reminded Powell of his statement in *Furman* that an equal protection argument would be available for a black defendant "who could demonstrate that members of his race were being singled out for more severe punishment than others charged with the same offense." He also cited Powell's reference to statistical evidence of racial disparities in death sentences for rape. Brennan accused the majority of missing the point. Whether any particular sentence resulted from racial bias was "irrelevant" to the question of whether a sentencing system created an unacceptable "risk" of arbitrary decisions. "This emphasis on risk acknowledges the difficulty of divining the jury's motivation in an individual case," he wrote. It was clear to Brennan that black defendants in Georgia—and most likely in other states—gambled with their lives in going to trial on capital charges. "Close analysis of the Baldus study," he wrote, "reveals that the risk that race influenced McCleskey's sentence is intolerable by any imaginable standard."

Brennan had retired by the time the Supreme Court made its last ruling in the *McCleskey* case, shortly before 3 a.m. on September 25, 1991. The justices rejected a final appeal by a 6–3 vote. The majority refused to consider a claim that prosecutors concealed from the trial jury the fact that the chief witness against McCleskey, Offie Evans, was a police informer who was promised a lighter sentence for his testimony. Two jurors who voted for the death penalty had changed their minds. "I believe if you take a life, death is the right punishment," juror Robert Burnette said. "But when you take that person's life you have to be sure beyond a shadow of a doubt that person committed the crime, and I don't feel that way about this case. If we knew more about Offie Evans, his credibility would have been shot to hell."

Justice Thurgood Marshall, who had already announced his retirement, wrote a last, stinging dissent: "In refusing to grant a stay to fully review McCleskey's claims, the Court values expediency over human life. Repeatedly denying Warren McCleskey his constitutional rights is unacceptable. Executing him is inexcusable."

Minutes after the Court's final ruling, Warren McCleskey was strapped into Georgia's electric chair. Prison officials had described him as a peacemaker among the violent inmates. McCleskey had these last words:

"I pray that one day this country, supposedly a civilized society, will abolish barbaric acts such as the death penalty." Thirteen minutes later, he was pronounced dead.

DURING HIS LAST three years on the Court, Justice Brennan continued to vote against capital punishment, but in most cases he was joined only by Thurgood Marshall. After the *McCleskey* decision, the Court's majority looked for cases that would broaden the scope of death penalty laws and speed up the pace of executions. Chief Justice Rehnquist took every opportunity to support this judicial effort. He assigned Justice Antonin Scalia in 1989 to write for a bare majority in upholding the execution of juvenile defendants. Kentucky and Missouri allowed judges to impose the death penalty on juvenile defendants—as young as fourteen—who were convicted of murder.

Scalia's opinion in *Stanford v. Kentucky* recounted in gory detail the crimes of Kevin Stanford and Heath Wilkins. Stanford was seventeen when he robbed a gas station in Jefferson County, Kentucky, and shot the clerk, Barbel Poore, in the head. Stanford later told a prison guard that "I had to shoot her" because she lived next door and could identify him. "Then after he said that he started laughing," the guard testified. Wilkins was sixteen when he robbed a convenience store in Avondale, Missouri, and stabbed to death Nancy Allen, the store's clerk and the mother of two young children. Wilkins later said he killed Allen because "a dead person can't talk."

The question before the Court in both cases was not guilt, but whether the Eighth Amendment barred the death penalty for juveniles. Scalia based his opinion on the fact that twenty-five states—exactly half—allowed the execution of persons under eighteen years of age. "This does not establish the degree of national consensus this Court has previously thought sufficient to label a particular punishment cruel and unusual," he wrote. Scalia then addressed the argument that juvenile executions had been rejected by "public opinion polls, the views of interest groups, and the positions adopted by various professional associations." He declined "the invitation to rest constitutional law upon such uncertain foundations." Any "national consensus" on this issue, Scalia wrote, must rest on laws "that the people have approved." Under this test, Kevin Stanford and Heath Wilkins could not challenge their death sentences.

Scalia viewed the glass as half full, while Brennan saw it as half empty.

Writing for the four dissenters, he noted that twelve states rejected the death penalty for persons under eighteen years of age, and that another fifteen did not allow capital punishment. He thus found a national consensus "that no one under 18 should face the death penalty." Brennan also differed with Scalia in considering "the opinions of respected organizations" as indicators of "contemporary standards" on the question. He listed thirty-three groups, from the American Bar Association to the West Virginia Council of Churches, that had filed briefs opposing capital punishment for persons under eighteen, and cited the laws of 132 countries that did not permit this penalty. "The views of organizations with expertise in relevant fields and the choices of governments elsewhere in the world," Brennan argued, "merit our attention as indicators whether a punishment is acceptable in a civilized society." But the groups and governments he cited did not vote in the Court's conference room.

By the end of 1989, the Death Row population jumped to 2,250. During that year, the Court approved the execution of mentally retarded convicts, and ruled that inmates sentenced to death had no constitutional right to lawyers in pursuing *habeas corpus* appeals. In both cases, Rehnquist joined the majority and Brennan dissented. Speaking as Chief Justice, Rehnquist had appeared before Congress to lobby for restrictions on federal *habeas corpus* petitions by state prisoners. This issue produced a head-on collision with Brennan in 1990. Rehnquist wrote for a majority of five in dismissing a *habeas* challenge by a South Carolina inmate, Horace Butler, who invoked his *Miranda* rights after an arrest for assault and battery. His lawyer told the police not to question Butler further. While Butler was still in jail, he was charged with killing a convenience-store clerk, Pamela Lane. Without consulting his lawyer, Butler signed a waiver form and confessed to the murder. Again, the defendant was a black male and the victim was a white female, and Butler received the death penalty.

The question in *Butler v. McKellar* was whether the police could disregard a request for counsel after one arrest in questioning a suspect for another crime. A recent Supreme Court decision said no, but Rehnquist declined to give this ruling a retroactive application. Even a violation of the new decision, Rehnquist wrote, would not "seriously diminish" the case against Butler. The issue was technical, but Brennan looked to its impact on Death Row inmates in complaining that Rehnquist's opinion "strips state prisoners of virtually *any* meaningful federal review of the constitutionality of their incarceration." Brennan looked directly at

Rehnquist in noting that justices who "pride themselves on their reluctance to play an 'activist' judicial role by infringing upon legislative prerogatives" did not "hesitate today to dismantle Congress' extension of federal habeas to state prisoners."

The final confrontation of Rehnquist and Brennan over capital punishment took place on July 19, 1990. A Virginia inmate, Richard Boggs, asked the Court for a stay of execution to consider evidence of his mental retardation. Boggs had been sentenced to die for the murder of an eighty-seven-year-old woman. Chief Justice Rehnquist received the application and referred it to the full Court, which rejected the stay by a vote of 7–2. In his last official statement before retirement, Brennan spoke for himself and Thurgood Marshall. "Adhering to our views that the death penalty is in all circumstances cruel and unusual punishment," Brennan wrote, "we would grant the application for stay of execution and the petition for writ of certiorari and would vacate the death sentence in this case." Within hours of the Court's decision, Richard Boggs died in Virginia's electric chair.

By the end of 1993, the population of Death Row, America, had grown to more than 3,000. Given the current rate of death sentences, if one inmate is executed every day from now on, this number will never decline. But there is still hope for some who claim unfairness or innocence. On March 1, 1993, Walter McMillian walked out of an Alabama courtroom. After six years on Death Row, the black inmate was cleared of charges that he murdered a white female during a convenience-store robbery. McMillian's lawyers proved that police had concealed evidence that he had been nowhere near the murder scene. The district attorney called the case "a horrible mistake." After his release, a reporter asked McMillian if the decision restored his faith in the judicial system. "No," he replied. "Not at all."

ELEVEN

"The Equal Protection of the Laws"

"Among the novel objects that attracted my attention during my stay in the United States," Alexis de Tocqueville wrote in 1835, "nothing struck me more forcibly than the general equality of conditions." Unburdened by feudalism and hereditary privilege, citizens of the new nation quickly achieved a fair measure of economic equality. But the "love of equality" the young French aristocrat observed among Americans was matched with an older and stronger principle, the love of liberty—or freedom—that English "freemen" brought to their new home. Tocqueville made a perceptive comment in *Democracy in America*: "Thus among the Americans it is freedom which is old—equality is of comparatively modern date."

Tocqueville had an acute eye for many facets of American society. On one issue, however, he was blind to reality. "The South contains an enormous slave population," he wrote, "a population which is already alarming, and still more formidable for the future." But he found nothing in the slave system that might threaten the stability of the United States. "It is indeed easy to discover different interests in the different parts of the Union," he wrote, "but I am unacquainted with any which are hostile to each other."

These separate observations of a nineteenth-century visitor have considerable relevance as Americans approach the twenty-first century. The principle of equality was, indeed, foreign to the original Framers. The preamble they drafted in 1787 spoke of the "Blessings of Liberty" and made no mention of equality. Four years later, another group of Framers added a Bill of Rights to the Constitution, including the Fifth Amendment, which protects all persons against deprivation of "liberty" without "due process of law." Again, the Constitution did not mention equality.

Significantly, the liberty that both groups of Framers guaranteed to Americans was limited to those who were white. Even with the Bill of Rights, the Constitution remained a lily-white charter. Black Americans—the vast majority held in slavery—were denied any kind of liberty.

The Constitution did not recognize the principle of equality until 1868, more than thirty years after Tocqueville wrote that slavery was "alarming" but not threatening to the Union. Like many people before and after the Civil War, he failed to recognize that liberty cannot exist without equality. The Fourteenth Amendment, which guarantees the "equal protection of the laws" to every American, was adopted only because the "liberty" to own slaves was purchased at the cost of 600,000 lives in a tragic civil war.

Ever since the Fourteenth Amendment became binding on the states, the Supreme Court has struggled with its interpretation. The other Civil War amendments—the Thirteenth and Fifteenth—spoke directly of race and protected the rights of former slaves. The Equal Protection clause of the Fourteenth Amendment, however, protects "any person" from official discrimination. It makes no mention of race or slavery, which has led to questions about the intent of its framers. Did they mean, as the Court held in the *Civil Rights Cases* in 1883, that African Americans—the victims of slavery—were not its intended beneficiaries? Or, as the Court said with unintended irony, that they were no longer the "special favorites" of the Constitution? Did the Congress that adopted the Fourteenth Amendment intend to prohibit racial segregation in public schools? Does the Equal Protection clause allow whites to challenge affirmative action programs designed to redress centuries of official discrimination?

The Supreme Court has grappled with questions of racial discrimination for more than a century, without any more success than the other branches of government. The constitutional issues go back to the Jim Crow laws of the nineteenth century, which replaced slavery with segregation. One case symbolized the conflict over the Equal Protection clause. Louisiana passed a law in 1890 that required racial separation on all railroad cars. Two years later, Homer Plessy was arrested for sitting in a car reserved for white passengers. Plessy described himself as "of seven-eighths Caucasian and one-eighth African blood," and had passed as white in New Orleans. State law, however, prohibited those with *any* black ancestry from mixing with whites in public places.

Ruling in *Plessy v. Ferguson* in 1896, the Supreme Court upheld Jim

Crow laws. The Court's opinion accepted the arguments of white supremacy. "Legislation is powerless to eradicate racial instincts," Justice
Henry Brown wrote. "If one race be inferior to the other socially, the
Constitution of the United States cannot put them upon the same plane."
The Louisiana law, Brown stated in passing, was no "more obnoxious
to the Fourteenth Amendment than the acts of Congress requiring separate schools for colored children in the District of Columbia," laws first
enacted the same year as the amendment's adoption.

The sole dissenter in *Plessy*, Justice John Harlan, put his objections
into a widely quoted statement: "Our Constitution is color-blind, and
neither knows nor tolerates classes among citizens. In respect of civil
rights, all citizens are equal before the law." But even Harlan admitted
the reality of white supremacy. "The white race deems itself to be the
dominant race in this country," he wrote. "And so it is, in prestige, in
achievements, in education, in wealth and in power." Harlan cited no
evidence for this statement, nor did he need to. He simply expressed the
reality of race relations at the end of the nineteenth century.

The real heart of the Jim Crow system was not in railroad cars but in
public schools. Keeping blacks "in their place" began with inferior and
segregated education. Armed with the *Plessy* decision, southern states
forced black children into separate—and unequal—schools. The National Association for the Advancement of Colored People launched a
legal campaign in the 1930s against school segregation. Under the leadership of Thurgood Marshall, NAACP lawyers first attacked segregation
in graduate schools in border states. They followed up victories in these
cases with a final assault on the citadel of segregation, elementary schools
in the Deep South. In 1950, Marshall argued—and lost—the first segregation case in South Carolina. Along with four other cases from
Virginia, Delaware, the District of Columbia, and Kansas, the school
segregation issue reached the Supreme Court in 1952. Marshall relied
on the Equal Protection clause in attacking the unequal education provided to black students in segregated schools.

Ruling in May 1954, the Supreme Court supported Marshall in a
unanimous opinion. Chief Justice Earl Warren spoke for the Court. In
construing the Equal Protection clause, he wrote, "we cannot turn the
clock back to 1868 when the Amendment was adopted, or even to 1896
when *Plessy v. Ferguson* was written." Warren rested his opinion on the
psychological stigma that segregation imposed on black children. He cited
the reports of Dr. Kenneth Clark, a noted psychologist whose doll studies

showed that black children identified black dolls as "most like me" but preferred white dolls as "prettier than me." Warren concluded from these "social facts" that black children suffered from "a feeling of inferiority as to their status in the community that may affect their hearts and minds in a way unlikely ever to be undone."

THE *Plessy* AND *Brown* DECISIONS form the backdrop to the conflicts of Justices Brennan and Rehnquist over the Equal Protection clause. As the intellectual leader of the Warren Court, Brennan took the lead in restoring this clause to the purpose the Court defined in 1886 of preventing "unjust and illegal discriminations" on racial grounds. Without dissent, the justices held in *Yick Wo v. Hopkins* that the San Francisco sheriff had illegally denied business licenses to Yick Wo and two hundred other Chinese laundry owners solely because of their race. Justice Stanley Matthews, writing for the Court, found a "broad and benign" purpose in the Equal Protection clause. Its protections "are universal in their application," he wrote, and apply "to all persons" in every state "without regard to any differences of race, of color, or of nationality."

Despite its strong language and unanimous support, the Court tossed the *Yick Wo* opinion onto the constitutional scrap heap for almost a century. It was simply ignored in the *Plessy* decision and later discrimination cases. Justice Brennan finally dusted off *Yick Wo* in 1982, in a case that struck down a Texas law that barred the use of state funds to educate the children of illegal aliens, most of them Mexican. Writing for the Court in *Plyler v. Doe*, Brennan said the Equal Protection clause "was intended to work nothing less than the abolition of all caste-based and invidious class-based legislation." He did not deny the power of states to deal with public problems by making "classifications that roughly approximate the nature of the problem perceived" by lawmakers. The Court sought "only the assurance that the classification at issue bears some fair relationship to a legitimate public purpose."

This part of the *Plyler* opinion simply restated the "rational basis" test the Court applied to "economic and social legislation." Brennan had said nothing so far that might upset Rehnquist and other defenders of judicial "deference" to lawmakers. His next paragraph, however, drew a line between the two sides. The justices "would not be faithful to our obligations under the Fourteenth Amendment if we applied so deferential a standard to every classification," Brennan continued. "The Equal Protection Clause was intended as a restriction on state legislative action inconsistent with elemental constitutional premises. Thus we have treated as presumptively invidious those classifications that disadvantage a 'suspect class,' or that impinge upon the exercise of a 'fundamental right.' With respect to such classifications, it is appropriate to enforce the mandate of equal protection by requiring the State to demonstrate that its classification has been precisely tailored to serve a compelling governmental interest."

Brennan moved on to elaborate the "strict scrutiny" test, first stated by Justice Harlan Fiske Stone in Footnote Four of his *Carolene Products* opinion in 1938. Stone wrote that laws "directed at particular religious, or national, or racial minorities," or which reflected "prejudice against discrete and insular minorities," should be subjected to a "searching judicial inquiry." Brennan cited Stone's footnote in his *Plyler* opinion. "Some classifications are more likely than others to reflect deep-seated prejudice rather than legislative rationality in pursuit of some legitimate objective," he wrote. Illegal aliens from Mexico, derided as "wetbacks" by many Texans, were certainly the objects of prejudice. "Legislation predicated on such prejudice," Brennan wrote, "is easily recognized as incompatible with the constitutional understanding that each person is to be judged individually and is entitled to equal justice under the law."

Brennan then shifted from "suspect class" analysis to the protection of "fundamental rights" against state restrictions. "In determining whether a class-based denial of a particular right is deserving of strict scrutiny under the Equal Protection Clause," he wrote, "we look to the Constitution to see if the right infringed has its source, explicitly or implicitly," in that document. Brennan looked beyond the narrow text for the "implicit" meanings of the Constitution. He faced a problem in the *Plyler* case. The Court's precedents made clear that illegal aliens were not a "suspect class" and that education was not a "fundamental right" under the Constitution.

These obstacles did not deter Brennan. He returned to the *Brown* opinion for guidance, quoting Chief Justice Warren's statement that education "is the very foundation of good citizenship." Racial segregation imposed a stigma on black children who were relegated to separate and unequal schools. Brennan based his *Plyler* opinion on these related concepts. Without adequate education, he wrote of the Mexican children, "the stigma of illiteracy will mark them for the rest of their lives." Brennan linked the original intent of the Equal Protection clause with its contemporary meaning. "Equal protection of the laws," he stated in a 1965 speech, "means equal protection today, whatever else the phrase may have meant in other times." In Brennan's view, the Court was obligated to respond to a century of social change.

NOT SURPRISINGLY, Justice Rehnquist dissented in the *Plyler* case, although he did not write separately. He did, however, elaborate a fundamentally different vision of the Equal Protection clause in a series of dissenting opinions. Writing in 1972, he noted that "the Constitution does not speak of 'fundamental personal rights,' but speaks of the equal protection of the laws and prohibits the denial thereof." Only those rights "found in the language of the Constitution, and not elsewhere," deserve judicial protection, he argued. Rehnquist dismissed the concept of fundamental personal rights as "a judicial superstructure, awkwardly engrafted upon the Constitution" by activist justices on the Warren Court.

Rehnquist took a narrow view of the Constitution. When the Court looks for rights beyond its clear text, he wrote, "it is doing nothing less than passing policy judgments upon the acts of every state legislature in the country." He denied that the Constitution allowed only laws that were "logical" or "just" in their application. "It requires only that there be some conceivable set of facts that may justify the classification involved," he said. Rehnquist refused to join Brennan in looking at society today for the meaning of the Equal Protection clause. He turned back the clock a full century in searching for the intent of the Framers on the reach of this provision. He found what he sought in "the traditional presumption of constitutionality" accorded to lawmakers by nineteenth-century justices. Rehnquist delivered this lecture in a solo dissent, objecting to a ruling that states could not deny insurance benefits to illegitimate children.

In another solo dissent, Rehnquist denied that the Fourteenth Amendment protected the members of "suspect" classes other than racial minorities. "The principal purpose of those who drafted and adopted the Amendment was to prohibit the states from invidiously discriminating by reason of race," he wrote. Rehnquist found no "historical evidence" that the Equal Protection clause was intended to protect members of any other "discrete and insular minorities" from laws that reflected prejudice against them. In disputing this twentieth-century proposition, Rehnquist cited a nineteenth-century case. Ruling in 1873, the Supreme Court rejected in the *Slaughterhouse Cases* any role as the "perpetual censor upon all legislation of the States, on the civil rights of their own citizens," even those rights protected by the Fourteenth Amendment. Writing exactly a century after this restrictive decision, Rehnquist adopted its language as his credo in Equal Protection cases.

Writing again as a solo dissenter in 1977, Rehnquist attacked a century of judicial precedent on the Equal Protection clause. If the Court "had developed a consistent body of doctrine which could reasonably be said to expound the intent of those who drafted and adopted that Clause," he wrote, "there would be no cause for judicial complaint, however unwise or incapable of effective administration one might find those intentions." Rehnquist, however, was full of complaints. He denounced the Court's decisions in equal protection cases as "an endless tinkering with legislative judgments, a series of conclusions unsupported by any central guiding principle."

Rehnquist had no doubt as to what that principle should be. He found it on the battlefields of Gettysburg and Antietam. The Equal Protection clause, he wrote, "makes sense only in the context of a recently fought Civil War." Its sole purpose was "the protection of blacks" against official discrimination. With some hesitation, Rehnquist agreed that other racial minorities and those singled out on the basis of national origin, which he called "the first cousin of race," also deserved judicial protection. But he drew the line at this point. Those who were not distinguished by skin color or accent should fend for themselves in legislative chambers. Without listing any cases, Rehnquist denounced "a century of decisions" in which the Court wielded the Equal Protection clause as a judicial "cat-o'-nine tails" to whip lawmakers who punished minorities.

THE GULF BETWEEN Brennan and Rehnquist over the Equal Protection clause was at its widest in school integration cases. Two decades after the *Brown* decision, the Supreme Court still faced cases that tested judicial orders to enforce that ruling. By the early 1970s, most southern states had surrendered to federal authority and the Second Reconstruction was under way. In the continuing civil war over race, the battlefront had shifted to northern cities and the rallying cry became "Stop the busing!" Conservative politicians responded to constituent pressure with a flurry of bills designed to block judicial busing orders.

The political leadership for this movement came from President Richard Nixon. Early in 1970, with midterm congressional elections approaching, he turned to Attorney General John Mitchell for advice on the best legislative strategy against busing. Mitchell delegated the task to William Rehnquist, who then headed the Office of Legal Counsel in the Justice Department. Rehnquist had already gone on record against busing in Phoenix, Arizona. He jumped into the assignment with enthusiasm, and sent his boss two lengthy memoranda in March 1970.

In the first, Rehnquist wrote that "the critical issue" in northern cities was that of "de facto segregation" based largely on housing patterns. His memo posed this question: "Does the Constitution require a school district to take affirmative steps to achieve 'racial balance' among its schools, even though the 'balance' existing stems from residential segregation or other factors for which the school board is not responsible?" Rehnquist answered with the concepts of "freedom of choice" and "neighborhood schools," the Nixon administration's code words for opposition to busing. In his second memo, Rehnquist noted that the legality of school zoning plans depended on "how the local Federal District judge sizes up the state of mind of the various school board members." If judges decided that such plans would perpetuate racial segregation, they could order busing as a remedy.

To avoid the prospect of "inserting federal courts still further into the business of operating schools," Rehnquist proposed a constitutional amendment to strip federal judges of any power over local school boards. The draft he gave Mitchell was aimed directly at the Equal Protection clause: "No provision of the Constitution shall be construed to prohibit the United States, any state, or any subdivision of either from assigning persons to its educational facilities on the basis of geographical boundaries provided only that such boundaries are reasonably related to school capacity, availability of transportation, safety or other similar considerations."

Approving a constitutional amendment requires the votes of two-thirds of the House and Senate. Democrats controlled both chambers of Congress in 1970, and Nixon knew that Rehnquist's amendment had no chance in an election year. So he dropped the issue until his reelection campaign in 1972. During this period, a major Supreme Court ruling affected Nixon's election strategy. Upholding a judicial busing order from Charlotte, North Carolina, the Court rejected the Justice Department's opposition to the plan. Not only was the opinion in *Swann v. Charlotte-Mecklenburg* unanimous, but its author was Chief Justice Warren Burger, appointed by Nixon for his conservative views. Burger sounded like Earl Warren in writing that the power of federal courts "to remedy past wrongs is broad" and that judges should employ "close scrutiny to determine that school assignments are not part of state-enforced segregation."

Nixon reacted to the *Swann* decision with strong words. "I am opposed to busing for the purpose of achieving racial balance in our schools," he said in a televised speech. "I believe it is wrong when an eight-year-old child who was once able to walk to a neighborhood school is now forced to travel two hours a day on a bus." Nixon called for "action to stop" busing, but he rejected Rehnquist's proposal, saying that "the constitutional amendment approach has a fatal flaw: It takes too long." He urged Congress instead to "call an immediate halt to all new busing orders" through legislation. Nixon made another move, shortly after the election, in placing Rehnquist on the Supreme Court. His public opposition to busing in Phoenix put the new justice on the same side as the president.

REHNQUIST QUICKLY justified Nixon's confidence in him. He dissented in 1973 from a decision that ordered strong remedies, including busing, for *de facto* segregation in Denver, Colorado. His position would make it difficult for judges to order busing in cities where schools had never been segregated by law. Rehnquist not only took on Justice Brennan, who wrote for the Court in *Keyes v. School District No. 1*; he also challenged all the cases that followed *Brown* in providing judicial remedies for school segregation.

Wilfred Keyes and other parents of black and Hispanic children in Denver asked a federal judge in 1969 to order the school board to redraw district lines in the largely black Park Hill area. They claimed the board had created a school zone and constructed a small elementary school to keep minority students out of neighboring white schools. The record showed only one "Anglo" child among the 423 students at the Barrett school.

Federal judge William Doyle, appointed by President John F. Kennedy, held after a lengthy trial that the board had intentionally segregated the Park Hill schools and ordered the redrawing of district lines to achieve greater racial balance. The plaintiffs then asked for citywide remedies, arguing that *de jure* segregation in one area of the district affected all the city's schools. Judge Doyle denied this request, holding that the situation outside the Park Hill area was "more like *de facto* segregation" and that "the court cannot order desegregation in order to provide a better balance" of the races.

In his lengthy opinion, Justice Brennan reviewed the history of school-board actions in Denver and statistics of racial composition in each school. He found "uncontroverted evidence" that Denver had deliberately seg-regated minority students and thus maintained a dual school system that violated the Equal Protection clause. "This is not a case," Brennan conceded, "where a statutory dual system has ever existed" by force of law. But that did not matter, because "common sense dictates the con-clusion that racially inspired school board actions have an impact beyond the particular schools that are the subject of those actions." In the Denver case, "proof of state-imposed segregation in a substantial portion of the district will suffice to support a finding by the trial court of the existence of a dual system."

Brennan then addressed the board's claim that it simply applied a "neighborhood school policy" and that any racial imbalance in the schools was "necessarily the result of residential patterns and not of pur-posefully segregative policies." He replied by quoting Chief Justice Bur-ger's unanimous opinion in the *Swann* case, decided two years earlier: "All things being equal, with no history of discrimination, it might well be desirable to assign pupils to schools nearest their homes. But all things are not equal in a system that has been deliberately constructed and maintained to enforce racial segregation." Holding that the plaintiffs had shown "a prima facie case of intentional segregation" in Denver's schools, the Court sent the case back to Judge Doyle for further hearings, with the burden on the board to prove it had not acted to segregate the schools.

In his first major segregation opinion, Rehnquist argued strenuously against extending the *Brown* decision to this case. The laws struck down in *Brown*, he noted, required "that Negro children and white children attend separate schools" and that there be "no race mixing whatever in the population of any particular school." He stressed that neither Col-orado nor the city of Denver ever "had a statute or ordinance of that description." Consequently, even proof of "manipulative drawing of at-tendance zones in a school district the size of Denver does not necessarily result in denial of equal protection to all minority students" in the city.

Rehnquist had written, as a Supreme Court law clerk in 1952, that "*Plessy v. Ferguson* was right and should be reaffirmed" by the Court in the *Brown* case. He later denied that these words reflected his own thoughts, attributing them to his former boss, Justice Robert Jackson, who voted in *Brown* to overrule the *Plessy* decision. Whatever his feelings as a clerk, Rehnquist accepted *Brown* as a justice. But he read the case narrowly, and denied that its prohibition of official segregation imposed "an affirmative duty to integrate" schools that no longer separated the races by law.

One of the most significant cases that followed *Brown* was *Green v. School Board*, which held in 1968 that school districts with "state-compelled dual systems" had "the affirmative duty to take whatever steps might be necessary to convert to a unitary system in which racial discrimination would be eliminated root and branch." Justice Brennan cited this decision in his *Keyes* opinion, but Rehnquist blasted the "drastic extension" of the *Brown* ruling in the *Green* case. "I can see no constitutional justification for it," he complained, in cases that did not involve segregation by law. Brennan replied in a footnote that Rehnquist's position echoed a lower-court decision in 1955 that the Constitution "does not require integration. It merely forbids discrimination." That decision, he noted, had been expressly overruled by the Supreme Court. Brennan reminded his colleague that "*Green* remains the governing principle."

The Court's strong decision in *Keyes* did not sway either President Nixon or Justice Rehnquist. Nixon repeated his old refrain: "I am opposed to compulsory busing for the purpose of achieving racial balance in our schools. I continue to believe in the neighborhood school—in the right of children to attend schools near their homes with friends who live near them." But the justices kept a firm grip on busing cases. The same day the Court decided *Keyes* in 1973, Gary Penick and other parents of minority students filed suit against the school board in Columbus, Ohio. Four years later, after a lengthy trial, federal judge Robert Duncan— placed on the bench by Richard Nixon—held that the Columbus schools "were openly and intentionally segregated on the basis of race when *Brown* was decided in 1954. The Court has found that the Columbus Board of Education has never actively set out to dismantle this dual system." Duncan ordered extensive remedial steps, including busing.

Reviewing this order in 1979, the Supreme Court reaffirmed the principles of *Brown* and *Green*, and the remedial approaches of *Swann* and *Keyes*. Writing for the Court in the *Penick* case, Justice Byron White found in all these cases "an affirmative duty to desegregate" whenever official action resulted in segregation. "Each instance of a failure or refusal to fulfill this affirmative duty continues the violation of the Fourteenth Amendment," he added.

Once again, Rehnquist dissented, this time with greater rhetorical heat. The trial judge's order, he wrote, "is as complete and dramatic a displacement of local authority as is possible in our federal system." He accused the Court's majority of adopting a policy of "integration uber alles." And he denounced the "superficial methodology" of Justice White's opinion, calling it a "lick and a promise" approach to the issue of racial balance. Rehnquist complained that the *Penick* decision relieved plaintiffs in school cases "from any showing of a causal nexus between intentional segregative actions and the conditions they seek to remedy." He burrowed into the case record and came out persuaded that Columbus officials had neutrally followed the "neighborhood school concept" and "employed the most objective criteria possible" in locating schools and drawing attendance zones. Finally, he likened the Court's majority to Pontius Pilate in washing its hands of "disparate results" in school cases, and compared his colleagues to "a bevy of Platonic Guardians" who ignored the public will. "Whether the Court's result be reached by the approach of Pilate or Plato," he concluded, "I cannot subscribe to it."

Justice White ignored this fulmination, but he reminded Rehnquist that "the Equal Protection Clause was aimed at all official actions, not just those of state legislatures." And he pointed to the *Keyes* decision as demonstrating that "there is no magical difference between segregated schools mandated by statute and those that result from local segregative acts and policies." White also answered Rehnquist's boast that he had "a better grasp of the historical and ultimate facts" than the trial judge who "lived with the case over the years." Digging through the record, without good reason to suspect the lower court of serious error, struck White as asserting for the Court "an omnipotence and omniscience that we do not have and should not claim."

These lectures from Brennan and White, buried in the small type of footnotes, had no discernible effect on Rehnquist's determination to end judicial oversight of school desegregation. He predicted in his *Penick* dissent that school cases "will certainly be with this Court as long as any of its current Members," and he outlasted both Brennan and White on the bench. Rehnquist finally won a majority to his hands-off position in 1991, in a case that began in 1961. Robert Dowell and other black parents had sued the Oklahoma City school board and won an order that included busing to achieve racial balance. In 1977, the board successfully asked the federal court to terminate the order, arguing that it had ended all vestiges of segregation.

The former plaintiffs returned to court in 1985, claiming the city's schools had become "resegregated" over the past seven years. They showed that more than half of the elementary schools had greater than 90 percent majorities of one race. The district judge denied their request for further remedies, but a federal appellate court reversed this decision, holding that the original order had "a life of its own" and could be revived even after its demise.

Rehnquist had become Chief Justice by the time the Court decided *Board of Education v. Dowell* in 1991, and he was determined to use it to kill off another six hundred federal desegregation orders. With Brennan in retirement, and White now on his side, he assigned the opinion to himself. He was finally able to send the *Swann* and *Green* cases to the constitutional graveyard. "We think it is a mistake," he wrote, "to treat words such as 'dual' and 'unitary' as if they were actually found in the Constitution." They were not, of course, any more than the words "school" or "student." Public education, as Chief Justice Warren noted in the *Brown* opinion, hardly existed when the Equal Protection clause was ratified in 1868. But much had changed in a century. "Today, education is perhaps the most important function of state and local government," Warren wrote in 1954. Local officials had a constitutional duty to eliminate every vestige of segregation, the Court had ruled in later cases. Rehnquist disagreed. "From the very first," he wrote in *Dowell*, "federal supervision of local school systems was intended as a temporary measure to remedy past discrimination." Once those local officials complied with court orders for "a reasonable period of time," any further resegregation of the schools was beyond the power of federal judges to remedy.

Justice Brennan could not answer this opinion, although his vote would not have changed the outcome. The Supreme Court nominees of Presidents Reagan and Bush gave Rehnquist his majority. Justice Thurgood Marshall spoke in dissent for the black children of Oklahoma City, as he spoke for an earlier generation of black children in arguing the *Brown* case. He returned to that case for the basic holding that "separate educational facilities are inherently unequal." Marshall noted that schools in Oklahoma City had been segregated for sixty-five years. He disagreed with Rehnquist "that 13 years of desegregation was enough" to overcome this legacy of discrimination. Marshall repeated the *Brown* concept of "stigmatic injury" that racial separation imposed on black children. This concept, he wrote in *Dowell*, "explains our unflagging insistence that formerly *de jure* segregated school districts extinguish all vestiges of school segregation."

Unlike Rehnquist, Marshall viewed the decisions in the cases that followed *Brown* as still alive. Taken together, he wrote, they held that "the reemergence of racial separation" could "revive the message of racial inferiority implicit in the former policy of state-supported segregation." With proper evidence of resegregation, judges could respond by reviving desegregation orders to carry out the *Brown* mandate. But the Court's unanimity in *Brown* had dissolved; Marshall now wrote only for himself and two other dissenters. Five months later, he decided to join Brennan in retirement.

Marshall was not on the bench when another school case returned in 1992 to the Court's docket. This case was *Brown v. Board of Education*, the same case that began in 1951 in Topeka, Kansas, and that Marshall guided to the Supreme Court. Oliver Brown and his daughter Linda, now Linda Smith, were joined by her children, Charles and Kimberly, in asking a federal judge to order further steps to end racial imbalance in the Topeka schools.

Judge Richard Rogers—appointed by President Gerald Ford—conducted a lengthy trial in 1986 at which Linda Smith testified about her experiences as a child in Topeka's segregated schools. Other witnesses detailed the continuing racial imbalance, showing that the percentage of black students in elementary schools ranged from 7 to 62. The judge agreed that the board's "neighborhood school approach has achieved a high level of integration, but not racial balance by any means." He ruled, however, that the board had done enough to promote integration and that the *Brown* case "has reached an appropriate denouement."

But the case was not over. A federal appellate panel reversed Judge Rogers and ruled that "there is a current condition of segregation in Topeka. Contrary to the district court, we are convinced that this condition is causally connected to the prior *de jure* system of segregation." Judge Stephanie Seymour, who wrote the opinion, had been active in civil rights work and was appointed by President Jimmy Carter. She read the *Swann* and *Penick* cases as holding that "plaintiffs need only show that current racial disparities exist, not that such disparities are the result of current *intentional* segregation" by the board. Ruling that Topeka had not done enough to promote integration, the panel kept the *Brown* case alive.

After Marshall retired in 1991, Chief Justice Rehnquist wrote a tribute to a colleague with whom he rarely agreed in equal protection cases; he lauded Marshall as "a champion of minorities and the poor" and singled out his "notable victory" in the *Brown* case. The next year, Rehnquist voted to send that historic case, now more than forty years old, back to the appellate panel for "reconsideration" in light of his *Dowell* opinion, from which Marshall had vigorously dissented. But the advocate in *Brown* did not live to see whether its principle of equality in education would long endure.

BY THE TIME Justice Rehnquist joined the Court, the major battles over the civil rights laws of the 1960s had been fought and won by Justice Brennan and his liberal allies. Even conservatives like Tom Clark and John Harlan, who generally supported states' rights against federal power, agreed that Congress could outlaw discrimination in public accommodations and protect the voting rights of southern blacks. Rehnquist was already on record against civil rights laws. He had opposed a public accommodations ordinance in Phoenix, arguing in 1964—while Congress was debating a national law—that "a measure of our traditional freedom would be lost" if restaurant owners had to admit an "unwanted customer" to their premises.

In December 1968, a member of the Moose Lodge in Harrisburg, Pennsylvania, brought an "unwanted customer" to its dining room as his guest. Although the constitution of the Loyal Order of Moose urged its members to "encourage tolerance of every kind," the Moose limited membership to "acceptable white persons of good character." Tolerance did not extend to the black guests of white members. This black guest, however, was Leroy Irvis, majority leader of the Pennsylvania legislature, whose white members used the Moose Lodge—a block from the state capitol—as a watering hole. Irvis sued the lodge, claiming it was a "place of public accommodation" under state and federal law and had violated his equal protection rights. A federal court upheld his claim and ordered the state to revoke the lodge's liquor license until it ended the racial exclusion policy.

The *Moose Lodge v. Irvis* case was argued the month after Rehnquist joined the Court, and he chose it for his first major opinion. The primary issue stemmed from the lodge's status as a private club whose facilities could be used only by members and guests. Irvis, however, claimed that regulation by the Pennsylvania Liquor Control Board constituted "state action" that subjected the lodge to civil rights laws. The Supreme Court had adopted the "state action" doctrine in 1948, ruling in *Shelley v. Kraemer* that racially restrictive covenants in housing deeds could not be judicially enforced because they required state officials to uphold private discrimination.

Rehnquist knew the *Shelley* case from personal experience. During Senate hearings in 1986 on his nomination as Chief Justice, he faced questions about restrictive deeds he had twice signed. The deed to his Phoenix home barred its sale to anyone not of the "Caucasian race." And in 1974, Rehnquist signed a deed for a summer home in Vermont that prohibited its sale to "anyone of the Hebrew race." This restriction was specifically typed in to change the previous deed and was called to his attention in a letter from the realtor. Rehnquist claimed, however, that "I did not recall the letter" and that he found the restrictions "obnoxious" and unenforceable under the *Shelley* decision.

Writing in the *Moose Lodge* case, fourteen years before his restrictive deeds became public, Rehnquist had no compunction in citing *Shelley* against Leroy Irvis. He quoted its holding that the Equal Protection clause "erects no shield" against private racial discrimination. The question, however, was not whether the lodge was a private club but whether its regulation by the liquor board constituted "state action." Rehnquist admitted there was "no easy answer" to this question. But he found an answer, and a way around the *Shelley* case, in holding that the liquor regulations were "neutral" on the question of racial discrimination. Despite the admittedly "pervasive" nature of state control over liquor sales, Rehnquist found that the regulations did not "foster or encourage racial discrimination" by the state.

Justice Brennan wrote for three dissenters in blasting Rehnquist's "complete disregard of the fundamental value underlying the 'state action' doctrine." Quoting an earlier case, he described that value as demanding that "no State shall in any significant way lend its authority to the sordid business of racial discrimination." The state of Pennsylvania, Brennan noted, "dictates and continually supervises virtually every detail" of establishments with liquor licenses. This degree of regulation, he argued, brought even private clubs like the Moose Lodge within the "state action" doctrine and the reach of civil rights laws.

Leroy Irvis lost this round of the *Moose Lodge* case, but the savvy politician won the final decision. He persuaded the Pennsylvania Supreme Court that the Moose Lodge, by admitting guests to its dining facilities, was a place of public accommodation and was subject to state laws against racial discrimination. Because this decision was based solely upon state law, it could not be reviewed by the U.S. Supreme Court. The lodge tried anyway, but the justices decided without dissent in December 1972 that the appeal did not raise "a substantial Federal question" and should be dismissed. The Moose Lodge in Harrisburg now allows its members to bring guests of any race.

THE DECLINE OF BUSING as a political issue in the late 1970s did not signal a new era of harmony in race relations. Conflict merely shifted from schools to factories and offices, and the conservative slogan of "Stop the busing!" shifted to "End the quotas!" Disgruntled white males, claiming to be victims of reverse discrimination, sought recognition as the newest minority group. They argued that affirmative action programs, designed to promote job equality for racial minorities, violated the Equal Protection clause. Lawyers who represented white challengers to these programs often quoted the sentence in Justice Harlan's *Plessy* dissent that "Our Constitution is color-blind, and neither knows nor tolerates classes among citizens." They did not, however, quote his observation in the same paragraph that whites were the "dominant race" in education, wealth, and power and "will continue to be for all time."

The Supreme Court first tried to dodge the issue of racial quotas. Ruling in 1974, the justices dismissed the appeal of Marco DeFunis, who had been denied admission to the University of Washington law school, although thirty-six minority applicants with lower test scores and grades were admitted. DeFunis sued the university in state court under the Equal Protection clause, and a trial judge ordered his admission. By the time the state supreme court reversed this decision, he was in his second year of law study. Rehnquist joined the Court's majority in *DeFunis v. Odegard* by dismissing the case as moot because DeFunis would graduate before a final decision. Brennan dissented from this decision. "Few constitutional questions in recent history have stirred as much debate," he wrote, "and they will not disappear. They must inevitably return to the federal courts and ultimately to the Court."

It hardly required prophetic skill to predict that a similar case would reach the Court. It arrived in 1978 as *Regents v. Bakke*. Allen Bakke had been rejected twice, in 1973 and 1974, by the University of California medical school at Davis. He was an aerospace engineer in his thirties; most other schools told Bakke he was "too old" to begin medical study. Bakke sued the university in state court because the Davis medical school reserved sixteen places out of one hundred in each class for "disadvantaged" minority students. The trial judge agreed with Bakke's equal protection claim, but refused to order his admission pending appeal. The case thus lacked the mootness issue of *DeFunis*. Reflecting the political heat of the affirmative action battle, the *Bakke* case attracted a record number of *amicus* briefs by interested groups. The lineup on each side reflected the growing division over affirmative action within the civil rights coalition, with the NAACP behind the university and the American Jewish Committee with Bakke.

The *Bakke* case also split the Supreme Court down the middle, with four justices on Bakke's side and four with the medical school. Justice Lewis Powell finally broke the tie with a Solomonic decision: both sides won and both lost. Powell actually wrote two separate opinions. Rehnquist joined one that struck down the school's numerical quota and ordered Bakke's admission. Powell wrote in this opinion that racial distinctions "are inherently suspect and thus call for the most exacting judicial examination," words he lifted almost verbatim from Justice Stone's famous Footnote Four in the *Carolene Products* case. Ironically, Rehnquist joined this citation to the "strict scrutiny" doctrine he had consistently denounced.

Another irony of Powell's opinion was his reversal of Chief Justice Warren's view of the Fourteenth Amendment. "The clock of our liberties," Powell wrote, "cannot be turned back to 1868." He stole the words from Warren, who wrote in *Brown* that "we cannot turn the clock back to 1868 when the Amendment was adopted" in considering the issue of school segregation. Warren felt the time had come to protect blacks against unequal education; Powell believed enough time had been devoted to "remedial action" for minorities and that the "white majority" deserved judicial protection against discrimination.

Powell was unwilling, however, to rule that schools could *never* consider race as a factor in admissions. Justice Brennan spent months talking with him and brokering the Court's resolution of the *Bakke* case. Powell's second opinion, joined by the Court's liberals, held that the Davis medical school could employ "a properly devised admissions program involving the competitive consideration of race and ethnic origin" as positive factors. He pointed with pride at Harvard, his alma mater, which gave race a "plus" in admissions decisions but substituted "goals" for quotas. Brennan underlined this holding in a concurring opinion: "Government may take race into account when it acts not to demean or insult any racial group, but to remedy disadvantages cast on minorities by past racial prejudice," he wrote. Powell had written privately to Brennan that he "could put whatever 'gloss' on the several opinions you think proper." One scholar later said that the *Bakke* decision was Brennan's "most significant victory" during the years of the Burger Court. "If not for Brennan," he added, "it is probable that the Burger Court would have ruled all racial preferences unconstitutional."

Although neither side "won" the *Bakke* case, Brennan had rescued affirmative action from its conservative foes. He went on to write a series of majority opinions in subsequent cases. The first, and most important, involved a 1974 agreement between the United Steelworkers union and the Kaiser Aluminum Company to begin an affirmative action program for training unskilled production workers to become skilled craftsmen. At that time, blacks made up fewer than 2 percent of the craftsmen in the Kaiser plant in Gramercy, Louisiana. The voluntary agreement reserved 50 percent of the slots in the training program for blacks, until they reached their proportion of 39 percent in the local workforce. Brian Weber, a white production worker, sued both the union and the company after he was turned down for the program. He based his suit on a federal law—Title VII of the 1964 Civil Rights Act—that made it unlawful for employers "to deprive any individual of employment opportunities" because of race. Because *Steelworkers v. Weber* promised to affect millions of workers, it attracted dozens of *amicus* briefs. It also split the civil rights coalition of blacks and Jews, with the NAACP on the union's side and the Anti-Defamation League behind Weber.

Brennan's majority opinion in the *Weber* case, decided in 1979, highlights his skill in gaining votes from the Court's center group. Justice Potter Stewart had joined the conservatives in *Bakke*, but he shifted in *Weber* to support a more sweeping quota plan. Brennan tailored his opinion to fit Stewart's dislike of expansive federal power. "We emphasize at the outset the narrowness of our inquiry," he wrote. Because the plan of the union and company "does not involve state action," Brennan held that Brian Weber had no claim under the Equal Protection clause. There was some irony in this statement. Brennan had argued in the *Moose Lodge* case that the "pervasive" nature of state liquor regulations imposed the "state action" doctrine on a small private club. Giant corporations like Kaiser were subject to pervasive state and federal regulation in such areas as health and safety standards, wages and hours, and smokestack emissions.

Brennan finessed the "state action" problem by stressing that the craft-training program was "voluntarily adopted by private parties to eliminate traditional patterns of racial segregation." He glossed over the fact that both the union and the company had federal guns at their heads, having each been found in violation of discrimination laws by the Equal Employment Opportunity Commission. Their agreement was about as "voluntary" as those of John Dillinger's victims to empty their cash drawers. Brennan also slid around the clear wording in Title VII that outlawed *all* job discrimination by race. He admitted that a "literal" reading of the law supported Weber and that his position "is not without force." Brennan responded by picking through the *Congressional Record* for quotes by the law's sponsor, Senator Hubert Humphrey, that its primary concern was "the plight of the Negro in our economy."

After this selective reading of the legislative record, Brennan concluded that the federal law's prohibition of job discrimination "does not condemn all private, voluntary, race-conscious affirmative action plans." The purpose of such plans was "to break down old patterns of racial segregation and hierarchy," a goal the nation had endorsed many times, from *Brown* to *Bakke*. Brennan carefully stuck to the facts of the *Weber* case and disavowed any intent to "detail the line of demarcation between permissible and impermissible affirmative action plans." His opinion was hardly a judicial masterpiece; however desirable the goal of placing more blacks in good jobs, it smacked of "result-oriented" judging and political calculation. One politician, in fact, had taken a highly visible stand while Brennan was writing his opinion. "The *Weber* case is one on which the Attorney General will take a stand," President Jimmy Carter said at a televised press conference. "We want to protect the right of people for employment, not only for equal employment but also for affirmative action." The Justice Department had, in fact, joined the suit and argued against Weber in the Supreme Court.

The president approved the outcome, but Brennan's opinion drew an unusually harsh response from Chief Justice Burger, who accused his colleague of "totally rewriting" the law "to reach a 'desirable' result." Burger quoted the warning of Justice Benjamin Cardozo that no judge should act as "a knight-errant, roaming at will in pursuit of his own ideal of beauty or of goodness." Burger made clear the object of his rebuke. "What Cardozo tells us," he told Brennan, "is beware the 'good result,' achieved by judicially unauthorized or intellectually dishonest means on the appealing notion that desirable ends justify the improper judicial means. For there is always the danger that the seeds of precedent sown by good men for the best of motives will yield a rich harvest of unprincipled acts of others also aiming at 'good ends.'"

Justice Rehnquist went further in his dissent, scorning any suggestion that Brennan acted from good motives. Writing in 1979, he suggested that the majority opinion "could more appropriately have been handed down five years from now, in 1984, a year coinciding with the title of a book from which the Court's opinion borrows, perhaps subconsciously, at least one idea." Quoting from George Orwell's *1984*, Rehnquist compared Brennan to the government official in Oceania whose speech denouncing the current enemy, Eurasia, was interrupted by someone handing him a scrap of paper. "He unrolled and read it without pausing in his speech. Nothing altered in his voice or manner, or in the content of what he was saying, but suddenly the names were different." The former enemy suddenly became an ally. "The banners and posters with which the square was decorated were all wrong!"

Without using the word "newspeak," Orwell's term for such political turnabouts, Rehnquist accused the majority of acting "much like the Orwellian speaker earlier described, as if it had been handed a note" with instructions to change positions. He pointed to an earlier ruling in which the Court read the legislative history of Title VII to ban *all* racial discrimination. "Now we are told that the legislative history of Title VII shows that employers are free to discriminate on the basis of race," Rehnquist complained. "Our earlier interpretations of Title VII, like the banners and posters decorating the square in Oceania, were all wrong."

Even for Rehnquist, who often employs sarcasm in dissent, this is strong language. He continued in this vein, dismissing Brennan's opinion as "a *tour de force* reminiscent not of jurists such as Hale, Holmes, and Hughes, but of escape artists such as Houdini," in wriggling out of the words of Title VII. Rehnquist also examined the legislative history, and also quoted Senator Humphrey. "The truth," Humphrey had said in

Senate debate, "is that this title forbids discriminating against anyone on account of race. This is the simple and complete truth about Title VII." Rehnquist concluded that his "thorough examination of the congressional debates" had exposed "the magnitude of the Court's misinterpretation of Congress's intent" to bar even "voluntary" affirmative action plans that set racial quotas. His enemy had not changed from the time he joined the Court. "There is perhaps no device more destructive to the notion of equality than the *numerus clausus*—the quota," Rehnquist wrote in his *Weber* dissent.

Brennan let the sarcasm pass without comment; he had more votes than Rehnquist on this issue. Using his *Weber* opinion as precedent, Brennan turned back challenges to similar affirmative action plans during the presidency of Ronald Reagan, who declared in 1986 his goal of eliminating quotas in all federal programs. The Justice Department changed sides in pending cases, appearing before the Supreme Court on behalf of white challengers. One case involved the fire department in Cleveland, Ohio. Black and Hispanic firefighters had sued the city in 1980, claiming discrimination in promotions to officer ranks. City officials agreed to settle the case by reserving specified numbers of officer positions—sixteen of forty to lieutenant, three of twenty to captain—for minorities. After a federal judge approved the settlement, white union members challenged the decree, arguing that it violated their rights under both Title VII and the Equal Protection clause.

Once again, Brennan read the statute to permit "employers and unions voluntarily to make use of reasonable race-conscious affirmative action" in all aspects of employment. Writing in *Firefighters v. Cleveland* in 1986, he cited *Weber* and saw no reason to distinguish between private and public employers. Because the holding under federal law was clear, the Court did not address the equal protection claims of the white firefighters. Rehnquist again dissented and quoted Senator Humphrey as opposing any plans—voluntary or mandatory—designed "to achieve a certain racial balance" in workplaces. And he repeated his strictures against "the evil of court-sanctioned racial quotas."

Brennan wrote for six justices in the *Firefighters* case. From this highwater mark, his majority began slipping. The next year, he spoke for only five in a similar job-promotion case. In 1972, the NAACP sued the Alabama Department of Public Safety for refusing in the thirty-seven years of its existence to hire a single black state-police trooper. The federal government—under the Nixon administration—joined the plaintiffs, along with a rejected black applicant, Philip Paradise. Federal judge Frank Johnson, who firmly supported civil rights, found a "blatant and continuous pattern and practice of discrimination" by the state police. He ordered the one-to-one hiring of black and white troopers until blacks made up about one-quarter of the state-police force.

By the time this case reached the Court in 1987, the issue had shifted from the hiring of black troopers to discrimination in the officer ranks. Judge Johnson had followed up his initial order with another one-to-one racial decree, to ensure that one-quarter of officers were black. Political factors also shifted over time. President Reagan ordered the Justice Department to switch sides. The case was now called *United States v. Paradise*, with Alabama on the sidelines, cheering in an *amicus* brief for its former opponent, the Justice Department. Clinging to a bare majority, Justice Brennan wrote a "narrowly tailored" opinion that stressed the state's continuing failure to implement Judge Johnson's original decree. Brennan, in fact, used the term "narrowly tailored" so often—five times—that his ruling fit the case like a glove.

Even so, Brennan lost the vote of Justice Sandra O'Connor, a member of the Court's center bloc. Her dissent, which Rehnquist joined as Chief Justice, turned Alabama's failure to comply with Judge Johnson's initial hiring order on its head. Johnson had issued his one-to-one promotion order for the officer ranks before the state reached the 25-percent quota for troopers. The state, in fact, had not come close to compliance to that first order. Because of this, O'Connor reasoned, the "one-to-one promotion quota" for officers was unlawful because it "far exceeded the percentage of blacks in the trooper force," which she defined as the "relevant work force" in setting quotas. The state's "recalcitrance" in complying with Judge Johnson's initial order, as O'Connor put it, became an advantage in contesting his later order.

POLITICAL FACTORS outside the Court continued to affect decisions within its chambers. Justice Lewis Powell, a crucial swing vote in equal protection cases, joined Brennan in both the Cleveland and Alabama cases. His retirement in 1987 gave President Reagan the chance to make the eighth consecutive nomination by a Republican president. His first effort to fill Powell's seat with Judge Robert Bork, whose voluminous writings bristled with hostility to equal protection claims, ended in a crushing Senate defeat. Reagan took a second right-hand swing with Judge

Douglas Ginsburg, who quickly withdrew after reporters sniffed marijuana on his breath (which did not disqualify a later nominee, Clarence Thomas, or a later president, Bill Clinton). Reagan finally connected with Anthony Kennedy, a federal appellate judge from California and friend of Attorney General Edwin Meese. Brad Reynolds, Meese's assistant and the administration's most fervent opponent of affirmative action, predicted that Kennedy "would come out the right way 99 out of 100 times" on the Supreme Court.

Kennedy's later votes on flag burning and abortion showed that Reynolds had been overconfident. But the newest justice did give the Reagan administration—and Rehnquist—a majority in job-discrimination cases. The Chief Justice celebrated by assigning himself the opinion in *Martin v. Wilks*, a Title VII case that began in 1974 in Birmingham, Alabama. Black municipal employees in several departments reached agreement with city officials on consent decrees that set hiring and promotion goals. Several years later, a group of white firefighters sued the city, claiming they had been passed over for promotion in favor of less-qualified blacks. A federal judge dismissed their suit because the white firefighters had not been parties to the original litigation.

Rehnquist wrote for the new majority in 1989, ruling that "a person cannot be deprived of his legal rights in a proceeding to which he is not a party." This statement was both true as a general proposition and questionable in the Birmingham case. The white firefighters had not asked to intervene in the original suit even though they were aware of its potential impact on them. The city and the black plaintiffs both argued that allowing disgruntled groups to challenge settlements years later would disrupt all the progress toward job integration. Rehnquist disagreed and ordered the trial court to reopen the case and add the white firefighters as parties.

Writing for the four dissenters, including Brennan, Justice John Paul Stevens emphasized "the vast difference between persons who are actual parties to litigation and persons who merely have the kind of interest that may as a practical matter be impaired by the outcome of a case." Admitting that the consent decrees "will necessarily have an adverse impact on whites, who must now share their job and promotion opportunities" with blacks, Stevens wrote that the white firefighters chose to "remain on the sidelines" in the original suit and should take the consequences of that decision.

Justice Kennedy provided the fifth vote in another job-discrimination case, decided the same month in 1989. The issue in *Wards Cove Packing Co. v. Atonio*, which also began in 1974, involved the hiring practices of an Alaska salmon cannery. The basic facts were not disputed: the vast majority of unskilled jobs on the cannery line were filled by Filipinos and Alaska natives, while whites held most of the skilled and white-collar jobs. The parties agreed this was a "disparate impact" case under the provisions of Title VII. But they differed over which side had the burden of proving any intent to discriminate. The packing company raised a "business necessity" defense, arguing that the available labor pool for cannery-line workers contained few whites and that few nonwhites had applied for skilled jobs. The workers, represented by their union, responded that the company employed nepotism and separate hiring channels to segregate the workforce. The Reagan administration took the company's side in the *Wards Cove* case.

The Supreme Court majority took a narrow path through a thicket of statistics. Chief Justice Rehnquist made a shrewd choice in assigning the opinion to Byron White, who generally upheld civil rights claims against governments. But this was a private case, and White usually took the side of business against workers. His opinion gave the cannery workers an even harder job than gutting salmon. White imposed on them "the burden of disproving" the company's claim that it acted out of "business necessity" in choosing workers for the two job categories. He added to this burden the task of showing that the number of "qualified" nonwhites who applied for skilled and white-collar jobs approached the number who were hired. Without such proof, he wrote, "the employer's selection mechanism probably does not operate with a disparate impact on minorities." The company's lawyer couldn't have put it better.

Justice Brennan joined the dissent of Justice Harry Blackmun, who complained that "a bare majority of the Court" had taken several "major strides backwards in the battle against race discrimination." The salmon-canning industry "takes us back to a kind of overt and institutionalized discrimination," he wrote, that "resembles a plantation economy." Blackmun accused the majority of "upsetting the longstanding distribution of burdens of proof in Title VII disparate-impact cases." Even with ample statistical evidence of job disparity, it "would be impossible" for plaintiffs to disprove a "business necessity" claim. Blackmun also accused the majority of gutting Title VII. "Sadly, this comes as no surprise," he wrote.

"One wonders whether the majority still believes that race discrimination—or, more accurately, race discrimination against non-whites—is a problem in our society, or even remembers that it ever was."

Blackmun was not alone in wondering about the Court's attitude toward racial discrimination. The civil rights coalition, although fractured in recent years, responded to *Wards Cove* and similar employment cases with demands for congressional action. Because these decisions rested on judicial interpretation of federal law, they could be reversed by Congress. After a fierce political battle over the next two years, President George Bush reluctantly signed the *Civil Rights Act of 1991*, which undid nine Supreme Court rulings, including those in *Martin v. Wilks* and *Wards Cove*. Before its overwhelming passage by Congress, Bush denounced the bill as a "quota" plan. He changed his tune when he signed the new law in the Rose Garden, surrounded by civil rights leaders. "This historic legislation strengthens the barriers and sanctions against employment discrimination," the President said. The pictures of Bush signing the law he had opposed perfectly illustrate the politics of the Constitution.

TWELVE

"WELL QUALIFIED BY CHARACTER
AND EDUCATION"

IN THEIR DEBATE over the Fourteenth Amendment, Justices Rehnquist and Brennan at least agreed that it bans official segregation by race.
But the Court is often confronted with a more difficult question: Does
the Equal Protection clause also ban discrimination against members of
other groups? Rehnquist has consistently answered "no" and has pressed
his belief that only "racial minorities" come within its reach. Brennan
has responded that the clause was intended to invalidate laws based on
"deep-seated prejudice" against any group.

These conflicting answers reflect more than disputes over the intent
of those who framed the Civil War amendments. They are rooted in
divergent conceptions of American society. Conservatives like Rehnquist
believe that every person now has an equal chance to achieve the American dream. Judges and lawmakers have removed legal barriers to participation in the polity and economy. Blacks no longer live in slavery,
women can vote, aliens can become citizens, and poor people can achieve
prosperity if they work hard. Conservatives stress that the Constitution
speaks only of "persons" and not of "minorities." Brennan and other
liberals point to the social and psychic barriers that remain from the era
of slavery and legal patriarchy. They also note the persistence of poverty
and its disabling impact, especially on children. Liberals note that the
Constitution was first designed to "promote the general welfare" of all
Americans, not the wealth of any individual. As Kenneth Karst has put
it, the two sides differ in defining how people "belong" in America.

One group does not fully "belong" in the United States. Aliens cannot
take part in the political process, and their civil rights are restricted. More
than 1.5 million people are currently lawful alien residents, while esti-
mates of those who entered the country illegally range from 3 to 6 million.

One case in particular puts this issue into sharp focus, against a backdrop of "deep-seated prejudice" toward a distinctive minority. Back in 1914, Takao Ozawa applied for American citizenship. He was born in Japan but had lived in the United States for twenty years. The Supreme Court agreed without dissent that Ozawa would be a model citizen. Evidence that he was "well qualified by character and education for citizenship is conceded," wrote Justice George Sutherland, who lauded his qualifications. "He was a graduate of the Berkeley, California, High School, had been nearly three years a student in the University of California, had educated his children in American schools, his family had attended American churches and he had maintained the use of the English language in his home." It would be hard to imagine a more ideal American.

Ozawa faced just one obstacle in his quest to become a citizen: he was not a "free white person" and was thus excluded by federal naturalization laws, first passed by Congress in 1790. After a federal judge rejected his petition, Ozawa appealed to the Supreme Court. His case reached the justices in 1922, two years before Congress passed an immigration law that imposed restrictive "national origin" quotas on such "undesirable" groups as Italians and Poles. Asians had already been barred from immigration, beginning with the Chinese Exclusion Act in 1882. Congress added Japanese to the restricted list in 1906 and branded this entire national group as "ineligible for citizenship" in the future. Takao Ozawa, however, became a lawful resident of the United States before this law. He relied on the Due Process clause of the Fifth Amendment in challenging federal power to limit citizenship on racial grounds.

Solicitor General James Beck, a former Wall Street lawyer, spoke for the government in Ozawa v. United States. One biographer noted that Beck's "old New England" colonial ancestry "always meant much to him." This racial heritage shaped Beck's argument to the Supreme Court. "The men who settled this country," he told the justices, "were white men from Europe and the men who fought the Revolutionary War, framed the Constitution and established the government, were white men from Europe and their descendents. They were eager for more of their kind to come, and it was to men of their own kind that they held out the opportunity for citizenship in the new nation." Beck defended the racial bias in the naturalization laws. "Citizenship has always been deemed a choice possession," he said, "and the men of 1790 gave it only to those whom they knew and regarded as worthy to share it with them, men of their own type, white men."

With a bow of regret, the Supreme Court rejected Ozawa's appeal. "It is the duty of this Court to give effect to the intent of Congress," Sutherland explained. The Constitution gave Congress authority to "establish a uniform rule of naturalization," a power the courts did not question. The historical record made clear, Sutherland wrote, that Congress intended "to confer the privilege of citizenship upon that class of persons whom the fathers knew as white, and to deny it to all who could not be so classified." Limitation of citizenship to whites had been "welded into the structure of our national polity by a century of legislative and administrative acts and judicial decisions," he added. Sutherland assured Ozawa that the Court did not imply "any suggestion of individual unworthiness or racial inferiority" in its decision. "We have no function in the matter other than to ascertain the will of Congress and to declare it," he piously declared.

Not one constitutional law casebook includes Beck's argument in the *Ozawa* case. But his words speak volumes about the hostility toward aliens that has infected American law and politics for more than a century. There is an ironic twist in our history. Before 1875, Congress erected no barriers to immigrants. "Any person from any part of the world was welcome," one scholar noted. The new nation, expanding in territory and trade, needed farmers and laborers. Congress did not care about their national origin or citizenship status, as long as they could lift a hoe or hammer. Until the end of the nineteenth century, in fact, twenty-two states and territories allowed aliens to vote. Membership in the political community did not depend on citizenship, but merely on residence.

Several factors combined to change this welcoming attitude. One stemmed from the Japanese military victory over Russia in 1905, reviving American fears of a "Yellow Peril" in the Pacific. Another came from the militance of groups like the Industrial Workers of the World, whose members—including many aliens—engaged in sabotage and strikes against "capitalist oppression." Fears of aliens were later fanned by government propaganda in World War I portraying Germans as bestial "Huns" who raped Belgian nuns. Hostility increased after the 1919 founding of the American Communist Party, whose members included many Russian aliens. During the "Red Scare" that followed the Bolshevik Revolution, federal agents herded 10,000 aliens into jail cells; several hundred were later deported under the wartime Sedition Act. During the 1920s, nativist groups—including a resurgent Ku Klux Klan—denounced "alien" influences in American culture and pressured Congress to restrict immigration. Mixed into a boiling political cauldron, these factors turned aliens into a "suspect" group, accused of sedition, sabotage, and subversion.

Although overt hostility toward aliens declined after World War II, the second "Red Scare" of McCarthyism emphasized the foreign roots of American communism. Even the science fiction craze of the 1950s gave the word "alien" a sinister meaning. More important, the increase of illegal migration in the 1960s and 1970s, largely from Mexico, fueled political attacks on aliens. The term "wetback" became a common epithet. Speaking in 1972, President Richard Nixon deplored "the problem of illegal aliens" from Mexico and blamed them for adding to "the unemployment problem" in the United States. Even liberal politicians joined the nativist chorus. Representative Leo Ryan, a California Democrat, told Congress in 1973 that welfare officials in his state "look at need rather than entitlement and provide these unfortunates with food, clothing, shelter, and medical care, all at taxpayer expense." He asked his colleagues to protect those who "pay the costs of unentitled public services."

CONGRESS AND SEVERAL state legislatures responded with laws that deprived *all* aliens—even lawful residents—of public benefits. The new breed of "poverty lawyers," often financed by federal grants, promptly challenged these laws under the Equal Protection clause and won a string of legal victories. Appeals from state officials confronted the Supreme Court with cases that raised, in the words of Justice Harry Blackmun, "another aspect of the widening litigation in this area" of equal protection law.

Blackmun wrote for a unanimous Court in the first test of state laws barring resident aliens—those lawfully in the United States—from public benefits for which they paid taxes. The plaintiff in this case, Carmen Richardson, emigrated from Mexico to Arizona in 1956, having married an American citizen. After her husband died and she became disabled at the age of sixty-four, she applied in 1969 for welfare benefits. She was rejected, however, because Arizona law imposed a fifteen-year residency requirement on aliens. Carmen Richardson fell two years short of eligibility. Aided by lawyers from Legal Services for the Elderly Poor, she sued the Arizona welfare director and won a lower-court ruling on equal protection grounds.

Despite their eagerness to strike down the Arizona law in *Graham v.*

Richardson, the justices faced clear precedent on the other side. Ruling in another Arizona case that restricted the employment of aliens, the Court held in 1915 that states could limit benefits from public funds "to its citizens as against both aliens and the citizens of other States." The same year, the justices upheld a similar ruling from the New York courts written by Benjamin Cardozo, an esteemed state judge who later joined the Supreme Court. "Whatever is a privilege rather than a right," he wrote, "may be made dependent upon citizenship. In its war against poverty, the state is not required to dedicate its own resources to citizens and aliens alike." Cardozo anticipated by fifty years the War on Poverty of President Lyndon Johnson, but Blackmun quoted his opinion during the presidency of Richard Nixon, who waved a white flag in this war.

Political changes in the White House, however, did not sway the Court's decisions in this area. Justice Blackmun's opinion in *Graham v. Richardson* reflected the renewed vitality of the Equal Protection clause. He acknowledged Cardozo's opinion as the judicial doctrine of its time. "But this Court has now rejected the concept that constitutional rights turn on whether a governmental benefit is characterized as a 'right' or a 'privilege.' "

Blackmun conceded that states retain "broad discretion" to choose between different groups in handing out public benefits, if the choice has a "reasonable basis" in facts the lawmakers relied upon. He cited the 1955 opinion in *Williamson v. Lee Optical Co.* for the principle of judicial deference in economic matters. But this doctrine was subject to the overriding principle that classifications based on race, national origin, or alienage "are inherently suspect and subject to close judicial scrutiny." Blackmun trumped *Williamson* with Footnote Four of the *Carolene Products* case. "Aliens as a class are a prime example of a 'discrete and insular' minority," he wrote, "for whom such heightened judicial solicitude is appropriate." Arizona had not shown a "compelling interest" in denying welfare benefits to Carmen Richardson, a lawful resident of the state for many years.

Blackmun wrote this opinion during his second year on the Court. Both Blackmun and his fellow Minnesotan Chief Justice Burger had been appointed by President Nixon, and they voted together more than 80 percent of the time. The fact that Blackmun and Burger, the most conservative justices, were joined in *Richardson* by William Brennan and Thurgood Marshall, the most liberal, underscores the judicial consensus that the Equal Protection clause protects lawful aliens from discrimination. Blackmun's reliance on *Carolene Products* and the "strict scrutiny" test added an exclamation point to the Court's unity on this issue.

Starting in the next Court term, unanimity ended with the arrival of William Rehnquist. From his first vote, the newest justice maintained a consistent position in alien cases. He began his unbroken string in 1973, dissenting from a decision that struck down a New York law barring aliens from state civil-service positions. Justice Blackmun again wrote for the Court in *Sugarman v. Dougall*. Patrick Dougall—a native and citizen of Guyana—had been employed until 1970 by a New York job-training program supported by federal grants. When the Nixon administration cut off funding, New York absorbed Dougall and 450 other workers into the state's Manpower Career and Development Agency. The state conceded that Dougall did an excellent job in his administrative position. Two months later, he was abruptly fired because he lacked American citizenship.

Not surprisingly, given the recent precedent of the *Richardson* decision, the Supreme Court struck down the New York law. Justice Blackmun again wrote for the Court and again cited the *Carolene Products* decision. The only complicating issue was New York's arguments that state workers must give "undivided loyalty" to their tasks, and that aliens with "competing obligations to another power" might fall short in patriotism. Blackmun responded that New York required citizenship of a "sanitation man, class B," but not for its legislators or governor. The ban on alien employees, he dryly noted, "has no application at all to positions that would seem naturally to fall within the State's asserted purpose" of employee loyalty.

Justice Rehnquist stood alone in this case. His dissenting opinion reeked of scorn for *Carolene Products* and the application of "strict scrutiny" to the claims of aliens. Judicial decisions that the Fourteenth Amendment protected them, he wrote, "are simply irrelevant to the question of whether that Amendment prohibits legislative classifications based upon this particular status." Rehnquist scored the majority for failing to articulate "any constitutional foundation" for its decision. He read judicial history as holding "time and again that legislative classifications on the basis of citizenship were subject to the 'rational basis' test of equal protection," stubbornly holding to the test his colleagues had rejected in both *Richardson* and *Dougall*.

Rehnquist's narrow view of the "rational basis" test allowed him to imagine *any* reason a lawmaker might vote to bar aliens from public employment. He found this an easy task, with the categories of "we" and "them" as convenient guides. "It is not irrational," Rehnquist wrote, "to assume that aliens as a class are not familiar with how we as individuals treat others and how we expect 'government' to treat us." Aliens were more likely, he continued, to come from countries "in which political mores do not reject bribery" as a basis for official decisions. He also argued that aliens might adopt a "contemptuous attitude" toward public service and lack "the same rapport that one familiar with our political and social mores" would show with real Americans. Rehnquist even suggested that Dougall and other aliens "could rationally be expected" to fail in their assigned tasks because they would not appreciate "that such positions exist" to serve the public. Over his solitary dissent, the Court restored Patrick Dougall to the job he had performed without any complaint of bribery or disrespect.

JUSTICE REHNQUIST continued to dissent in alien cases after *Sugarman*, but he no longer stood alone. Members of the Court's center group began to join him, although the votes shifted from one case to the next. Justices Brennan, Stevens, and Marshall supported the claims of aliens in every case, and Blackmun agreed in all but one. Chief Justice Burger had joined Blackmun's "strict scrutiny" opinions, more likely because of his aversion to solo dissents than from sympathy with aliens. After the *Sugarman* decision, Burger lined up solidly with Rehnquist. Justices Stewart, Powell, and White became the swing votes as the Court backed away from "strict scrutiny" in a wide range of equal protection cases. This doctrinal reversal had less to do with changes on the Court—its membership remained stable from 1975 to 1981—than with the conservative shift of the public, most evident in the demise of the Equal Rights Amendment. Aliens suffered along with women from the Court's retreat to the "rational basis" test that Rehnquist championed.

This judicial change was more of a gradual erosion than a sudden earthquake. The Court's majority continued to support aliens in several cases that followed *Sugarman*. One involved a Chinese refugee, Mow Sun Wong, who abandoned a career as an electrical engineer and moved to San Francisco. Hampered by language problems, he finally gave up his search for engineering jobs and applied for work as a janitor in federal buildings. He completed training in a state program and also filed a declaration of intent to become an American citizen. But federal officials would not allow Mr. Wong to mop their floors. Congress had passed a law in 1883—the year after the Chinese Exclusion Act—barring aliens from all civil-service jobs.

Supported by the American Civil Liberties Union, Wong and four other Chinese resident aliens sued Robert Hampton, chairman of the U.S. Civil Service Commission. They relied on the Due Process clause of the Fifth Amendment, which protects "any person" against deprivation of liberty. After a federal judge ruled in Hampton's favor, an appellate panel reversed the decision. Arguing the government's appeal to the Supreme Court, Solicitor General Robert Bork denied that the Fifth Amendment restricted federal power over aliens. Because the Constitution gave Congress the authority to make rules about naturalization, he claimed, the government needed "no justification" for its ban on alien workers.

The Supreme Court rejected this hard-line position in 1976, the Bicentennial of the Declaration of Independence, which proclaimed that "all men are created equal." The Court's opinion in *Hampton v. Mow Sun Wong* did not note the irony that many who signed that document were foreign-born; American "citizenship" was not defined in legal terms for another century. Justice Brennan, the senior member of the majority, assigned the *Hampton* opinion to John Paul Stevens, the Court's junior member. Stevens fully met the expectations of his mentor. He described aliens as members of a "discrete and insular minority" and wrote that the federal rule against their employment "deprives a discrete class of persons of an interest in liberty on a wholesale basis."

Stevens followed Brennan in looking to "social facts" for judicial support, writing that lawmakers in 1883 were inclined "to regard 'foreigners' as a somewhat less desirable class of persons than American citizens." That "provincial attitude," he continued, "has been implicitly repudiated by our cases requiring that aliens be treated with the dignity and respect" accorded to American citizens. Stevens concluded that the federal law "has deprived these respondents of liberty without due process of law and is therefore invalid." With this ruling, the Supreme Court finally placed Mow Sun Wong on the federal payroll.

Writing for the Court's four dissenters, Rehnquist first denied that *anyone*, citizen or alien, has a "liberty" interest in federal employment under the Fifth Amendment. He also accused the majority of undermining "the exclusive power of Congress" to deal with aliens. From these premises, Rehnquist concluded that federal officials have no duty to "demonstrate why they chose to exclude aliens from the civil service." The decision to bar Mow Sun Wong and other aliens from federal jobs, he continued, was "a political decision reserved to Congress, the wisdom of which may not be challenged in the courts."

Rehnquist also berated the majority for using "classic equal protection analysis" in a case that did not involve state law. This argument involved an esoteric—but important—constitutional doctrine. The Court ruled in 1954 that the Due Process clause of the Fifth Amendment "incorporates" the Equal Protection clause of the Fourteenth Amendment. The "reverse incorporation" doctrine thus prohibits discrimination by federal officials. Rehnquist was upset that the Court used *Mow Sun Wong* to fuse "the concepts of equal protection and procedural and substantive due process" into a potent judicial weapon. Such an expansive doctrine violated his belief that federal laws regarding aliens were "not subject to judicial scrutiny" for any reason.

The following year, the Court struck down a New York law that barred aliens from financial aid in higher education if they did not declare an intent to apply for American citizenship. This was another five-to-four decision, although Justices Blackmun and White shifted sides from the *Mow Sun Wong* decision. The plaintiff in this case, Jean-Marie Mauclet, was a French national whose wife and child were both American citizens. He applied for tuition assistance at the state university in Buffalo and was turned down because he declared that "I do not wish to relinquish my French citizenship at this time."

As the senior majority justice, Brennan assigned the *Nyquist v. Mauclet* opinion to Harry Blackmun, rewarding him for returning to the fold on this issue. Blackmun dusted off his *Richardson* opinion and repeated his statement that classifications based on alienage are "inherently suspect and subject to close judicial scrutiny." He found no "compelling reason" for New York to penalize aliens like Mauclet, who "pay their full share of the taxes" that support tuition-assistance programs.

Rehnquist spoke in unusually soft tones in his dissent. He bent over backward in soothing the concerns of Justice Blackmun. "I think one can accept the premise of *Graham v. Richardson*," he wrote, "and therefore agree with the Court that classifications based on alienage are inherently suspect, but nonetheless feel that this case is wrongly decided." Rehnquist even agreed that "all aliens are, at some time, members of a discrete and insular minority" as long as federal law made them "powerless" to change their status to American citizenship. But his sympathy with Blackmun's opinion ended at this point. Jean-Marie Mauclet was eligible to apply for citizenship but had rejected this choice. Even though state law forced Mauclet to choose between his French citizenship and tuition benefits, Rehnquist did not consider this an "impermissible burden" on his constitutional rights. Soft words could not conceal the hard fact that one more vote would end judicial sympathy for aliens.

JUSTICE BYRON WHITE finally provided the fifth vote for a new majority in alien cases. In three decisions between 1978 and 1982, the Court removed what Chief Justice Burger called "the high hurdle of 'strict scrutiny' " that state laws had failed to clear. The Court simply took a detour around the *Richardson* and *Dougall* cases. Burger assigned the first opinion to himself. Edmund Foley had applied to become a New York State trooper. Like many officers, he was Irish, but he had not yet become an American citizen and was turned down for the job.

Burger professed tolerance in *Foley v. Connelie* for those who lacked citizenship. "As a nation we exhibit extraordinary hospitality to those who come to our country," he wrote, "which is not surprising for we have often been described as 'a nation of immigrants.' " He acknowledged that the Court had applied "close scrutiny of restraints imposed by States on aliens" in past cases. "But we have never suggested that such legislation is inherently invalid, nor have we held that all limitations on aliens are suspect." Burger cited Justice Blackmun's *Dougall* opinion for this proposition.

Blackmun had in fact written that states could exclude aliens from "an appropriately designated class of public office holders." But he limited this exclusion to those in "high public offices that have to do with the formulation and execution of state policy." Blackmun was referring to governors and cabinet members. Burger placed state troopers in this special category, arguing that "the police function fulfills a most fundamental obligation of government to its constituency." During the Court's conference on the *Foley* case, Burger used more pungent words: "I'd sooner let an alien be a mayor before I'd let him be a policeman." In his opinion, he admitted that police officers "do not formulate policy, *per se*, but they are clothed with authority to exercise an almost infinite variety of discretionary powers." Having turned Blackmun's narrow exception into a gaping hole, Burger then removed the warning sign. "The

State need only justify its classification by a showing of some rational relationship" of the law to the necessity of protecting New York motorists from alien troopers.

Surprisingly, Blackmun joined this decision, writing in concurrence that New York lawmakers could "rationally conclude" that the duties of troopers "are basic to the function of state government." The dissenters stood more firmly behind the *Dougall* opinion than its author. Justice Stevens, speaking for Brennan and Marshall, wrote that it "plainly teaches us that the burgeoning public employment market cannot be totally foreclosed to aliens." He disputed Burger's lumping together of those who shape and those who execute policy. "Since the police officer is not a policymaker in this country," Stevens wrote, "the total exclusion of aliens from the police force must fall." But Edmund Foley did not get his trooper's badge.

Blackmun returned to dissent in the next alien case, also from New York. Susan Norwick, born in Scotland and a British subject, applied in 1973 for an elementary-school teaching certificate. She had all the qualifications but one, American citizenship. New York excluded aliens from teaching as well as policing. Five justices upheld the law in *Ambach v. Norwick*, decided in 1979. Justice Lewis Powell wrote for the majority and relied heavily on the previous year's *Foley* decision. Public school teachers were required, he said, to lead students in flag salutes and other "patriotic exercises" for which "loyalty" was essential. New York lawmakers could rationally conclude that Susan Norwick and other aliens might lack the ability to "foster in the children of the state moral and intellectual qualities which are essential in preparing to meet the obligations of citizenship in peace or in war," as state law required.

Justice Powell noted that New York teachers were required to take courses in American and state history, but he left the Court's history lesson to Justice Blackmun, who spoke for the four dissenters. "These New York statutes, for the most part," Blackmun wrote, "have their origin in the frantic and overreactive days of the First World War when attitudes of parochialism and fear of the foreigner were the order of the day." The law barring aliens from the classroom was passed in 1918, when the targets were German "Huns" and Russian "Bolsheviks" and the British were our loyal allies. Blackmun also pointed to the anomaly that aliens could serve on New York school boards but could not teach in nursery schools. Of course, he noted wryly, "board members teach no classes, and rarely if ever are known or identified by the students." Even the state education commissioner who had been sued by Susan Norwick was not required to be a citizen.

The Court moved in the next alien case from the Atlantic to the Pacific Coast, reflecting the volatile political issue of Mexican immigration. Jose Chavez-Salido applied in 1974 for a job in Los Angeles as "Deputy Probation Officer, Spanish-speaking." He seemed highly qualified; although born in Mexico, he came with his parents to California as a child and had been a legal resident for twenty-six years. He earned a bachelor's degree in Mexican-American studies from California State College in Long Beach, and he scored 95 out of 100 on the qualifying examination for the probation-officer position. But he failed the citizenship test.

Only this last fact appeared in the Court's opinion in *Cabell v. Chavez-Salido*, decided in 1981. The lack of citizenship was the only relevant issue to Justice Byron White, whose majority opinion did not even mention Jose Chavez-Salido's name. White also did not mention Justice Blackmun, whose dissent stated the facts of the case. He did, however, include Blackmun's opinions in *Richardson* and *Dougall* in a listing of a dozen cases that began with *Yick Wo* in 1886 and ended with *Norwick* in 1979. White's purpose in lining up these equal protection cases was to shoot them down. Taken together, he wrote, the decisions "illustrate a not unusual characteristic of legal development: broad principles are articulated, narrowed when applied to new contexts, and finally replaced when the distinctions they rely upon are no longer tenable."

White's rhetoric obscured the majority's real purpose: the final dismantling of the "strict scrutiny" test. What had become untenable were not laws that discriminated against aliens, but decisions that struck down these laws. White spoke in this opinion for the newest justice, Sandra O'Connor, President Reagan's first nominee. After noting that *Richardson* and *Dougall* both dealt with economic benefits, White wrote for the conservative majority that "we have concluded that strict scrutiny is out of place when the restriction primarily serves a political function" of state government. He concluded that California probation officers, like New York state troopers, "sufficiently partake of the sovereign's power to exercise coercive force over the individual that they may be limited to citizens."

Justice Blackmun, soft-spoken in person, rarely raised his voice in judicial opinions. But he felt wounded by this decision and accepted Brennan's invitation to speak for the dissenters. "In my view," he wrote, "today's decision rewrites the Court's precedents, ignores history, defies common sense, and reinstates the deadening mantle of state parochialism in public employment." Blackmun accused the majority of "misstating the standard of review it has long applied" in alien cases and of "thoroughly eviscerating" his *Dougall* opinion. California had no good reason to bar Jose Chavez-Salido from a job for which he was "superbly qualified" by training and background. "I can only conclude," Blackmun wrote, that the California law "stems solely from state parochialism and hostility toward foreigners who have come to this country lawfully." The signs that once read "No Irish Need Apply" had been replaced with new ones written in Spanish.

Justice Brennan remained quiet during this extended judicial debate. He had not written any opinions in the alien cases, deferring to Justice Blackmun in this field. When he finally spoke in 1982, Brennan assigned the majority opinion in *Plyler v. Doe* to himself. This case began in 1975 when the Texas legislature passed a law that withheld state funds from school districts that enrolled children who were not "legally admitted" to the United States. Lawyers from the Mexican-American Legal Defense and Education Fund filed suit in 1977 against James Plyler, superintendent of the Tyler district in East Texas. The previous year, Jimmy Carter had become president and the Justice Department joined the suit on the children's side. A raft of church and civil rights groups filed *amicus* briefs for the plaintiffs, while groups that lobbied for restrictive immigration laws supported the Texas statute. Federal district judge William Justice, appointed in 1968 by his longtime friend Lyndon Johnson, ruled for the alien children, holding that depriving them of education did not foster any legitimate state interest.

Justice Brennan assumed a daunting task in this case. First, as the anonymous name "Doe" suggests, the aliens who filed suit had entered the United States illegally—many by wading across the Rio Grande from Mexico into Texas. Second, the Supreme Court had consistently rejected claims that illegal aliens constituted a "suspect class" under the "strict scrutiny" doctrine. Third, the plaintiffs were children who sought a free public education as a "fundamental right." But the Court had also ruled that the Constitution did not provide such a right. Finally, Brennan had to persuade a member of the Court's center group to change sides from decisions that rejected the claims of *legal* aliens.

Brennan's opinion showed a mastery of constitutional interpretation, or what some might call manipulation. Confronted with recent precedent that barred the "strict scrutiny" test, he looked instead to the "fundamental conceptions of justice" that shored up the constitutional structure. These concepts were located not in the text of the Constitution but in the principles that animated its framers. More was involved in this case, Brennan wrote, "than the abstract question whether [the Texas law] discriminates against a suspect class, or whether education is a fundamental right." He found a basic principle in the notion that no person should be punished for having a "disabling status" over which they have no control.

The parents of the undocumented students, Brennan agreed, had broken the immigration laws and could be deported. But their children had not voluntarily chosen their illegal status. He quoted a decision holding that punishing children for the misdeeds of their parents "is contrary to the basic concept of our system that legal burdens should bear some relationship to individual responsibility or wrongdoing." Brennan tied this premise to the Equal Protection clause by observing that a law "imposing special disabilities upon groups disfavored by virtue of circumstances beyond their control suggests the kind of 'class or caste' treatment that the Fourteenth Amendment was designed to abolish."

Brennan could not simply declare the Texas law unconstitutional on this basis. He needed to answer the state's claim that its policy served the "legitimate public purpose" of conserving tax funds. He responded with two related arguments, both rooted in "social facts" from the public record. First, the presence in the United States of several million illegal aliens "raises the specter of a permanent caste of undocumented resident aliens, encouraged by some to remain here as a source of cheap labor, but nevertheless denied the benefits that our society makes available to citizens and lawful residents." Members of this "underclass" are "virtually defenseless against any abuse" or exploitation. "The children who are plaintiffs in these cases are special members of this underclass," Brennan added.

Because most of these children will remain in the United States and later join the job force, Brennan reasoned that their only hope for escaping the underclass is education. He cited the Court's landmark *Brown* decision of 1954 for the proposition that "education has a fundamental role in maintaining the fabric of our society." It also "provides the basic tools by which individuals might lead economically productive lives to the benefit of us all." In Brennan's view, barring undocumented children from school was a form of official abuse. "The stigma of illiteracy will mark them for the rest of their lives," he wrote in a clear reference to the *Brown* holding that segregation imposed a stigma that marked black children.

From this perspective, Brennan measured the savings to Texas in tax funds against the costs to society of its policy. "It is difficult to understand precisely what the State hopes to achieve by promoting the creation and perpetuation of a subclass of illiterates within our boundaries," he wrote, "surely adding to the problems and cost of unemployment, welfare, and crime. It is thus clear that whatever savings might be achieved by denying these children an education, they are wholly insubstantial in light of the costs involved to these children, the State, and the Nation." Brennan concluded that it was "difficult to conceive of a rational justification for penalizing these children for their presence within the United States." With Brennan as schoolmaster, Texas had failed the most lenient constitutional measure, the "rational basis" test.

Brennan secured his majority in *Plyler* with the vote of Justice Lewis Powell, who generally sided with the conservatives in alien cases. Powell, in fact, had written the opinion in another Texas school-funding case, *San Antonio v. Rodriguez*, holding that education was *not* a "fundamental" constitutional right. And he almost always supported state and local governments. But Powell had served as president of the Richmond, Virginia, school board, and he knew the disabilities imposed on children by poor education. He wrote a separate concurrence in *Plyler* to underline "the unique character" of the case and make clear his belief "that strict scrutiny is not appropriately applied to this classification."

Even the dissenters professed sympathy for the undocumented children. Chief Justice Burger, who wrote for all four, considered it "senseless for an enlightened society to deprive any children—including illegal aliens—of an elementary education." But his sympathy had limits. He suggested that if "illegal alien children can be identified for purposes of this litigation, their parents can be identified for purposes of prompt deportation." Burger also rejected the notion that the children suffered because of their parents' acts. Texas penalized the children, he wrote with emphasis, "on the basis of *their own* illegal status, not that of their parents."

Burger had even less sympathy for Brennan's opinion, which to him smacked of judicial "policymaking" and of trespassing on legislative turf. The Chief paid a backhanded tribute to his colleague's skill at "patching together bits and pieces" of constitutional doctrine to construct "a theory custom-tailored to the facts of these cases." But he deplored the result of this creative jurisprudence. "If ever a court was guilty of an unabashedly result-oriented approach, this case is a prime example," Burger scolded. The only issue, he added, was whether states were free "to differentiate between persons who are lawfully within the state and those who are unlawfully there." That was the "dispositive" question to the dissenters, including Justice Rehnquist, and their answer was simple: yes.

ANOTHER MINORITY GROUP has much in common with aliens, and has also appealed to the Supreme Court for protection. Discrimination against illegitimate children is rooted in England's "bastardy" laws, designed to protect the aristocracy against claims from the many children born to the servants of noblemen. The concept of "family" has affected the Court's treatment of both groups. Just as aliens remain outside the American political family, illegitimates are not real members of the social family defined by middle-class norms.

The concept of "family" has very different meanings to Justices Brennan and Rehnquist. One case—which did not involve illegitimate children—illustrates their dispute, and highlights the factors of race and class in judicial decisions. Inez Moore, a sixty-three-year-old black woman, lived in East Cleveland, Ohio, and provided a home for two grandsons, Dale and his cousin John, whose mother died when he was a baby. Because the municipal housing code defined a "family" as only parents and their children, Moore was charged by city officials with harboring an "illegal occupant" and sentenced to five days in jail. The Ohio Supreme Court upheld her conviction and the American Civil Liberties Union took her appeal to the U.S. Supreme Court, which decided the case in 1977.

Inez Moore escaped her jail term by a single vote, provided by Justice Lewis Powell, whom Brennan rewarded with the opinion in *Moore v. East Cleveland*. Powell shied away from the Equal Protection clause and based the decision on the Due Process clause, writing that "the institution of the family is deeply rooted in this Nation's history and tradition" and that the concept was not limited to "members of the nuclear family."

Brennan added a concurrence "to underscore the cultural myopia" of those who limited the term "family" to parents and children. "In today's America," he wrote, "the 'nuclear family' is the pattern so often found in much of white suburbia. The Constitution cannot be interpreted, however, to tolerate the imposition by government upon the rest of us of white suburbia's preference in patterns of family living." He cited more than a dozen books and articles that included "social facts" about the "extended families" that had become "a prominent pattern—virtually a means of survival—for large numbers of the poor and deprived minorities of our society."

Justice Rehnquist, who grew up in an affluent Milwaukee suburb of traditional nuclear families, joined the dissenting opinion of Justice Potter Stewart, who came from even greater affluence in Cincinnati. Stewart backed the power of local governments "to say what a 'family' is" and to limit residence to those who fit that definition. He quoted an earlier opinion that upheld a similar housing code because it established "zones where family values, youth values, and the blessings of quiet seclusion and clean air make the area a sanctuary for people." Stewart also defended the East Cleveland ordinance as "rationally designed" to enforce "minimum health and safety standards." John and Dale Moore could presumably not learn "family values" from their grandmother in crowded and unhealthy East Cleveland. Both Stewart and Rehnquist voted to uphold Inez Moore's jail term for sheltering her grandchildren.

Building on the premise that governments can define what a "family" is, Rehnquist argued that lawmakers can exclude illegitimate children from this definition, even those who live with their parents. He stood alone on this issue in most cases, although other justices sometimes voted with him to uphold laws barring illegitimates from state benefits. Rehnquist explained his position in *Weber v. Aetna Casualty Co.*, one of his first major opinions. This Louisiana case, decided in 1972, began when Henry Stokes died in an industrial accident. He had four legitimate children, whose mother had been committed to a mental hospital, and two illegitimate children with Willie Mae Weber, with whom he lived before his death. All six children applied for death benefits under the state workmen's compensation law, but the claim of the two children labeled in the Louisiana code as "bastards" was denied.

The Supreme Court reversed this ruling in a brief opinion that relied on its 1968 decision in *Levy v. Louisiana*, which struck down a similar death-benefits law. Writing for the Court in *Levy*, Justice William Douglas admitted that in the area of "social and economic legislation, we give great latitude" to state lawmakers. He cited for this proposition his 1955 opinion in *Williamson v. Lee Optical*. Douglas, however, noted in *Levy* that "basic civil rights" cannot be infringed by "invidious discrimination"

against any group. He asked a simple question: "Why should the illegitimate child be denied rights merely because of his birth outside
wedlock?"

Writing a solo dissent in the *Weber* case, Rehnquist had a quick answer:
Douglas was right in *Williamson* and wrong in *Levy*. Because the Constitution does not grant any rights to illegitimate children, the Court must
apply the "rational basis" test to the challenged law. Rehnquist read the
minds of Louisiana lawmakers, who "might rationally presume that the
decedent would have preferred the compensation to go to his legitimate
children." Rehnquist imagined "another possible legislative purpose" for
the law. In order to promote "responsible family relationships," the Louisiana statute "might be considered part of that statutory pattern designed
to discourage formation of illicit family relationships." Once again, Rehnquist substituted "mights" and "possibles" for any sure knowledge of what
the lawmakers—or Henry Stokes—really intended.

Rehnquist turned his *Weber* dissent into a broadside attack on the
"strict scrutiny" test and the "fundamental personal rights" doctrine. He
expressed his opinion of the latter term by putting it in quotation marks
a dozen times. Rehnquist said little about illegitimate children, although
he exhumed and discussed at length the *Lochner* decision of 1905 to
make the point that his colleagues—like earlier activist judges—were
"passing policy judgments upon the acts of every state legislature in the
country." The motive for this judicial assault seems clear. Under Brennan's leadership, the Court was coming closer to applying the "strict
scrutiny" test to any distinctive minority group. Rehnquist was determined
to block this move, or at least to slow its progress until the Court's
composition changed.

While he waited, Rehnquist continued to vote against the claims of
illegitimate children. His opinions revealed a firm belief in traditional
family structure and values. In one solo dissent in 1973, he found a
"rational basis" for a New Jersey law that allowed welfare benefits only
to families in which the parents were "ceremonially married to each
other" and living with legitimate children. The other justices cited the
Weber decision and held that benefits "are as indispensable to the health
and well-being of illegitimate children as to those who are legitimate."
Rehnquist, however, felt that states could decide that "ceremonial marriage" was essential to the "particular type of family" that made up one
of the "core units of our social system." The same year, dissenting in
another welfare case, Rehnquist argued that lawmakers were entitled to

limit benefits to "the family as we know it—a household consisting of related individuals." The family that Rehnquist knew best was in Shorewood Village, Wisconsin. But only a minority of Americans now live in a traditional nuclear family.

THE PREMISE of the "strict scrutiny" test is that the Equal Protection clause outlaws discrimination on the basis of "immutable" characteristics, which no person can or should be forced to change. Race and national origin are certainly immutable, even if some people fall into hard-to-define categories. Aliens can change their status through naturalization, but must usually wait several years for citizenship. Parents can acknowledge their illegitimate children, but cannot backdate marriage certificates. One status that *can* be changed—at least for some—is poverty. Many people are born into families whose poverty goes back several generations, but the trait is not inherited, despite the claims of modern Social Darwinists. Poverty is also a relative concept, subject to changing definitions; the federal government's official poverty line has shifted many times over the years.

The Supreme Court has also shifted in poverty cases. During the 1960s, the justices usually supported the claims of indigents to government benefits. Justice Brennan wrote for a majority in 1969 that states could not impose a one-year residency rule on welfare recipients like Vivian Thompson, an unwed mother who was denied benefits after she moved from Massachusetts to Connecticut. She and others who moved across state lines, Brennan wrote, were deprived of aid "upon which may depend the ability of the families to obtain the very means to subsist—food, shelter, and other necessities of life." His opinion in *Shapiro v. Thompson* did not rely on "suspect class" analysis, however, but on the "fundamental right" of interstate travel and movement.

The *Shapiro* decision did not help many poor people. One year later, the Court upheld a Maryland law that placed a cap on welfare payments to needy families, regardless of their size. The majority ruled in *Dandridge v. Williams* that in "the area of economics and social welfare, a State does not violate the Equal Protection Clause merely because the classifications made by its laws are imperfect." When he joined the Court in 1972, two years after the *Dandridge* decision, Justice Rehnquist warmly embraced its doctrine of judicial deference. His first opinion in a welfare case held that Texas could limit benefits under the Aid to Families with

Dependent Children (AFDC) program to 50 percent of the "full standard of need" as defined by federal law. The state's lawmakers showed more solicitude for elderly welfare recipients, who received a full 100 percent of aid, and for the totally disabled, who were allotted 95 percent of the federal standard.

Ruth Jefferson, a mother of five, challenged this policy on equal protection grounds. Her suit alleged a racial and ethnic bias on the part of Texas lawmakers, since blacks and Chicanos made up 87 percent of AFDC recipients but less than half of those in the elderly and disabled groups. Writing for the Court in *Jefferson v. Hackney*, Rehnquist rejected the "naked statistical argument" of bias. He did not dispute the evidence of racial disparity, but responded that few governmental programs "could survive" equal protection scrutiny under a "constitutional theory" that "would render suspect each difference in treatment among the grant classes, however lacking in racial motivation and however otherwise rational the treatment might be." Rehnquist dodged the question of whether the Court *should* apply the "strict scrutiny" test to claims of racial bias in the *Jefferson* case. He simply answered that "we do not find it required by the Fourteenth Amendment."

Clearly uncomfortable with racial issues, Rehnquist took refuge in precedent that dealt with eyeglasses. He paraphrased the *Williamson* opinion of Justice William Douglas. "So long as its judgments are rational, and not invidious," he wrote, "the legislature's efforts to tackle the problems of the poor and the needy are not subject to a constitutional straightjacket." Once again, Rehnquist evaded the issue of "invidious" racial bias. Determined to find a "rational basis" for the Texas welfare law, he suggested that "the State may have concluded that the aged and infirm are the least able" of the needy groups "to bear the hardships of an inadequate standard of living." Speaking to Ruth Jefferson and her five children, whose monthly welfare check had been cut to $120, Rehnquist explained that "it is not irrational for the State to believe that the young are more adaptable than the sick and elderly, especially because the latter have less hope of improving their situation in the years remaining to them."

Justice Thurgood Marshall, dissenting with Justice Brennan, doubted this altruistic motive for the welfare cuts. "The record contains numerous statements by state officials," he noted, "that AFDC is funded at a lower level than the other programs because it is not a politically popular program." Elderly white people, he might have added, turn out on Election Day in large numbers, while black and Hispanic children cannot even vote.

CHILDREN WHO LIVE in poverty—like the five kids of Ruth Jefferson—have little hope of "improving their situation" if their schools are crumbling and lack basic facilities. The most important case to children since the *Brown* decision began in 1968 on the dusty streets of Edgewood, the Hispanic barrio in San Antonio, Texas. Demetrio Rodriguez, a Navy veteran who worked as a civilian mechanic for the Air Force, had tried without success to persuade Edgewood school officials to repair the elementary school three of his sons attended. Bricks were falling off the walls and only the first floor could be used. Even worse, half the teachers were not certified and worked on emergency permits. Rodriguez helped organize the Edgewood District Concerned Parents Association and took a delegation to see the superintendent, Dr. Jose Cardenas, who explained that schools were funded by property taxes and that Edgewood—which already taxed itself at the highest possible rate— could not raise enough money from its tax base to improve the schools.

Rodriguez refused to give up. He walked the streets and found six other parents willing to join a lawsuit against city and state officials. A sympathetic lawyer, Arthur Gochman, agreed to represent them without charge. He based the suit on equal protection grounds, arguing that the property tax system of school funding subjected Edgewood students— more than 90 percent Hispanic—to "wealth" and racial discrimination. Gochman decided to dramatize the case by comparing Edgewood, the county's poorest district, with its richest, Alamo Heights. Many of San Antonio's lawyers and doctors lived in this affluent "Anglo" suburb, where all the teachers were certified and 40 percent had master's degrees.

Gochman showed a panel of federal judges that Edgewood had a property tax base of $5,429 per student, while the Alamo Heights figure was $45,095. Adding state and federal funds to the $26 Edgewood raised per pupil through property taxes, the district spent $356 on each student. The Alamo Heights district, even at the lowest tax rate, raised $333 for each student and spent a total of $594 on each. Gochman put his case into a nutshell with this figure: Edgewood parents would have to tax themselves at twenty times the Alamo Heights rate to match their property tax revenues. But state law did not permit any higher rate. "The Texas system makes it impossible for poor districts to provide quality education," he argued.

Federal judge Adrian Spears, who wrote the panel's opinion, agreed. Nominated by President John Kennedy, he lived in Alamo Heights and knew the disparities with Edgewood. Spears ruled that the Texas property tax system violated the Equal Protection clause. He further held that "wealth" discrimination was "suspect" under the Constitution and that education was a "fundamental" right, as Gochman had argued. Not only had Texas been "unable to demonstrate compelling state interests" in basing school funding on property values, Spears wrote, but it had failed "even to establish a reasonable basis" for the existing system. The state had flunked the "rational basis" test, the easiest constitutional question.

The state's appeal to the Supreme Court gave its officials another chance to pass the judicial test. This time, they prevailed in 1973 by one vote. Justice Lewis Powell, a former school-board president, wrote for the majority—which included Justice Rehnquist—in *San Antonio v. Rodriguez*. He put the basic question in these words: "We must decide, first, whether the Texas system of financing public education operates to the disadvantage of some suspect class or impinges upon a fundamental right explicitly or implicitly protected by the Constitution, thereby requiring strict judicial scrutiny." If so, Texas would be required to equalize funding between all school districts. If not, the Court would apply the "rational basis" test to the challenged system.

Powell began by asking whether poor people belonged to a "suspect class." He gave two answers, both negative. The Edgewood parents "have not defined the term 'poor' with reference to any absolute or functional level of impecunity," he wrote. Consequently, they could not show that the property tax system "operates to the particular disadvantage of any class fairly definable as indigent, or as composed of persons whose incomes are beneath any designated poverty level." Arthur Gochman had, in fact, shown that most Edgewood families had incomes below the federal "poverty line," but the case was premised on the "poverty" of their property, which supported their schools. Powell also wrote that Edgewood's children did not suffer "an absolute deprivation" of education, but simply "a poorer quality education" than those in Alamo Heights. He reminded Demetrio Rodriguez that "the Equal Protection Clause does not require absolute equality or precisely equal advantages" to his children.

Turning to the question of whether education is a "fundamental right,"

Powell looked to the welfare cases for support. The Court had ruled that "the central importance of welfare benefits to the poor was not an adequate foundation for requiring the State to justify its law by showing some compelling state interest." If basic levels of food and shelter were not guaranteed by the Constitution, the Edgewood children were in trouble. Powell answered the question for them. "Education, of course, is not among the rights afforded explicit protection under our Federal Constitution," he wrote. "Nor do we find any basis for saying it is implicitly so protected."

Arthur Gochman had developed a "nexus" theory that connected education and the First Amendment. "In asserting a nexus between speech and education," Powell phrased this argument, "the right to speak is meaningless unless the speaker is capable of articulating his thoughts intelligently and persuasively." He answered that Texas was required only to provide the Edgewood students with "the basic minimal skills" of education. The state had no duty to help them develop "the most *effective* speech" they might use to demand better schools.

Powell explained why he rejected Gochman's "nexus" theory. He relied on the slippery-slope argument that lawyers and judges love to make. The "logical limitations" on this theory "are difficult to perceive," he wrote. "How, for instance, is education to be distinguished from the significant personal interests in the basics of decent food and shelter?" If the Court gave any one of these interests the status of a "fundamental right," then poor people in Edgewood could demand not only schools equal to those in Alamo Heights, but equal steaks and swimming pools. Without mentioning the word "socialism," Powell conjured up the ghost of Karl Marx in his opinion.

Demetrio Rodriguez later said that some of his fellow workers called him a Communist for starting the lawsuit. "I told them, I'm no more Communist than you are. We don't have to have the Communists come over here. We are doing the harm to this country by not having equal education. That's the only thing you can give a poor people. Give them an education and they'll be better citizens."

Justice Thurgood Marshall expanded on these words in a sixty-seven-page dissent, his longest opinion in any case and a reflection of his strong feelings. "I cannot accept such an emasculation of the Equal Protection Clause," he told the majority. The lawyer who guided the *Brown* case to the Supreme Court denounced the *Rodriguez* decision as "a retreat from our historic commitment of equality of opportunity" for poor children of any racial or ethnic group. Marshall quoted Chief Justice Earl Warren's holding in *Brown* that education "is the very foundation of good citizenship." Demetrio Rodriguez did not demand, he suggested, that the Edgewood schools must make his children the *best* citizens in San Antonio, only that they become *good* citizens.

Marshall answered Powell with citations to more than fifty Supreme Court decisions upholding claims to "fundamental rights" that the Constitution did not spell out in capital letters. He agreed that deciding which rights the Court should protect was a "difficult" task. But he denied that "the process need necessarily degenerate into an unprincipled, subjective 'picking-and-choosing' between various interests" with no constitutional guidance. Marshall accepted the "nexus" theory and noted that the Court had acknowledged "fundamental rights" as disparate as procreation, voting in state elections, and access to the criminal appellate process. "This is the real lesson that must be taken from our previous decisions involving interests deemed to be fundamental," he wrote. Education was the most fundamental right that Marshall, who devoted his career to getting poor children into good schools, could imagine.

Justice Brennan added only two paragraphs to Marshall's dissent, which he joined. He wrote separately to underscore his agreement with the "nexus" theory. There was "no doubt" in Brennan's mind "that education is inextricably linked to the right to participate in the electoral process and to the rights of free speech and association guaranteed by the First Amendment." This linkage meant that "any classification affecting education must be subjected to strict scrutiny" under the Equal Protection clause. Texas officials conceded that their property tax system "cannot pass constitutional muster under this stricter standard of review," Brennan noted. He believed the Constitution required that states provide *all* parents—mechanics and judges alike—equal funds to educate their children.

Justice Brennan was on the losing side in the *Rodriguez* case. But his position ultimately prevailed. For many years, Brennan urged lawyers to raise constitutional claims in state courts, whose judges are free to expand the protections of the federal Constitution in construing their state charters. Many civil rights and civil liberties groups have taken this advice and have won significant legal victories for their constituents. Lawyers for the Mexican-American Legal Defense and Education Fund asked Demetrio Rodriguez in 1985 to place his name on a lawsuit based on the Texas constitution, which provides a right to education. He agreed, and the Texas supreme court ruled in 1989 that the state legislature must equalize school-district funding. The lawmakers did not finally comply with this judicial order until 1993, after they faced a possible contempt citation. Rodriguez waited twenty-five years for this victory; by this time, he had retired from his job and all his children had graduated from high school. But his grandchildren now go to better schools in San Antonio.

Not all schools in America have improved since the Supreme Court decided the *Rodriguez* case in 1973. Most states continue to base funding on the property tax system, and there are more poor children in poor schools. Federal statistics reported in 1973 that 14 percent of American children—one of every seven—lived in poverty. This figure concealed a substantial racial and ethnic disparity. Fewer than 10 percent of white children lived in poor families, while 40 percent of blacks and 28 percent of Hispanics were raised in poverty. The most recent figures are even more depressing. In 1992, the poverty level rose to the highest rate in thirty years. Children suffered the most, and the youngest bore the greatest burden: 25 percent of those under six, and 22 percent of all children, lived below the poverty line. These figures—which hide the faces of more than 13 million children—impose an enormous burden on public schools. Without equal funding for all districts, the educational gap between rich and poor children will grow wider and deeper. The Supreme Court, however, still holds to its *Rodriguez* decision and the claim that America's children have no fundamental right to education.

THIRTEEN

"Not on a Pedestal, but in a Cage"

Myra Bradwell had all the makings of an outstanding lawyer. She was educated in the best schools in Illinois and taught school before she married a state judge. Although she raised two children, she wanted a career outside the home and established the *Chicago Legal News*. Her legal reporting was so highly respected that the state courts made the contents of her journal admissible as evidence in trials. Encouraged by her husband to study law, she passed the licensing exam with flying colors. The final step to law practice was admission by the state supreme court, a formality in most cases. To her surprise, Myra Bradwell received a letter stating that her application had been rejected. The only reason given was gender: women could not practice law in Illinois.

This was a clear case of sex discrimination, and Bradwell appealed to the U.S. Supreme Court. Senator Matthew Carpenter of Wisconsin argued her case. The right to practice law, he told the justices, belonged to "every American citizen as a matter of right" and could not be denied to Bradwell "on the ground of her sex" alone. Congress had recently passed a Civil Rights Act—based on the Fourteenth Amendment—that barred racial discrimination. That constitutional provision, Carpenter argued, "protects every citizen, black or white, male or female."

Senator Carpenter made a compelling argument, but he spoke a century too early. The Court ruled against Myra Bradwell in 1873, shortly after holding in the *Slaughterhouse Cases* that the Fourteenth Amendment was intended only to protect blacks from official discrimination. The *Slaughterhouse* majority expressed doubt that any other group "will ever be held to come within the purview of this provision." Dissenting from this holding, Justice Joseph Bradley wrote that states could not restrict the rights "which belong to every citizen," regardless of race. The

Fourteenth Amendment protected "every right and privilege belonging to a freeman," he stated.

Bradley used the term "freeman" in the most literal sense. His concurring opinion in *Bradwell v. State* expressed the prevailing attitude of men about the role of women in society. "Man is, or should be, woman's protector and defender," he wrote. "The natural and proper timidity and delicacy which belongs to the female sex evidently unfits it for many of the occupations of civil life," including the legal profession. Bradley argued that "the family institution is repugnant to the idea of a woman adopting a distinct and independent career from that of her husband." He looked beyond the Constitution for precedent. "The paramount destiny and mission of woman are to fulfill the noble and benign offices of wife and mother. This is the law of the Creator."

God may have intended Myra Bradwell to stay out of courtrooms and remain in her kitchen, but the Illinois judges had a change of heart. Several years after the Supreme Court decision, she was admitted to practice; her daughter Bessie followed in her footsteps and became a lawyer. But the Bradwells were unique in their careers. What began as a trickle of women in a male-dominated profession remained a trickle for another century; not until the 1970s did women make up more than 5 percent of American lawyers. And not until then did the Supreme Court agree with Senator Carpenter that the Fourteenth Amendment protected women as well as blacks.

Historical parallels can sometimes be instructive. President Abraham Lincoln issued the Emancipation Proclamation in 1863, freeing slaves from bondage. Congress later passed a civil rights act that barred discrimination on the basis of race, and also approved a constitutional amendment designed to secure equal rights for black citizens. The Emancipation Proclamation for women came a century later, stated most clearly in Betty Friedan's 1963 book, *The Feminine Mystique*. She spoke for millions of women who chafed in their assigned roles as "wife and mother," unable to break the grip of cultural stereotypes. Congress later passed a civil rights act that barred discrimination on the basis of sex, and also approved a constitutional amendment to secure equal rights for women.

The Supreme Court's decision in 1883 in the *Civil Rights Cases* gutted the first law designed to protect a group from official discrimination. The demise in 1983 of the Equal Rights Amendment ended the effort to give similar protection to another group. Historical parallels can be pressed only so far, and this one ends in the Court's marble chamber. The justices have agreed that blacks constitute a "suspect class" under the Fourteenth Amendment, but have refused to extend the same protection to women. The reasons for this difference are rooted less in the Constitution than in social, political, and cultural factors that go back centuries, if not millennia. "Wives, be subject to your husbands," commanded Paul in the Bible, and the English common law obeyed. The American colonies followed suit, and the biblical injunction became imbedded in the laws of most states. Women could not own property, serve on juries, hold public office, or bring suit in their own names. They could not even vote until the Constitution was amended in 1920. Most laws that treated women differently than men remained on the books for another fifty years. Women are the majority that is treated like a minority.

Even laws intended to protect women from burdens placed upon men reflected stereotypes of the "weaker sex." The Supreme Court upheld in 1908 an Oregon statute that limited the workday of women to ten hours. The justices distinguished this law from their *Lochner* ruling in 1905, which struck down a New York law that limited bakers to a ten-hour day. The Court held in *Muller v. Oregon* that "history discloses the fact that woman has always been dependent upon man." Laws that treat women differently "are not imposed solely for her benefit, but also largely for the benefit of all," wrote Justice David Brewer. Most of these laws, in reality, placed women at a disadvantage in relation to men.

MUCH LIKE THE ABOLITIONIST MOVEMENT, which achieved its primary goal—the end of slavery—but failed to eradicate prejudice and discrimination against blacks, the Suffragist movement gained women the right to vote but could not overcome gender stereotypes and legal barriers against women. African Americans had to launch a second movement to end segregation, and women followed their example with a feminist movement that focused on the Equal Rights Amendment to the Constitution. Congress held hearings on the ERA in 1970, and the House of Representatives approved it that year by the overwhelming vote of 350–15. Although more than eighty senators had sponsored the ERA resolution, it never reached a vote that year, and the legislative process started over in 1971.

Feminist groups also followed the civil rights model in using litigation to attack discrimination. The first case to reach the Supreme Court seemed an unlikely vehicle for constitutional change. The justices agreed in 1971 to review an obscure probate case from Idaho. *Reed v. Reed* had none of the elements of legal drama. Richard Reed, a teenager, died in 1967 and left no will to devise his estate, valued at less than $1,000. His adoptive parents had divorced, and Sally Reed and her former husband, Cecil, both applied to administer Richard's modest estate. The county probate judge appointed Cecil Reed, relying on an Idaho law that "males must be preferred to females" in selecting estate administrators. Sally Reed appealed to the Idaho Supreme Court, arguing that the law violated the Equal Protection clause of the Fourteenth Amendment, but the judges upheld the statute as a reasonable way to spare probate courts the burden of conducting hearings to choose estate administrators.

The *Reed* case attracted the attention of the American Civil Liberties Union, which had recently set up a Women's Law Project under the direction of Ruth Bader Ginsburg, one of the first female graduates of Columbia Law School. The ACLU offered to take Sally Reed's appeal to the Supreme Court, and Ginsburg drafted the brief. Political supporters of the ERA also took an interest in the case. Representative Martha Griffiths, a Michigan Democrat, had pushed the ERA through the House, while Senator Birch Bayh of Indiana, who chaired the Subcommittee on Constitutional Amendments, worked the Senate floor. Both lawmakers signed *amicus* briefs for Sally Reed, Griffiths for the American Veterans Committee and Bayh for the National Federation of Business and Professional Women's Clubs. The Supreme Court decided the case in late 1971, between the House and Senate votes that finally sent the ERA to state legislatures in March 1972.

The justices ruled unanimously that the Idaho law violated the Equal Protection clause, and Chief Justice Burger took the opinion for himself. Because all the Court's prior decisions in gender-discrimination cases, going back to *Bradwell* in 1873, had upheld the challenged laws, Burger reached for precedent to an unlikely source, a 1920 case that involved state taxation of a fertilizer company. He quoted from *Royster Guano Co. v. Virginia* for the proposition that "all persons similarly situated shall be treated alike" by state law. Burger did not apply the "strict scrutiny" test because the Idaho statute failed even the lenient "rational basis" test. The mandatory preference for males, he wrote, was "the very kind of arbitrary legislative choice" the Equal Protection clause forbids.

Two years after the *Reed* decision, twenty-two states had ratified the Equal Rights Amendment, and prospects looked good for getting the necessary thirty-eight states well before the 1979 deadline. By 1973, however, ERA opponents had mobilized under the leadership of Phyllis Schlafly, a conservative Republican activist. Members of her "Stop ERA" group needed only thirteen states to block its passage, and they lobbied hard in southern and midwestern states.

The political debate over the ERA reached the Supreme Court's conference room in 1973, when the justices considered the case of Sharron Frontiero, another unlikely crusader for women's rights. She was an Air Force lieutenant who served as a physical therapist in Alabama. Her husband, Joseph, was a Vietnam veteran and full-time college student. Lt. Frontiero applied for housing and medical benefits, listing her husband as a dependent. The military brass rejected her application, because her husband's veterans benefits covered more than half of his monthly expenses. If their genders were reversed, the Frontieros would have automatically received benefits. The federal law that provided military benefits included a legislative "presumption" that wives of personnel were financially dependent on their husbands, with no requirement of proof.

Lt. Frontiero sued the Secretary of Defense, making an equal protection argument under the Due Process clause of the Fifth Amendment. A panel of federal judges ruled against her, in an opinion by Judge Richard Rives, who was born in the nineteenth century and served in the Mexican campaign against Pancho Villa. He relied on the *Reed* decision in applying the "rational basis" test to the law. Searching for reasons that it might pass the test, Rives wrote that "Congress apparently reached the conclusion that it would be more economical to require married female members claiming husbands to prove actual dependency than to extend the presumption of dependency to such members." He did not explain why this requirement of additional forms and possible hearings would be a "rational" way to save time and money. He even noted the burden on Lt. Frontiero of "having to traverse the added red tape" in proving her husband's financial dependency. But the military is famous for Catch-22 regulations. Perhaps conscious of changing attitudes, Rives felt compelled to disavow "romantic paternalism" or "Victorianism" as motivations for the law he upheld.

The *Frontiero v. Richardson* case reached the Supreme Court at a bad time for supporters of women's rights. Lawmakers in eleven states had rejected the ERA, and prospects for ratification looked grim. Hoping to win from the Supreme Court what state lawmakers refused to give them, feminist groups joined the case, and Ruth Bader Ginsburg pressed in oral argument for extending "suspect class" protection to women. She won the case but not the argument. With only one dissent, the Court voted in 1973 to strike down the challenged section of the military-benefits law.

Justice Brennan volunteered to write the majority opinion. His first draft took a narrow approach, citing *Reed* and flunking the law under the "rational basis" test. Justice Byron White, however, had been impressed with Ginsburg's argument and sent Brennan a note, saying that "I would think that sex is a suspect classification, if for no other reason than the fact that Congress has submitted a constitutional amendment making sex discrimination unconstitutional." Brennan realized that applying "strict scrutiny" in the *Frontiero* case might add judicial weight to the legislative battle for the ERA. And if the amendment fell short of ratification, the Court could accomplish its purpose by constitutional interpretation.

Brennan answered White by redrafting his opinion to state that "classifications based upon sex, like classifications based upon race, alienage, and national origin, are inherently suspect and must therefore be subjected to close judicial scrutiny." This new draft picked up the support of Justices William Douglas and Thurgood Marshall, which gave Brennan four votes for the "strict scrutiny" position. But he lost the support of Chief Justice Burger and Justices Lewis Powell, Potter Stewart, and Harry Blackmun. These four justices would still vote against the law, but they refused to move beyond the *Reed* case and the "rational basis" test. Powell wrote to Brennan that "I see no reason to consider whether sex is a 'suspect' classification in this case. Perhaps we can avoid confronting that issue until we know the outcome of the Equal Rights Amendment."

The legal issues in *Frontiero* had become hostage to the political fate of the ERA. Brennan decided to take the initiative and responded to Justice Powell that he did not "see that we gain anything by awaiting what is at best an uncertain outcome" of the ratification battle. The final opinion included the "strict scrutiny" language of the earlier draft and cited more than a dozen books, articles, and government reports that documented the "social facts" of gender discrimination. "There can be no doubt that our Nation has had a long and unfortunate history of sex discrimination," Brennan wrote. "Traditionally, such discrimination was rationalized by an attitude of 'romantic paternalism' which, in practical effect, put women, not on a pedestal, but in a cage."

To show that paternalism had become "firmly rooted in our national consciousness," Brennan quoted at length from Justice Bradley's opinion in the *Bradwell* case. "As a result of notions such as these," he continued, "our statute books gradually became laden with gross, stereotyped distinctions between the sexes and, indeed, throughout much of the 19th century the position of women in our society was, in many respects, comparable to that of blacks under the pre–Civil War slave codes." Brennan acknowledged that "the position of women in America has improved markedly in recent decades." He also conceded that "women do not constitute a small and powerless minority" in American society. But he cited statistics that "women are vastly underrepresented in this Nation's decisionmaking councils" and noted that there had "never been a female President, nor a female member of this Court." Based on this evidence, Brennan concluded that "any statutory scheme which draws a sharp line between the sexes, *solely* for the purpose of achieving administrative convenience," ran afoul of the Equal Protection clause.

Brennan fell one vote short of achieving for women the status of a "suspect class" for constitutional protection. Four justices agreed with the outcome but refused to move beyond the *Reed* decision. In his concurrence, Justice Powell chided Brennan for dragging the Court into the political battle over the ERA. "By acting prematurely and unnecessarily," he wrote, "the Court has assumed a decisional responsibility at the very time when state legislatures, functioning within the traditional democratic process, are debating the proposed Amendment." Powell worried that "democratic institutions are weakened, and confidence in the restraint of the Court is impaired, when we appear unnecessarily to decide sensitive issues of broad social and political importance at the very time they are under consideration within the prescribed constitutional processes."

One justice, however, felt the military regulations were "in all respects constitutional." William Rehnquist filed a solo dissent in the *Frontiero* case, noting simply that he agreed with the lower-court decision of Judge Rives. Dissenters are not required to write opinions, but Rehnquist usually expressed his views—often in sharp words—when he thought the majority had strayed from the path of judicial deference. Perhaps he was afraid he might push one of the concurring justices into Brennan's welcoming embrace. At any rate, Rehnquist had already outlined his position on the ERA, stating in a 1970 Justice Department internal "Brief in Opposition" his belief that the ERA would be "almost certain to have an adverse effect on the family unit as we have known it."

Claims of gender discrimination are not, of course, limited to women. The Court faced the issue of whether men are equally protected by the

Fourteenth Amendment in the 1977 case of *Califano v. Goldfarb*, which challenged a federal law requiring widowers, but not widows, to show proof of dependency on the deceased spouse in order to collect Social Security survivors' benefits. Hannah Goldfarb worked as a New York City school secretary for twenty-five years before she died in 1968. Her husband, Leon, was turned down for benefits because he could not show that Hannah had provided 75 percent of the family income, the test applied by officials in widower cases. With ACLU support, Leon Goldfarb sued Joseph Califano, the Secretary of Health, Education and Welfare. A federal court struck down the law on equal protection grounds, holding that it constituted "invidious discrimination" against males. When the case reached the Supreme Court, Ruth Bader Ginsburg argued for Goldfarb.

Five justices voted against the law, and Brennan wrote for a plurality of four. He relied on *Reed* and *Frontiero* in rejecting laws that "rest only upon 'old notions' and 'archaic and overbroad' generalizations" about gender differences. Assumptions that all widows were financially dependent on their husbands struck him as an archaic notion. The regulation failed the "rational basis" test, Brennan wrote, because the "only conceivable justification" for presuming dependency by widows was that "it would save the Government time, money, and effort simply to pay benefits to all widows" rather than requiring both sexes to prove dependency. But claims of "administrative convenience" could not justify gender discrimination, against women or men. Justice John Stevens joined the outcome, but wrote separately that he considered the statute a legislative "accident" rather than deliberate discrimination.

Once again, Rehnquist was willing to scrap recent precedent. Writing for the four dissenters, he conceded that *Reed* and *Frontiero* provided "support in our cases for the result reached by the Court." But he warned against applying "heightened levels of scrutiny" to social-insurance legislation. This was one area, he claimed, where courts should defer to claims of "administrative convenience," because of "congressional concern for certainty in determination of entitlement and promptness in payment of benefits." Rehnquist did not cite any evidence that the challenged law would achieve these goals. He simply said the law was "rationally justifiable" and "explainable as a measure to ameliorate the characteristically depressed condition of aged widows."

.   .   .

THE UNCERTAIN FATE of the ERA became tangled with the most divisive national issue since the *Brown* decision: abortion. Shortly before the Court decided *Frontiero*, seven justices had ruled in *Roe v. Wade* that the Constitution embodied a "right of privacy" that was "broad enough to encompass a woman's decision whether or not to terminate her pregnancy," as Justice Harry Blackmun wrote for the majority. This decision sparked a political battle that has not yet ended, and that has forced the Supreme Court to rule on dozens of state and federal laws designed to restrict or even outlaw abortions.

The abortion issue reached the Court through a litigation campaign that feminist groups consciously modeled on the NAACP crusade against school segregation. Lawyers for both groups pursued a strategy of building on victories in "easy" cases to establish precedent for the "hard" cases. Civil rights lawyers started with graduate schools in border states before they moved against elementary schools in the Deep South. Lawyers in the feminist movement made their first attack on a Connecticut law that prohibited doctors from prescribing contraceptives to married couples. The 1965 case of *Griswold v. Connecticut* was "easy" by any measure. The state's lawyer had trouble describing the law's purpose, finally settling on the promotion of "marital fidelity" as the best reason. Access to contraceptives, he suggested, might plant thoughts of adultery in the minds of errant spouses. Arguing for Estelle Griswold, director of the Planned Parenthood clinic in New Haven, Yale law professor Thomas Emerson attacked the law for infringing personal "liberty" under the Due Process clause of the Fourteenth Amendment. Emerson was a close friend of Justice William Douglas, who volunteered to write the majority opinion.

Given the state's weak argument, the Supreme Court could easily have struck down the Connecticut law under the "rational basis" test. The *Griswold* case, however, reached the justices at the height of the Warren Court's "activist" phase, and the majority was eager to expand the scope of the Due Process clause. Justice Douglas had personal reasons for taking this case. He had lived in New Haven as a Yale law professor, and had no love for Yankee bluenoses. He also wanted to explain why judicial deference to state lawmakers in economic cases, which his 1955 opinion in *Williamson v. Lee Optical* had defended, should not extend to personal liberties. Although his *Griswold* opinion rested on solid precedent, Douglas wrote like a law professor. Building on earlier cases that protected rights of speech, press, and assembly, he found in them suggestions "that specific guarantees in the Bill of Rights have penumbras, formed by emanations from those guarantees that help give them life and substance." His use of terms from astronomy—a penumbra is the shadow of a partial eclipse—and chemistry—emanations are gases that flow from radioactive decay—gave critics of the *Griswold* decision an opening to ridicule the Court.

Despite its arcane terminology, the *Griswold* decision actually rested on conventional "notions of privacy surrounding the marital relationship," as Douglas wrote. He described the "right of privacy" as one that is "older than the Bill of Rights—older than our political parties, older than our school system." Douglas, who had recently married for the fourth time, waxed poetic about the institution. "Marriage is a coming together for better or for worse, hopefully enduring, and intimate to the degree of being sacred." He asked in tones of horror if Americans would "allow the police to search the sacred precincts of marital bedrooms for telltale signs of the use of contraceptives?" Behind the hyperbole was a principle that Justice Louis Brandeis described in softer tones as "the right to be left alone," free from state interference in our personal lives.

Justice Brennan found an even more expansive basis for the *Griswold* decision in the Constitution. Along with Chief Justice Warren, he joined a concurring opinion of Justice Arthur Goldberg, who dusted off the Ninth Amendment, virtually ignored by the Court since its ratification in 1791. "The enumeration in the Constitution, of certain rights," the amendment read, "shall not be construed to deny or disparage others retained by the people." What did these words mean? Conservative commentators warned that the Ninth Amendment could become a Pandora's Box in the hands of activist judges. Goldberg did nothing to calm their fears. The Framers "believed that there are additional fundamental rights, protected from governmental infringement," he wrote, "which exist alongside those fundamental rights specifically mentioned in the first eight constitutional amendments." Goldberg argued that "the right of privacy in the marital relation is fundamental and basic—a personal right 'retained by the people' within the meaning of the Ninth Amendment." Hardly any claim, responded the advocates of judicial restraint, could not be supported by citation to this wild-card amendment.

The *Griswold* decision allowed Justice Brennan to take the next "easy" step toward abortion rights with his 1972 majority opinion in *Eisenstadt v. Baird*. This case began in 1969 with a lecture at Boston University by Bill Baird, an abortion-rights activist. During his talk, Baird showed the student audience an array of contraceptive devices, and at the end he handed a package of vaginal foam to a young woman. Boston police officers, who showed up in response to complaints from Catholic groups, promptly arrested Baird under a Massachusetts law that provided a maximum five-year prison term for anyone who "exhibits" or "gives away" any "drug, medicine, instrument or article whatever for the prevention of conception." The law made an exception—added by the legislature after the *Griswold* decision—for physicians who prescribed contraceptives for married persons. After a federal appellate panel reversed Baird's criminal conviction, the Suffolk County sheriff, Thomas Eisenstadt, appealed to the Supreme Court.

Much like the *Griswold* case, the state's lawyers had trouble in describing the law's purpose. They first cited the state court ruling that the law prevented the distribution of contraceptives which "may have undesirable, if not dangerous, physical consequences." But they had no evidence that Emko vaginal foam was dangerous. They next claimed the law was necessary to "promote marital fidelity," but Brennan's opinion noted that allowing married persons to obtain contraceptives erased any "deterrent effect on extramarital sexual relations." Their final argument was that the law protected morals by "regulating the private sexual lives of single persons." Brennan responded that it "would be plainly unreasonable to assume that Massachusetts has prescribed pregnancy and the birth of an unwanted child as punishment for fornication," by making contraception illegal for unmarried persons.

Brennan sidestepped the issue of whether access to contraception was a "fundamental human right" under the Due Process clause, as the appellate panel had ruled. He looked instead to the Equal Protection clause in holding that "whatever the rights of the individual to access to contraceptives may be, the rights must be the same for the unmarried and the married alike." He then moved the Court beyond the *Griswold* decision. "If the right of privacy means anything," he wrote, "it is the right of the *individual*, married or single, to be free from unwarranted governmental intrusion into matters so fundamentally affecting a person as the decision whether to bear or beget a child." The Court took the last step in Brennan's opinion on the judicial path that ended with abortion rights.

THE FEROCIOUS POLITICAL and legal battles that followed the 1973 decision in *Roe v. Wade* have obscured the fact that abortion was not then a significant public issue. Street crime was the big issue, pushed by President Richard Nixon, who was soon distracted by another criminal problem, the Watergate scandal. Nixon did not make a public statement about the *Roe* decision, and there is no evidence he asked William Rehnquist his views on abortion before appointing him to the Court. Not until Ronald Reagan became president did abortion become the litmus test for judicial candidates.

Perhaps the most significant fact about the *Roe* case—in light of later partisan debate over abortion—is that three of Nixon's four appointees to the Supreme Court voted to support abortion rights. Chief Justice Warren Burger and Lewis Powell joined Harry Blackmun's majority opinion. Another Republican justice, Potter Stewart, added his vote to those of William Douglas, William Brennan, and Thurgood Marshall. Republicans, in fact, outnumbered Democrats in the majority.

Justice Blackmun was the Court's least partisan member, and his *Roe* opinion avoided any political issues. He wrote like a history professor, delving into Greek and Roman law, English common and statutory law, and the evolution of medical practice and opinion on abortion. Blackmun noted that the medical profession, which opposed abortion in the nineteenth century because of the dangers of infection, shifted to support after the development of antiseptic surgery and antibiotic medicines. After a thorough canvass of medical history, Blackmun reviewed the legal history of abortion and concluded that judges had never ruled that a fetus was a "person" under the Fourteenth Amendment.

These factors persuaded Blackmun that Texas had not demonstrated any "compelling state interest" in making abortion unlawful before the point of fetal "viability," which he defined as the last trimester of pregnancy. "If the State is interested in protecting fetal life after viability," he wrote, "it may go so far as to proscribe abortion during that period, except when it is necessary to preserve the life or health of the mother." This was hardly the kind of "penumbral" opinion that Justice Douglas wrote in the *Griswold* case. In planting the right of privacy within the Constitution, Blackmun traced its roots to a long line of cases "relating to marriage, procreation, family relationships, and child rearing and education." Blackmun's opinion acknowledged "the sensitive and emotional nature of the abortion controversy" and "the vigorous opposing views" on both sides. But this moderate approach to the issue did not satisfy those with deep religious scruples against abortion, or those who worshiped at the temple of judicial deference.

In his dissenting opinion, Justice Rehnquist did not reveal his theological views, but he sounded like a debater with a well-thumbed dictionary. He disputed Blackmun's claim that "the right of 'privacy' is involved in this case," responding that a medical operation "is not 'private' in the ordinary sense of that word." Rehnquist presumably meant that allowing a doctor into the operating room turned the medical procedure into a public event. Suggesting that "privacy" was limited to physical settings, he cited a case that protected bookies who took bets from the "privacy" of a telephone booth. This dictionary approach to legal concepts clashed with Blackmun's holding that "privacy" goes beyond places, and involves relations between individuals and officials over personal decisions.

Rehnquist said nothing about the dilemma of a woman who faced an agonizing decision about her pregnancy. Instead, he equated the legislative decision over abortion to that of whether opticians should be allowed to grind eyeglasses without a prescription. He cited his favorite case, *Williamson v. Lee Optical*, for the proposition that the judicial test "traditionally applied in the area of social and economic legislation is whether or not a law such as that challenged has a rational relation to a valid state objective." Rehnquist did not identify, or even imagine, any "rational basis" for the Texas law; he simply asserted that "the Court's sweeping invalidation of any restrictions on abortion during the first trimester is impossible to justify" under the *Williamson* standard. To Rehnquist, abortion was the kind of "social and economic" issue that should be decided, not by women and doctors, but by "the majority sentiment" of voters and lawmakers.

THE DEBATE OVER women's rights took a sharp turn after the *Roe* decision, as abortion became the dividing issue. Feminist groups turned their energies from the campaign to ratify the Equal Rights Amendment and mobilized to defeat legislative curbs on abortion, particularly the Hyde Amendment, which ended federal Medicaid funding for abortions, a measure named after its sponsor, Representative Henry Hyde, an Illinois Republican. By 1974, as one historian of the ERA wrote, its supporters knew "how little time they had left" for ratification.

Increasingly, feminists looked to the Supreme Court for support, hoping that the *Reed* and *Frontiero* cases would hold up as precedent. They were encouraged by a January 1974 decision striking down a regulation of the Cleveland, Ohio, school board that forced pregnant teachers out of their classrooms after the fourth month of pregnancy. Jo Carol LaFleur, who taught a junior high class of girls with behavior problems, was told in 1971 that she must take mandatory pregnancy leave without pay for at least a year. She refused to sign the papers, but school officials took her off the payroll. Ironically, as LaFleur later explained, several of her students—one just twelve years old—were pregnant themselves. "I thought I was actually contributing," she said, "partly by being a good role model. I'm a married woman, going to a doctor, getting good care; I can do some good." Determined to fight back, she found legal help from the Women's Action Equity League, an advocacy group for working women.

LaFleur's trial was conducted by federal judge James Connell, a crusty seventy-three-year-old who did not conceal his sympathy with the school board's chief witness, the seventy-two-year-old former superintendent, Mark Schinnerer. Asked to explain why he drafted the regulation, Schinnerer said that students "giggled" at pregnant teachers. Judge Connell quoted from this testimony in ruling that the policy was "entirely reasonable" as an effort to spare pregnant teachers from "children pointing, giggling, laughing and making snide remarks" about their condition. A federal appellate panel was not so bound to Victorian notions of feminine delicacy. "Basic rights such as those involved in the employment relationship," Judge George Edwards wrote, "cannot be made to yield to embarrassment."

Seven justices agreed with the appellate panel in *Cleveland v. LaFleur.* Potter Stewart was a natural choice to write for the Court: the case came from his home state of Ohio; he and Judge Connell had both been appointed by President Eisenhower; and Stewart had served on the appellate court that decided the case. His opinion took an expansive view of women's rights. "This Court has long recognized that freedom of personal choice in matters of marriage and family life is one of the liberties protected by the Due Process Clause of the Fourteenth Amendment," he wrote, citing *Griswold* and *Roe* for support. He also quoted from Brennan's opinion in the *Baird* case on the right "to be free of unwarranted governmental intrusion" in decisions about childbearing. Completing a pregnancy was just as much protected from official restrictions as terminating one.

Stewart turned an old legal doctrine into a new weapon against discrimination. An "irrebuttable presumption" is one that establishes a fact without any exceptions; presuming that drivers whose blood alcohol exceeds a certain level are legally drunk is an example. The Cleveland schools presumed that teachers could no longer function after their fourth month of pregnancy; they barred Jo Carol LaFleur from rebutting this presumption with evidence that she was capable of teaching until the school year ended. Stewart concluded that the board's regulations "employ irrebuttable presumptions that unduly penalize a teacher for deciding to bear a child."

Justice Rehnquist dissented, and used his opinion—which Chief Justice Burger joined—to show off his political-science degrees. He looked back to the days before the English Parliament, when "controversies were determined on an individualized basis without benefit of any general law." He lectured his errant colleagues. "Most students of government," he wrote, consider the shift to a system of codified rules "to have been a significant step forward in the achievement of a civilized political society. It seems to me a little late in the day for this Court to weigh in against such an established consensus."

Rehnquist replied to his soft-spoken colleague with sarcasm. "My Brother Stewart," he wrote, "enlists the Court in another quixotic engagement in his apparently unending war on irrebuttable presumptions." Rehnquist saw nothing wrong with such presumptions as a tool of efficient administration. The whole process of lawmaking, he noted, was based on drawing lines that some may consider unfair. Stewart's opinion, he complained, could support the argument of "a twenty-year-old who insists that he is just as able to carry his liquor as a twenty-one-year-old." Rehnquist again cited the *Williamson* case for support. "It has been said before," he wrote, "but it bears repeating here: All legislation involves the drawing of lines, and the drawing of lines necessarily results in particular individuals who are disadvantaged by the line drawn being virtually indistinguishable from those individuals who benefit from the legislative classification."

Rehnquist did not answer Stewart's question of how Cleveland's rule might benefit *any* pregnant teacher. After all, they could apply at any time for leave without pay. If school officials could show that any teacher—pregnant or not—was disabled, they could provide medical leave with pay. But the regulation took *every* pregnant teacher out of her classroom, removed her from the payroll, and sent her home for a year. Jo Carol LaFleur had an answer for Rehnquist. "I couldn't believe that anybody would yank from an inner-city school a person who was specially trained to teach there and *wanted* to teach," she said.

STEWART'S OPINION in *LaFleur* sounded very much like Brennan. But he switched sides in another pregnancy case, just five months later. Chief Justice Burger rewarded Stewart with the majority opinion in *Geduldig v. Aiello*, which tested California's disability insurance program. Carolyn Aiello required surgery to terminate an ectopic pregnancy, which could have threatened her life without treatment. She applied for insurance to pay for her operation, but was turned down by state officials. California law provided that "in no case shall the term 'disability' or 'disabled' include any injury or illness caused by or arising in connection with pregnancy," before or after any medical procedure.

Stewart's opinion in *Geduldig* echoed Rehnquist, down to citation of the *Williamson* case. "Particularly with respect to social welfare programs," he wrote, "so long as the line drawn by the State is rationally supportable, the courts will not interpose their judgment as to the appropriate stopping point." What accounted for this abrupt shift? The reasons are unclear, but Stewart was a classic judicial centrist, deferential to legislative will unless he felt that lawmakers made "arbitrary" distinctions between groups. Even so, he had to stretch to uphold the California disability law. The *Geduldig* case, he argued, was "a far cry" from *Reed* and *Frontiero*, which involved "discrimination based upon gender as such." In contrast, the California insurance program "does not exclude anyone from benefit eligibility because of gender but merely removes one physical disability—pregnancy—from the list of compensable disabilities."

From this point, Stewart's opinion read like a passage from *Alice in Wonderland.* "The program divides potential recipients into two groups," he wrote, "pregnant women and nonpregnant persons. While the first group is exclusively female, the second includes members of both sexes." His conclusion was stunning in its logical rigor. "There is no risk from which men are protected and women are not," he wrote. "Likewise, there is no risk from which women are protected and men are not." Somewhere in this equation, the connection of women and pregnancy was erased.

Writing in dissent, Justice Brennan passed up the opportunity for sarcasm. He stuck to the facts of the case, noting that the disability plan covered *every* medical procedure for males, including prostatectomies and circumcision, which only men could have. The only disabilities excluded from coverage were pregnancy and its life-threatening complications, which only women could experience. "In effect," Brennan wrote, "one set of rules is applied to females and another to males." Turning to the majority opinion, he asked for an explanation of "what differentiates the gender-based classification employed in this case from those found unconstitutional in *Reed* and *Frontiero*."

Stewart answered Brennan in a footnote. Because the disability plan did not "effect an invidious discrimination against the members of one sex or the other," lawmakers could exclude pregnancy from coverage "on any reasonable basis," he wrote. He suggested that the "reasonable basis" for excluding pregnancy from coverage was money. The problem with women was that they "contribute about 28 percent of the total disability insurance fund and receive back about 38 percent of the fund in benefits." Adding coverage for pregnancy might cost the state more than $100 million each year. Avoiding this financial burden seemed reasonable to Stewart. Not surprisingly, Brennan disagreed. Restating his belief that all gender discrimination was subject to "strict judicial scrutiny," he replied that California's "interest in preserving the fiscal integrity of its disability insurance program simply cannot render the State's use of a suspect classification constitutional." But the "suspect class" argument had not prevailed in *Frontiero* and it failed again.

The next pregnancy case, which reached the Supreme Court in 1976, matched the General Electric Company against its female employees. Martha Gilbert, an assembly-line worker at a GE factory in Salem, Virginia, became pregnant in 1971 and applied for disability benefits under the company's insurance program. After her claim was denied, she filed suit under Title VII of the federal Civil Rights Act of 1964, which outlawed gender discrimination by companies with more than twenty-five employees. Gilbert won favorable rulings from a federal district judge and an appellate panel, which distinguished the *Geduldig* ruling on the ground that Congress had broad powers to enforce the Equal Protection clause of the Fourteenth Amendment. The *Gilbert* case drew a flock of *amicus* briefs, pitting the Chamber of Commerce and the National Association of Manufacturers against the AFL-CIO and the Women's Law Project. Even the Westinghouse company supported its business rival on this issue.

Six justices voted in *General Electric v. Gilbert* for the company, and Chief Justice Burger assigned the majority opinion to Rehnquist. He outdid Potter Stewart in divorcing women from pregnancy. Rehnquist did not argue with the facts of life, but he disputed the medical dictionary. "Pregnancy is, of course, confined to women," he conceded, "but it is in other ways significantly different from the typical covered disease or disability." Rehnquist argued that pregnancy "is not a 'disease' at all," but is "often a voluntarily undertaken and desired condition," making the risk of complications a matter of choice, much like betting on racehorses. Emma Furch, one of the *Gilbert* plaintiffs, lost her bet when she took pregnancy leave and was later hospitalized for a pulmonary embolism. Her claim was rejected by company bureaucrats because she had first applied for benefits as a pregnant woman. The effect of Rehnquist's opinion was to advise Furch that she should have suffered her embolism before she became pregnant. Like much advice, this came too late to be helpful.

Brennan usually avoided disparaging words in his dissents, but he blasted Rehnquist's opinion as "purely fanciful" and one that "offends common sense" in disavowing any gender bias in the company's benefits program. He wrote that "the Court simply disregards a history of General Electric practices that have served to undercut" the status of women workers. Brennan quoted the company's first report on its benefit plan as saying that women were excluded because they "did not recognize the responsibilities of life, for they probably were hoping to get married soon and leave the company." He faulted the majority for failing to recognize that "contemporary disability programs are not creatures of a social or cultural vacuum devoid of stereotypes and signals concerning the pregnant woman employee."

Rehnquist's opinion in *Gilbert* did not survive the wrath of women workers. Disillusioned with the courts, they turned to Congress, which overturned the decision in 1978 with passage of the Pregnancy Discrimination Act. The politics of the Constitution dictated a change in strategy. With the Supreme Court no longer an ally, feminist groups again followed the civil rights coalition in moving from litigation to lobbying.

IMPORTANT CONSTITUTIONAL debates often take place over issues many people would consider trivial. Should boys in Oklahoma wait until they reach twenty-one to purchase beer, while girls can buy a six-pack at eighteen? Can males in California be punished for having sex with girls under eighteen, while females are exempted from the law? Both questions reached the Supreme Court, and Justices Brennan and Rehnquist differed in both over the application of the Equal Protection clause in gender cases. Significantly, both cases involved challenges to state laws by teenage boys—the most rebellious group in society—who flouted social conventions of proper conduct.

Curtis Craig was eighteen when he sued Oklahoma Governor David Boren in federal court because state law barred him from purchasing beer with 3.2 percent alcohol, defined by state law as a "nonintoxicating" brew. The record suggests that the case was financed by the brewing industry. Young men drink a lot of beer, legally and otherwise, and there is profit to be made in selling it to them. After a federal court upheld the law, the Supreme Court agreed to review the decision. Seven justices voted in *Craig v. Boren* to strike down the law, and Brennan assigned the opinion to himself. Four members of the majority, however, stepped back from his strong position. Only Byron White and Thurgood Marshall joined all of Brennan's opinion.

Predictably, Brennan relied on *Reed* and *Frontiero* as precedent. "To withstand constitutional challenge," he wrote, "previous cases establish that classifications by gender must serve important governmental objectives and must be substantially related to achievement of those objectives." This was not the "strict scrutiny" test he had urged in *Frontiero*, but this "heightened scrutiny" or "intermediate" position put challenged laws to a much harder test than "rational basis" analysis. It was not a valid governmental objective, Brennan wrote, to foster " 'old notions' of role typing," whether they applied to males or females. Oklahoma would have to identify a better objective, which the state defined as "the enhancement of traffic safety." Brennan did not quarrel with this general goal, but he disputed the claim that preventing teenage boys from purchasing beer was "substantially related" to that objective.

The case record was crammed with statistics. Not surprisingly, Oklahoma's young men liked beer—84 percent said they preferred it to other beverages. Statistics also showed that more than 90 percent of those arrested for drunk driving were males. But eight out of ten Oklahoma drivers under twenty were males. Brennan was not impressed with these facts. "Plainly these statistical disparities between the sexes are not substantial," he wrote. He turned to other "social facts" for support. Citing a presidential commission report on *The Female Offender*, Brennan suggested that "social stereotypes" affected the official statistics, since males "who drink and drive are transformed into arrest statistics, whereas their female counterparts are chivalrously escorted home" by the police. He concluded that "the relationship between gender and traffic safety becomes far too tenuous to satisfy *Reed's* requirement that the gender-based difference be substantially related to achievement of the statutory objective." What was sauce for the goose became sauce for the gander in Oklahoma.

Writing in dissent, Rehnquist complained that Brennan had disguised the "strict scrutiny" test in new clothes. The majority's application of "an elevated or 'intermediate' level scrutiny," he wrote, "raises the question of why the statute here should be treated any differently from countless legislative classifications unrelated to sex which have been upheld under a minimum rationality standard." Needless to say, Rehnquist cited the *Williamson* case for this proposition. Conceding, strictly for argument, that laws which reflect "a history or pattern of past discrimination" might require some higher level of scrutiny, he found "no suggestion in the Court's opinion that males in this age group are in any way particularly disadvantaged, subject to systematic discriminatory treatment, or otherwise in need of special solicitude from the courts." Rehnquist rejected suggestions that teenage boys belonged to a "suspect class," and that the right to purchase beer was a "fundamental" aspect of liberty.

Rehnquist had even less use for statistics than Brennan. Once again, he substituted "coulds" and "mights" for evidence of legislative intent. Oklahoma lawmakers "could have believed," he suggested, that young men drink more than females, and that they "might" drive drunk more often if they could purchase 3.2-percent beer. Of course, any teenage girl in Oklahoma could purchase beer for any boy, without much fear of arrest. The law was not an effective deterrent, but that did not bother Rehnquist. He would not substitute "our own preferences" as judges for decisions of "the popularly elected branches" of government on this issue.

Studies are hardly needed to show that teenage drinking often leads to sex. The Court faced the issue of sex by minors in *Michael M. v. Sonoma County Superior Court*, decided in 1981. Like most states, California has a statutory rape law that imposes criminal penalties on males who have intercourse with females under eighteen. Unlike laws that punish the use of force or threats to have sex with an unwilling person, statutory rape supposedly involves consensual sex. The notion behind these laws is that women under the statutory age—which varies among states—are not sufficiently mature to give their consent.

The facts in the *Michael M.* case would seem to support a forceful rape charge, but both parties were juveniles—which is why their full names were not revealed—and evidence of force was limited. This case began on a warm Saturday night at a bus stop, when Michael, who was seventeen, started flirting with Sharon, who was sixteen. Both teenagers had been drinking, and as their flirting progressed they moved from the bus stop into some bushes and began kissing. Sharon initially rebuffed Michael's demands to have sex, but after he "slugged" her two or three times she submitted to intercourse. The record is unclear about how the police learned of these acts, but after Michael's arrest for statutory rape his lawyer moved to dismiss the charge because the law discriminated on gender grounds. The California Supreme Court applied the "strict scrutiny" test, but upheld the law for serving the "compelling state interest" of deterring "illegitimate teenage pregnancies" and limiting the number of abortions that followed them.

When the case reached the Supreme Court, Justices Stewart, Powell, and Blackmun switched sides from the *Craig* decision and voted to uphold the California law. Justice Rehnquist wrote for the Court, but only for a plurality of four, as Blackmun refused to join the opinion. With a tenuous majority, Rehnquist took a narrow approach. He cited the *Craig* decision—from which he dissented—for the proposition that "the traditional minimum rationality test takes on a somewhat 'sharper focus' when gender-based classifications are challenged." This bow to precedent, however, ignored Brennan's majority opinion and cited only a footnote in Powell's concurrence.

Although he dismissed the "strict scrutiny" test applied by the California judges, Rehnquist faced the problem of identifying the "important governmental objective" behind the law, which had been passed in 1850 with no surviving legislative record. Once again, "mays" and "mights" took the place of solid evidence. Some lawmakers, Rehnquist wrote, "may have been concerned about preventing teenage pregnancies," others by desires to protect female "chastity," and still others motivated by "religious and moral attitudes toward premarital sex." Choosing from this menu, he professed "great deference" to the state's asserted interest in preventing teenage pregnancy.

This was one of very few opinions in which Rehnquist cited "social facts" to support his ruling. Unable to rely upon the "rational basis" test, he was forced to find an "important governmental objective" for the statutory rape law. Looking to the record, he documented the burdens of teenage pregnancy, noting that about 1 million girls between fifteen and nineteen became pregnant in 1976, that more than two-thirds of these pregnancies were illegitimate, and that "most teenage mothers drop out of school and face a bleak economic future." Poverty, however, did not concern Rehnquist as much as abortion. "Of particular concern to the State," he wrote, "is that approximately half of all teenage pregnancies end in abortion." Addressing the claim of gender discrimination, Rehnquist argued that if "the risk of pregnancy itself constitutes a substantial deterrence to young females," then a "criminal sanction imposed solely on males thus serves to roughly 'equalize' the deterrents on the sexes." That was his answer to the equal protection argument.

In his dissent, Justice Brennan reacted with unusual petulance to the rejection of the "heightened scrutiny" test he had "so carefully developed" in the *Craig* case. He directed his fire not so much at Rehnquist—whose position was clear—but at Stewart and Blackmun, who explained their shifting votes in concurring opinions. Both justices reasoned that limiting punishment to males was justified because only females could become pregnant. This argument struck Brennan as a logical fallacy. He publicly scolded Blackmun, who had privately complained to him that Rehnquist "substituted a lower level of scrutiny" than was required by the *Craig* decision. Blackmun had concluded "without explanation," Brennan wrote, that the California law would effectively deter teenage pregnancies. "My Brethren seem not to recognize," he continued, "that California has the burden of proving that a gender-neutral statutory rape law" would be less effective in deterring teenage sex.

Brennan aimed his final blast at all the justices who rejected the "heightened scrutiny" test. "Because they fail to analyze the issue in these terms," he wrote, "I believe they reach an unsupportable result." Returning to the plurality opinion, Brennan turned the tables on Rehnquist, accusing him in effect of disguising the "rational basis" test in new clothes. Because the legislative history contained "no mention whatever of pregnancy prevention" as the law's purpose, he added, California had relied upon "outmoded sexual stereotypes" to justify the law. Brennan lost this argument, however, and the Court turned further to the right in gender cases.

DEBATES OVER DRINKING ages and statutory rape laws raised difficult legal questions, but they did not even approach abortion as political issues. During the 1980 presidential campaign, abortion became a major partisan issue for the first time. There was no shortage of irony in this debate.

President Jimmy Carter opposed abortion on personal grounds, but most leading Democrats took a "pro-choice" position. His Republican opponent, Ronald Reagan, had signed a liberal abortion statute as California's governor, but the GOP platform adopted the "pro-life" position. When the antiabortion Hyde Amendment came before the Supreme Court, Carter placed his administration behind a statute that was drafted by a Republican.

The justices could hardly have ignored the political implications of *Harris v. McRae*, the case that tested the Hyde Amendment. Another irony of this case is that it pitted two black women against each other. Patricia Harris, an honors graduate of Howard Law School, served President Carter as Secretary of Health and Human Services, while Cora McRae was an indigent, unmarried woman who sought an abortion with Medicaid assistance. Harris was joined as a defendant by Representative Henry Hyde and Senator Jesse Helms, the most ferocious Republican opponents of abortion in Congress. And the Hyde Amendment was defended before the Supreme Court by Solicitor General Wade McCree, the second African American to serve in this post. It is unlikely that either Harris or McCree felt comfortable in supporting Hyde and Helms and opposing Cora McRae.

The justices seemed equally uncomfortable with this case. A bare majority supported the Hyde Amendment, and Chief Justice Burger assigned the opinion to Potter Stewart, whose moderate voice might calm the debate on this divisive issue. His opinion simply added confusion to the clamor. Stewart had supported abortion rights in the *Roe* case, but he retreated in *Harris* to his usual position of supporting governmental action. He had trouble in reconciling the two cases. Conceding that *Roe* protected "the freedom of a woman to decide whether to terminate a pregnancy," Stewart denied that the Hyde Amendment obstructed that right for poor women.

Stewart resorted to Orwellian newspeak in evading the word "poverty" in his opinion. "The Hyde Amendment," he wrote, "places no governmental obstacle in the path of a woman who chooses to terminate her pregnancy, but rather, by means of unequal subsidization of abortion and other medical services, encourages alternative activity deemed in the public interest." The "alternative activity" that Stewart urged on Cora McRae was that she bear the child she did not want to have. If she had anything close to Stewart's income, McRae could have paid for an abortion. Because she lacked the funds, she had to endure a judicial lecture.

"The financial constraints that restrict an indigent woman's ability to enjoy the full range of constitutionally protected freedom of choice," Stewart wrote, "are the product not of governmental restrictions on access to abortions, but rather of her indigency." One senses that the patrician justice was uncomfortable around poor people.

Although Justice Brennan consistently supported abortion rights, he wrote just two opinions in abortion cases. He never discussed this unusual reticence, but he may have felt it would be unwise as a Catholic to speak against his church's doctrine on this divisive issue. He felt compelled, however, to write dissenting opinions from rulings that penalized women who could not pay for abortions in private clinics. Perhaps he wanted to remind other Catholics that concern for the poor had greater biblical sanction than opposition to abortion.

Brennan first wrote in a 1977 case that upheld a state version of the federal Hyde Amendment. Three years later, he wrote another dissent in *Harris v. McRae*. "I write separately to express my continuing disagreement with the Court's mischaracterization of the nature of the fundamental right recognized in *Roe v. Wade*," he began. Not only did *Roe* establish that a pregnant woman "has the right to be free from state interference with her choice to have an abortion"; it also required that "the State must refrain from wielding its enormous power and influence in a manner that might burden the pregnant woman's freedom to choose whether to have an abortion."

Brennan was clearly upset by Stewart's claim that the Hyde Amendment was "rationally related to the legitimate governmental objective of protecting potential life." He responded with unusually sharp words. "As a means of delivering health services," he wrote, "the Hyde Amendment is completely irrational. As a means of preventing abortions, it is concededly rational—brutally so. But this latter goal is constitutionally forbidden." Brennan argued that the law expressed nothing more than "legislative hostility to abortions" and that it penalized poor women who could not fight back.

Turning to the provision that denied Medicaid coverage for life-threatening illnesses whose treatment might require an abortion, Brennan tried "to put this decision in human terms." The consequence, he wrote, "is to leave indigent sick women without treatment simply because of the medical fortuity that their illness cannot be treated unless their pregnancy is terminated. Antipathy to abortion, in short, has been permitted not only to ride roughshod over a woman's constitutional right to terminate her pregnancy in the fashion she chooses, but also to distort our Nation's health-care programs."

Brennan followed these strong words with a judicial sermon. He drew his texts from two historic Supreme Court cases: the *Carolene Products* opinion, in which Justice Harlan Stone devised the "strict scrutiny" test to protect minorities, and the *Barnette* opinion, in which Justice Robert Jackson wrote that constitutional rights "may not be submitted to vote; they depend on the outcome of no elections." Brennan did not cite these cases in his *McRae* dissent, but he employed their approaches in denouncing the Hyde Amendment as "a transparent attempt by the Legislative Branch to impose the political majority's judgment of the morally acceptable and socially desirable preference on a sensitive and intimate decision that the Constitution entrusts to the individual."

Brennan's sermon was not over. "Worse yet," he continued, "the Hyde Amendment does not foist that majoritarian viewpoint with equal measure upon everyone in our Nation, rich and poor alike; rather, it imposes that viewpoint only upon that segment of our society which, because of its position of political powerlessness, is least able to defend its privacy rights from the encroachments of state-mandated morality." In no other opinion, during more than three decades on the Court, did Brennan speak with such force and passion about the rights of people who stood alone before the tanks of the legislative majority.

AFTER HIS *McRae* DISSENT, Justice Brennan moved to the sidelines in the judicial battles over abortion. Before his retirement in 1990, he voted with Justices Blackmun and Marshall to strike down every legislative restriction on abortion rights. The Court's moderates, Justices Stewart and Powell, joined this group in most cases until 1989. By that time, the original *Roe* majority had lost four members to retirement. One of the new justices, John Stevens—placed on the Court by President Gerald Ford—generally supported abortion rights. But the three justices appointed by President Ronald Reagan had passed the litmus test of the Republican platform, which demanded that all federal judicial nominees oppose abortion. Sure enough, all three—Justices O'Connor, Scalia, and Kennedy—voted in 1989 with the original *Roe* dissenters, Justices Rehnquist and White, to uphold state restrictions on abortion in *Webster v. Reproductive Health Services*. The medical staff of a Missouri clinic that offered abortion services had sued the state's attorney general, William

Webster, to challenge a law barring doctors from "encouraging or counseling" pregnant women to have abortions.

Three years before the *Webster* case, Rehnquist had dissented in a
similar case, in which the Court struck down a Pennsylvania law that
forced doctors to tell pregnant women that abortion was a risky procedure.
In that case, *Thornburgh v. American College of Obstetricians and Gynecologists*, Rehnquist agreed with Justice White that the Court should
reverse the *Roe* decision. The retirement in 1987 of Justice Powell, who
had joined the *Thornburgh* majority, shifted the Court's balance with his
replacement by Anthony Kennedy. The Court's junior member voted in
the *Webster* case with Rehnquist, who now sat in the center seat as Chief
Justice.

With five votes to uphold the Missouri law, Rehnquist rewarded himself with the Court's opinion. He could not, however, convince Justice
O'Connor to join his hard-line opinion. After the justices sent a blizzard
of draft opinions among their chambers, Rehnquist accepted his defeat
and decided to write a plurality opinion in the *Webster* case. Adopting
the *Alice in Wonderland* approach of Justice Stewart, Rehnquist argued
that the Missouri law only limited "a woman's ability to obtain an abortion
to the extent that she chooses to use a physician affiliated with a public
hospital." Writing from his position as an affluent male, Rehnquist advised poor women that paying a private doctor for an abortion was "considerably less burdensome" than undergoing an illegal operation or
bearing an unwanted child. Most likely, few poor women read this well-
meaning advice in the pages of *United States Reports*.

Writing in dissent for Justices Brennan and Marshall, the author of
Roe expressed his outrage in very personal terms. "I fear for the future,"
Justice Blackmun wrote. "I fear for the liberty and equality of the millions
of women who have lived and come of age in the sixteen years since *Roe*
was decided. I fear for the integrity of, and public esteem for, this Court."
He accused Rehnquist and his allies of overruling *Roe* without having
the courage to say so. "The plurality opinion is filled with winks, and
nods, and knowing glances to those who would do away with *Roe* explicitly, but turns a stone face to anyone in search of what the plurality
conceives of as the scope of a woman's right under the Due Process
Clause to terminate a pregnancy free from the coercive and brooding
influence of the State."

Blackmun portrayed the result of overruling *Roe* in grim words. He
forecast that "every year hundreds of thousands of women, in desperation,

would defy the law, and place their health and safety in the unclean and unsympathetic hands of back-alley abortionists, or they would attempt to perform abortions upon themselves, with disastrous results. Every year, many women, especially poor and minority women, would die or suffer debilitating physical trauma, all in the name of enforced morality or religious dictates or lack of compassion, as it may be." Blackmun knew that the shift of one vote would finish the demolition job that Rehnquist had begun. Only the reluctance of Justice Sandra O'Connor had blocked the Chief Justice in the *Webster* case. "For today, at least, the law of abortion stands undisturbed," Blackmun wrote with foreboding. "For today, the women of this Nation still retain the liberty to control their destinies. But the signs are evident and very ominous, and a chill wind blows."

THREE YEARS AFTER the *Webster* decision, the chill wind had seemingly intensified to gale force. The retirements of Justices Brennan and Marshall offered President George Bush the chance to give Rehnquist a solid majority to overturn *Roe*, with or without the vote of Justice O'Connor. The newest justices, David Souter and Clarence Thomas, differed greatly in demeanor but were widely expected to vote with Rehnquist when the next abortion case reached the Court. But, like the weather, the votes of Supreme Court justices can never be predicted with certainty.

Still, it seemed likely that Rehnquist could bank on the support of Justices White, Scalia, Kennedy, Souter, and Thomas in *Planned Parenthood v. Casey*, which reached the Court in 1992. Justice Blackmun had complained in *Webster* that the plurality "invites every state legislature to enact more and more restrictive abortion regulations in order to provoke more and more test cases," and lawmakers in several states proved him right. A Pennsylvania statute won the race to the Court, raising issues of mandatory counseling by doctors on abortion risks, notification of husbands by married women seeking abortions, and parental consent for minors.

The Court's chamber was packed for the oral arguments in *Casey*, and everyone knew that the future of *Roe* was at stake. All the lawyers urged the Court to substitute a firm judicial voice for the winks and nods of the *Webster* case. Solicitor General Kenneth Starr spoke for the Bush administration in arguing that *Roe* be reversed. Justices O'Connor and Souter prodded Starr with tough questions. After he ducked a question from Justice Stevens about whether the federal government considered a fetus to be a "person" with constitutional rights, O'Connor shot back that *Roe* had already decided that question. And Souter asked if the "rational basis" test that Starr urged as the proper standard would allow a total prohibition of abortion. Starr admitted that such a ban would raise "serious questions." But the arguments ended without any hint of the final decision.

As the Court's term neared its end in June 1992, the *New York Times* ran a front-page story under the headline, "Changed Path for Court? New Balance Is Held by Three Cautious Justices." Linda Greenhouse wrote that "effective control of the Court has passed to a subgroup of the majority, a moderately conservative middle group of three Justices." Next to her article were pictures of Justices O'Connor, Kennedy, and Souter. "The group's hallmarks," Greenhouse continued, "appear to be a generally cautious approach to deciding cases, a hesitancy to overturn precedents and a distaste for aggressive arguments, whether those presented to the Court or those made by the Justices themselves in written opinions." Many Court observers had detected Justice O'Connor's extreme distaste for the sarcasm and hyperbole in Justice Scalia's opinions, although Greenhouse made no mention of this. "This group does not always vote together, but when it does, its views prevail," she noted.

Three days after this article appeared, "the judgment of the Court" in *Casey* was announced in an opinion by Justices O'Connor, Kennedy, and Souter. Linda Greenhouse had it right; they voted together and they prevailed. "After considering the fundamental constitutional questions resolved by *Roe*, principles of institutional integrity, and the rule of *stare decisis*, we are led to conclude that the essential holding of *Roe v. Wade* should be retained and once again reaffirmed," they wrote. Justices Blackmun and Stevens joined this part of their opinion to save *Roe* from reversal by one vote. Almost lost in the media uproar was the fact that the three "moderate" justices also voted with Rehnquist, White, Scalia, and Thomas to uphold all parts of the Pennsylvania law except the spousal notification provision.

Speaking for himself, Justice Blackmun shifted his metaphors from wind to fire. The *Webster* decision had threatened to "cast into darkness the hopes and visions of every woman in this country" who believed the Constitution protected "the right to reproductive choice," he wrote. "All that remained between the promise of *Roe* and the darkness of the plurality was a single, flickering flame," the one vote that saved *Roe* from being snuffed out. "But now, just when so many expected the darkness to fall, the flame has grown bright," Blackmun exulted. He praised the opinion of the three moderates as "an act of personal courage and constitutional principle." But he would not hold a victory party. "I am eighty-three years old," he wrote in a remarkable personal statement. "I cannot remain on this Court forever, and when I do step down, the confirmation process for my successor may well focus on the issue before us." Blackmun knew full well that the future of *Roe* would probably hinge on the outcome of the presidential campaign being waged as he wrote. "And I fear for the darkness as four Justices anxiously await the single vote necessary to extinguish the light," he concluded.

The *Webster* plurality became the *Casey* minority on the basic issue of abortion as a constitutional right. Chief Justice Rehnquist took a defiant stand in dissent. "We believe that *Roe* was wrongly decided, and that it can and should be overruled consistently with our traditional approach to *stare decisis* in constitutional cases," he wrote. That approach was that any precedent could be overturned once a fifth vote emerged. But that last vote eluded Rehnquist's grasp. The presidential victory of Bill Clinton in 1992 ended the string of ten straight Supreme Court appointments by Republicans. And the retirement of Justice Byron White in 1993 moved Rehnquist one vote further from his goal. White's replacement by Ruth Bader Ginsburg, who had argued for women's rights before the Court, reduced the number who would overturn *Roe* to three. Justice Blackmun, who many observers felt would retire in despair, took new hope and decided to stay on the bench for one more term. He left the Court in 1994 with his judicial legacy intact, confident that his successor would support abortion rights. Speaking of the *Roe* decision, with President Bill Clinton at his side, Blackmun called it "a step that had to be taken as we go down the road toward the full emancipation of women."

It would be wrong to conclude, however, that the chill wind of the *Webster* decision has become a warm summer breeze. The Court upheld most of the abortion restrictions in *Casey*, and the Equal Rights Amendment is still not part of the Constitution. Battles over women's rights and reproductive choice will certainly continue, in the political arena and the Court's chamber. But the descendents of Myra Bradwell are doing well, and the first woman Chief Justice is probably practicing law—or on the bench—right now.

FOURTEEN

"Which Side Are You On?"

On July 20, 1990, a steamy Friday afternoon in Washington, D.C., Justice William Brennan sat alone in his chambers and composed a brief letter to President George Bush. "The strenuous demand of court work and its related duties required or expected of a justice," he wrote, "appear at this time to be incompatible with my advancing age and medical condition. I therefore retire effective immediately as an associate justice of the Supreme Court of the United States." A gallbladder operation had weakened him, and a recent stroke had produced episodes of confusion. After thirty-four years on the Court, Brennan knew he could no longer function at full capacity. Fifteen years earlier, he had witnessed the agonizing slide into senility of his liberal ally William Douglas. Brennan was determined to leave the bench with the dignity that he consistently urged his colleagues to give every American.

Three days later, President Bush announced his nomination of Judge David Souter to the Supreme Court. "Let me pay tribute," he said, "to the Justice whose retirement from the Court created the vacancy: Justice William Brennan. His powerful intellect, his winning personality and, importantly, his commitment to civil discourse on emotional issues that, at times, tempt uncivil voices have made him one of the greatest figures of our age." Reporters may have smiled at these words, knowing that Bush differed with Brennan on every important issue before the Court—abortion, affirmative action, and flag-burning among them. Political convention requires presidents to say polite things about retiring justices. In this case, however, Bush probably spoke with sincerity about his ideological foe. Not one person who knew Brennan ever questioned the force of his mind, his personal warmth, or his dedication to the Court as an institution. Debates with Brennan over legal issues never became personal, as they had for such combative personalities as Felix Frankfurter and Hugo Black.

Chief Justice William Rehnquist joined the tributes to the man who sat opposite him at the Court's conference table, the senior associate justice who some called the "shadow chief justice" in the parlance of British politics. Rehnquist spoke of his colleague in frankly political terms. He recalled meeting Brennan in 1972, after Warren Burger had replaced Earl Warren as Chief Justice. Rehnquist had looked forward to joining a new conservative majority in reversing the Warren Court's liberal decisions. He acknowledged that "the skills which Bill Brennan brought to the work of judging enabled him on numerous occasions to put together majorities espousing the side of individual rights in which he believed so deeply."

Like the president, Rehnquist also linked Brennan's political savvy with the "personal warmth and friendliness" that enabled him to charm and cajole reluctant justices into joining his opinions. From opposite ends of the political spectrum, the Court's two dominant members battled over the Constitution for almost two decades. But the senior associate justice did not hand over his sword in surrender. Speaking with a combination of respect and regret, Rehnquist agreed that "the enduring legacy of Justice Brennan—the high value which he placed on claims of individual constitutional rights asserted against the authority of majoritarian self-government—is in no danger of being forgotten or disregarded simply because he has left the bench."

In his tribute to Brennan, Rehnquist clearly stated the central issue that divided the two justices. During their years together, the Supreme Court decided hundreds of cases that matched claims of individual rights against governmental powers. These conflicts—over issues of individual liberty, criminal law, minority rights, and personal autonomy—reflect the political divisions in American society between liberals and conservatives, with those in the center often holding the balance of power. The preceeding chapters have examined one hundred cases—out of some 2,700 in which Brennan and Rehnquist both voted—which pitted individuals against governmental bodies or officials, or raised private claims based on state law. They agreed in only two of these one hundred cases, voting to reverse a Georgia decision that banned the movie *Carnal Knowledge* and to reject an "emotional distress" claim by the Reverend Jerry Falwell against *Hustler* magazine. In the other ninety-eight cases, Brennan voted for the individual litigants and Rehnquist against their claims.

This division graphically illustrates the politics of the Constitution. A labor song from the 1930s asked, "Which side are you on?" Whether the conflict takes place at a West Virginia coal mine or in the Supreme Court chamber, the question is equally relevant.

THERE IS LITTLE DOUBT that most law professors and legal commentators take Brennan's side in his conflict with Rehnquist. Most of them went to school and came of age during the Warren Court era, and absorbed the liberal doctrine of individual rights. They sided with people like Rosa Parks and Father Daniel Berrigan, who defied oppressive laws, and they deplored the bully-boy tactics of officials like Governor Orval Faubus and Senator Joseph McCarthy. An entire generation of lawyers, writers, and teachers looked to Justice Brennan for guidance and inspiration. He became their prophet, and his opinions their Bible. There is little exaggeration in comparing Brennan to Saint Paul as a propagator of the faith. "He who loves his neighbor has fulfilled the law," Paul told the Romans. Brennan tried his best to turn this admonition into constitutional doctrine.

After Brennan's retirement, his acolytes filled the law reviews with paeans of praise. Professor Laurence Tribe of Harvard Law School, whose massive treatise *American Constitutional Law* made him the modern Blackstone, set the tone. "What makes Justice Brennan's accomplishments so remarkable and so timeless," he wrote, "is that they created not a mere sandcastle to be washed away by the political vicissitudes of the Court's ebb and flow, but a well-founded legal edifice that will withstand constitutional tides for decades to come." Casting Brennan as the "architect of the Bill of Rights," Tribe canvassed his opinions and concluded that he "did not view cases in isolation from one another. Rather, he saw them as building materials from which a constitutional vision could be elaborated." Brennan's "unparalleled ability to detect related themes in different cases, and to see the constitutional structure whole," Tribe wrote, "will give ageless strength to his judicial handiwork."

Professor Owen Fiss of Yale Law School, who served Brennan as a law clerk during the Warren Court era, wrote of this period that "it was Brennan who by and large formulated the principle, analyzed the precedents, and chose the words that transformed the ideal into law. Like any master craftsman, he left his distinctive imprint on the finished product." Fiss recalls Brennan's legendary ability to charm his colleagues into agreement with his positions. "In conference," he wrote, "Justice Brennan always had more than one vote. Who could possibly resist him when he grabbed you by the elbow, or put his arm around your shoulder, and began, 'Look, pal'?" Fiss portrayed Brennan as a diminutive version of Lyndon Johnson, the champion elbow-grabber, but without Johnson's power to punish those who resisted his blandishments. In what another clerk called "taking the pulse," Brennan offered only the force of argument in return for judicial votes.

Another former clerk recounts a story of Brennan's personal charm. "A tradition among law clerks at the Court," wrote Virginia Seitz, "is to take the other justices to lunch one at a time. When the very conservative law clerks of one very conservative justice took Justice Brennan to lunch, they considered him their arch-enemy. I asked one of them, upon his return, how it had gone. He paused, and then said a bit defensively, 'Well, if everyone were as wonderful as Justice Brennan, his legal philosophy would work.' "

To appropriate a phrase from the 1960s, the message of these tributes is that "the personal is political." Frank Michelman, a former clerk and now a Harvard law professor, spoke bluntly on this question after Brennan's retirement. "The point is that there's finally no dissecting the man from the judge," he wrote, "Brennan in person from Brennan in robes. The fellow man *is* the caring judge; the visionary man, the committed judge. In that special union of the personal and the judicial lies, I believe, a key to understanding Justice Brennan's greatness."

More than other commentators, Michelman looked into Brennan's mind to explain his judicial philosophy. "Justice William Brennan is our living, legendary, judicial activist," he wrote. "So it is natural to ask: What does Justice Brennan know? What, in substance, *is* his theory of the Constitution?" Michelman identified two basic values in Brennan's jurisprudence: "commitments to the protection of individual liberty and to the furtherance of dialogic exchange—'critically interactive' exchange thriving on difference, dissent, and disruption—in the many, varied forums of public life." These are not two independent ideas but "complementary aspects of one, unified vision." In other words, Brennan has fused the personal and the political in his constitutional ethos, "political" in the broader sense of public life. Individuals have rights that are personal, but these rights only become operational within a political system that allows and fosters "dialogic exchange" between persons with different, and often antagonistic, values and interests. The Constitution was designed, in this view, to mediate this dialogue, balancing the broad powers of government with the protection of individual rights.

Michelman expands on this dialogic theme. "Freedom, then, is a social and political, not just a personal, condition," he writes. "With striking regularity, Justice Brennan's civil liberties opinions fuse the personal and political aspects of constitutional rights, tightly bonding their value to individual claimants with their social value as structural supports for critically interactive, democratic public life." The conditions of real dialogue, of course, require that both parties allow the other to speak freely, that they listen carefully, and treat one another as equals. These conditions are not always met when one party is a government official and the other is a person with little influence, or someone with a grievance. For Brennan, explains Michelman, "the logic of democratic self-government by the people implies that every law-dispensing office is a site of a critically interactive encounter." Laws or official acts that violate the conditions of equal dialogic exchange also violate the Constitution.

This aspect of Brennan's constitutional ethos draws on the individualistic philosophy of John Stuart Mill and notions of a "free marketplace" of competing ideas. It helps to explain Brennan's opinions in First Amendment cases, but not those in equal protection cases, where the claim of right is based on group membership, such as race or gender. Here is where his jurisprudence fuses the personal and political, and where his concern with "social facts" becomes most evident. "He certainly knows and shares the view," Michelman writes, "that laws and their regulatory consequences can have 'cultural meanings' that limit individuals' prospects by the persuasive images they help to cast of social groups and the characters and capacities of group members and their consequent effects on mind and spirit." Brennan's opinions in cases such as *Frontiero v. Richardson* and *Plyler v. Doe,* striking down laws that discriminated against women and aliens, reflect this concern for stereotypical images and cultural prejudice as constitutionally illegitimate. Michelman explains that Brennan "simply refused to suppress from his judicial assessments of law's effects on individuals his awareness of law's involvement in the social phenomenon of group-based identification."

The jargon of academic jurisprudence should not obscure the basic theme that runs through all of Brennan's opinions: law is not an abstract set of rules, but a social institution that mediates, as he put it, "the relationship between one human being and another." Perhaps the best example of this concern is his dissent in *McCleskey v. Kemp,* where

Brennan imagines a conversation between a Death Row inmate and his lawyer. This creative dialogic exchange captures the essence of a constitutional vision that is grounded in human reality, and that takes into account the corrosive effect on human relationships of stereotype, prejudice, and the abuse of official power. Professor Michelman asked, "What does Justice Brennan know?" He certainly knows this reality, in its many forms and contexts, and this knowledge informs and shapes his judicial opinions.

THE TRIBUTES OF FORMER law clerks are likely, of course, to shower praise on any justice, certainly one with Brennan's warmth and charm. Professor Michelman has already elevated Brennan to the Supreme Court's pantheon as "the foremost judicial architect of American constitutionalism since John Marshall." A better test of his enduring influence is in the comments of critics. Judge Richard Posner, who sits on the U.S. Courts of Appeals after a distinguished academic career, falls into both categories of former clerk and present critic. He clerked in the 1962 term, during the heyday of the Warren Court. "The Brennan chambers were the cockpit of the revolution," Posner recalls. He then shared his boss's liberal views, and worked "with enthusiasm, indeed with relish," on the cases decided in that momentous Court term, which included *Gideon v. Wainwright* and *Abington Township v. Schempp*.

Judge Posner has since moved to the political right, which gives him a unique perspective on his former boss. "The political liberalism that is the salient feature of Justice Brennan's judicial opinions is, I am convinced, not the product of commitment to a doctrine," he writes. "It is the emanation of a warm, generous, and good-hearted person." Posner differs with Michelman—who clerked during the prior term—in suggesting that Brennan never developed a distinctive constitutional doctrine. He suggests instead that Brennan simply put his personal views into his opinions, and slighted the Constitution. "Justice Brennan has not pretended that the constitutional revolution in which he has played a leading role was dictated by the text of the Constitution or by the intentions of its Framers," Posner chides. "He has striven, in the American pragmatic tradition, for concrete results and will be judged in history by the results achieved, both intended and unintended." Although he now regrets those results, Posner adds that "I trust that no one will question the *effectiveness* with which Justice Brennan has pursued his conception of the judicial role, or the impact of his work on contemporary legal and social thought." Posner believes that the key to this powerful impact on the law "lies in a personality warm and serene, and in a character that can fairly be described as noble."

Other critics, writing from a greater distance, agree with Posner on Brennan's "engaging personality" but differ on the question of his political doctrine. During the 1980s, members and supporters of the Reagan administration filled the pages of conservative journals with denunciations of Brennan, portraying him as a black-robed Svengali who hypnotized his colleagues and made them see "fundamental rights" that were not there. These critics portrayed their diminutive adversary in almost superhuman terms. Writing in William Buckley's *National Review* in 1984, Stephen Markman and Alfred Regnery—Republican officials in the Senate and the Justice Department—asserted that "there is no individual in this country, on or off the Court, who has had a more profound and sustained impact upon public policy in the United States" than Brennan.

Markman and Regnery attributed Brennan's "stunning influence on Court and country" to his "ability to strike the sort of judicial compromise that was beyond the grasp of those who, like Black or Douglas, had even more ideological and absolute views of the Constitution." This backhanded compliment took issue with Posner's view of Brennan as a judicial pragmatist, unencumbered by a political agenda. These critics dismissed Brennan's reputed pragmatism as the kind of "two steps forward, one step back" approach of the Soviet Bolsheviks before they took absolute power. "Primarily," the Reagan officials wrote, "what Brennan has done has been to package and market his beliefs more attractively than have some of his ideological brethren." This was high praise indeed from officials of an administration that had mastered the skills of political packaging and marketing.

The Reagan administration wheeled out bigger guns after Justice Brennan, speaking in 1985, responded to the demand of Attorney General Edwin Meese that the Supreme Court adopt his "jurisprudence of original intent." Without naming Meese, Brennan replied that his views were "little more than arrogance cloaked as humility." Meese waited a year before authorizing his combative deputy, William Bradford Reynolds, who headed the Justice Department's civil rights division, to take on Brennan directly. Reynolds had his own bone to pick with Brennan, having personally argued and lost an affirmative action case, *Firefighters v. Cleveland*, in which Brennan wrote the majority opinion in July 1986.

Two months later, Reynolds traveled to Missouri to make his attack before a law school audience, but the attorney general's press office made sure the news media had advance copies of the speech. The front-page headline in the *New York Times* read "Aide in Justice Dept. Holds That Brennan Has 'Radical' Views."

Reynolds rushed through his introductory remarks, eager to attack the "fundamentally flawed jurisprudence" of Justice Brennan. He went through, almost line by line, the speech in which Brennan had accused his boss of "arrogance" and "facile historicism." Reynolds took a few liberties with the historical record himself. "Justice Brennan's fundamental point made unabashedly and apparently without qualifications," he said, "is that the Constitution is essentially a 'dead letter,' a document that has probably outlived its usefulness except as a fond memory to celebrate every so often." Brennan had actually said that "the genius of the Constitution rests not in any static meaning it may have had in a world that is dead and gone, but in the adaptability of its great principles to cope with current problems and current needs." This is a far cry from calling it a "dead letter," but Reynolds had another message to deliver.

Without mentioning the *Firefighters* decision, Reynolds faulted Brennan's view of the Equal Protection clause as one that "would have shocked the Framers" of the Fourteenth Amendment. "Justice Brennan's radically egalitarian jurisprudence," he claimed, "is a theory that seeks not limited government in order to secure individual liberty, but unlimited judicial power to further a personalized egalitarian vision of society." Reynolds hinted darkly at sinister forces. "Where did Justice Brennan's definition of the Fourteenth Amendment's promise come from?" he demanded to know. "And further, why is it that it looks suspiciously more like a political or social agenda than a theory of law?" Consciously or not, Reynolds echoed Senator Joseph McCarthy, demanding to know Brennan's views on "the Communist conspiracy" at his Supreme Court confirmation hearing.

Reynolds ended his assault by answering his own rhetorical questions: "This theory and its policy particulars derive primarily from a liberal social agenda in which Justice Brennan shares. And that agenda has little or no connection with the Framers' Constitution, Bill of Rights, or any subsequent amendment." Brennan's approach to the Constitution, Reynolds might have added, also had little or no connection with the conservative social agenda of the Reagan administration for which Reynolds spoke.

Over the years, Brennan has almost entirely escaped serious criticism in law reviews, largely because most law professors share his constitutional views; this is certainly true in the elite schools from which they graduate and in which they teach after a judicial clerkship and perhaps a short stint in practice. Brennan has become a virtual icon to the law professoriate. One vocal exception is Professor Lino Graglia, who teaches constitutional law at the University of Texas. Best known for *Disaster by Decree*, a book that heatedly criticized the Supreme Court's school integration decisions, Graglia added his voice in 1986 to the conservative assault on Brennan in the pages of the journal *Commentary*. His lengthy article did not discuss any of Brennan's decisions, but attacked the speech in which Brennan had criticized Attorney General Meese. Like other critics, Graglia agreed that "Justice Brennan—although his name is probably unknown to the great majority of his fellow citizens—has surely been our most important government official" over the past three decades. He achieved this position of unelected power, Graglia charged, by practicing "constitutional law without the Constitution."

Graglia based his critique of Brennan on the proposition that "the function of judges is to apply, not to make, the law." This narrow view of the judicial role is, of course, central to the conservative philosophy that stresses the power of electoral majorities over minorities, looks with disfavor on claims of "fundamental rights," and demands that judges apply the "original intent" of the Framers. Graglia made clear his opposition to "judicial intervention in the political process in the name of protecting individual rights from majority rule." In his view, "although the Constitution does create some individual rights, they are actually rather few, fairly well-defined, and rarely violated." In listing these few rights, Graglia argued that the Bill of Rights applies "only to the federal government," and that the "clear historic purpose" of the Fourteenth Amendment was to prohibit state racial discrimination "but not otherwise to change fundamentally the constitutional scheme." This is, of course, almost a verbatim reiteration of the position Justice Rehnquist argued in his 1976 speech at the University of Texas, "The Notion of a Living Constitution." From these premises, Graglia concluded that government officials and lawmakers have "little occasion or desire to violate the Constitution." His Panglossian notion leaves minorities with little to fear and judges with little to do.

Professor Graglia heaped scorn on Brennan's argument that, underlying the specific provisions of the Constitution, the Framers meant to protect "the human dignity of every individual." Admitting his temptation "to dismiss Justice Brennan's rapturous statements as mere flights of poetic fancy or utopian ecstasy," he took them seriously as the justification "for the Court's assumption and exercise of enormous government power." At bottom, Graglia's dispute with Brennan and his fellow "judicial activists" is political, and goes back to the Madisonian dilemma of balancing majority power with minority rights. From opposite ends of the political spectrum, Graglia and Brennan view the judicial role in antithetical terms.

Even at the retirement party of the most beloved person, there is always one churlish fellow, muttering "good riddance" from the sidelines. William F. Buckley played this role with characteristic acerbity, complaining in his *National Review* that Brennan "used the rhetoric of equality and individual rights to transform the federal structure, in which power had been dispersed through innumerable institutions, into a Washington-based liberal oligarchy." Buckley rejoiced—prematurely, it seems—that Brennan's retirement "means the liberal domination of the Supreme Court has finally ended," but he sourly predicted that "the damage that William Brennan did may never be undone."

Those who lauded Brennan and those who lamented his work agreed on two things: his enormous influence on the Court and the enduring legacy of his opinions. Our understanding of Brennan's constitutional vision is sharpened, however, by viewing it in contrast with that of his judicial opposite, William Rehnquist.

CHIEF JUSTICE REHNQUIST is entitled by the Constitution to serve "during good Behaviour," until his retirement or death. Until he leaves the Court, his former law clerks will not deliver the tributes that were showered on Brennan. Many fewer of Rehnquist's clerks became law professors—they have mostly gone into corporate practice—and only a handful have written about his jurisprudence. Consequently, most of the commentaries thus far have been critical, which is not surprising in view of the liberal cast of the law professoriate. As with Brennan, his opinions and articles are the best source for Rehnquist's legal philosophy. But there is enough outside commentary to provide a preliminary assessment of his judicial output and impact.

One former clerk has offered an overview of Rehnquist's constitutional approach. Robert Giuffra, a Yale law graduate who clerked during the 1988 term and now practices with a Wall Street firm, wrote in 1991 that "Rehnquist's jurisprudence is consistent and well formed. It has three central themes. First, he is deferential to the popularly elected branches of government. Second, he believes that judges should base their decisions on the Constitution's text as understood in the context of the times when it was written. Third, he has a deep respect for the values of federalism and state autonomy."

This is an accurate distillation of Rehnquist's opinions over two decades. But it is notably devoid of nuance, of any recognition of competing values and interests. It sounds more like a checklist of "do's and don'ts." Defer to government, look for "original intent," and support the states. Deciding cases by this formula becomes almost automatic, and the results are highly predictable. One empirical study of Rehnquist's decisions, published in 1983, employed these three factors and found they predicted his votes—depending on the category of cases—between 85 and 100 percent of the time. A comparable study of Brennan's decisions would undoubtedly find similar percentages on the other side. The factors Giuffra has identified are simply the starting point in assessing Rehnquist's judicial approach.

Judicial reasoning is more important to law professors than the outcome of cases. Rehnquist has taken a beating on this score from liberal critics such as Owen Fiss, who clerked for Brennan and now teaches at Yale Law School. Writing in 1982 in the *New Republic*, Fiss and Charles Krauthammer, the journal's senior editor, raked Rehnquist over the coals. Much like Brennan's critics, they attributed great influence to their adversary. Warren Burger then sat as Chief Justice, but they dismissed him as a figurehead. "There is a vision that informs its work and shapes our politics," Fiss and Krauthammer wrote of the Supreme Court. "The source of that vision, however, is not Warren Burger. It is William Rehnquist."

His liberal critics gave Rehnquist due credit for craftsmanship. His opinions "have been clear, lucid, brief, and mercifully free of bureaucratese," they wrote. "He gets to the point quickly and does not decorate his opinions with authorities he has neither read nor understood." But the applause ended there. "On the other hand," Fiss and Krauthammer continued, "his opinions fall radically short of the ideals of the profession. He repudiates precedents frequently and openly, and if that is impossible (because the precedent represents a tradition that neither the Court nor society is prepared to abandon), then he distorts them."

This is a serious charge, akin to accusations of judicial fraud. Fiss and Krauthammer cited an opinion in which Rehnquist portrayed the historic *Debs* case of 1895, which tested a judicial injunction against a nationwide strike of railway workers, as "an armed conspiracy that threatened the interstate transportation of the mails." Rehnquist suggested in effect that Eugene Debs, the union leader and four-time Socialist presidential candidate, was stopping trains and throwing off the mail. Given the government's massive deployment of troops to break the strike, this version of the railway strike did not agree with those of most historians.

The Supreme Court is not, however, a scholarly seminar, and the *Debs* case was ancient history when Fiss and Krauthammer wrote. They moved to 1976 in charging that Rehnquist "manipulates trial records" to support his decisions. This charge had more substance. Without naming the case, which was *Rizzo v. Goode,* they claimed that Rehnquist "tried to discredit the findings of a trial court, affirmed by a court of appeals, that a pattern of police harassment of minorities had occurred in Philadelphia." Dismissing this evidence, "Rehnquist saw only isolated incidents" of police misconduct. A fair reading of the case record supports the claim that Rehnquist ignored the trial judge's findings in his zeal to support the police.

Fiss and Krauthammer took issue with Giuffra's argument that Rehnquist was a judicial conservative who based his decisions on respect for states' rights and deference to legislative will. They portrayed him as a judicial activist in sheep's clothing. "Rehnquist's championing of state autonomy may make him a hero to conservatives," they wrote, "but that acclaim would be ill-deserved. He is no conservative as the term is ordinarily understood in the law, but rather a revisionist of a particular ideological bent." Fiss and Krauthammer disputed each of Giuffra's claims about his former boss. "He repudiates precedents," they charged; "he shows no deference to the legislative branch; and he is unable to ground state autonomy in any textual provision of the Constitution." The clerk and the critics painted entirely different pictures of Justice Rehnquist.

Law professors are expected to criticize—in the academic sense of the word—the opinions and jurisprudence of Supreme Court justices. Federal judges, whose decisions are subject to review and reversal, hardly ever speak or write critically of their judicial superiors. One who did, however, offered a trenchant critique of Justice Rehnquist's notion of judicial review. William Justice, a federal district judge appointed by President Lyndon Johnson, ruled in 1978 in *Plyler v. Doe* that Texas schools could not bar the children of illegal aliens from classrooms, a decision the Supreme Court upheld in 1982, with Rehnquist in the minority. Between those two decisions, Judge Justice answered Rehnquist's attack on "The Notion of a Living Constitution," his 1976 Texas law school speech, with his own critique of "A Relativistic Constitution," his label for Rehnquist's constitutional approach.

Justice faulted Rehnquist on two major points. First, he compared Rehnquist's conception of democracy with that of the Constitution, and found great differences. Rehnquist equates democracy with pure majoritarianism, admitting to few—if any—limits on the powers of electoral majorities. His votes in the cases discussed in this book certainly display no recognition of these limits, since he voted against the exercise of governmental powers in just one case out of one hundred. Noting that the Constitution "unquestionably contains some distinctly non-majoritarian elements," notably the "no law" limits in the Bill of Rights, Justice accused Rehnquist of importing "some extra-constitutional notion of democracy" into his jurisprudence. Unwilling to acknowledge any real limits on majority rule within the Constitution itself, Rehnquist looks instead to a model of untrammeled electoral power the Framers expressly rejected in adding the Bill of Rights to the Constitution.

The second point of this critique, closely linked to the first, was that Rehnquist based his adherence to "pure majoritarianism" on a "moral relativism" that was equally foreign to the Framers. According to Judge Justice, Rehnquist believed that, "since no value can be demonstrated to be intrinsically better or worse than any other, a particular value is *authoritative* only when it can claim majority support." Rehnquist did, in fact, argue in his Texas speech that laws "take on a form of moral goodness because they have been enacted into positive law." What is lawful is therefore moral, he concludes, because the Constitution embodies no moral values that limit the power of majorities, certainly not the value of "human dignity" espoused by Justice Brennan. To complete Rehnquist's jurisprudential equation, morality is defined by the commands of positive law.

In his Texas speech, Rehnquist cited the *Lochner* dissent of Justice Oliver Wendell Holmes to support his belief in judicial deference to legislative will. Holmes argued in this 1905 case—striking down a state limitation on the work hours of bakers—that the Constitution "is not intended to embody a particular economic theory" and that judges should therefore not interfere with legislative decisions on economic issues. This citation to *Lochner* is revealing. Rehnquist has imported this principle into cases that deal with the most intimate decisions of personal life. Even abortion, he argued in *Roe v. Wade,* is the kind of "economic and social" issue that elected lawmakers should be allowed to decide without judicial interference.

Judge Justice agreed that Rehnquist derived his "moral relativism" from Holmes, but traced its roots instead to *Buck v. Bell,* the 1927 decision in which Holmes upheld a state law that allowed the sterilization of supposedly "feebleminded" persons. In this case, Justice wrote, "Holmes employed his habitually relaxed deference to legislative choice." This *Buck* decision "may shock us," he added, but Rehnquist "professed to swallow whole" the principle of moral relativism that Holmes advanced. Justice denied, however, that the Framers intended to give lawmakers such power over individuals. "The main deficiency of philosophical relativism as a constitutional principle," he wrote, "is that it is clearly a latter-day excrescence."

Unlike Rehnquist, Justice found in the Constitution not the absence of moral values but an "intense concern with the nature and quality of human existence," rooted in the explicitly moral values of the Declaration of Independence and the *Federalist* papers. The purpose of constitutional limits on majorities, Justice claimed, was "to bind future generations" to such basic moral values as liberty and equality. He argued that "if the relativism of Holmes and Justice Rehnquist had been conceived to be true by the Framers, there would have been no reason for any rights to have been written into a constitution" as judicially enforceable limits on legislative power.

Justice directed two rhetorical questions at Rehnquist. Suppose the Framers wanted to protect religious freedom, he asked. They could simply have passed a religious-freedom law, subject to future revision or repeal. Or if they disliked slavery, "a statute would have been sufficient, and would have left later majorities more free to change their minds." Justice made clear his disagreement with Rehnquist's "substitution of his own relativist majoritarian ideals for those embodied in the Constitution, a substitution which I cannot accept at all." In the end, the district judge accused the Chief Justice of placing "in majority sentiment a degree of legitimacy that is simply undeserved" in a system based on constitutional limitations.

DURING A PERIOD of eighteen years, William Brennan and William Rehnquist waged a battle over the Constitution, conducted largely behind the marble walls of the Supreme Court. This was not a personal conflict, with raised voices and strained relations. The general public had little idea that these two genial men, who sat beside each other on the bench for the last four years of Brennan's tenure, each headed a Court faction that sought to influence the votes of judicial "moderates" to prevail in the conference room. It is a measure of their persuasive abilities that, of the thirty-nine cases discussed in this book in which both men wrote opinions, Brennan prevailed in twenty and Rehnquist in nineteen. And few people understood how their antithetical constitutional approaches reflected a fundamental disagreement over the role of justices in deciding cases. Much like the two poles of a magnet, each exerted a strong pull over the center but neither overcame the other's force.

Although Brennan has left the Supreme Court bench, he retains his title and office and works almost daily in his chambers, talking and corresponding with a legion of friends and former clerks. As the Court ended its term in 1994, Rehnquist remained as Chief Justice, although he is eligible, at sixty-nine, to retire with full pension. Chief Justices, however, have a tradition of longevity. Four in this century—Charles Evans Hughes, Harlan Fiske Stone, Earl Warren, and Warren Burger—served into their late seventies. And Justice Oliver Wendell Holmes set the Court's all-time longevity record when he retired in 1932 at the age of ninety-one. The factor of life tenure for federal judges makes it impossible to predict when any justice will leave the Court.

The facts of political life, however, make it virtually certain there will never be a "Rehnquist Court" in the sense that we speak of the "Hughes Court" or the "Warren Court," one dominated by a Chief Justice with a solid majority on most issues. That is not to say that Rehnquist has not prevailed on very important issues; he certainly has on capital punishment. But he fell one vote short in his campaign to overturn *Roe v. Wade,* and most likely will never gain a majority to outlaw abortion.

The election in 1992 of President Bill Clinton, and his appointment of Ruth Bader Ginsburg to replace Justice Byron White, ended the dream of conservatives that the Supreme Court—with Rehnquist at the helm—

would extend their influence well into the twenty-first century. The Court is far from liberal domination, but the "moderates" have now taken effective control. Ironically, it seems that Justice Brennan's replacement, David Souter, might fulfill the promise of President Bush that in choosing him, "I have looked for the same dedication to public service and strength of intellect exemplified by Justice Brennan." Souter has hardly become another Brennan—perhaps no justice ever will—but he refuses to join the right-wing faction of Rehnquist, Scalia, and Thomas. Statistics of judicial voting make this clear. During the 1987 Court term, after the appointment of Justice Anthony Kennedy, Rehnquist was on the winning side in nine of twelve cases decided by 5–4 votes. Brennan joined only two of the winning coalitions in that term. But in the 1991 term, after Souter replaced Brennan, Rehnquist prevailed in only four of the fourteen one-vote decisions, while Souter was in the majority in thirteen of these cases. In the most important of these cases, *Planned Parenthood v. Casey*, Sandra O'Connor and Anthony Kennedy joined Souter in blocking Rehnquist's drive to overturn *Roe v. Wade*.

With four decades of experience in partisan and judicial politics, Rehnquist can have no illusions about his declining influence. He knows the Court's history and the effect of political tides on its composition. Speaking in 1984, during the Reagan years, he noted that "a President who sets out to 'pack' the Court seeks to appoint people to the Court who are sympathetic to his political or philosophical principles. There is no reason in the world why a president should not do this." Rehnquist confessed that "even a 'strong' President determined to leave his mark on the Court—a President such as Lincoln or Franklin Roosevelt—is apt to be only partially successful." Between 1969 and 1991, four Republican presidents tried to "pack" the Court with ten successive justices. This partisan effort to make the Court a conservative bastion failed because, as Rehnquist acknowledged, each justice is "thoroughly independent of his colleagues" and becomes free to vote without fear of defeat at the next election. If Bill Clinton serves two terms as president, he will almost certainly nominate a successor to William Rehnquist as Chief Justice.

Although the "Rehnquist Court" is now more liberal than its Chief, conservatives still dominate the lower federal courts. Between them, Presidents Reagan and Bush appointed more than 60 percent of all sitting district judges, and almost 70 percent at the appellate level. These were not affirmative-action jobs; only 12 percent were female and 3 percent were black. But the Republicans did not practice age discrimination; they appointed a record number of judges in their forties and even thirties. This cadre of conservative judges will remain on the bench for three or four decades. But the balance will shift as the federal judiciary grows. President Clinton assumed office with more than 130 judicial vacancies to fill, and Congress will create more judgeships to meet a swelling federal caseload—much of it created by the Republican "war on drugs." This shifting balance will create more work for the Supreme Court, as divergent rulings by liberal and conservative judges force the justices to resolve the conflicts among the lower courts.

A FINAL VERDICT in the case of Brennan vs. Rehnquist cannot be rendered until the judicial records of both men have become history. We can, however, look back and examine the impact of each justice on American law and society. Writing in 1991, Professor Owen Fiss painted a vivid picture of the nation at the time Brennan joined the Court, well worth quoting at length. "In the 1950s, America was not a pretty sight. Jim Crow reigned supreme. Blacks were systematically disenfranchised and excluded from juries. State-fostered religious practices, like school prayers, were pervasive. Legislatures were grossly gerrymandered and mal-apportioned. McCarthyism stifled radical dissent, and the jurisdiction of the censor over matters considered obscene or libelous had no consti-tutional limits. The heavy hand of the law threatened those who publicly provided information and advice concerning contraceptives, thereby im-periling the most intimate of human relationships. The states virtually had a free hand in the administration of justice. Trials often proceeded without counsel or jury. Convictions were allowed to stand even though they turned on illegally seized evidence or on statements extracted from the accused under coercive circumstances. There were no rules limiting the imposition of the death penalty. These practices victimized the poor and disadvantaged, as did the welfare system, which was administered in an arbitrary and oppressive manner."

Fiss identified fifteen areas in which the Supreme Court had limited constitutional rights at the time Justice Brennan took his seat in 1956. Over the next thirty-four years, on each of these issues, Brennan wrote or joined opinions that extended the Constitution's reach and expressed his conception of "human dignity." The cases discussed in this book make clear that Brennan was only partially successful in his constitutional quest. None of the rights he championed is now free of some restraint, whether it be speech, abortion, or freedom from self-incrimination. But people like Jacinta Moreno, Don Aguillard, and Sharron Frontiero can thank Brennan for the rights they were granted by the Supreme Court.

Justice Rehnquist has achieved his own victories over the past two decades. He has largely prevailed on such issues as capital punishment, *habeas corpus* review, and governmental liability. The lives of people like Warren McCleskey, Ruth Jefferson, and Joshua DeShaney were affected—in one case, ended—by Rehnquist's votes and opinions. This is not to say that either justice was motivated by hostility or sympathy to these individual litigants. But it bears repeating that Supreme Court decisions affect real people, and that choosing between the principles of "dignity" and "deference" makes a real difference to them.

Supreme Court justices are placed on the bench by elected officials who owe their positions to the electorate. How we vote in elections for senators and presidents will affect the outcome of the Court's decisions in years and decades to come. This is an awesome power, one that every American should ponder before entering the voting booth. Justices Brennan and Rehnquist have offered persuasive arguments on either side of a continuing constitutional debate. But in the end, the decision is ours.

Bibliographic Note

As I noted in the Preface, the published opinions of the U.S. Supreme Court are the primary source for this book. They are available in *United States Reports*, which is the Court's official reporter. For those who are unfamiliar with legal notation, cases are cited in the Notes by volume, page, and year, in this form: Laird v. Tatum, 408 U.S. 1 (1973).

This citation form is followed in reporters of the lower federal courts. Opinions from the federal district courts are published in the *Federal Supplement* and are cited with the district and state abbreviated: COPPAR v. Rizzo, 357 F.Supp. 1289 (E.D.Pa. 1973) was decided in the Eastern District of Pennsylvania. Opinions from the federal courts of appeal are published in the *Federal Reporter, 2d Series*, and citations include the circuit number (the District of Columbia is a separate circuit): Brown v. Board of Education, 892 F.2d 851 (10th Cir. 1989).

My accounts of numerous Supreme Court cases have been supplemented with data from the briefs and records in these cases. These include briefs of the parties and of *amicus* groups, and excerpts of trial records. They are available on microfiche in law school libraries, and are filed by Supreme Court term and case docket number, in this form: Briefs and Record, U.S. Dept. of Agriculture v. Moreno, 72-534. This case was filed in the 1972 Supreme Court term and was given the docket number 534.

Another useful source is the collection of briefs and oral argument transcripts in significant cases, edited by Philip Kurland and Gerhard Casper and published as *Landmark Briefs and Arguments of the Supreme Court*, available in law school and many university libraries. Tape recordings and transcripts of all Supreme Court cases argued since the 1955 term are available in the new National Archives building in suburban Washington, D.C. Edited recordings of oral arguments in several cases discussed in this book are available in the collection I edited with Stephanie Guitton, *May It Please the Court.*

This book also draws on several books that are cited in the notes. Some deserve mention here. A basic study of the Supreme Court, which examines how cases reach the Court and how justices decide them, is David M. O'Brien's book, *Storm Center: The Supreme Court in American Politics.* My notion of "social facts" in Supreme Court jurisprudence draws on the fine work of Harry N. Hirsch in A *Theory of Liberty.* Bernard Schwartz has written two detailed studies of cases decided by the Warren and Burger courts, drawing on unpublished opinion drafts and conference notes: *Super Chief: Earl Warren and His Supreme Court—A Judicial Biography* and *The Ascent of Pragmatism: The Burger Court in Action.*

Two journalistic accounts of the Court provide "backstage" details of important cases: Bob Woodward and Scott Armstrong covered the Burger court from 1969 to 1976 in *The Brethren: Inside the Supreme Court,* and David Savage reported on the Rehnquist court from 1986 to 1991 in *Turning Right: The Making of the Rehnquist Supreme Court.* Neither book is documented, although each adds personal flavor and political intrigue to the cases that Schwartz dissects in his work.

There are no full-scale, documented biographies of either Justice Brennan or Chief Justice Rehnquist. Kim Isaac Eisler has written a journalistic biography in A *Justice for All: William J. Brennan, Jr., and the Decisions That Transformed America.* This book has no notes and little discussion of Brennan's judicial philosophy. Steven Wermiel, who covered the Supreme Court for the *Wall Street Journal,* is currently writing an authorized biography of Justice Brennan that will draw on his private papers and extensive interviews with him and with his former law clerks.

I have no knowledge of any biography of Rehnquist in the works. Two academic studies have examined his judicial philosophy. Sue Davis, in *Justice Rehnquist and the Constitution,* and Donald E. Boles, in *Mr. Justice Rehnquist: Judicial Activist,* both conclude that Rehnquist is a committed judicial activist with a conservative political agenda and little regard for judicial precedent.

Although I have not cited his work in this book, I want to acknowledge the influence of Fred Rodell, the late Yale Law School professor and legal realist. His book, *Nine Men: A Political History of the Supreme*

Court from 1790 *to* 1955, helped to shape my understanding of the Supreme Court as a political institution and of justices as unelected politicians. Any work in jurisprudence that fails to recognize these factors—and most recent books in this field ignore them—seems to me the kind of "sterile formalism" that separates law from social reality.

Notes

Preface

xi–xii   Brennan and Rehnquist voting statistics were compiled from the annual surveys of Supreme Court voting published in the *Harvard Law Review* (November issues, 1973–1990).

xiii   Tocqueville: David M. O'Brien, *Storm Center: The Supreme Court in American Politics*, 2d ed. (New York: Norton, 1990), 209.

    Marshall: Marbury v. Madison, 5 U.S. 137 (1803), 176.

    Jackson: *The Struggle for Judicial Supremacy* (New York: Hippocrene Books, 1979), 287.

    Biddle: Quoted by Edward Ennis, interview by author, 23 October 1981.

Chapter 1

3   Byrnes: David O'Brien, *Storm Center: The Supreme Court in American Politics*, 2d ed. (New York: Norton, 1990), 225.

4   Richmond school cases: *School Board of Richmond v. State Board of Education of Virginia*, 412 U.S. 92 (1973).

    Tax-dependents law: *Food Stamp Act of 1964*, Title 7, *U.S. Code*, sec. 2012(3)(e)[1971].

5   Quote on college students: 116 *Congressional Record* 41979.

    Hippy commune law: *Food Stamp Act*, Title 7, *U.S. Code*, sec. 2012(3)(e)[1971].

    Holland: 116 *Congressional Record* 44439.

    Pollack on FRAC: *Time*, 2 August 1976, 41.

5–6   Pollack on child diseases and Butz: Remarks at Freedom from Hunger Conference of American Bar Association, 1 *Human Rights* (1971), 114–16.

6–7   Affidavits in Moreno case: Briefs and Record, *U.S. Department of Agriculture v. Moreno*, 413 U.S. 528 (1973), Docket No. 72-534.

7   Brickfield and Smith: Transcript of hearing of 5 April 1972, Briefs and Record in Moreno case.

8   Brickfield, Robinson, and McGowan: Transcript of hearing of 14 April 1972, Briefs and Record in Moreno case.

8–10   McGowan: *Moreno v. United States Dept. of Agriculture*, 345 F.Supp. 310 (D.D.C. 1972), 313–16; "Developments in the Law—Equal Protection," 82 *Harvard Law Review* (1969), 1065; *Dandridge v. Williams*, 397 U.S. 471 (1970).

11   Government petition and brief: Briefs and Record in the Moreno case.

11–12   Pollack brief: Briefs and Record in the Moreno case.

12   Randolph data: Senate Judiciary Committee, *Confirmation Hearings on Federal Appointments*, 1991, serial J-101-6, 50–61.

12–13   Supreme Court arguments: Transcript of Arguments, *United States Dept. of Agriculture v. Moreno*, Supreme Court Library, Washington, D.C.

13   Order in Richmond school cases: *School Board of Richmond v. State Board of Education of Virginia*, 412 U.S. 92 (1973), 93.

14   Brennan: Stephen J. Friedman, ed., *An Affair with Freedom: A Collection of Opinions and Speeches* (New York: Atheneum, 1967), 335.
Rehnquist: William H. Rehnquist, *The Supreme Court* (New York: Morrow, 1989), 228.

15–16   Brennan: *United States Dept. of Agriculture v. Moreno*, 531–38.

16–17   Douglas: *United States Dept. of Agriculture v. Moreno*, 544–45.

17–18   Rehnquist: *United States Dept. of Agriculture v. Moreno*, 545–547; *Williamson v. Lee Optical Co.*, 348 U.S. 483 (1955), 487–88.

18   Stewart: *Dandridge v. Williams*, 485.
Douglas: *Williamson v. Lee Optical Co.*, 487–88.
Rehnquist: *United States Dept. of Agriculture v. Moreno*, 547.

18–19   Article on Supreme Court decisions: *New York Times*, 26 June 1973.

19   Butz resignation: *New York Times*, 5 October 1976.

CHAPTER 2

23–4   Brennan: "A Fine Judge Ready for His Biggest Job," *Life*, 29 October 1956, 115–16.

24   Hagerty and Brennan: *New York Times*, 30 September 1956.

25   Krock and Shanley: *New York Times*, 2 October 1956.

25–7   Brennan biographical data: This account draws largely on Jack Alexander, "Mr. Justice from New Jersey," *Saturday Evening Post*, 28 September 1957, 25; see also Kim Isaac Eisler, *A Justice for All: William J. Brennan, Jr., and the Decisions That Transformed America* (New York: Simon and Schuster, 1993).

28   Brennan in Fifth Amendment case: *In Re Pillo*, 93 A.2d 176 (N.J. 1952), 179–81.
Comment on Brennan: Daniel Berman, "Mr. Justice Brennan," *The Nation*, 13 October 1956, 298–300.

28–9   Burlesque theater case: *Adams Theater Co. v. Keenan*, 96 A.2d 519 (N.J. 1953), 520–23.

29–30   Union officer case: *Hazelton v. Murray*, 121 A.2d 1 (N.J. 1956), 2–5.

30   Tenant eviction case: *Kutcher v. Housing Authority of Newark*, 119 A.2d 1 (N.J. 1955), 2–5.

30   Brennan speech: *Congressional Record*, March 19, 1957, 3940–41.

31–3   Brennan confirmation hearings: *Congressional Record*, March 19, 1957, 3937–44.

33   Brennan: *Jencks v. United States*, 353 U.S. 57 (1957), 72.

34   Brennan: *Congressional Record*, March 19, 1957, 3938–39.

35   Pope Leo XIII: Rev. John F. Cronin, *Catholic Social Principles* (Milwaukee, Wis.: Bruce, 1950), 303.
Pope Pius XII: Cronin, *Catholic Social Principles*, 65.

35–6   Brennan: "Reason, Passion, and 'The Progress of the Law,' " 10 *Cardozo Law Review* 2 (1988), 15–23.

36   Harlan: *Poe v. Ullman*, 367 U.S. 497 (1961), 542.

36–9   Brennan: "The Constitution of the United States: Contemporary Ratification," 27 *South Texas Law Review* 433 (1986), 433–45.

39–41   Brennan: *Goldberg v. Kelly*, 397 U.S. 254 (1970), 256–57, 262–71.

41–2   Brennan from Cardozo Lecture: "Reason, Passion, and 'The Progress of the Law,' " 19–23.

CHAPTER 3

43   Mitchell: Richard Kleindienst, *Justice: Memoirs of Attorney General Richard Kleindienst* (Ottawa, Ill.: Jameson Books, 1985), 122.

45   Moore: Kleindienst, *Justice*, 122.

45–6   Nixon: Bob Woodward and Scott Armstrong, *The Brethren* (New York: Simon and Schuster, 1980), 189.

46   Reaction of Rehnquist children: *Time*, 1 November 1971, 17.

46–7   Nixon: *Public Papers of the Presidents*, 1971, 1055–56; RN: *The Memoirs of Richard Nixon* (New York: Grosset and Dunlap, 1978), 424.

47–8   Rehnquist biographical data: This account is drawn from John A. Jenkins, "The Partisan: A Talk with Justice Rehnquist," *New York Times Magazine*, 3 March 1985; U.S. Census data on Shorewood Village, Wisconsin, *Characteristics of the Population—Wisconsin*, 1940, 666, 671, 676; *New York Times*, 22 October 1971.

48   Rehnquist letter to *Stanford Daily*: *Congressional Record*, 18 November 1971 [collection of Rehnquist's writings and speeches, cited below as Rehnquist Writings], 42148 (letter published 13 August 1948).

49–50   Rehnquist to Phoenix City Council: Rehnquist Writings, 42131 (testimony of 15 June 1964).

50   Rehnquist letters: Rehnquist Writings, 42132 (published 21 June 1964 and 9 September 1967).

51–2   Rehnquist: Rehnquist Writings, 42132–34.

52   *Newsweek* quote: 14 June 1971, 28.
Rehnquist on civil disobedience: Rehnquist Writings, 42134–35.

53   Rehnquist on Cambodia: Rehnquist Writings, 42135–36.
Rehnquist on bail: Rehnquist Writings, 42145.

54   Rehnquist on wiretapping and surveillance: Rehnquist Writings, 42145–46.
Ervin and Rehnquist: Rehnquist Writings, 42139.

54–5   Rehnquist testimony on ERA: Rehnquist Writings, 42135.

55   Rehnquist memo on ERA: Washington *Post*, 10 September 1986.

56   ABA report: Senate Judiciary Committee, *Nominations of William H. Rehnquist and Lewis F. Powell, Jr.*, 1971, serial Y4.J89/2:R 26/2, 1–4. (Cited below as Judiciary Hearings) Hurlbut and Bork: Judiciary Hearings, 9–10.

56–7   McClellan and Rehnquist: Judiciary Hearings, 16–21.

57   Ervin: Judiciary Hearings, 21–23.

57–8   Hart and Rehnquist: Judiciary Hearings, 26–27.

58   Rehnquist article: "Who Writes Decisions of the Supreme Court?" *U.S. News and World Report*, 13 December 1957, 74–75.
Kennedy and Rehnquist: Judiciary Hearings, 55.
Rehnquist to Tunney: Judiciary Hearings, 76.

58–9   Bayh and Rehnquist: Judiciary Hearings, 69–72.

60   Rehnquist memo: *Newsweek*, 13 December 1971, 32.
Rehnquist letter: Washington *Post*, 9 December 1971.
Douglas: Washington *Post*, 10 December 1971.

61   Bayh and Senate vote: *Congressional Record*, December 10, 1971, 46196–97.

61–3   Rehnquist: "The Notion of a Living Constitution," 54 *Texas Law Review* 693 (1976), 704–6.

63   Shapiro: "Mr. Justice Rehnquist: A Preliminary View," 90 *Harvard Law Review* 293 (1976), 294–95.
Riggs: "The Judicial Philosophy of Justice Rehnquist," 16 *Akron Law Review* 555 (1983), 601–4.

64   Rauh: Judiciary Hearings, 340.
Rehnquist: Jenkins, "The Partisan," 100–101.

CHAPTER 4

65   Peckham: *Lochner v. New York*, 198 U.S. 45 (1905), 53.

66   Kennedy and Rehnquist: Senate Judiciary Committee, *Nominations of William H. Rehnquist and Lewis F. Powell, Jr.*, 1971, serial Y4.J89/2:R 26/2, 159–60.
Medical report: *Lochner v. New York*, 70.
Weismann: *New York Times*, 19 April 1905.

66–7   Weismann brief: Philip B. Kurland and Gerhard Casper, eds., *Landmark Briefs and Arguments of the Supreme Court* (Bethesda, Md.: University Publications of America), 14:663, 674, 662.

67   Brandeis brief in *Muller*: Kurland and Casper, *Landmark Briefs*, 16:63–178.
Mayer brief in *Lochner*: Kurland and Casper, *Landmark Briefs*, 14:725, 733.
Peckham: *Lochner v. New York*, 57, 59, 64.

67–8   Holmes: *Lochner v. New York*, 75.

68–70   Rehnquist on *Lochner* and *Dred Scott*: "The Notion of a Living Constitution," 54 *Texas Law Review* 693 (1976), 701–4.

70–1   Stone: *United States v. Carolene Products Co.*, 304 U.S. 144 (1938), 151–53.

71–2   New Deal cases: Peter Irons, *The New Deal Lawyers* (Princeton: Princeton University Press, 1993); *Schechter Poultry Co. v. United States*, 295 U.S. 495 (1935); *United States v. Butler*, 297 U.S. 1 (1936).

72   Butler and Stone: *Morehead v. Tipaldo*, 298 U.S. 587 (1936), 610–11, 632.

72–3   Brant: Irons, *The New Deal Lawyers*, 278.

73   Hughes in hotel case: *West Coast Hotel v. Parrish*, 300 U.S. 379 (1937), 399, 391.

73–4   Hughes in steel case: *National Labor Relations Board v. Jones & Laughlin Steel Corp.*, 301 U.S. 1 (1937), 41.

74   Wheat case: *Wickard v. Filburn*, 317 U.S. 111 (1942), 120.

75   Stone to Lehman: Alpheus T. Mason, *Harlan Fiske Stone: Pillar of the Law* (New York: Viking Press, 1956), 515.
Nazi rule in Austria: *New York Times*, 14 April 1938.
Goebbels: *Time*, 11 April 1938, 19.
Mississippi lynching: *New York Times*, 14 April 1937.
Bilbo: Robert L. Zangrando, *The NAACP Crusade Against Lynching, 1909–1950* (Philadelpia: Temple University Press, 1980), 150.
Barron case: *Barron v. Baltimore*, 32 U.S. 243 (1833), 250.

76   Gitlow case: *Gitlow v. New York*, 268 U.S. 652 (1925), 666–67.
Cardozo: *Palko v. Connecticut*, 302 U.S. 319 (1937), 325–27.

77   Gunther: "Forward: In Search of Evolving Doctrine on a Changing Court: A Model for a Newer Equal Protection," 86 *Harvard Law Review* 1 (1972), 8.
Bork: Robert H. Bork, *The Tempting of America: The Political Seduction of the Law* (New York: Free Press, 1989), 58–61.

77–8   Rehnquist: *Sugarman v. Dougall*, 413 U.S. 634 (1973), 655–57.

78   Bork: *The Tempting of America*, 60.

78–9   Flag salute cases: Peter Irons, *The Courage of Their Convictions: Sixteen Americans Who Fought Their Way to the Supreme Court* (New York: Free Press, 1988), 15–35.

79   Maris: *Gobitis v. Minersville School Dist.*, 21 F.Supp. 581 (E. Pa. 1937), 584–88.

79–80   Frankfurter: *Minersville School Dist. v. Gobitis*, 310 U.S. 586 (1940), 595–600.

80   Stone: *Minersville School Dist. v. Gobitis*, 601–7.

80–1   Reaction to Gobitis decision: Irons, *The Courage of Their Convictions*, 22–23.

81–2   Jackson: *West Virginia State Board of Education v. Barnette*, 319 U.S. 624 (1943), 630, 638–62.

82–3   Frankfurter: *West Virginia State Board of Education v. Barnette*, 646–48, 651–56, 661–67.

83–4   Japanese American internment: Peter Irons: *Justice at War: The Story of the Japanese American Internment Cases* (Berkeley: University of California Press, 1993), 3–74.

84   Stone: *Hirabayashi v. United States*, 320 U.S. 81 (1943), 96–105.

84–5   Black: *Korematsu v. United States*, 323 U.S. 214 (1944), 216–224.

85   Murphy: *Korematsu v. United States*, 323 U.S., 236–39.
       Black: Irons, *Justice at War*, 356.

85–6   Patel: *Korematsu v. United States*, 584 F.Supp. 1406 (N.D.Cal. 1984), 1417–20.

86   Smith Act: *U.S. Statutes at Large* 54 (1940), 673.
       Hobbs and McCormack: 86 *Congressional Record* 9031.

87   Dennis case: *Dennis v. United States*, 341 U.S. 494 (1951), 508, 542.

87–8   Little Rock case: Irons, *The Courage of Their Convictions*, 107–16; *Bates v. Little Rock*, 361 U.S. 516 (1960), 522.

88   Draft card case: 111 *Congressional Record* 19871–72; *United States v. O'Brien*, 391 U.S. 367 (1968), 381, 383–86.

88–9   Armband case: Irons, *The Courage of Their Convictions*, 233–52; *Tinker v. Des Moines*, 393 U.S. 503 (1969), 511, 522–25.

89–90 Swimming pool case: *Palmer v. Thompson*, 403 U.S. 217 (1971), 224–25.

90   Chinese laundry case: *Yick Wo v. Hopkins*, 118 U.S. 356 (1886), 373–74.
       Frankfurter: *Minersville School Dist. v. Gobitis*, 593.
       Stone: *Minersville School Dist. v. Gobitis*, 607.

CHAPTER 5

93   Burger: *Laird v. Tatum*, 408 U.S. 1 (1972), 2–3, 13.
       Douglas: *Laird v. Tatum*, 408 U.S., 28.
       Brennan: *Laird v. Tatum*, 408 U.S., 38–40.
       Rehnquist: *Congressional Record*, November 18, 1971, 42145–46.
       Quote about baseball case: John P. MacKenzie, "The Rehnquist Recusal," *Washington Monthly*, May 1974, 54–59.

94   Rehnquist on recusal motion: *Laird v. Tatum*, 409 U.S. 824 (1972), 825–26, 835.

94–5   Rehnquist: *Paul v. Davis*, 424 U.S. 693 (1976), 697, 699, 702.

95–6   Brennan: *Paul v. Davis*, 714, 721–22, 734–35.

96–7   Rizzo case: *COPPAR v. Rizzo*, 357 F.Supp. 1289 (E.D.Pa. 1973), 1291, 1298–99, 1320–22.

97–8   Rehnquist: *Rizzo v. Goode*, 423 U.S. 362 (1976), 365, 368, 371–73, 376–78.

98–9   Blackmun: *Rizzo v. Goode*, 384–87.

99–100 Rehnquist: *United States v. Salerno*, 481 U.S. 739 (1987), 741–43, 746–47.

100–101 Marshall: *United States v. Salerno*, 755, 762–67.

101–2   Rehnquist: *Bell v. Wolfish*, 441 U.S. 520 (1979), 533–35, 558–62.

102 Marshall: *Bell v. Wolfish*, 578.

102–3 Stevens: *Bell v. Wolfish*, 579–80, 584–87.

103–4 Carlson case: *Carlson v. Green*, 446 U.S. 14 (1980), 16.

104 Brennan in Bivens case: *Bivens v. Six Unknown Federal Narcotics Agents*, 403 U.S. 388 (1971), 392, 395.
Brennan: *Carlson v. Green*, 18, 22.

105 Rehnquist: *Carlson v. Green*, 32, 53.

105–6 Rehnquist: *Davidson v. Cannon*, 474 U.S. 344 (1986), 345–48.

106 Brennan: *Davidson v. Cannon*, 349.

106–8 Rehnquist: *DeShaney v. Winnebago County*, 489 U.S. 189 (1989), 191–94, 202–3, 195–96.

108–9 Brennan: *DeShaney v. Winnebago County*, 203–5, 208–12.

109–10 Rehnquist: *Cruzan v. Missouri Dept. of Health*, 497 U.S. 261 (1990), 266, 277–87.

111 Brennan: *Cruzan v. Missouri Dept. of Health*, 302, 321–30.

112 Nancy Cruzan's death: *New York Times*, 19 December 1990; 20 December; 27 December; Editorial, "After the Cruzan Case," *America*, 2 January 1991, 51.

CHAPTER 6

113 Brewer: *Church of the Holy Trinity v. United States*, 143 U.S. 457 (1892), 471.
San Diego cross case: *San Diego Voters' Guide*, 1992; La Jolla *Light*, 27 August 1992.

114 Religion statistics: *Statistical Abstract of the United States*, 1992, Tables 76–79.
Tocqueville: *Democracy in America* (New York: Oxford University Press, 1946), 232–33, 236–37.

115 Falwell and Buchanan: *New York Times*, 23 August 1992, national edition.
Puritan laws: George Dow, *Everyday Life in the Massachusetts Bay Colony*, 200, 102; *Church of the Holy Trinity v. United States*, 49.

116–17 Waite: *Reynolds v. United States*, 98 U.S. 145 (1878), 16–67.

118 Cantwell case: *Cantwell v. Connecticut*, 310 U.S. 296 (1940), 303–4.

119 Everson case: *Everson v. Board of Education*, 330 U.S. 1 (1947), 15–18.

119–20 Engel case: *Engel v. Vitale*, 370 U.S. 421 (1962), 422, 425.

120 Reaction to *Engel v. Vitale* decision: Bernard Schwartz, *Super Chief: Earl Warren and His Supreme Court* (New York: New York University Press, 1983), 441–42.
Clark: *Abington Township v. Schempp*, 374 U.S. 203 (1963), 213, 222–23.

121–2 Brennan: *Abington Township v. Schempp*, 231, 234, 303–4, 295, 241.

122 Burger: *Lemon v. Kurtzman*, 403 U.S. 602 (1971), 612–13.

122–3 Brennan: *Marsh v. Chambers*, 463 U.S. 783 (1983), 805–6, 821.

123 Rehnquist: *Cruz v. Beto*, 405 U.S. 319 (1972), 325; *Committee for Public Education v. Nyquist*, 413 U.S. 756 (1973), 813.

123–5 Rehnquist: *Wallace v. Jaffree*, 472 U.S. 38 (1985), 106, 92, 98, 107, 92, 107, 112, 110, 112–13, 99.

125–6 Powell: *Committee for Public Education v. Nyquist*, 760–61, 794.

126 Rehnquist: *Committee for Public Education v. Nyquist*, 805, 812–13.

126–7 Brennan: *Meek v. Pittenger*, 421 U.S. 349 (1975), 374; quoting Burger in *Lemon v. Kurtzman*, 622–23.

127 Rehnquist: *Meek v. Pittenger*, 395; quoting Douglas in *Zorach v. Clauson*, 343 U.S. 306 (1952), 313.

127–8 Brennan: *Grand Rapids School Dist. v. Ball*, 473 U.S. 373 (1985), 382, 379, 385.

128 Rehnquist: *Grand Rapids School Dist. v. Ball*, 401.

128–9 Brennan: *Aguilar v. Felton*, 473 U.S. 402 (1985), 414.

129 Rehnquist: *Aguilar v. Felton*, 421.
Reaction to *Grand Rapids School Dist. v. Ball* and *Aguilar v. Felton*, decisions: Edd Doerr, "Church and State," *The Humanist*, September–October 1985, 39; David Carlin, "Negative Liberty," *Commonweal*, September 1985, 455.

130 Rehnquist: *Stone v. Graham*, 449 U.S. 39 (1980), 40–41, 44–45.

130–1 Stevens: *Wallace v. Jaffree*, 41, 56–57.

131 Rehnquist: *Wallace v. Jaffree*, 92, 113.

131–2 Epperson case: *Epperson v. Arkansas*, 393 U.S. 97 (1968), 108.

132 Aguillard case: *Edwards v. Aguillard*, 482 U.S. 578 (1987), 592–93.
Brennan: *Edwards v. Aguillard*, 586–87, 593.

132–3 Scalia: *Edwards v. Aguillard*, 634–40.

133 Reaction to *Edwards v. Aguillard* decision: James Wall, "Supreme Court on 'Flat Souls'," *Christian Century*, 1–8 July 1987, 579; Nathan Glazer, *New Republic*, 21 October 1987, 17–18.

133–4 Kennedy: *Lee v. Weisman*, 112 S.Ct. 2649 (1992), 2661, 2665.

134 Scalia: *Lee v. Weisman*, 2679–86.
Burger: *Marsh v. Chambers*, 786–87, 792.

135 Brennan: *Marsh v. Chambers*, 796–800.

135–6 Burger: *Lynch v. Donnelly*, 465 U.S. 668 (1984), 671, 678–79, 683–85.

136 Brennan: *Lynch v. Donnelly*, 696–97, 725.

137 O'Connor: *Allegheny County v. ACLU*, 492 U.S. 573 (1989), 626, 635.
Brennan: *Allegheny County v. ACLU*, 639, 644.

137–8 Kennedy: *Allegheny County v. ACLU*, 657, 660–61, 664.

138 Fordice: *New York Times*, 18 November 1992, national edition.

139 Brennan: *Sherbert v. Verner*, 374 U.S. 398 (1963), 402–3.

139–40 Burger: *Thomas v. Review Board*, 450 U.S. 707 (1981), 717.

140 Rehnquist: *Thomas v. Review Board*, 722–23.
Brennan: *Hobbie v. Florida*, 480 U.S. 136 (1987), 143–44.

141 Rehnquist: *Goldman v. Weinberger*, 475 U.S. 503 (1986), 505–7.
Brennan: *Goldman v. Weinburger*, 513, 518, 524.

CHAPTER 7

143 Griswold: Peter Irons and Stephanie Guitton, eds., *May It Please the Court: The Most Significant Oral Arguments Made Before the Supreme Court Since 1955* (New York: New Press, 1993), p. 175.

144 Brennan: *New York Times v. United States*, 403 U.S. 713 (1971), 726.
Black: *Tinker v. Des Moines*, 393 U.S. 503 (1969), 515–26.
Holmes: *Schenck v. United States*, 249 U.S. 47 (1919), 52.

144–5 Ethredge case: Macon, Georgia, *Telegraph*, 24 March 1992; Denver *Post*, 27 April 1992. Accounts of this and the following cases are based on articles from the ACLU Press Clips, compiled by the ACLU Education Department. I am grateful to Loren Seigel for sending them to me.

145 Riggi case: Wheeling, West Virginia, *Intelligencer*, 3 October 1992.

145–6 Jones case: Idaho *Statesman*, 7 November 1992.

146 Roth case: Minneapolis *Star Tribune*, 31 October 1992.

146–7 Cooper case: Marysville, California, *Appeal-Democrat*, 22 January 1992.

147 Hines case: Logansport, Indiana, *Tribune*, 30 September 1992.
Hicks: Dallas *Morning News*, 5 March 1992.

147–8 English sedition law: Leonard Levy, *Freedom of Speech and Press in Early American History* (New York: Harper & Row, 1963), 10–11.

148 Zenger case: Nat Hentoff, *The First Freedom: The Tumultuous History of Free Speech in America* (New York: Delacorte, 1980), 63–68.
Wilson: Levy, *Freedom of Speech*, 202.

148–9 Sedition Act: Hentoff, *The First Freedom*, 82.

149–50 Holmes: *Schenck v. United States*, 49–52.

150 Holmes: *Abrams v. United States*, 250 U.S. 616 (1919), 629–30.

151 Sanford: *Gitlow v. New York*, 268 U.S. 652 (1925), 666, 669.
Smith Act: *Dunne v. United States*, 320 U.S. 790 (1943); Francis Biddle, *In Brief Authority* (Garden City, NY: Doubleday, 1962), 151–52.

152 Vinson: *Dennis v. United States*, 341 U.S. 494 (1951), 509–10.
Harlan: *Yates v. United States*, 354 U.S. 298 (1957), 319–20.

152–3 Ku Klux Klan case: *Brandenberg v. Ohio*, 395 U.S. 444 (1969), 445–47.

153 Sound amplifier case: *Kovacs v. Cooper*, 36 U.S. 77 (1949).
Skokie case: David Hamlin, *The Nazi-Skokie Conflict: A Civil Liberties Battle* (Boston: Beacon Press, 1981).

154 Warren: *United States v. O'Brien*, 391 U.S. 367 (1968), 376–81.
Fortas: *Tinker v. Des Moines*, 505–6.

154–5 Murphy: *Chaplinsky v. New Hampshire*, 315 U.S. 568 (1942), 569–72.

155–6 Brennan: *New York Times v. Sullivan*, 376 U.S. 254 (1964), 270–76; Anthony Lewis, *Make No Law: The Sullivan Case and the First Amendment* (New York: Random House, 1991).

156–7 Rehnquist: *Rosenfeld v. New Jersey*, 408 U.S. 901 (1972), 909.

157 Burger: *Rosenfeld v. New Jersey*, 909.
Rehnquist: *Papish v. Board of Curators*, 410 U.S. 667 (1973), 670, 675–76.

157–8 Brennan: *Lewis v. City of New Orleans*, 415 U.S. 130 (1974), 131–34.

158 Blackmun: *Lewis v. City of New Orleans*, 140.

158–9 Rehnquist: *Parker v. Levy*, 417 U.S. 733 (1974), 743, 756–58.

159 Stewart: *Parker v. Levy*, 782–83.

159–60   Powell: *Smith v. Goguen*, 415 U.S. 56 (1974), 572–76.

160   Rehnquist: *Smith v.Goguen*, 594–604.

161   Rehnquist: *Spence v. Washington*, 418 U.S. 405 (1974), 417–23.

162–3   Brennan: *Texas v. Johnson*, 491 U.S. 397 (1989), 409, 418–19, 414.

163   Kennedy: *Texas v. Johnson*, 420–21.

163–4   Rehnquist: David Savage, *Turning Right: The Making of the Rehnquist Supreme Court* (New York: John Wiley & Sons, 1992), 283; *Texas*, 434, 422–27, 430–31, 435.

164   Mitchell and Dole: *Congressional Record*, June 22, 1989, S7185–89.

164–5   Kerrey: *Congressional Record*, August 1, 1989, E2763.

165   Flag Protection Law: *United States v. Eichman*, 496 U.S. 310 (1990).
Rehnquist: Savage, *Turning Right*, 327.

CHAPTER 8

166   Jefferson: Nat Hentoff, *The First Freedom: The Tumultuous History of Free Speech in America* (New York: Delacorte, 1980), 297–98.
Prosecutor in Roth case: Petitioner's certiorari brief, 65, *Roth v. United States*, 354 U.S. 476 (1957).

167   Kefauver: *Congressional Record*, June 28, 1956, 11174.

167–8   Brennan: *Roth v. United States*, 484–87, 489–92.

168   Harlan: *Roth v. United States*, 496–98.
Douglas: *Roth v. United States*, 512–14.

168–9   Brennan: *Jacobellis v. Ohio*, 378 U.S. 184, 188, 191–96 (1964); Bob Woodward and Scott Armstrong, *The Brethren* (New York: Simon and Schuster, 1980), 194.

169–70   Stewart: *Jacobellis v. Ohio*, 197.

170   Waggoner: *Congressional Record*, June 23, 1964, 14271.
Brennan: *Memoirs v. Massachusetts*, 383 U.S. 413 (1966), 415–20.

170–1   Brennan: *Ginzburg v. United States*, 383 U.S. 463 (1966), 466–76.

171   Black: *Ginzburg v. United States*, 476.
Nixon: *Public Papers of the Presidents*, 1969, 796.

171–2   Rehnquist: *California v. LaRue*, 409 U.S. 109 (1972), 111–18.

172   Brennan: *California v. LaRue*, 123.
Burger: *Miller v. California*, 413 U.S. 14 (1973), 24–25, 30–32.

173   Rehnquist: *Jenkins v. Georgia*, 418 U.S. 153 (1974), 55–65.

173–4   Rehnquist: *Hamling v. United States*, 418 U.S. 87 (1974), 104, 129.

174   Brennan: *Hamling v. United States*, 144, 149–51.

175   Blackmun: *Southeastern Promotions v. Conrad*, 420 U.S. 54 (1975), 549, 552.
Rehnquist: *Southeastern Promotions v. Conrad*, 572–73.

175–6   Rehnquist: *Renton v. Playtime Theaters*, 475 U.S. 41 (1986), 44, 50–53.

176   Brennan: *Renton v. Playtime Theaters*, 57–60.

177   Tocqueville, *Democracy in America* (New York: Oxford University Press, 1946), 118.

Brennan: *New York Times v. Sullivan*, 273.

Powell: *Gertz v. Welch*, 418 U.S. 323 (1974), 351–52.

177–8   Rehnquist: *Time v. Firestone*, 424 U.S. 448 (1976), 450–58.

178   Brennan: *Time v. Firestone*, 476–81.

178–9   Burger: *Richmond Newspapers v. Virginia*, 448 U.S. 555 (1980), 573.

179   Brennan: *Richmond Newspapers v. Virginia*, 584–85.

Rehnquist: *Richmond Newspapers v. Virginia*, 605–06.

180–1   Brennan: *Island Trees School Dist. v. Pico*, 457 U.S. 853 (1982), 859, 863–64, 867–68, 872–75.

181   Powell: *Island Trees School Dist. v. Pico*, 897–903.

Rehnquist: *Island Trees School Dist. v. Pico*, 904–9, 915.

182–3   White: *Hazelwood School Dist. v. Kuhlmeier*, 484 U.S. 260 (1988), 262–65, 269–73.

183–4   Brennan: *Hazelwood School Dist. v. Kuhlmeier*, 277–78, 281–85, 291.

184   Rehnquist: *Hustler Magazine v. Falwell*, 485 U.S. 46 (1988), 54; Rodney A. Smolla, *Jerry Falwell v. Larry Flynt: The First Amendment on Trial* (New York: St. Martin's Press, 1988).

185–6   Brennan: *Carey v. Brown*, 447 U.S. 455 (1980), 459–65.

186   Rehnquist: *Carey v. Brown*, 475–76.

186–7   O'Connor: *Frisby v. Schultz*, 487 U.S. 474 (1988), 476–79, 484–88.

187   Brennan: *Frisby v. Schultz*, 492–98.

187–8   O'Connor: *Boos v. Barry*, 485 U.S. 312 (1988), 315–19.

188   Brennan: *Boos v. Barry*, 334–38.

Rehnquist: *Boos v. Barry*, 338–39.

CHAPTER 9

189   Warren: *Miranda v. Arizona*, 384 U.S. 436 (1966), 457.

189–90   Nixon: *New York Times*, 9 August 1968.

190   Warren: *Miranda v. Arizona*, 457.

191   Warren: *Terry v. Ohio*, 392 U.S. 1 (1968), 23–31.

191–2   Brennan on Terry case: Bernard Schwartz, *Super Chief: Earl Warren and His Supreme Court* (New York: New York University Press, 1983), 692–93.

192   Brennan: *Florida v. Royer*, 460 U.S. 491 (1983), 513.

Rehnquist: *Cady v. Dombrowski*, 413 U.S. 433 (1973), 439.

White: *Florida v. Royer*, 494–95, 507.

193   Brennan: *Florida v. Royer*, 510–12.

Rehnquist: *Florida v. Royer*, 519–30.

193–4   Clark: *Mapp v. Ohio*, 367 U.S. 643 (1961), 655, 659.

194   Reagan: *Public Papers of the Presidents*, 1981, 842.

Rehnquist: *Robbins v. California*, 453 U.S. 420 (1981), 437.

194–5   Rehnquist: *Cady v. Dombrowski*, 435–39, 449.

195   Brennan: *Cady v. Dombrowski*, 450–54.

Brennan: *New York v. Belton*, 453 U.S. 454 (1981), 464–70.

195–6   Rehnquist: *Robbins v. California*, 438–43; *United States v. Peltier*, 422 U.S. 531 (1975), 542.

196   Brennan: *United States v. Peltier*, 551–62.

197   Harlan: *Hurtado v. California*, 110 U.S. 516 (1884), 548.
Rehnquist: *Cupp v. Naughton*, 414 U.S. 141 (1973), 142–49.

197–8   Brennan: *Cupp v. Naughton*, 150–55.

198   Stewart: *Carter v. Kentucky*, 450 U.S. 288 (1981), 289–94, 304.
Rehnquist: *Carter v. Kentucky*, 308–10.

198–9   Marshall: *Ake v. Oklahoma*, 470 U.S. 68 (1985), 70–73, 83.

199   Rehnquist: *Ake v. Oklahoma*, 88–92.

200   Powell: *Chambers v. Mississippi*, 410 U.S. 284 (1973), 285–90, 294–302.

200–1   Rehnquist: *Chambers v. Mississippi*, 308–13.

201–2   Rehnquist: *Wainwright v. Sykes*, 433 U.S. 72 (1977), 74–77, 81, 86–91.

202–3   Brennan: *Wainwright v. Sykes*, 100, 113–18.

204   Black: *Gideon v. Wainwright*, 372 U.S. 335 (1963), 344.

204–5   Rehnquist: *Scott v. Illinois*, 440 U.S. 367 (1979), 373.

205   Brennan: *Scott v. Illinois*, 375–78, 380, 388–89.

205–6   Brennan: *Evitts v. Lucey*, 469 U.S. 387 (1985), 389–92, 39.

206   Rehnquist: *Evitts v. Lucey*, 406–11.

206–7   Rehnquist: *United States v. MacCollum*, 426 U.S. 317 (1976), 34–28.

207   Brennan: *United States v. MacCollum*, 332–34.

208   Rehnquist: *Ross v. Moffitt*, 417 U.S. 600 (1974), 603–5, 610–11, 615–16.
Douglas: *Ross v. Moffitt*, 620–21.

209–10   Rehnquist: *Rummel v. Estelle*, 445 U.S. 263 (1980), 272–76; quote from *Weems v. United States*, 217 U.S. 349 (1910), 366.

210–11   Powell: *Rummel v. Estelle*, 288, 307.

211   Powell: *Hutto v. Davis*, 454 U.S. 370 (1982), 380.
Brennan: *Hutto v. Davis*, 381–88.

CHAPTER 10

213   Colonial history: George Dow, *Everyday Life in the Massachusetts Bay Colony*, 199–210.

214   Reagan: *Public Papers of the Presidents*, 1988, 1203.
Bush: *Public Papers of the Presidents*, 1991, 582.
Clinton: *New York Times*, 22 February 1992, national edition.

215   Amsterdam: Philip B. Kurland and Gerhard Casper, eds., *Landmark Briefs and Arguments of the Supreme Court*, 73:841, 872.

215–16   White: Kurland and Casper, *Landmark Briefs*, 73:848–49.

216   Facts of case: *Furman v. Georgia*, 408 U.S. 238 (1972), 239–40.
Blackmun: *Furman v. Georgia*, 405.
Stewart: *Furman v. Georgia*, 309–10.

216–17   Brennan: *Furman v. Georgia*, 257–69.

217   Warren: *Trop v. Dulles*, 356 U.S. 86 (1958), 87–89, 100–101.

217–19   Brennan: *Furman v. Georgia*, 270–82.

219   Brennan on Stephens case: *Glass v. Georgia*, 471 U.S. 1080 (1984), 1087–92.
Brennan: *Furman v. Georgia*, 291–305.
Criticism of Brennan: Leonard Levy, *Original Intent and the Framers' Constitution* (New York: Macmillan Publishing Co., 1988), 372–73.

219–20   Brennan: "The Constitution of the United States: Contemporary Ratification," 27 *South Texas Law Review* 433 (1986), 443–44.

220–1   Rehnquist: *Furman v. Georgia*, 466–668.

221   Nixon: *Public Papers of the Presidents*, 1972, 214–16.

222–4   Stewart: *Gregg v. Georgia*, 428 U.S. 153 (1976), 173–75, 179–82, 187–207.

224   Brennan: *Gregg v. Georgia*, 229–31; citing L. S. Tao, "Beyond *Furman v. Georgia*: The Need for a Morally Based Decision on Capital Punishment," 51 *Notre Dame Lawyer* 722 (1976), 736.
White: *Gregg v. Georgia*, 222–26.

225   Stewart: *Woodson v. North Carolina*, 428 U.S. 280 (1976), 288–93.

225–6   Rehnquist: *Woodson v. North Carolina*, 308–12, 316–24.

227   Rehnquist: *Roberts v. Louisiana*, 431 U.S. 633 (1977), 636–37, 642–49.

227–8   White: *Coker v. Georgia*, 433 U.S. 584 (1977), 596–98.

228   Burger: *Coker v. Georgia*, 612, 621.

228–9   Burger: *Lockett v. Ohio*, 438 U.S. 586 (1978), 589–94, 604–5.

229   Rehnquist: *Lockett v. Ohio*, 628–29, 633.

230   White: *Pulley v. Harris*, 465 U.S. 37 (1984), 38–39, 44–45, 51–55.

231   Brennan: *Pulley v. Harris*, 60–61, 64–67.

232   Harris execution: San Francisco *Chronicle*, April 22, 1992, 1, 8.

233   Boger and the Baldus study: David Savage, *Turning Right: The Making of the Rehnquist Supreme Court* (New York: John J. Wiley & Sons, 1992), 82–84.

233–4   Forrester: *McCleskey v. Zant*, 580 F.Supp. 338 (N.D.Ga. 1984), 350–80.

234   Boger and law clerk: Savage, *Turning Right*, 83, 95.

235   Powell: *McCleskey v. Kemp*, 481 U.S. 279 (1987), 292–93, 297, 313.

235–7   Brennan: *McCleskey v. Kemp*, 345, 321, 328–30, 344, 331, 322–23, 325.

237–8   McCleskey execution and Marshall: *New York Times*, 24 September 1991; 26 September 1991.

238   Scalia: *Stanford v. Kentucky*, 492 U.S. 361 (1989), 365–67, 370–77.

239   Brennan: *Stanford v. Kentucky*, 384–90.
Rehnquist: *Butler v. McKellar*, 494 U.S. 407 (1990), 409–10.
Brennan: *Butler v. McKellar*, 417, 432.

240   Brennan: *Boggs v. Muncy*, 497 U.S. 1043 (1990); *New York Times*, 20 July 1990.
McMillian: *New York Times*, 1 March 1993, national edition.

CHAPTER 11

241   Tocqueville: *Democracy in America* (Oxford ed.), 1, 555, 558, 263–65.

242   *Civil Rights Cases*, 109 U.S. 3 (1883), 25.

242–3   Brown: *Plessy v. Ferguson*, 163 U.S. 537 (1896), 551–52.

243–4   Warren: *Brown v. Board of Education*, 347 U.S. 483 (1954), 492, 494–95.

244   Matthews: *Yick Wo v. Hopkins*, 118 U.S. 356 (1886), 374, 369.

244–5   Brennan: *Plyler v. Doe*, 457 U.S. 202 (1982), 213–17.

245   Stone: *United States v. Carolene Products*, 304 U.S. 144 (1938), 153, fn. 4.
Brennan: *Plyler v. Doe*, 216–17, 222–23.

246   Brennan: "The Role of the Court," in Stephen J. Friedman, ed., *An Affair with Freedom: A Collection of Opinions and Speeches* (New York: Atheneum, 1967), 329.
Rehnquist: *Weber v. Aetna Casualty & Surety Co.*, 406 U.S. 164 (1972), 179–81.

246–7   Rehnquist: *Sugarman v. Dougall*, 413 U.S. 634 (1973), 649–50.

247   Rehnquist: *Trimble v. Gordon*, 430 U.S. 762 (1977), 777–79.

248   Rehnquist: Donald Boles, *Mr. Justice Rehnquist: Judicial Activist, The Early Years* (Ames, Ia.: Iowa State University Press, 1987), 90–94.

248–9   Burger: *Swann v. Charlotte-Mecklenburg Board of Education*, 402 U.S. 1 (1971), 15, 26.

249   Nixon: *Public Papers of the Presidents*, 1972, 425–26.

250   Brennan: *Keyes v. School Dist. No. 1*, 413 U.S. 189 (1973), 191–93, 199–203, 211–14.

250–1   Rehnquist: *Keyes v. School Dist. No. 1*, 254–55, 258.

251   Green case: *Green v. School Board*, 391 U.S. 430 (1968), 437–38.
Rehnquist: *Keyes v. School Dist. No. 1*, 258.
Brennan: *Keyes v. School Dist. No. 1*, 200–201.
Nixon: *Public Papers of the Presidents*, 1973, 773.

251–2   White: *Columbus Board of Education v. Penick*, 443 U.S. 449 (1979), 452, 459.

252   Rehnquist: *Columbus Board of Education v. Penick*, 489, 513, 492, 501, 503, 525.
White: *Columbus Board of Education v. Penick*, 457.
Rehnquist: *Columbus Board of Education v. Penick*, 525.

252–3   Rehnquist: *Board of Education of Oklahoma City v. Dowell*, 111 S.Ct. 630 (1991), 633–35, 637.

253–4   Marshall: *Board of Education of Oklahoma City v. Dowell*, 639–42.

254   Rogers: *Brown v. Board of Education*, 671 F.Supp. 1290 (D.Kan. 1987), 1311.
Seymour: *Brown v. Board of Education*, 892 F.2d 851 (10th Cir. 1989), 886, 862.

255   Rehnquist on Marshall
Rehnquist: *Arizona Republic*, 24 June 1964.

255–6   Moose Lodge case: *Irvis v. Scott*, 318 F.Supp. 1246 (E.D.Pa. 1970), 1247.

256   Shelley case: *Shelley v. Kraemer*, 334 U.S. 1 (1948).
Rehnquist and restrictive deeds: Donald Boles, *Mr. Justice Rehnquist: Judicial*

Activist, The Early Years (Ames, Ia.: Iowa State University Press, 1987), 87.

Rehnquist: *Moose Lodge No. 107 v. Irvis*, 407 U.S. 163 (1972), 172–79.

257 Moose Lodge case: *New York Times*, 20 August 1972; 12 December 1972.

257–8 Brennan: *DeFunis v. Odegard*, 416 U.S. 312 (1974), 350.

258–9 Powell: *Regents v. Bakke*, 438 U.S. 265 (1978), 291, 295.

259 Brennan: *Regents v. Bakke*, 325.

Comment on Brennan: Bernard Schwartz, *The Ascent of Pragmatism: The Burger Court in Action* (Reading, Mass.: Addison-Wesley, 1989), 279–80.

259–60 Brennan: *Steelworkers v. Weber*, 443 U.S. 193 (1979), 200–202, 209.

260 Carter: *Public Papers of the Presidents*, 1979, 847.

261 Burger: *Steelworkers v. Weber*, 218–19.

261–2 Rehnquist: *Steelworkers v. Weber*, 219–22, 226–52.

262 Reagan: *Public Papers of the Presidents*, 1986, 207.

Brennan: *Firefighters v. Cleveland*, 478 U.S. 501 (1986), 516.

Rehnquist: *Firefighters v. Cleveland*, 541–42.

263 Brennan: *United States v. Paradise*, 480 U.S. 149 (1987), 154, 166–86.

O'Connor: *United States v. Paradise*, 196–200.

264 Reynolds: David Savage, *Turning Right: The Making of the Rehnquist Supreme Court* (New York: John Wiley, 1992), 172–82.

Rehnquist: *Martin v. Wilks*, 490 U.S. 755 (1989), 759–69.

Stevens: *Martin v. Wilks*, 769, 791–92.

265 White: *Wards Cove Packing Co. v. Atonio*, 490 U.S. 642 (1989), 653–61.

265–6 Blackmun: *Wards Cove Packing Co. v. Atonio*, 661–62.

266 Civil Rights Act of 1991: *Congressional Quarterly Almanac*, 1991, 251–61.

CHAPTER 12

267 Rehnquist: *Sugarman v. Dougall*, 413 U.S. 634 (1973), 649–50.

Brennan: *Plyler v. Doe*, 457 U.S. 202 (1982), 213.

268 Sutherland: *Ozawa v. United States*, 260 U.S. 178 (1922), 189.

Beck: *Ozawa v. United States*, 187–88.

269 Sutherland: *Ozawa v. United States*, 194–98.

Immigration quote: Milton Konvitz, *The Alien and the Asiatic in American Law* (Ithaca, NY: Cornell University Press, 1946), 1.

270 Nixon: *Public Papers of the Presidents*, 1972, 695.

Ryan: *Congressional Record*, May 9, 1973, 15106.

Blackmun: *Graham v. Richardson*, 403 U.S. 365 (1971), 366.

271 Arizona case: *Truax v. Raich*, 239 U.S. 33 (1915), 39–40.

Cardozo: *People v. Crane*, 108 N.E. 427 (1915), 429–30.

Blackmun: *Graham v. Richardson*, 371–74.

272 Blackmun: *Sugarman v. Dougall*, 641–43.

272–3 Rehnquist: *Sugarman v. Dougall*, 651–64.

274 Stevens: *Hampton v. Mow Sun Wong*, 426 U.S. 88 (1976), 102–3, 107, 116–17.

274–5   Rehnquist: *Hampton v. Mow Sun Wong*, 118–24.

275   Blackmun: *Nyquist v. Mauclet*, 432 U.S. 1 (1977), 5, 7, 12.

275–6   Rehnquist: *Nyquist v. Mauclet*, 17–18, 21.

276   Burger: *Foley v. Connelie*, 435 U.S. 291 (1978), 294.

Blackmun: *Sugarman v. Dougall*, 648, 643.

Burger in conference: Bernard Schwartz, *The Ascent of Pragmatism: The Burger Court in Action* (Reading, Mass.: Addison-Wesley, 1989), 235.

276–7   Burger: *Foley v. Connelie*, 296–97.

277   Blackmun: *Foley v. Connelie*, 302.

Stevens: *Foley v. Connelie*, 311.

Powell: *Ambach v. Norwick*, 441 U.S. 68 (1979), 74–79.

277–8   Blackmun: *Ambach v. Norwick*, 82.

278   White: *Cabell v. Chavez-Salido*, 454 U.S. 432 (1982), 436, 439, 445.

278–9   Blackmun: *Cabell v. Chavez-Salido*, 448–49, 462–63.

279–81   Brennan: *Plyler v. Doe*, 217–23, 230.

281   Powell: *Plyler v. Doe*, 236–38.

281–2   Burger: *Plyler v. Doe*, 242–45.

282   Powell: *Moore v. East Cleveland*, 431 U.S. 494 (1977), 503–4.

282–3   Brennan: *Moore v. East Cleveland*, 507–8.

283   Stewart: *Moore v. East Cleveland*, 539.

Douglas: *Levy v. Louisiana*, 391 U.S. 68 (1968), 71.

284   Rehnquist: *Weber v. Aetna Casualty & Surety Co.*, 406 U.S. 164 (1972), 179–80, 183–85.

Rehnquist: *New Jersey Welfare Rights Org. v. Cahill*, 411 U.S. 619 (1973), 621–22.

284–5   Rehnquist: *United States Dept. of Agriculture v. Moreno*, 413 U.S. 528 (1973), 546.

285   Brennan: *Shapiro v. Thompson*, 394 U.S. 618 (1969), 627.

Maryland case: *Dandridge v. Williams*, 397 U.S. 471 (1970), 485.

286   Rehnquist: *Jefferson v. Hackney*, 406 U.S. 535 (1972), 546–49.

286–7   Marshall: *Jefferson v. Hackney*, 575.

287–8   Rodriguez case: Peter Irons, *The Courage of Their Convictions: Sixteen Americans Who Fought Their Way to the Supreme Court* (New York: Free Press, 1988), 283–93.

288–9   Powell: *San Antonio Independent School Dist. v. Rodriguez*, 411 U.S. 1 (1973), 17, 19–24, 33–37.

289   Rodriguez: Irons, *The Courage of Their Convictions*, 299, 302.

289–90   Marshall: *San Antonio v. Rodriguez*, 98, 111, 102–3.

290   Brennan: *San Antonio v. Rodriguez*, 62–63.

CHAPTER 13

292   Carpenter: *Bradwell v. State*, 83 U.S. 130 (1873), 136.

Slaughterhouse majority: *Slaughterhouse Cases*, 83 U.S. 36 (1873), 81.

292–3   Bradley dissent: *Slaughterhouse Cases*, 123.

293   Bradley concurrence: *Bradwell v. State*, 141.

294 Brewer: *Muller v. Oregon*, 208 U.S. 412 (1908), 421–22.
ERA history: Mary Frances Berry, *Why ERA Failed: Politics, Women's Rights, and the Amending Process of the Constitution* (Bloomington, Ind.: University of Indiana Press, 1986), 63.

295 Burger: *Reed v. Reed*, 404 U.S. 71 (1971), 76–77.

296 Rives: *Frontiero v. Laird*, 341 F.Supp. 201 (M.D.Ala. 1972), 206–9.

297 White and Powell to Brennan: Bernard Schwartz, *The Ascent of Pragmatism: The Burger Court in Action* (Reading, Mass.: Addison-Wesley, 1989), 222–25.

297–8 Brennan: *Frontiero v. Richardson*, 411 U.S. 677 (1973), 684–86.

298 Powell: *Frontiero v. Richardson*, 691.
Rehnquist: *Frontiero v. Richardson*, 691.

299 Brennan: *Califano v. Goldfarb*, 430 U.S. 199 (1977), 215–17.
Stevens: *Califano v. Goldfarb*, 223.
Rehnquist: *Califano v. Goldfarb*, 224–25, 242.

300 Blackmun: *Roe v. Wade*, 410 U.S. 113 (1973), 113.
Griswold arguments: Philip B. Kurland and Gerhard Casper, eds., *Landmark Briefs and Arguments of the Supreme Court*, 61:430, 423.

300–1 Douglas: *Griswold v. Connecticut*, 381 U.S. 479 (1965), 484–86.

301 Goldberg: *Griswold v. Connecticut*, 488, 499.

301–2 Brennan: *Eisenstadt v. Baird*, 405 U.S. 438 (1972), 440–50, 453.

303 Blackmun: *Roe v. Wade*, 129–64.

304 Rehnquist: *Roe v. Wade*, 172–73.
ERA history: Berry, *Why ERA Failed*, 67.

304–5 LaFleur case: Peter Irons, *The Courage of Their Convictions: Sixteen Americans Who Fought Their Way to the Supreme Court* (New York: Free Press, 1988), 307–9, 311–12.

305–6 Stewart: *Cleveland v. LaFleur*, 414 U.S. 32 (1974), 639–40, 648.

306 Rehnquist: *Cleveland v. LaFleur*, 657–70.

306–7 LaFleur: Irons, *The Courage of Their Convictions*, 320.

307 Stewart: *Geduldig v. Aiello*, 417 U.S. 484 (1974), 495–97.

307–8 Brennan: *Geduldig v. Aiello*, 501.

308 Stewart: *Geduldig v. Aiello*, 494–97.
Brennan: *Geduldig v. Aiello*, 503–4.

308–9 Rehnquist: *General Electric v. Gilbert*, 429 U.S. 125 (1976), 136.

309 Brennan: *General Electric v. Gilbert*, 148–50, 159–60.

310–11 Brennan: *Craig v. Boren*, 429 U.S. 190 (1976), 191–99, 202–4.

311 Rehnquist: *Craig v. Boren*, 217–19, 225–27.

311–13 Rehnquist: *Michael M. v. Superior Court*, 450 U.S. 464 (1981), 468–73.

313 Blackmun to Brennan: Schwartz, *The Ascent of Pragmatism*, 231.
Brennan: *Michael M. v. Superior Court*, 489.

314–15 Stewart: *Harris v. MacRae*, 448 U.S. 297 (1980), 312–15.

315–16 Brennan: *Harris v. MacRae*, 329–30, 325, 330–32.

317 Rehnquist in Pennsylvania case: *Thornburgh v. American College of Obstetricians and Gynecologists*, 476 U.S. 474 (1986), 788 (joining White's dissent).

Rehnquist: *Webster v. Reproductive Health Services*, 492 U.S. 460 (1989), 509.

317-18   Blackmun: *Webster v. Reproductive Health Services*, 538, 557-60.

318-19   Starr: Philip B. Kurland and Gerhard Casper, eds., *Landmark Briefs and Arguments of the Supreme Court*, 1991 Term Supplement, 1214, 1226.

319   Greenhouse article: *New York Times*, 2 June 1992.
Casey decision: 60 *U.S. Law Week* 4817.

319-20   Blackmun: 60 *U.S. Law Week* 4826, 4820.

320   Rehnquist: 60 *U.S. Law Week* 4826.

CHAPTER 14

321   Brennan: David Savage, *Turning Right: The Making of the Rehnquist Supreme Court* (New York: John J. Wiley & Sons, 1992), 348-49.
Bush: *Public Papers of the Presidents*, 1990, 1046.

322   Rehnquist: *Journal of Supreme Court History*, 1991, 1-2.

323   Tribe: "Architect of the Bill of Rights," ABA *Journal*, February 1991, 47-48.

323-4   Fiss: "A Life Lived Twice," 100 *Yale Law Journal* (1991), 1117, 1119, 1128.

324   Seitz: *Judicature*, February-March 1991, 243.

324-6   Michelman: "A Tribute to Justice William J. Brennan, Jr.," 104 *Harvard Law Review* (1990), 22-23, 25-27, 31-32.

326-7   Posner: "Tribute to Brennan," 13-15.

327   Markman and Regnery: "The Mind of Justice Brennan: A 25-Year Tribute," *National Review*, 18 May 1984, 30-38.

328   Times headline: *New York Times*, 13 September 1986, A1.
Reynolds: "Seeking Equal Liberty in an Egalitarian Age," 52 *Missouri Law Review* (1987), 586-92.

329-30   Graglia: "How the Constitution Disappeared," *Commentary*, February 1986, 19-24.

330   Buckley: "The Oligarch," *National Review*, 20 August 1990, 12.

331   Giuffra: "The Rehnquist Court," 22 *Toledo Law Review* (Spring 1991), 522.
Statistics on Rehnquist: Riggs and Profitt, "The Judicial Philosophy of Justice Rehnquist," 16 *Akron Law Review* 555 (Spring 1983), 601-4.

321-2   Fiss and Krauthammer: "The Rehnquist Court," *New Republic*, 10 March 1982, 14.

333   Justice: "A Relativistic Constitution," 52 *University of Colorado Law Review* 18 (1980), 21, 24.
Rehnquist on positive law: "The Notion of a Living Constitution," 54 *Texas Law Review* 693 (1976), 703-4.

333-4   Holmes: *Lochner v. New York*, 198 U.S. 45 (1905), 74-76.

334   Rehnquist on abortion: *Roe v. Wade*, 410 U.S. 113 (1973), 172-73.

334-5   Justice: "A Relativistic Constitution," 26-28.

336   Bush: *Public Papers of the Presidents*, 1990, 1047.
Rehnquist: Donald Boles, *Mr. Justice Rehnquist: Judicial Activist, The Early Years* (Ames, Ia.: Iowa State University Press, 1987), 61-62.

337   Fiss: "A Life Lived Twice," 1188.

Table of Cases

Abington Township v. Schempp, 374 U.S. 203 (1963)

Abrams v. United States, 250 U.S. 616 (1919)

Adams Theater Co. v. Keenan, 96 A.2d 519 (N.J. 1953)

Aguilar v. Felton, 473 U.S. 402 (1985)

Ake v. Oklahoma, 470 U.S. 68 (1985)

Allegheny County v. ACLU, 492 U.S. 73 (1989)

Ambach v. Norwick, 441 U.S. 68 (1979)

Barron v. Baltimore, 32 U.S. 243 (1833)

Bates v. Little Rock, 361 U.S. 516 (1960)

Beauharnais v. Illinois, 343 U.S. 250 (1952)

Bell v. Wolfish, 441 U.S. 520 (1979)

Bivens v. Six Unknown Federal Narcotics Agents, 403 U.S. 388 (1971)

Board of Education of Oklahoma City v. Dowell, 111 S.Ct. 630 (1991)

Boggs v. Muncy, 497 U.S. 1043 (1990)

Boos v. Barry, 485 U.S. 312 (1988)

Bradwell v. State, 83 U.S. 130 (1873)

Brandenberg v. Ohio, 395 U.S. 444 (1969)

Brown v. Board of Education, 374 U.S. 483 (1954); *Brown v. Board of Education*, 671 F.Supp. 1290 (D.Kan. 1987); *Brown v. Board of Education*, 892 F.2d 851 (10th Cir. 1989)

Butler v. McKellar, 494 U.S. 407 (1990)

Cabell v. Chavez-Salido, 454 U.S. 432 (1982)

Cady v. Dombrowski, 413 U.S. 433 (1973)

Califano v. Goldfarb, 430 U.S. 199 (1977)

California v. LaRue, 409 U.S. 109 (1972)

Cantwell v. Connecticut, 310 U.S. 296 (1940)

Carey v. Brown, 477 U.S. 455 (1980)

Carlson v. Green, 466 U.S. 14 (1980)

Carter v. Kentucky, 450 U.S. 288 (1981)

Chambers v. Mississippi, 410 U.S. 284 (1973)

Chaplinsky v. New Hampshire, 315 U.S. 568 (1942)

Church of the Holy Trinity v. United States, 143 U.S. 457 (1892)

Civil Rights Cases, 109 U.S. 3 (1883)

Cleveland v. LaFleur, 414 U.S. 32 (1974)

Coker v. Georgia, 433 U.S. 584 (1977)

Columbus Board of Education v. Penick, 443 U.S. 449 (1979)

Committee for Public Education v. Nyquist, 413 U.S. 756 (1973)

Craig v. Boren, 429 U.S. 190 (1976)

Cruz v. Beto, 405 U.S. 319 (1972)

Cruzan v. Missouri Department of Health, 497 U.S. 261 (1990)

Cupp v. Naughton, 414 U.S. 141 (1973)

Dandridge v. Williams, 397 U.S. 471 (1970)

Davidson v. Cannon, 474 U.S. 344 (1986)

DeFunis v. Odegard, 416 U.S. 312 (1974)

Dennis v. United States, 341 U.S. 494 (1951)

DeShaney v. Winnebago County, 489 U.S. 189 (1989)

Dred Scott v. Sandford, 60 U.S. 393 (1857)

Dunne v. United States, 320 U.S. 790 (1943)

Edwards v. Aguillard, 482 U.S. 578 (1987)

Eisenstadt v. Baird, 405 U.S. 438 (1972)

Engel v. Vitale, 370 U.S. 421 (1962)

Epperson v. Arkansas, 393 U.S. 97 (1968)

Everson v. Board of Education, 330 U.S. 1 (1947)

Evitts v. Lucey, 469 U.S. 387 (1985)

Firefighters v. Cleveland, 478 U.S. 501 (1986)

Florida v. Royer, 460 U.S. 491 (1983)

Foley v. Connelie, 435 U.S. 291 (1978)

Frisby v. Schultz, 487 U.S. 474 (1988)

Frontiero v. Richardson, 411 U.S. 677 (1973); *Frontiero v. Laird*, 341 F.Supp. 201 (M.D.Ala. 1972)

Furman v. Georgia, 408 U.S. 238 (1972)

Geduldig v. Aiello, 417 U.S. 484 (1974)

General Electric v. Gilbert, 429 U.S. 125 (1976)

Gertz v. Welch, 418 U.S. 323 (1974)

Gideon v. Wainwright, 372 U.S. 335 (1963)

Ginzburg v. United States, 383 U.S. 463 (1966)

Gitlow v. New York, 268 U.S. 652 (1925)

Glass v. Georgia, 471 U.S. 1080 (1984)

Goldberg v. Kelly, 397 U.S. 254 (1970)

Goldman v. Weinberger, 475 U.S. 503 (1986)

Graham v. Richardson, 403 U.S. 365 (1971)

Grand Rapids School Dist. v. Ball, 473 U.S. 373 (1985)

Green v. School Board, 391 U.S. 430 (1968)

Gregg v. Georgia, 428 U.S. 153 (1976)

Griswold v. Connecticut, 381 U.S. 479 (1965)

Hamling v. United States, 418 U.S. 87 (1974)

Hampton v. Mow Sun Wong, 426 U.S. 88 (1976)

Harris v. MacRae, 448 U.S. 297 (1980)

Hazelton v. Murray, 121 A.2d 1 (N.J. 1956)

Hazelwood School Dist. v. Kuhlmeier, 484 U.S. 260 (1988)

Hirabayashi v. United States, 320 U.S. 81 (1943)

Hobbie v. Florida, 480 U.S. 136 (1987)

Hurtado v. California, 110 U.S. 516 (1884)

Hustler magazine v. Falwell, 485 U.S. 46 (1988)

Hutto v. Davis, 454 U.S. 370 (1982)

Island Trees School Dist. v. Pico, 457 U.S. 853 (1982)

Jacobellis v. Ohio, 378 U.S. 184 (1964)

Jefferson v. Hackney, 406 U.S. 535 (1972)

Jencks v. United States, 353 U.S. 57 (1957)

Jenkins v. Georgia, 418 U.S. 153 (1974)

Keyes v. School Dist. No. 1, 413 U.S. 189 (1973)

Korematsu v. United States, 323 U.S. 214 (1944); *Korematsu
  v. United States*, 584 F.Supp. 1406 (N.D.Cal. 1984)

Kovacs v. Cooper, 336 U.S. 77 (1949)

Kutcher v. Housing Authority of Newark, 119 A.2d 1 (N.J.
  1955)

Laird v. Tatum, 408 U.S. 1 (1972); 409 U.S. 824 (1972)

Lee v. Weisman, 112 S.Ct. 2649 (1992)

Lemon v. Kurtzman, 403 U.S. 602 (1971)

Levy v. Louisiana, 391 U.S. 68 (1968)

Lewis v. City of New Orleans, 415 U.S. 130 (1974)

Lochner v. New York, 198 U.S. 45 (1905)

Lockett v. Ohio, 438 U.S. 586 (1978)

Lynch v. Donnelly, 465 U.S. 668 (1984)

McCleskey v. Kemp, 481 U.S. 279 (1987); *McCleskey v. Zant*,
  580 F.Supp. 338 (N.D.Ga. 1984)

McCollum v. Illinois, 335 U.S. 203 (1948)

Mapp v. Ohio, 367 U.S. 643 (1961)

Marbury v. Madison, 5 U.S. 137 (1803)

Marsh v. Chambers, 463 U.S. 783 (1983)

Martin v. Wilks, 490 U.S. 755 (1989)

Meek v. Pittenger, 421 U.S. 349 (1975)

Memoirs v. Massachusetts, 383 U.S. 413 (1966)

Michael M. v. Sonoma County Superior Court, 450 U.S. 464 (1981)

Miller v. California, 413 U.S. 14 (1973)

Minersville School Dist. v. Gobitis, 310 U.S. 586 (1940); *Gobitis v. Minersville School Dist.*, 21 F.Supp. 581 (E.D.Pa. 1937)

Miranda v. Arizona, 384 U.S. 436 (1966)

Moore v. East Cleveland, 431 U.S. 494 (1977)

Moose Lodge No. 107 v. Irvis, 407 U.S. 163 (1972); *Irvis v. Scott*, 318 F.Supp. 1246 (E.D.Pa. 1970)

Morehead v. Tipaldo, 298 U.S. 587 (1936)

Muller v. Oregon, 208 U.S. 412 (1908)

National Labor Relations Board v. Jones & Laughlin Steel Corp., 301 U.S. 1 (1937)

New Jersey Welfare Rights Org. v. Cahill, 411 U.S. 619 (1973)

New York Times v. Sullivan, 376 U.S. 254 (1964)

New York Times v. United States, 403 U.S. 713 (1971)

New York v. Belton, 453 U.S. 454 (1981)

Nyquist v. Mauclet, 432 U.S. 1 (1977)

Ozawa v. United States, 260 U.S. 178 (1922)

Palko v. Connecticut, 302 U.S. 319 (1937)

Palmer v. Thompson, 403 U.S. 217 (1971)

Papish v. Board of Curators, 410 U.S. 667 (1973)

Parker v. Levy, 417 U.S. 733 (1974)

Paul v. Davis, 424 U.S. 693 (1976)

People v. Crane, 108 N.E. 427 (1915)

Pillo, In Re, 93 A.2d 176 (N.J. 1952)

Planned Parenthood v. Casey, 60 U.S. Law Week 4817 (1992)

Plessy v. Ferguson, 163 U.S. 537 (1896)

Plyler v. Doe, 457 U.S. 202 (1982)

Poe v. Ullman, 367 U.S. 497 (1961)

Pulley v. Harris, 465 U.S. 37 (1984)

Reed v. Reed, 404 U.S. 71 (1971)

Regents v. Bakke, 438 U.S. 265 (1978)

Renton v. Playtime Theaters, 475 U.S. 41 (1986)

Reynolds v. United States, 98 U.S. 145 (1878)

Richmond Newspapers v. Virginia, 448 U.S. 555 (1980)

Rizzo v. Goode, 423 U.S. 362 (1976); *COPPAR v. Rizzo*, 357 F.Supp. 1289 (E.D.Pa. 1973)

Robbins v. California, 453 U.S. 420 (1981)

Roberts v. Louisiana, 431 U.S. 633 (1977)

Roe v. Wade, 410 U.S. 113 (1973)

Rosenfeld v. New Jersey, 408 U.S. 901 (1972)

Ross v. Moffitt, 417 U.S. 600 (1974)

Roth v. United States, 354 U.S. 476 (1957)

Rummel v. Estelle, 445 U.S. 263 (1980)

San Antonio Independent School Dist. v. Rodriguez, 411 U.S. 1 (1973)

Schechter Poultry Co. v. United States, 295 U.S. 495 (1935)

Schenck v. United States, 249 U.S. 47 (1919)

School Board of Richmond v. State Board of Education of Virginia, 412 U.S. 92 (1973)

Scott v. Illinois, 440 U.S. 367 (1979)

Shapiro v. Thompson, 394 U.S. 618 (1969)

Shelley v. Kraemer, 334 U.S. 1 (1948)

Sherbert v. Verner, 374 U.S. 398 (1963)

Slaughterhouse Cases, 83 U.S. 36 (1873)

Smith v. Goguen, 415 U.S. 56 (1974)

Southeastern Promotions v. Conrad, 420 U.S. 54 (1975)

Spence v. Washington, 418 U.S. 405 (1974)

Stanford v. Kentucky, 492 U.S. 361 (1989)

Steelworkers v. Weber, 443 U.S. 193 (1979)

Stone v. Graham, 449 U.S. 39 (1980)

Sugarman v. Dougall, 413 U.S. 634 (1973)

Swann v. Charlotte-Mecklenburg Board of Education, 402 U.S. 1 (1971)

Terry v. Ohio, 392 U.S. 1 (1968)

Texas v. Johnson, 491 U.S. 397 (1989)

Thomas v. Review Board, 450 U.S. 707 (1981)

Thornburgh v. American College of Obstetricians and Gynecologists, 476 U.S. 474 (1986)

Time v. Firestone, 424 U.S. 448 (1976)

Tinker v. Des Moines, 393 U.S. 503 (1969)

Trimble v. Gordon, 430 U.S. 762 (1977)

Trop v. Dulles, 356 U.S. 86 (1958)

Truax v. Raich, 239 U.S. 33 (1915)

United States Dept. of Agriculture v. Moreno, 413 U.S. 528 (1973); *Moreno v. United States Dept. of Agriculture*, 345 F.Supp. 310 (D.D.C 1972)

United States Dept. of Agriculture v. Murray, 413 U.S. 508 (1973)

United States v. Butler, 297 U.S. 1 (1936)

United States v. Carolene Products Co., 304 U.S. 144 (1938)

United States v. Eichman, 496 U.S. 310 (1990)

United States v. MacCollum, 426 U.S. 317 (1976)

United States v. O'Brien, 391 U.S. 367 (1968)

United States v. Paradise, 480 U.S. 149 (1987)

United States v. Peltier, 422 U.S. 531 (1975)

United States v. Salerno, 481 U.S. 739 (1987)

Wainwright v. Sykes, 433 U.S. 72 (1977)

Wallace v. Jaffree, 472 U.S. 38 (1985)

Wards Cove Packing Co. v. Atonio, 490 U.S. 642 (1989)

Weber v. Aetna Casualty & Surety Co., 406 U.S. 164 (1972)

Webster v. Reproductive Health Services, 492 U.S. 460 (1989)

Weems v. United States, 217 U.S. 349 (1910)

West Coast Hotel v. Parrish, 300 U.S. 379 (1937)

West Virginia State Board of Education v. Barnette, 319 U.S. 624 (1943)

Wickard v. Filburn, 317 U.S. 111 (1942)

Williamson v. Lee Optical Co., 348 U.S. 483 (1955)

Woodson v. North Carolina, 428 U.S. 280 (1976)

Yates v. United States, 354 U.S. 298 (1957)

Yick Wo v. Hopkins, 118 U.S. 356 (1886)

Zorach v. Clauson, 343 U.S. 306 (1952)

Index

Abington Township v. Schempp (1963), 120–2, 129, 130, 326

abortion, 3, 16, 20–1, 69, 70, 186–7, 264, 300–4, 312–20, 334–6

Abrams v. United States (1919), 150, 163

Adams, Pres. John, 148, 149

Adams Theater Co. v. Keenan, 28–9

affirmative action, 242, 257–63, 327

AFL-CIO, 308

Agriculture, U.S. Department of, 4, 6

Agricultural Adjustment Act (1933), 72

Aguilar v. Felton (1985), 128–9

Aguillard, Don, 132, 338

Aid to Families with Dependent Children (AFDC), 39, 285–6

Air Force, U.S., 141, 145

Ake v. Oklahoma (1985), 198–9

alien cases, 267–82

Alien Registration Act, *see* Smith Act

Allegheny County v. ACLU (1989), 136–8

Ambach v. Norwick (1979), 277–8

American Bar Association (ABA), 44–5, 55–6, 239

American Civil Liberties Union (ACLU), 20, 137, 145–7, 151, 153, 180, 182, 187, 274, 282, 299;
   Women's Law Project, 295

American Jewish Committee, 258

American Library Association, 180

Americans for Religious Liberty, 129

American Veterans Committee, 295

amicus briefs, 20–2, 258, 259, 263, 279, 295, 308

Amsterdam, Anthony, 215–16, 222, 229, 230, 233

Andrews, Rep. George, 120

Anti-Defamation League of B'nai B'rith, 259

Army, U.S., 27, 30, 32, 83, 154; Air Corps, 48, 141; Intelligence, 54, 92–3; Special Forces, 158

assembly, right of, 146–7, 185–8

association, freedom of, 11, 16–17

Bail Reform Act (1984), 99–101

Baird, Bill, 301–2

Bakke, Allen, 258–9

Baldus, David, 233–5

Baptists, 115

Barron v. Baltimore (1833), 75–6, 221

Barry, Marion, 187

Bates v. Little Rock (1960), 87–8

Bayh, Sen. Birch, 57–61, 295

Beauharnais case (1952), 167

Beck, James, 268, 269

Bell v. Wolfish (1979), 101–3

Biddle, Atty. Gen. Francis, 151

Bilandic, Michael, 185

Bilbo, Sen. Theodore, 75

Bill of Rights, 9, 75–6, 82, 93, 95–6, 100, 103, 115, 124, 141, 196, 198, 204, 216, 217, 221, 241, 300–1, 323, 328, 329, 333; *see also specific amendments under* Constitution

birth control, *see* contraception

Bivens v. Six Unknown Federal Narcotics Agents (1971), 104

Black, Justice Hugo, 44, 82, 84–5, 89–90, 119, 120, 143–4, 155, 168, 169, 171, 176, 182, 322, 327

Blackmun, Justice Harry, 14, 16, 22, 44, 89, 183, 187, 297; abortion cases, 300, 303–4, 312, 313, 316–20; alien cases, 270–3, 275–9; death penalty cases, 216, 234; equal protection cases, 265–6; free expression cases, 158, 162; liberty cases, 98, 100, 103, 108; religion cases, 135, 136, 138

blacks, 143, 152, 337; death penalty and, 214, 215, 222, 225, 231, 233–7, 239, 240; discrimination against, 49–50, 60–1, 74–5, 87–90, 96–8; equal protection and, 241–67, 281, 293, 294; police and, 190–2, 203; poverty among, 20, 286, 291

Board of Education of Oklahoma City v. Dowell (1991), 252–5

Boger, John Charles, 233–5

Boggs v. Muncy (1990), 240

Boos v. Barry (1988), 187–8

Boren, Gov. David, 310

Bork, Robert, 19, 56, 61–2, 77, 78, 188, 263, 274

Bradley, Justice Joseph, 292–3, 297–8

Bradwell v. State (1873), 292–3, 295, 298, 320

Brandeis, Justice Louis, 67, 76, 111, 155, 301

Brandenberg v. Ohio (1969), 152–3

Brant, Irving, 72–3

Brennan, Agnes McDermott, 26

Brennan, Charlie, 26, 30

Brennan, Marjorie Leonard, 26

Brennan, William J., Sr., 25–6

Brennan, Justice William J., Jr.: abortion cases, 301–3, 315–18; alien cases, 271, 273–5, 277–82; appointment to Court, 23–5; assembly rights cases, 185–8; background of, 25–7; censorship cases, 180–4; criminal procedure cases, 190–3, 195–8, 202–11; death penalty cases, 212, 216–20, 224, 225, 231, 233, 235–40; equal protection cases, 244–7, 250–65, 267; food-stamp cases, 14–22; free expression cases, 144, 154–9, 161–3, 165; gender-discrimination cases, 297–9, 305, 307–13; historical context for views of, 65–90; judicial philosophy of, 33–42, 64, 323–31; liberty cases, 93, 95–6, 98, 100–6, 108–9, 111–12; McCarthy and, 30–3; on New Jersey Supreme Court, 23, 24, 27–31, 51; obscenity cases, 166–74; poverty cases, 285, 290; press freedom cases, 177–9, 184–5; religion cases, 113–14, 120–3, 125–9, 132–7, 139–42; retirement of, 321–2

Brewer, Justice David, 294

Brewer, Justice Joseph, 113, 114

Brickfield, Peter, 7–10

Bridges, Harry, 86

Brown, Justice Henry, 243

Brown v. Board of Education (1954), 8, 58, 60, 98, 243–5, 247, 249–51, 253–5, 258, 260, 280–1, 287, 289–9, 300

Brownell, Atty. Gen. Herbert, 23, 24

Bryan, William Jennings, 131

Buchanan, Patrick, 115

Buck v. Bell (1927), 334

Buckley, William F., 327, 330

Buddhism, 114, 123

Burger, Chief Justice Warren, 12–15, 37, 46, 89, 93, 331, 335; abortion cases, 303, 314; alien cases, 271, 273, 276–7, 281–2; censorship cases, 181, 184; criminal procedure cases, 190, 197, 206; death penalty cases, 224, 228, 229; equal protection cases, 248–50, 259, 261; free expression cases, 161; gender-discrimination cases, 295, 297, 307, 308; liberty cases, 93; obscenity cases, 171–3; press freedom cases, 177, 179; religion cases, 122, 124, 126–7, 134–6, 139–40

Burke, Edmund, 51

Bush, Pres. George, 19, 145, 164, 214, 253, 266, 318, 321, 322, 336, 337

Butler, Justice Pierce, 72

Butler v. McKellar (1990), 239–40

Butz, Earl, 6–10, 12, 19

Byrnes, Justice James, 3

Cabell v. Chavez-Salido (1981), 278–9

Cady v. Dombowski (1973), 194–5

Califano v. Goldfarb (1977), 299

California, University of, at Davis, 258–9

California v. LaRue (1972), 171–2

Cambodia, U.S. invasion of, 50, 53, 161

Cantwell v. Connecticut (1940), 118

capital punishment, *see* death penalty cases,

Cardozo, Justice Benjamin, 35, 41, 76, 261, 271

Carey v. Brown (1980), 185–6, 188

Carlin, David, 129

Carlson v. Green (1980), 103–6

Carpenter, Matthew, 292, 293

Carswell, Judge G. Harrold, 44, 55, 57, 58

Carter, Pres. Jimmy, 254, 260, 279, 314

Carter v. Kentucky (1981), 198

Catholics, 24–5, 34–5, 82, 114, 115, 118–20, 122, 125, 127–9, 133, 141, 315

censorship cases, 179–84

Central Committee for Conscientious Objectors, 93

Central Intelligence Agency (CIA), 46, 49, 54

Chambers v. Mississippi (1973), 200–1

Chaplinsky v. New Hampshire (1941), 154–5, 157, 164, 167

Chinese Exclusion Act (1882), 268, 274

Christian Century, 133

Christians, 113–14, 117, 123, 134–7; fundamentalist, 129, 130, 132, 133

Church and State, separation of, 115, 116, 119–24, 127, 129, 133, 138, 142

civil disobedience, 52, 88

Civil Rights Act (1964), Title VII of, 259–62, 264, 265, 308

Civil Rights Act (1991), 266

Civil Rights Cases (1883), 242, 293

Civil Service Commission, U.S., 274

Civil War, 69, 149, 150, 217, 242, 247, 267

Clark, Kenneth, 243

Clark, Justice Tom, 120–1, 152, 193–4, 255

"clear and present danger" test, 150, 152–3, 166, 167

clerks, 14–15

Cleveland v. LaFleur (1974), 305–7

Clinton, Pres. Bill, 214, 264, 320, 335–7

Coker v. Georgia (1977), 227–8

Cold War, 151, 152

Coleman, William, 4

Columbia University: Center on Social Welfare Policy and Law, 5; Law School, 74, 295

Columbus Board of Education v. Penick (1979), 251–2, 254

Committee for Public Education v. Nyquist (1973), 125–6

Communists, 30–3, 49, 58, 71, 74, 76, 86–7, 101, 151–2, 177, 269–70, 289, 328

competency to stand trial, 198–9

conflict of interest, 93

Congress, U.S., 57, 75, 86, 87, 105, 116, 120, 124, 141, 143, 165, 187, 188, 216, 220, 296, 297, 314, 337; bail denial laws, 99, 100; chaplain of, 134; civil rights laws, 49, 292, 293; death penalty laws, 214, 223, 239–40; and declaration of war, 53; food-stamp restrictions, 4, 6–8, 13, 15–16, 20, 21; during Great Depression, 70–73; integration and, 243, 248–9, 255, 266; naturalization and immigration laws, 268–70, 274–5; obscenity laws, 166, 171; Reconstruction era, 69, 94; sedition laws, 148, 149, 151; substantive evils and, 150, 152; during Vietnam War, 88; women's rights laws, 309; during World War II, 83, 84; *see also* House of Representatives, U.S.; Senate, U.S.

Constitution, U.S., 5, 12, 17–18, 20, 27, 29, 31, 38–40, 53–5, 58, 60, 64, 72–4, 77, 80–2, 90, 104, 110, 189, 193, 197, 202, 251, 266, 269, 300, 309, 319, 322–35; Establishment clause, 118–20, 123, 124, 127, 128, 130, 131, 133–5, 137, 138, 140; Framers of, 36, 37, 66, 69, 108, 121, 123, 128, 143, 147, 148, 177, 204, 212, 213, 216, 219, 221, 241–2, 301, 326, 328, 329, 333, 334; Free Exercise clause, 116, 120, 123, 128, 138–40; "liberty" clauses, 91–2, 96, 103, 111–12; "living," 3, 15, 39, 61–2, 68, 210; Supremacy clause, 80, 179

Amendments: First, 9, 16, 63, 71, 76, 87, 89, 241, 268, 274, 275, 289, 290, 296, 325 (*see also* censorship cases; expression, freedom of; obscenity cases; press, freedom of; religion, freedom of); Fourth, 53–4, 92, 104, 190–6; Fifth, 7–9, 28, 32, 35, 76, 91, 99, 190, 196, 213; Sixth, 191, 196, 203–5, 208, 209; Eighth, 191, 209, 211–13, 215, 217–20, 223, 224, 226, 228, 229, 231, 238; Ninth, 179, 301; Thirteenth, 149, 242; Fourteenth, 35, 39, 69–71, 79, 91, 94–5, 117, 131, 151, 186, 201, 205, 212, 215, 216, 267, 292–5, 299, 303, 328, 329 (*see also* due process; equal protection); Fifteenth, 242; Twenty-first, 171–2

contraception, 16, 300–2, 337

contract, right of, 65, 69, 72, 73

counsel, right to, 203–8

Craig v. Boren (1976), 310–13

criminal procedure cases, 53–4, 56–8, 63, 99–106, 189–211, 337

Criminal Syndicalism Act, 152

cruel and unusual punishment, 191, 209–11; *see also* death penalty cases

Cruz v. Beto (1972), 123

Cruzan v. Missouri Department of Health (1990), 109–12

Cupp v. Naughton (1973), 197–8

Dandridge v. Williams (1970), 9, 11, 12, 15, 18, 285–6

Darrow, Clarence, 131

Davidson v. Cannon (1986), 105–6

Davis, Edward III, 94

death penalty cases, 212–40, 337

Debs, Eugene V., 149, 332

Declaration of Independence, 34, 274, 334

deference, judicial, 21, 63, 64, 68, 69, 79–80, 86, 90, 123, 158, 164, 190, 285, 299, 300, 303, 331, 333–4

DeFunis v. Odegard (1974), 257, 258

Democratic party, 20, 23, 24, 43, 44,

49, 55–9, 61, 75, 145, 248, 303, 314

Dennis v. United States (1951), 87

DeShaney v. Winnebago County (1989), 106–9, 338

die, right to, 109–12

dignity, 21, 34–6, 38–9, 41, 62, 64, 190, 217–20, 321, 330, 337

Doerr, Edd, 129

Dole, Sen. Robert, 164

Dombrowski, Chester, 194–5

double jeopardy, 76, 190, 213

Dougall, Patrick, 272–3

Douglas, Elsie, 60

Douglas, Sen. Paul, 152

Douglas, Justice William O., 14, 17–18, 82, 127, 283, 286, 297, 321, 327; abortion cases, 300–1, 303; criminal procedure cases, 191, 208; free expression cases, 144, 155; liberty cases, 93, 96; obscenity cases, 168, 169, 172, 176

Dowell, Robert, 252

Doyle, Judge William, 249–50

Dred Scott v. Sandford (1857), 68–70

due process, 5, 8, 29, 35–7, 40–1, 53, 65, 71, 73, 76, 213, 241, 282; in alien cases, 268, 274, 275; criminal procedure and, 191, 197, 198, 206–7; death penalty and, 230; gender and, 296, 305; in liberty cases, 99–103, 109; privacy rights and, 300, 302, 317; substantive, 63, 69, 100, 103, 108

Dukakis, Gov. Michael, 214

Eastland, Sen. James, 55–6, 59, 60

education, right to, 69, 245, 253, 279–82, 288–91; *see also* schools

Edwards, Judge George, 305

Edwards v. Aguillard (1987), 132–4

Ehrlichman, John, 45

Eisenhower, Pres. Dwight D., 23–5, 45, 168, 305

Eisenstadt v. Baird (1972), 301–2, 305

Emancipation Proclamation, 293

Emerson, Ralph Waldo, 160, 161, 163

Emerson, Thomas, 300

Engel v. Vitale (1962), 119–21, 129, 130

Epperson v. Arkansas (1968), 131–2

Equal Employment Opportunity Commission, 260

equal protection, 5, 7–9, 15, 29, 71, 90, 186, 207, 241–66, 282, 325; aliens and, 267, 270, 271, 275, 280; death penalty and, 237; gender and, 295, 296, 298, 310, 313; poverty and, 285–91; privacy rights and, 302

Equal Rights Amendment (ERA), 50, 54–5, 273, 293–8, 300, 304, 320

Ernst, Morris, 167

Ervin, Sen. Sam, 54, 57

Espionage Act (1918), 149

Ethredge, Jesse, 144–5

Everson v. Board of Education (1947), 119, 126, 127, 133

Evitts v. Lucey (1985), 205–6

evolutionary theory, 131–3

exclusionary rule, 193–6

executive powers, 52–3

expression, freedom of, 63, 71, 76, 87, 143–65; obscenity and, 167, 168

fair trial, elements of, 191

Falwell, Rev. Jerry, 115, 184, 322

Families USA Foundation, 19

"family," concepts of, 282–5

Faubus, Orval, 323

Federal Bureau of Investigation (FBI), 33, 54, 83, 92

Federal Bureau of Narcotics, 104

Federal Bureau of Prisons, 103

Federalist papers, 220, 334

Firefighters v. Cleveland (1986), 262,
    327–8
Firestone, Russell, 177–8
Fiss, Owen, 323–4, 331–2, 337
flag cases, 159–65, 264
Florida v. Royer (1983), 192–3
Florida Supreme Court, 140
Flynt, Larry, 184
Foley v. Connelie (1978), 276–7
Food Research and Action Center
    (FRAC), 5, 21
food-stamp program, 4–22
Ford, Pres. Gerald, 254, 316
Fordice, Kirk, 138
Forrester, Judge Owen, 233–5
Fortas, Justice Abe, 44, 45, 89, 131–2,
    154, 167, 204
Frankfurter, Justice Felix, 15, 21, 79–
    83, 87, 90, 322
Friday, Herschel, 44–5, 56
Frisby v. Schultz (1988), 186–7
Frontiero v. Richardson (1972), 296–300,
    304, 307–8, 310, 325, 338
Fullam, Judge John, 96–7
"fundamental rights" doctrine, 284, 285,
    288–90, 302, 329
Furman v. Georgia (1972), 215–25, 231,
    237

Ginzburg v. United States* (1966), 170–1
Gitlow v. New York (1925), 76, 151
Giuffra, Robert, 331, 332
Glass v. Georgia (1984), 219
Glazer, Nathan, 133
Gobitis v. Minersville School Dist.
    (1937), 78–82, 86, 89, 90
Gochman, Arthur, 287–9
Goguen, Valarie, 159–60
Goldberg, Justice Arthur, 169, 301
Goldberg v. Kelley (1970), 39–2
Goldman v. Weinberger (1986), 140–1
Goldwater, Sen. Barry, 43, 49, 51, 55
Graglia, Lino, 329–30
Graham, Rev. Billy, 120
Graham v. Richardson (1971), 270–2,
    275, 276, 278
Grand Rapids School Dist. v. Ball
    (1985), 127–8
Great Depression, 20, 70–2, 74, 118,
    214
Greenhouse, Linda, 319
Green v. School Board (1968), 251, 253
Gregg v. Georgia (1976), 222–7, 229
Griffiths, Rep. Martha, 295
Griswold, Erwin, 4, 10, 12, 143, 144
Griswold v. Connecticut (1965), 16, 300–
    3, 305
Gunther, Gerald, 77

Geduldig v. Aiello (1974), 307–8
gender discrimination, 3, 292–99, 304–
    13
General Electric v. Gilbert (1976), 308–9
Gertz v. Welch (1974), 177, 178
Gideon v. Wainwright (1963), 203–5,
    209, 326
Gilbert, Martha, 308–9
Gilmore, Gary, 227
Ginsburg, Judge Douglas, 263–4
Ginsburg, Justice Ruth Bader, 295–7,
    299, 320, 335

habeas corpus cases, 201–3, 208, 209,
    233, 239–40, 338
Hagerty, James, 24
Hamilton, Alexander, 220
Hamling v. United States (1974), 173–4
Hampton v. Mow Sun Wong (1976),
    273–5
Hand, Judge Augustus, 29
Hand, Judge Brevard, 130–1
Harlan, Justice John (grandfather), 243,
    197, 257

Harlan, Justice John, 36, 44, 152, 168, 169, 255

Harris, Robert, 230–2

Harris v. MacRae (1980), 314–16

Hart, Sen. Philip, 57–8

Harvard Law Review, 9, 19

Harvard Legal Aid Society, 26

Harvard University, 49, 259; Law School, 4, 9, 19, 26

Haynsworth, Judge Clement, 44, 55, 57, 58

Hazelwood School Dist. v. Kuhlmeier (1988), 182–4

"heightened scrutiny" test, 310–11, 313

Heins, Marjorie, 146

Helms, Sen. Jesse, 314

Hicks, Judge Maryellen, 147

Hines, Jimmy, 147

Hispanics, 190, 249, 262; poverty among, 286–91

Hobbie v. Florida (1987), 140

Hobbs, Rep. Sam, 86–7

Holland, Sen. Spessard, 5, 15, 17

Holmes, Justice Oliver Wendell, 15, 67–8, 73, 76, 150–3, 155, 158, 159, 163, 221, 333–5

Hoover, J. Edgar, 74

House of Representatives, U.S., 54, 86–7, 164, 248, 294, 295; Un-American Activities Committee, 151

Howard Law School, 8

Hughes, Chief Justice Charles Evans, 73, 74, 335

Humphrey, Sen. Hubert, 152, 260–2

Hurlbut, John, 56

Hustler Magazine v. Falwell (1988), 184, 322

Hutto v. Davis (1982), 211

Hyde Amendment, 304, 314–16

illegitimate children, 282–5

"incorporation" doctrine, 204

Industrial Workers of the World, 269

insanity defense, 198–9

interested groups, briefs by, *see amicus* briefs

Internal Security Act (1950), 152

invasion-of-privacy cases, 184

Iran-Contra scandal, 45

irrebuttable presumptions, 30

Irvis, Leroy, 255–7

Island Trees School Dist. v. Pico (1982), 180–4

Jackson, Justice Robert, 45, 46, 49, 58–60, 81–2, 85–6, 90, 101, 251, 316

Jacobellis v. Ohio (1964), 169–70, 172, 173

Japanese-Americans, internment of, 83–6

Jefferson, Pres. Thomas, 116–17, 119, 120, 123, 124, 138, 142, 148–9, 166, 177

Jefferson v. Hackney (1972), 286–7, 338

Jehovah's Witnesses, 78–82, 86, 118, 139–40, 154

Jencks v. United States (1957), 33

Jenkins v. Georgia (1974), 173, 174

Jews, 82, 114, 115, 119, 123, 133, 134, 136–7, 140–1, 143, 152; civil rights and, 258, 259; discrimination against, 256; Nazis and, 75, 153; Orthodox, 138

Jim Crow laws, 74, 215, 242–3, 337

job-discrimination cases, 259–66

John Birch Society, 177

Johnson, Judge Frank, 263

Johnson, Gregory Lee, 162–5

Johnson, Pres. Lyndon B., 4, 5, 7, 43, 96, 143, 271, 279, 324, 333

Journeymen Bakers' Union, 66

"judicial restraint," 21, 64
Justice, Judge William, 279, 333–5
Justice Department, U.S., 7, 43, 45, 50, 52, 54, 57, 80–1, 93, 127, 156, 171, 248, 260, 262, 263, 279, 298, 327

Kaiser Aluminum Co., 259–60
Karst, Kenneth, 267
Kefauver, Sen. Estes, 167
Kennedy, Justice Anthony, 106, 107, 133–4, 137–8, 162, 163, 264, 265, 316–19, 336
Kennedy, Sen. Edward, 6, 57, 58, 66
Kennedy, Pres. John F., 5, 8, 119, 249, 288
Kent, Chancellor, 113, 117
Kerrey, Sen. Bob, 164–5
Keyes v. School Dist. No. 1 (1973), 249, 251, 252
King, Martin Luther, Jr., 52, 185
King, Rodney, 115
Kleindienst, Asst. Atty. Gen. Richard, 43, 46, 49
Korematsu v. United States (1944), 84–6
Krauthammer, Charles, 331–2
Krock, Arthur, 25
Ku Klux Klan, 143, 152, 185, 269
Ku Klux Klan Act (1871), 94–5
Kurland, Philip, 4
Kutcher v. Housing Authority of Newark (1955), 30

labor laws, 65–73
LaFleur, Jo Carol, 305–7
Laird v. Tatum (1972), 93–4
laissez-faire, 20, 66, 71
Lee v. Weisman (1992), 133
legislative prayer, 134–5
Lehman, Judge Irving, 75

Lemon v. Kurtzman (1971), 122–6, 128, 130, 132–5, 137–8, 140
Levy, Captain Howard, 158–9
Levy, Leonard, 219
Levy v. Louisiana (1968), 283–4
Lewis v. City of New Orleans (1974), 157–8
libel cases, 155–6, 167–8, 177, 178, 184
"liberty" cases, 91–112
Lillie, Judge Mildred, 44–5, 56
Lincoln, Pres. Abraham, 68, 293, 336
Lochner v. New York (1905), 65–73, 76, 284, 294, 333–4
Locke, John, 121
Lockett v. Ohio (1978), 228–9
Lovejoy, Elijah, 149
Lucey, Keith, 205–6
Lusky, Louis, 74, 75
Lynch v. Donnelly (1984), 135–7
lynch law, 74, 75
Lyon, Rep. Matthew, 148

MacCollum, Colin, 206–7
McCarthy, Sen. Joseph, 30–4, 152, 270, 323, 328, 337
McClellan, Sen. John, 56–7
McCleskey v. Kemp (1987), 232–8, 325–6, 338
McCormack, Rep. John, 87
McCollum v. Illinois (1948), 119
McCree, Sol. Gen. Wade, 314
McGovern, Sen. George, 221–2
McGowan, Judge Carl, 8–12, 16
McIntyre, Cardinal, 120
McMillian, William, 240
McRae, Cora, 314–16
Madison, Pres. James, 115, 123, 124, 156, 166
Mafia, 99, 112
Magna Carta, 197, 210, 217

majoritarianism, 51, 62, 67–8, 77, 304, 333

Mapp v. Ohio (1961), 193–4, 196

Marbury v. Madison (1803), 179, 220–1

Maris, Judge Albert, 79

Markman, Stephen, 327

Marsh v. Chambers (1983), 134–5

Marshall, Chief Justice John, 149, 179, 220–1, 326

Marshall, Justice Thurgood, 8, 14, 18, 60, 133, 162, 172, 177, 183, 297; abortion cases, 303, 310, 316–18; alien cases, 261, 273, 277; criminal procedure cases, 199, 202, 208, 211; death penalty cases, 212, 219, 234, 237, 238, 240; equal protection cases, 243, 253–5; liberty cases, 96, 98, 100–2, 108; poverty cases, 286–7, 289–90

Martin v. Wilks (1989), 264

Matthews, Justice Stanley, 244

Matusow, Harvey, 33

Mauclet, Jean-Marie, 275–6

Mayer, Julius, 67

Medicaid, 304, 314, 315

Meek v. Pittenger (1975), 126–7

Meese, Atty. Gen. Edwin, 36–7, 99, 264, 327–9

Memoirs v. Massachusetts (1966), 170

Mexican-American Legal Defense Fund, 279, 290

Michael M. v. Sonoma County Superior Court (1981), 311–13

Michelman, Frank, 324–6

Mill, John Stuart, 325

Miller v. California (1973), 172–5

Minton, Justice Sherman, 23–5

Miranda v. Arizona (1966), 40, 189–90, 201, 239

Mitchell, Sen. George, 164

Mitchell, Atty. Gen. John, 10, 43–6, 50, 51, 55, 248

Moore, Richard, 43–6

Moore v. East Cleveland (1977), 282–3

Moose Lodge No. 107 v. Irvis (1972), 255–7, 260

Moral Majority, 184

moral relativism, 62, 333–4

Morehead v. Tipaldo (1936), 72–3

Moreno vs. U.S. Department of Agriculture (1972), 6–22, 338

Mormons, 116–17, 139, 141

Muller v. Oregon (1908), 67, 294

Murphy, Justice Frank, 21, 25, 34, 82, 85, 155, 157

Muslims, 114, 123, 138

National Association for the Advancement of Colored People (NAACP), 8, 11, 20, 49, 59, 60, 87, 96, 243, 258, 259, 262, 300; Legal Defense and Education Fund, 215, 222, 229, 233

National Industrial Recovery Act (1933), 72

National Labor Relations Act, 73

National Labor Relations Board v. Jones & Laughlin Steel Corp. (1937), 73, 74

National Review, 327, 330

Nature of the Judicial Process, The (Cardozo), 35

Naughton, Hugh, 197

Navy, U.S., 83

Nazis, 75, 78, 143, 153

New Deal, 20, 40, 71–2, 74

New Jersey Supreme Court, 23, 24, 27–31

New Left Notes, 157

New Republic, 331

Newsweek magazine, 52, 59

New York v. Belton (1981), 195–6

New York Times, 18–19, 24, 25, 46, 75, 319, 328

New York Times v. Sullivan (1964), 155–6, 162, 177, 184, 188

Nixon, Pres. Richard M., 4, 12, 19, 21, 22, 64, 215, 262; aliens and, 270–2; anti-Communism of, 151; antiwar groups and, 54, 92–3; crime as campaign issue for, 189–90, 221–2, 303; defended by Rehnquist, 53–5; pornography and, 171, 173; school integration and, 247–9, 251; Supreme Court appointments of, 43–7, 51
Norwick, Susan, 277–8
Notre Dame Lawyer, 224
Nyquist v. Mauclet (1977), 275–6

O'Brien, David, 88
obscenity cases, 3, 28–9, 156–8, 161, 166–76, 337
O'Connor, Justice Sandra Day, 100, 103, 135, 137, 138, 186–8, 263, 278, 316–19, 336
O'Mahoney, Sen. Joseph, 31
"original intent," 327, 329
Ozawa v. United States (1922), 268–9

Palko v. Connecticut (1937), 76
Palmer v. Thompson (1971), 89–90
Papish v. Board of Curators (1973), 157
Parker v. Levy (1974), 158–9
Parks, Rosa, 323
Parrish, Elsie, 73
Patel, Judge Marilyn, 85–6
Paul v. Davis (1976), 94–5, 98
Peckham, Justice Rufus, 65–7
Penick, Gary, 251–2
Pennsylvania, University of: Law School, 12; Wharton School of Finance and Commerce, 26
Pentagon Papers, 143
People v. Crane (1915), 271
picketing cases, 185–8

Pico, Steven, 180–2
Planned Parenthood, 300
Planned Parenthood v. Casey (1992), 318–20, 336
Plessy v. Ferguson (1896), 50, 60, 242–4, 250–1, 257
Plyler v. Doe (1982), 244–6, 279–82, 325, 333
Poe v. Ullman (1961), 36
"police powers" doctrine, 73, 76, 153
Pollack, Ronald F., 5–9, 11, 12, 15, 16, 19, 21, 22
"Poor Laws," 20
pornography, *see* obscenity cases
Posner, Judge Richard, 326–7
poverty cases, 285–91
Powell, Justice Lewis, 14, 16, 22, 45, 46, 56, 59, 61, 160, 283, 288–90; abortion cases, 303, 312, 316, 317; alien cases, 273, 277, 281; censorship cases, 181, 182; criminal procedure cases, 200, 210, 211; death penalty cases, 223, 234–7; equal protection cases, 258–9, 263; gender-discrimination cases, 297, 298; liberty cases, 93, 100, 103, 106; press freedom cases, 177, 178; religion cases, 125–6, 133, 135
prayer: legislative, 134–5; in schools, 119–21, 123, 129–31, 133–5, 164, 337
"preferred freedoms" doctrine, 71
press, freedom of, 76, 148–9, 153, 176–9
presumption-of-innocence cases, 197–8
privacy rights, 16, 102, 179, 300–4, 317
probable cause, 190–2
Progressive movement, 66
Prohibition, 171–2
property rights, 49–50, 160
Protestants, 114, 118–20, 128, 133
public accommodations legislation, 49–50, 58–9, 255–7

Pulley v. Harris (1984), 230–3

Puritans, 115, 116, 213

Quakers, 79, 115

Randolph, A. Raymond, 12, 19

Rankin, Sol. Gen. J. Lee, 167

"rational basis" test, 17–18, 90, 244, 272, 273, 281, 284, 288, 295–7, 300, 312, 319

Rauh, Joseph, 64

Reagan, Pres. Ronald, 37, 106, 145, 194, 209, 233, 327, 336; abortion and, 303, 314, 316; affirmative action opposed by, 263–5; capital punishment supported by, 214; Christian Right and, 132; conservative political agenda of, 127, 328; protestors against, 161; Supreme Court appointments of, 107, 253, 278

Reconstruction era, 94

"Red Scares," 269–70

Reed, Justice Stanley, 82

Reed v. Reed (1971), 295–9, 304, 307–8, 310, 311

Regents v. Bakke (1978), 258–60

Regnery, Alfred, 327

Rehnquist, Jean, 47

Rehnquist, Marjorie Peck, 47

Rehnquist, Natalie, 46, 49, 55

Rehnquist, William Benjamin, 47

Rehnquist, Chief Justice William H.: abortion cases, 303, 304, 316–20; alien cases, 272–6, 282; appointment to Court of, 43–7, 55–61; assembly rights cases, 185–8; background of, 47–50; censorship cases, 181–4; criminal procedure cases, 190–211; death penalty cases, 215, 220–1, 224–9,

231, 238–40; equal protection cases, 246–58, 261–5, 267; food-stamp cases, 14, 15, 17–22; free expression cases, 144, 155–65; gender-discrimination cases, 298, 299, 306–9, 312–13; historical context for views of, 65–90; illegitimate children cases, 283–5; judicial philosophy of, 42, 48–55, 61–4, 329–38; liberty cases, 93–8, 100–3, 105–12; obscenity cases, 171–6; poverty cases, 285–6, 288; press freedom cases, 177–9, 184–5; religion cases, 113–14, 122–34, 137, 139–41; tribute to Brennan, 322

Reich, Charles, 40

religion, freedom of, 113–42

Renton v. Playtime Theaters (1986), 175–6, 188

Republican party, 20, 24, 27, 44, 45, 47, 49, 55, 59, 61, 66, 73, 74, 115, 161–2, 303, 314, 316, 327, 336, 337; Jeffersonian Republicans, 148

Revolutionary Communist Youth Brigade, 162

Reynolds, Robert, 182, 183

Reynolds, Asst. Atty. Gen. William Bradford, 264, 327–8

Reynolds v. United States (1878), 116–18

Richmond Newspapers v. Virginia (1980), 178–9

Rivers, Rep. Mendel, 88

Rives, Judge Richard, 296, 298

Rizzo v. Goode (1976), 96–8, 332

Robbins v. California (1981), 194–6

Roberts, Justice Owen, 73, 82

Roberts v. Louisiana (1977), 226–7

Robinson, Judge Spottswood, 8

Rodriguez, Demetrio, 287–91

Roe v. Wade (1973), 3, 16, 20–1, 102, 300, 302–5, 314–20, 334–6

Rogers, Richard, 254

Roosevelt, Pres. Franklin D., 14, 40, 71–3, 75, 83, 92, 214, 336

Ross v. Moffitt (1974), 208
Roth v. United States (1957), 166–72
Royer, Mark, 192–3
Royster Guano Co. v. Virgina (1920),
    295
Rummel v. Estelle (1980), 209–11
Rutledge, Justice Wiley, 82
Ryan, Msgr. John A., 34
Ryan, Rep. Leo, 270

Salerno, Anthony, 99, 100, 112
*San Antonio Independent School Dist. v.
    Rodriguez* (1973), 281, 287–91
Sanchez, Ermina, 6–7, 9, 11–13, 16
Sanford, Justice Edward, 151
Santeria, 114
Scalia, Justice Antonin, 106, 107, 132–
    4, 137, 162, 163, 187, 188, 238, 239,
    316, 318, 319, 336
Schechter Poultry Co. v. United States
    (1935), 72
Schenck v. United States (1919), 149–
    50, 158
Schlafly, Phyllis, 296
schools: evolution taught in, 131–3;
    funding of, 287–81; integration of, 3,
    4, 50, 59, 60, 87, 97, 98, 185, 243–
    4, 245, 247–55, 257, 258, 329; prayer
    in, 119–21, 123, 129–31, 133–5,
    164, 337; religious, government aid to,
    3, 125–9; *see also* education, right to
Scopes, John, 131
Scott v. Illinois (1979), 204–5
search-and-seizure cases, 190–6
secular humanists, 123
Sedition Act (1798), 148–9, 156, 177
"seditious libel," 147–8
Seitz, Virginia, 324
Selective Service System, 88
self-incrimination, protection against, 28,
    32, 190

Senate, U.S., 15, 25, 30–3, 44, 49, 55–
    61, 64, 93, 164, 188, 248, 262, 263,
    327; Subcommittee on Constitutional
    Amendments, 295
sentencing, harsh, 209–11
"separate but equal" doctrine, 50, 60,
    242–4, 250–1
Seventh-Day Adventist Church, 139,
    140
Seymour, Judge Stephanie, 254
Shanley, Bernard, 25
Shapiro, David, 63
Shapiro v. Thompson (1969), 285
Shelley v. Kraemer (1948), 256
Sherbert v. Verner (1963), 139–40
Slaughterhouse Cases (1873), 247, 292
slavery, 236, 241–2, 267, 293, 294, 298,
    334
Smith, Judge John Lewis, Jr., 7, 8
Smith Act (1940), 86–7, 151–2
Smith v. Goguen (1974), 159–61, 163,
    164
Social Darwinism, 20, 285
"social facts," 22, 39–40, 68, 81, 90,
    190, 244, 274, 297, 312
Socialist party, 149
Socialist Workers party, 30, 151
Souter, Justice David, 133, 318, 319,
    321, 336
Southeastern Promotions v. Conrad
    (1975), 175–6
Spears, Judge Adrian, 288
speech, freedom of, *see* expression, free-
    dom of
Spence v. Washington (1974), 161, 164
Stanford v. Kentucky (1989), 238
Stanford University Law School, 46, 48,
    56
stare decisis, principle of, 219, 319, 320
Starr, Sol. Gen. Kenneth, 318–19
"state action" doctrine, 256–7, 260
Steelworkers v. Weber (1979), 259–60,
    262

Stevens, Justice John Paul, 102–3, 106, 131, 183, 211, 223, 234, 264, 273, 274, 277, 299, 316, 319

Stevenson, Adlai, 24, 25

Stewart, Justice Potter, 14, 16, 18, 103, 120, 159, 169–70, 198, 216, 222–5, 259, 283, 297, 303, 305–8, 312–17

"stop and frisk" rule, 191–2

Stone, Chief Justice Harlan Fiske, 70–2, 74–7, 80, 82–5, 90, 139, 155, 245, 258, 316, 335

Stone v. Graham (1980), 130

"strict scrutiny" test, 17, 22, 70–1, 76–7, 80, 82, 84, 90, 284; in abortion cases, 312, 316; in alien cases, 272, 273, 276, 278, 280, 281; in equal protection cases, 245, 258; in flag cases, 162, 163; in gender-discrimination cases, 295, 297, 311; in poverty cases, 285, 286, 290; in religion cases, 139

Students for a Democratic Society (SDS), 51, 157

Sugarman v. Dougall (1973), 272–3, 276–9

Sullivan, L. B., 156

Supremacy clause, 27

Sutherland, Justice George, 268

Swann v. Charlotte-Mecklenburg Board of Education (1971), 248–51, 253, 254

Sykes, John, 201–3

Taft, Sen. Robert, 83

Tatum, Arlo, 93

Terry v. Ohio (1968), 191–3

Texas v. Johnson (1989), 162

Thomas, Justice Clarence, 133, 264, 318, 319, 336

Thomas v. Review Board (1981), 139–40

Thornburgh v. American College of Ob-stetricians and Gynecologists (1986), 317

Thurmond, Sen. Strom, 88

Time magazine, 5, 75

Time v. Firestone (1976), 177–8

Tinker, Mary Beth, 88–9, 154

Tinker v. Des Moines (1969), 88–9, 154, 182–3

Tocqueville, Alexis de, 11, 114, 177, 241, 242

Tribe, Laurence, 19, 323

Trop v. Dulles (1958), 217, 223, 225, 228

Truman, Pres. Harry S., 23, 152

Tunney, Sen. John, 57, 58

Twain, Mark, 180

Twyn, William, 148

Ulysses (Joyce), 29

Unitarians, 120

United States v. Butler (1936), 72

United States v. Carolene Products Co. (1938), 70–1, 74–5, 80, 162, 245, 258, 271, 272, 316

United States v. Eichman (1990), 165

United States v. Hirabayashi (1943), 84, 85

United States v. MacCollum (1976), 206–7

United States v. O'Brien (1968), 88, 90, 154

United States v. Paradise (1987), 262–3

United States v. Salerno (1987), 99–101

United Steelworkers union, 259–60

U.S. Department of Agriculture v. Murry (1973), 11, 12, 14, 15

U.S. News and World Report, 58

Vanderbilt, Judge Arthur T., 23, 24, 28

Vietnam War, 4, 50, 51–4, 88–9, 92–3, 143–4, 146, 154, 158–61, 163, 164, 171, 182

Vinson, Chief Justice Fred, 152

Waggoner, Rep. Joe, 170

Wainwright v. Sykes (1977), 201–3

Waite, Chief Justice Morrison, 116, 117

Wallace v. Jaffree (1985), 123–5, 130–1, 133

Walsh, Lawrence, 44–5

War on Poverty, 4, 39, 271

War Powers Act, 53

Wards Cove Packing Co. v. Atonio (1989), 265

Warren, Chief Justice Earl, 5, 14, 37, 53, 56–8, 88, 89, 154, 290, 300, 301, 323, 326, 335; criminal procedure cases, 189–91, 204; death penalty cases, 217, 223; equal protection cases, 243–6, 249, 253, 258; liberty cases, 95, 96; obscenity cases, 167, 168, 170; religion cases, 120, 122, 129

Washington, Pres. George, 131, 181, 184

Washington *Post*, 60

Watergate scandal, 54, 303

Weber, Brian, 259–60

Weber v. Aetna Casualty & Surety Co. (1972), 283–4

Webster v. Reproductive Health Services (1989), 21, 316–18, 320

Weems v. United States (1910), 210

Weinberger, Caspar, 141

Weisman, Deborah, 133, 134

Weismann, Henry, 66–7

Welch, Joseph, 30–1

welfare, 3–22, 39–41, 284–6, 289, 337

West Coast Hotel v. Parrish (1937), 73–4

West Virginia Council of Churches, 239

West Virginia State Board of Education v. Barnette (1943), 81, 83, 86, 316

White, Justice Byron, 14, 96, 106, 137, 161, 175, 192, 193, 251, 253, 265, 297, 310, 335; abortion cases, 316–20; alien cases, 273, 275, 276, 278; censorship cases, 181–3; death penalty cases, 216, 222, 224, 227–8, 230–1

Whittier, John Greenleaf, 160, 161, 163

Wickard v. Filburn (1942), 74

Williamson v. Lee Optical Co. (1955), 17–18, 172, 176, 271, 283, 284, 286, 300, 304, 306, 307, 311

Wilson, James, 148

Women's Action Equity League, 305

Wong, Mow Sun, 273–5

Woodson v. North Carolina (1976), 225–6, 229

World War I, 149–50, 157, 269, 277

World War II, 27, 47–8, 79–80, 83–6, 118, 151, 157, 160, 163, 217

Wright, Charles Alan, 215

Wright, Richard, 180

Yasui, Minoru, 84

Yates v. United States (1957), 152

Yick Wo v. Hopkins (1886), 90, 244, 278

Young Conservative Alliance, 187

Zenger, John Peter, 148, 179

A Note on the Type

The text of this book was set in Electra, a typeface designed by W. A. Dwiggins (1880–1956). This face cannot be classified as either modern or old style. It is not based on any historical model; nor does it echo any particular period or style. It avoids the extreme contrasts between thick and thin elements that mark most modern faces and attempts to give a feeling of fluidity, power, and speed.

Composed by PennSet, Bloomsburg, Pennsylvania
Printed and bound by Arcata Graphics/Fairfield,
Fairfield, Pennsylvania
Designed by Anthea Lingeman